# Contents

# Note

There is no exact and explanatory title for the large body of people that was included within the Northern Ireland system as a 33% minority and was disfranchised by it. *"Catholic"* is sometimes used in preference to *"Nationalist"* in this book, on the understanding that the religious classification of political affairs has been historically established in Ireland by the force of a State which was very assertively Protestant. The British State sectarianised politics in Ireland.

The Irish did not assert a Catholic identity against a liberal regime. They were oppressed as Catholics by a Protestant regime, and it was therefore as Catholics that they had to achieve their freedom. When the island was Partitioned, the British State, though still being assertively Protestant in many respects, had developed a medium of political life that was not bound to religious denomination. But it excluded the Six Counties from that medium of political life when retaining them within the British state, and it established a system of sub-government whose political life centred on the Orange Order. In earlier times the Irish majority was excluded from politics by political Protestantism: in Northern Ireland a large minority was subordinated by essentially the same means and for the same purpose.

Policy may suggest a euphemistic or evasive title. But this is history, and there is no doubt that the local variant of the British State was run by a political system organised as Protestant, compelling the oppressed minority to act politically as a cohesive community of Catholics.

# Introduction

The year of 2014 marks a significant centenary for the Nationalists of the North of Ireland. A century earlier saw the climax of their struggle for Irish Home Rule and the great gamble of their leaders, including their own Joe Devlin, in supporting Britain's Great War.

Having gradually freed themselves from centuries of systematic oppression, the Northern Catholics entered a phase of rapid National development. They were in the vanguard of the movement for Home Rule and looked forward to being a major force in a self-governing Ireland within the Empire as promised by the British Liberal Government. And they were also part of a great social reform movement with their Liberal and Labour allies in the British State.

This was a great improvement on their experience over the previous three centuries. The Catholics of the North had barely survived England's colonial project in Ireland that had earmarked them for extermination and replacement by a Plantation. Their destiny to be cleansed from the lands intended to be colonised was no different from that of the rest of the Irish. But the Northern Catholics found themselves in a different situation from the rest of native Ireland when the colony established amongst them, unlike the others, survived and developed into a substantial society around them.

And so the Catholics of the North found themselves with a colonial problem and the colony which had grown into industrial Belfast found itself with a native problem.

It started to go wrong for the Northern Catholics with the Ulster colonial rebellion, supported by the British Unionist Party, against the Liberal Home Rule proposal, intended to apply to the whole of Ireland. The Unionist Party was an alliance of the Conservative Party and Joe Chamberlain's social reform Liberals and it was the main British party of state.

The Ulster colony, unlike the Protestant ascendancy on the rest of the island, did not need the natives in order to exist and it objected to the Liberal proposal that the Imperial connection be reconstituted on democratic lines, with themselves in the position of a new minority. Ulster was a partner with Britain in the great Imperial project of 'civilising' the world and it was not about to submit to a majority operated by the less 'civilised' and 'backward' section of the native populace.

And so, in alliance with British Unionism, the Ulster colony frustrated the Imperial Home Rule future through the bringing of force into Irish politics.

In some desperation, and to prove loyalty to England in its vital hour, the Home Rule leaders entered into Britain's Great War on Germany in an attempt to circumvent the Unionist obstruction to Home Rule and on a pledge that the 'war for small nations' and for 'self-determination' would include Ireland.

But the Northern Catholics who supported Britain's Great War and who made a great 'blood sacrifice' for it found themselves victims of a Great Fraud. In 1920-1 they were separated from the rest of the Nation of which they formed a very significant and substantial part, just as the National development was entering its momentous phase.

And they not only got Partition but much, much worse—they got 'Northern Ireland.'

In 1920-1 the Catholic community in what was becoming the political construct of 'Northern Ireland', suffered a disaster not experienced by others on the island.

Britain not only Partitioned Ireland, cutting off the Catholics of the North from the rest of the Irish Nation, but also decided to cut off the Northern Catholics from the social reform movement they had been part of in the UK, placing them within a new political construct within which they were to form a permanent minority under the heel of the people who had deprived them of their historic destiny.

That act represented a Catastrophe for the Northern Catholics.

Michael Collins, fresh from fighting Britain to the negotiating table, arrived in Armagh in late 1921 and promised deliverance from the Catastrophe to the Northern Catholics. But in the following year he only succeeded in making things considerably worse for them. In attempting to manoeuvre around the 'Treaty' he signed, he used the Northern Catholics and IRA as pawns in a losing game with greatly demoralising consequences for them.

And then it turned out that the Boundary Commission did not report in the way that had been indicated to Collins.

The Northern Catholic predicament resulted from a revised Imperial design for the rest of the island of Ireland. The 'Treaty' of 1921 attempted to keep a hold on the part of Ireland that was being lost by utilising that which was still held.

Gerry Adams later wrote: "We were the unfortunate baggage of a Partitionist arrangement. We were the human flotsam floating about in the political limbo of an unfinished struggle" (*Twenty Turbulent Years*, Irish Times, 3.10.88). And Britain, for Imperial purposes of State, was determined that 'Northern Ireland' remained a political limbo no matter what effect it had on those who had to inhabit it.

The Catholics of the North were not only cut off from their own nation they were also shut out of the political life of the state they remained part of.

That State, which retained overall authority, constructed a false front in the Six Counties that helped absolve Westminster of responsibility for what was done in it.

So it is little wonder that the Northern Catholics withdrew within themselves to live their own lives until the day of deliverance arrived from the rest of the Nation. But that day never came.

The effect of all this was to confine the Northern Catholics in a type of political quarantine that was very detrimental to their well-being as a self-respecting community. And it took half a century, a popular insurrection, and a Twenty Eight Year War for them to transform their position within this confinement.

And that is what this book, in two volumes, 'Catastrophe' and 'Resurgence', is about.

*

There are very few books from the Northern Catholic perspective. Many books have been written about 'Northern Ireland', of course, but they are specific to the Six Counties and treat the Northern Catholics as a disconnected problem that periodically disturbed the peace and normality enjoyed by others. They, in effect, lock the Northern Catholics in the box into which they were placed in 1921. The implicit desire is that they live in peace and contentment in that box. In consequence, they contribute to the act of deliberate policy that created the problem in the first place and connive in a demand for the impossible.

Treating the problem of 'Northern Ireland' as being something specific to 'Northern Ireland' ignores the deeper cause of the Northern Catholic predicament. This approach cannot hope to illuminate Northern Nationalist behaviour. But then that seems to be the point.

In the last few years books have begun to appear that look at things from the Northern Catholic perspective. They are a start in understanding things in the formative 1918-25 period from a Northern Catholic view. Their area of interest is Northern Republicanism and that is not surprising after the experience of recent history. But Republicanism is not the central aspect of Northern Nationalism—it is just one part of a wider *continuum* whose other part has been much more substantial over the last century.

And Northern Republicanism is both a product of island-wide events and the specific experience of Six County existence. That should be clear from the events of recent years.

Northern Republicanism cannot be explained within itself. It is the product of a distinct community placed in a perverse political structure producing a peculiar predicament. Out of that came a 28-Year War and a movement to end it to the political advantage of that community.

The predicament that the Northern Catholic community found itself in naturally led it to seek ways out of it. As this volume shows, it sought escape routes in various directions and not only through the traditional route of re-unification with the rest of the Nation.

But all its escape attempts were foiled and that led it to utilise the element of force—an element that it was very familiar with as a community. That familiarity with force did not come from within the community itself but was something that community experienced externally as part of the origin of its predicament, and in its everyday existence since.

The Northern Catholic community itself came late to the use of force. It had been acting entirely through the normal constitutional channels of British parliamentary democracy in its pursuit of a very moderate political ambition when it was suddenly confronted by the main institution of British parliamentary democracy threatening force against it. A Unionist private army was formed around it in 1912 to resist its constitutional objective, and the regular army of the State, that it depended upon to implement the will of the Westminster Government, mutinied.

The mutineers became an indispensable element in Britain's waging of its Great War on Germany and that was that for Home Rule.

And yet the Northern Catholic community continued to pursue the constitutional road and sent its sons in large numbers in support of Britain's Great War and to die for it.

The political construct of 'Northern Ireland' was little more than an armed police and militia operation to subordinate the large minority within it, which had no constitutional means of seeking redress.

The Catholic community never really lay down but it was effectively subdued for nearly half a century. And then there was an almighty explosion.

*

This book comes out of a previous book written back in 1988. That book was called *From Civil Rights to National War*. It was part of a political initiative that originated in the Catholic community but which encompassed Protestants and which aimed to reconstitute politics in the North within the democratic political system of the state—of the British state which is the only state that has ever been in 'Northern Ireland'.

It took the "Two Nations" view as its starting point and as an accurate description of the political facts of the Northern situation. This had been advanced from Athol Street in West Belfast in the aftermath of the events of August 1969 to explain why the Ulster Protestant community would act as a national entity under any pressure that was applied to it, and that a necessary precondition to dialogue with it was a frank acknowledgement of its existence, and an end to telling it that it was really part of an all-Ireland nation.

The Nationalist Establishment in its political and academic forms had refused to adopt that approach and held to the view that Ulster Unionism was a deluded remnant of aristocracy and religious bigotry which would crumble under pressure. But it was the Nationalist Establishment's position that increasingly crumbled instead, under the pressure of the ensuing conflict.

The 1988 book was based on the idea that there was one great determining event in the politics of the North of Ireland. The entity known as 'Northern Ireland' had been established by the Westminster Government in 1920-1 for an ulterior Imperial purpose and not for the good governance of the Six Counties.

Since then 'Northern Ireland' had been systematically misgoverned as a region of the British State and had been excluded from the representative party system of that State. Undemocratic government within this annex of a democratic state left two hostile communities in a relationship of simple antagonism with each other, particularly because one was given the role of policing the other in perpetuity. And this system was bound to have political consequences, especially if it started to unravel, as it did at the turn of the decade between the 1960s and 1970s.

'Northern Ireland' had been cut off from State politics in 1921—from both the party politics of the UK and from that the emerging Irish State. It had been condemned to a routine of communal conflict by this decision of the Imperial Government and had been sealed off from normal political life.

The book was part of the project of democratising the North within the state. Seeing the assertion that Partition was the cause of the trouble in the North, and that the ending of Partition was necessary to peace, as a utopian pursuit, it looked for a settlement on the basis of ending the exclusion of the North from the democratic political life of the State. It concluded that it was the exclusion of the Six Counties from the democracy of the State that preserved and aggravated the antagonism of Protestant and Catholic on which the devolved system was imposed in 1921. And, in the era of democracy, which Britain was loudest in proclaiming across the world, democracy could not, without serious consequences, be flouted as Britain was flouting it in its 'Northern Ireland' region.

It generated a great deal of discussion in the Belfast media and the Annual Conferences of the British Parties. What it demonstrated through many years of intense effort was that the State was absolutely determined to keep 'Northern Ireland' out of its democracy, and the Ulster Unionists had become addicted to the routine of communal antagonism, seeing it as a guarantee of their continuing supremacy. They chose to be "Ulsterish" rather than British.

The democratisation project was given up as hopeless. Whitehall wouldn't allow it, Dublin wouldn't hear of it, and the Ulster Unionist, being paranoid about Britain, were scared of it.

The War was left to work itself out in a 'Northern Ireland' framework. The Unionists, choosing sectarian safety, were made to put up with the *Hillsborough Treaty* (1985). It threw them into a frenzy but proved irrelevant to the War. Then, trying to escape from Hillsborough, they had to submit to the Good Friday Agreement in 1998. The *Good Friday Agreement* ended the War by ending the pretence that 'Northern Ireland' was either a democratic state in itself or a democratic region of the democratic state it was part of, and by negating the majority status of Unionism in devolved government.

The State chose for its 'Northern Ireland' region a form of government that was undemocratic and sectarian. The apparent purpose for this was that it gave it continuing leverage on the politics of the South. In the North war was its inevitable outcome. After half a century the Catholic minority accepted this inevitability.

This book is a substantial extension of the small 1988 book and written in the light of things which never could be the same again.

The 1988 book dealt largely with the 1964-74 period and much of its content appears within this book. However, it has been brought up to date with many new chapters and expanded into two volumes. New chapters have been added to describe the position of the Northern Catholics before Partition and the origins of the perverse political entity of 'Northern Ireland' that they were confined within. These have helped deepen the understanding of the ingenious and devilish construct of 'Northern Ireland' which still forms the basis of the political problem.

Much of the information on the earlier period was gleaned through writing a book called, *The Rise and Fall of Imperial Ireland* and some other publications about the formative events. These provided a more thorough appreciation of the nature of the issue than appeared in the small book of 1988. Material written in the *Irish Political Review* (formerly Worker's Weekly and *The Northern Star*) over the last few decades, and published by Athol Books, is the basis for it.

The story of the present book finishes in early 1969, just at the point when the Civil Rights movement was gaining traction. Volume Two, *Resurgence*, continues the story thereafter and deals with the rise of Northern Republicanism and the political developments it generated.

**Pat Walsh**
*April 2014*

# CHAPTER ONE

# Before the Fall

The establishment of 'Northern Ireland' placed two distinct and antagonistic communities in a political structure that was designed to enhance that antagonism. So it is within these parameters that a history of it has to be written.

'Northern Ireland' was established by the British Government in 1920-1 to contain two communities with very distinct historical developments within a common territory. Since the existence, scale and character of the construct were all determined by the Imperial Government at Westminster this must be taken to have been its deliberate intention.

There was nothing inevitable about it. It was a conscious act of policy by the most experienced and greatest statesmen of the most powerful state in the world.

This act of policy had the effect of assigning particular roles to the two communities within the political entity established—roles that were quite different to those that had existed prior to the establishment of 'Northern Ireland'.

In the years leading up to 1920 the Catholic community of the North was part of an all-Ireland movement that was pressing for a measure of self-government that would be some recognition of nationhood. In the final decade of this campaign an Imperialist consciousness was injected into the movement for Home Rule through the relationship that was built with the Liberal Government in Britain and the willingness of the Irish Party leadership to resign themselves to a British Empire future.

The Ulster Protestant community, which had developed through the Imperial connection for a longer time attempted to resist this development of the whole of Ireland as a distinct component of the British Empire.

With the establishment of 'Northern Ireland' the quite different roles assigned to the two communities in 1921 had to be taken up and played out if the entity was to function at all. The majority community, the Protestants, had to take responsibility for keeping in check the minority, the Catholics, by various means. If they did not accomplish this then 'Northern Ireland', the entity assigned to them, would be no more.

And the Catholics caught within the boundaries of this Imperial contrivance had to also play a role—as a quiescent and subordinate permanent minority in a construct they found both antagonistic and obnoxious.

This book is about the political predicament which this placed the minority community in, when the entity of 'Northern Ireland' was established. But it must start out with the important fact that this minority was actually a majority prior to the act of creation of 'Northern Ireland' and it was, in fact, the most vigorous part of that majority at the time, looking to the future with relish and a great sense of anticipation, before the catastrophe of 1920-1 befell it.

## The Catholics Of Ulster

There is a largely forgotten publication from the Ulster Unionist campaign against Irish Home Rule called *The Truth About Ulster* that gives the Plantation view of the native. But it was produced in 1913 rather than 1613. It was written by Frank Frankfort Moore, a Presbyterian educated at the Belfast Academical Institute (Inst). He was a journalist with the *Belfast Newsletter* from 1876 until 1892 rising to the position of Assistant Editor before moving to London, where he wrote *The Truth About Ulster* during the Home Rule Crisis.

Moore made his career as a satirist in England but he began by satirising the idea of Irish Home Rule in books such as *Diary Of An Irish Cabinet Minister* (1893), *The Viceroy Of Muldoon*, and the *Rise And Fall Of Larry O'Lannigan, JP* (1893). *The Truth About Ulster* was written when Moore saw articles in the English press asking whether Ulster would really fight against Home Rule. Moore, believing this to be a ridiculous question, wrote in the first chapter, *Fighting Ulster*:

> "I felt inclined to ask myself when had Ulster not been fighting? She has been fighting for precisely the same 'Cause' at intervals during the past fifty years, and for nearly three hundred years previously she had been fighting with an enemy who was the same, although wearing a different uniform. So that I fancy the question of the hour should be, 'Will Ulster continue to fight?' rather than 'Will Ulster fight?'" (p.10)

Moore saw the struggle against Home Rule as the latest instalment of the ancient struggle of the colonist to keep the native down. The native had to be kept down because the coloniser had not succeeded in exterminating him. That might seem a rather blunt way of putting it but it was put very explicitly like this by Moore.

*The Truth About Ulster* referred to the Biblical programme of extermination to explain why the pacification of Ireland did not lead to a perpetual peace for the colonists:

> "...the efforts at colonisation made by the early, if not the earliest, masters of the art of pacification in Ulster were too faithfully framed on the lines of the Act of Settlement formulated by Moses in respect of Palestine, to have any greater chance of success in Ulster than it had in Asia Minor.
> "And be it remembered also that the failure in both cases was due to the

same cause, namely, the incompleteness of the conquests which were to result in perpetual peace. The scheme of colonisation recommended to the Israelitish brotherhood was a simple one, and I should not like to be the one to stand up and say in the presence of a congregation of Ulster Presbyterians that it did not come direct from God.

"It was neither more nor less than a policy of extermination. The instructions for carrying it out may be read in detail in a certain chapter of Exodus. The original inhabitants of the land were to 'be wiped out, men, women, and children, especially the children unborn'. Truly an effective, if somewhat drastic, scheme of 'planting' a colony.

"But in framing it, unfortunately, neither the humanity of man nor the cupidity of the children of Israel was taken into account, and the result was what God's mouthpiece prophesied it would be: the colonists were commanded to spare no one, and assured that if they did, they would find that the survivors of the massacre would become as thorns in their sides for evermore. But the colonists were weak enough to do some sparing, and of course the prophecy as to the result was realised; for those of the Philistines who were allowed to live became as thorns in their sides, even those whom the cupidity of the Israelites had saved in order that they might be turned into slaves.

"Exactly the same thing has happened in Ulster. The colonists of the Plantation instituted by James I. wanted their wood to be hewn for them and their water to be drawn for them; therefore they spared a reasonable number of the original Irish who were quarrelling among themselves, and so (according to the statesmanship of the Middle Ages and of a long time afterwards) should have been swept out of existence altogether; and these survivors became as thorns in their flesh, especially when they were hewing wood or drawing water; and so they have remained to the present day.

"Ulster is still a colony in the midst of the hostile people who, though they have never (generally speaking) recovered more of their old position than allows of their quarrelling among themselves, are still, as hewers of wood and drawers of water, always ready to fling a faggot at the head of their task-master.

"That is, in very truth, what the constant fighting in Ulster has meant. It has been the attempt of the subject race to rebel against the ascendancy. In all the other provinces of Ireland some progress has been made by the conquered race during the past hundred years or so toward regaining the ascendancy which they once enjoyed; and the dominant ones have for long thought it prudent to suspend their domineering; but in Ulster there has never been a need for them to do so. They have always looked with indignant eyes at the attempts of the Hivites and the Hittites and the Jebusites to regain their original position, and called such attempts by the name of rebellion. They have been fighting since the days of the siege of Derry against the intermittent rebellions of the native Irish, who had become their servants; and now when it is suggested to them that these servants should become their masters, some newspaper folk inquire with a seriousness that has its comic side to anyone who knows Ulster and the history of Ulster: 'Will Ulster fight?'" (The Truth about Ulster, pp. 12-15).

Whilst the English *"civilising"* of Ireland during the seventeenth century involved the destruction of Gaelic society, there were not the population resources necessary to entirely supplant an exterminated native population with enough colonists. The Catholic natives also survived in the Plantation area because the Government instructions were not implemented as thoroughly as they should have been. The Plantation needed labour and native labour came cheaper than English or Scottish. So the natives survived in pockets within the Plantation. Extermination proved unworkable as a practical policy and the natives lived to fight another day, remaining a thorn in the side of the Plantation. They naturally wanted to undo it after what it had done to them.

## The Catholics Of Belfast

The area around what became Chapel Lane was the place in which a small Catholic population first gathered in Belfast. The Catholics of Belfast in the late 18th Century were minuscule in number and they congregated around the city boundaries, where St Mary's Chapel was built. This chapel, which looked more like a Presbyterian meeting-house, was the centrepiece of Catholic existence in Belfast and was established in an obscure lane on the west side of the town with the help of Protestant money. The Protestant Volunteers paraded there in 1784, forming a guard of honour for the priest, in a long-remembered opening ceremony.

Martha M'Tier was one of the few to anticipate future developments regarding the Catholic community after being in Chapel Lane. She wrote to her brother, William Drennan, the United Irishman, in 1802:

"The R. Catholics here, now, a large, tho' poor & unknown body... at their Chapel there is more news than any other place... Christmas Eve for the first time in this place there was a singing procession in the street. I begin to fear these people, & think like the Jews, they will regain their native land." (Belfast Politics, Athol Books edition, p.263)

It was in this area, where the Falls Road meets the town centre, that some of the great political events of Catholic politics occurred. Wee Joe Devlin, the mighty leader of Catholic Belfast, had his election office here. For a time he managed the bar, Kelly's Stores — where the United Irish once talked about a rising. And just down the road in Berry Street he built his National Club for his Hibernians — from where the first Irish Volunteers mustered to join the British Army in France in 1914.

It was here also that St. Mary's Hall stood, where Padraig Pearse, Jim Larkin and Eamon De Valera all spoke at public meetings and where Devlin and Redmond accepted Partition on Black Friday in 1916. It was at St. Mary's Hall that Catholic refugees gathered, seeking protection after being driven out of other areas of the Six Counties, as 'Northern Ireland' came into existence, were provided for; here that General O'Duffy established an IRA H.Q. during the Truce, right in the heart of the Unionist citadel, as Michael Collins promised to deliver Catholics from Partition; and here, too, that the Specials re-occupied for Unionism the Republican headquarters, as Collins' offensive against the North began to disintegrate as he was boxed in by the Treaty he signed.

And it was here that Northern Catholics came together after the catastrophe of 1920-25 through Cahir Healy and Devlin to form the National League which became the Nationalist Party.

In the 19th Century a large Catholic working-class accumulated in Belfast along with the progress of industrialisation in the city. These unskilled Catholic workers who were drawn from the outlying areas of the Ulster Plantation entered the town with the growth of the mills and began to organise an existence for themselves in areas that largely remain to this day. The building of chapels, convents and schools in these areas helped define them as Catholic and forge a distinct identity within the Protestant city.

The Catholics of Belfast regarded themselves as a part of the people of Ireland, temporarily dominated by an alien intrusion. They did the menial work for the alien intrusion within its great economic development but never subordinated themselves to it.

Belfast was a unique city in Ireland. It had nothing to do with the official Plantation and was not the result of Viking or Norman effort. It was a city built entirely by the enterprise of Ulster Protestants outside the auspices of the British State. It was, therefore, very much a creation of the Ulster Protestant, mostly Presbyterian, settler and was seen as such. When Catholic numbers began to increase in the city toward the middle of the century a sense of threat emerged. In the higher-skilled and higher-paid areas of employment where Protestants predominated they sought to maintain their advantage over the Catholic migrants and make these areas exclusive to their kind.

Half way through the century it looked as though Catholics might become a majority in Belfast as they had become earlier in the century in Dublin. This thought led to periodic violent confrontations between the communities, particularly over the ownership of territory and the marching through it. The rural Catholics that came to the city began to emulate the Protestant customs of marching and engaging in symbolic displays of identity. This produced the periodic communal conflict that characterised the town.

But there was no repeat of what happened in Dublin: the much more substantial Protestant community of Ulster supplied the developing shipbuilding and engineering industries and swelled the non-Catholic population of the city in the latter part of the nineteenth century. And the Great Hunger of 1847-8 decimated the Catholic population of the island by at least a quarter and probably much more and meant that Belfast received smaller numbers of Catholic migrants than it would have done. Catholics remained a minority in the city for another century and a half and the comparative strength of Catholic Ireland to Protestant Ulster declined to about 4:1 rather than the potential 15:1 that would have existed if Britain had not availed of the Famine to reduce the Irish numbers.

## The 'Invasion' Of Ulster

As the threat of being swamped by Catholic numbers was averted by the Famine this seemed to secure the Protestant supremacy in the city. But the continuation of conflict in the areas between the territory of the two communities showed that the feeling of threat had not gone away. Two decisive political events in the 1880s accentuated this 'siege mentality' among Ulster Protestants.

The first was the 1884 Franchise Act which established male household suffrage. This great act of democratisation under the Union produced what Unionists in the North-East called "the invasion of Ulster" and the re-appearance of the Northern Catholics on the stage of history.

In 1885 the Home Rule Party from having not a single MP in Ulster captured 17 of the 33 Ulster seats in the Westminster Parliament with a massive turn-out of 90 per cent. The Reform Act of 1884 gave the vote to all male householders who owned or rented property. As a result, the Irish electorate rose from 225,000 to 740,000. Before the 1884 Reform only 4% of Irish people had the vote but after it roughly 16% of the population were enfranchised. This created a much enlarged Catholic electorate in Ulster that included not just the small middle class but many agricultural labourers and urban workers. The 'invasion of Ulster' was accompanied by the decimation of Unionists MPs on the rest of the island as democracy kicked-in.

The democratisation resulting in the 'invasion of Ulster' meant that Unionists began to feel the Catholic presence again for the first time in two centuries. It also signalled the beginning of the predominance of the Home Rule Party amongst the mass of Ulster Catholics. Previously, many of the smaller numbers of Catholic electors had voted Liberal to keep out the Ascendancy/Landlord candidate. It brought a substantial section of the masses into politics for the first time and it was the appearance of the Catholic element of this enfranchisement that shook up the political situation and frightened the Unionists of the North-East.

The second was the introduction of a Home Rule Bill in 1886.

A politically active and demanding Catholic majority was now very visible across Ireland. This was achieved through clerical mobilisation of the Catholic masses and more effective Nationalist organisation. So it was not just the numerical swamping by the Catholic masses that alarmed Protestant Unionists but the developing Nationalist efficiency in democratic politics that confronted them for the first time.

So in 1900 there were two very distinct and antagonistic communities existing in Ulster. The Protestant Unionist community felt itself to be a superior settler community which maintained a strong degree of racial purity from the natives and built industrial Ulster as part of the British Empire understanding its achievements as being based on its Protestant religion. It was *"a great governing race"* but it also had a 'siege-mentality' against the Catholic masses that were seemingly growing stronger and were believed to be threatening to overwhelm it.

The Catholic Nationalist community saw itself as a native people, long-suffering of proscriptions and expulsions, and resentful at being treated as inferior by the alien intrusion. It had a strong sense of grievance against both the Protestants and the British Government. It maintained an attachment to "the ancient faith," for which it was constantly derided, keeping the faith as a response to the attacks upon it and in order to reach out to something of greater substance beyond the locally-dominant English, Protestant world.

Then the adoption of Irish Home Rule as an Imperial policy by one section of the London Establishment threatened to fundamentally change the power relationship between Protestant Ulster and Catholic Ireland. That had the effect of sharpening the ancient conflict that existed between the two communities in Ulster.

But at this stage no one dreamt of putting these two peoples within a local political construction to play out the long-standing conflict.

## Joe Devlin And Belfast

To understand the position of what was to be the contrived minority in 'Northern Ireland' we must comprehend how the Ulster Catholics were reduced from a leading role in the Irish Nation to that of a marginalised cast-off in a detached backwater.

The world was their oyster—including its vast Imperial expression— but their future became a clam.

The vanguard position which the Northern Catholics had attained in the national movement before their great decline had been achieved under the leadership of Joe Devlin of West Belfast.

Joe Devlin had a rapid rise to power and influence over the first decade or so of the twentieth century. He had been asked by John Dillon to lead the 1798 centenary commemorations in Belfast on behalf of the Irish National Federation and was then appointed to the National Directory of the United Irish League/Home Rule Party in 1900, just after the great reconciliation from the Parnell split.

Belfast and Ulster generally, were anti-Parnellite strongholds — much more so than other areas in the country. In the 1892 elections anti-Parnell candidates received 98 per cent of the votes in the constituencies that were contested by Parnellites. The Parnellite newspaper, *The Belfast Morning News*, was swallowed up by the new anti-Parnellite *Irish News*. When Parnell visited the city in 1891 Devlin had, apparently, jumped on his carriage taunting the Chief with the words, "*Kitty O'Shea! Kitty O'Shea!*"

After the healing of the split Devlin was elected (unopposed) MP for North Kilkenny in February 1902 and accompanied the Parnellite, Willie Redmond, brother of the new Chairman of the Parliamentary Party, on a substantial fund-raising tour of the United States. This was followed by tours of Canada, Australia and New Zealand on behalf of the Party. In 1903, he became the Party's General Secretary and then MP for West Belfast in 1906, winning the seat by 16 votes when an independent unionist split the Protestant vote.

From 1896, Devlin engaged in a struggle with Bishop Henry's Belfast Catholic Association, which was the organising body for Catholic representation in the city. Henry had established a strict clerical control of Nationalist political organisation in the city and felt that any dilution of this would be dangerous in separating religion and politics. Devlin was frustrated at the clerical dictation of policy in Belfast and when The Irish News refused to support him he began his own weekly, *The Northern Star*. This contained a combination of Irish nationalism and social reformism, which Devlin felt was lacking from the Irish Party's policy on account of it being a mainly rural and small town phenomenon and having little feel for industrial Belfast. But in 1897 Bishop Henry's Belfast Catholic Association trounced Devlin's Irish National Federation in the municipal elections in West Belfast winning all the seats.

In the 1904 municipal elections Henry's Catholic Association managed again to see off Devlin's challenge but the tide turned against the Bishop shortly after. Devlin began to win the battle for control of Belfast Catholic politics by 1905, when he wrested control of *The Irish News* from the supporters of Bishop Henry, and joined the Board of the newspaper. He then absorbed Henry's supporters into his organisation after a number of priests deserted the Bishop, unhappy at his dictation. In July 1905 Devlin accepted the position of President of the Ancient Order of Hibernians (Board of Erin).

Devlin's experience of the AOH in America led him to see the usefulness of developing an organisation of similar power and influence in Ireland. He was impressed by its large membership, the wealth at its disposal and the patronage it could utilise. Also it was a Catholic, rather than a clerically controlled organisation that could be used as a social, economic and political instrument within the Catholic community outside of the control of the Bishops. The Church wanted control over all social life within the Catholic community (including even whist drives and dances held with permission of the Parish Priest). Devlin conceived the AOH being an alternative to the clerical direction of Catholic social life writing in *The Northern Star* of January 1908 that he wanted "a public hall in every parish in Ireland" where people "would become acquainted with the language and music of Ireland" and where could be held "dances and merry meetings".

So the AOH would have a similar objective to many of the national organisations that were growing up in Ireland although the direction of the Parliamentary Party would place these activities within the Imperial ambit rather than being as a force for separatism.

Devlin also concluded that the AOH was a much better suited organisation to industrial Belfast than the rural-orientated United Irish League which had been founded by William O'Brien on the basis of "the land for the people". And it would give the Party the very thing it lacked—popular participation and activism and a sense of vigour in its internal life.

The AOH was to act decisively as Devlin's instrument in spreading his power southwards.

## Powerful 'Wee Joe'

With control of the Parliamentary Party in Belfast and a seat on the Board of the *Irish News*, Devlin consolidated his position in Ulster. This established him as part of a triumvirate at the top of the Irish Parliamentary Party with John Dillon and the Chairman, John Redmond.

But it soon became clear that Devlin was the most substantial of the Home Rule Leaders. Tim Healy famously called him the *"pocket Demosthenes"*. And Cruise O'Brien, for example, wrote in *The Leader* (19.02.10):

"Mr. Devlin is the most powerful man in Ireland. He is far more powerful, for example, than Mr. Redmond, who has too many of the qualities which distinguished Burke to make him the darling of the crowd. He is more powerful than Mr. Dillon whose rigid and rather puritanical type of mind disdains to pander to the populace. Mr. Devlin, in a word, is the triumph of the commonplace man... Mr. Devlin, nay Joe Devlin, who calls him Mister?—he is the man whom we all love and understand and would, in some cases, die for."

Devlin, unlike Redmond and Dillon, was not a gentleman. He was a working-class self-made man. The fact that he had rose so highly from his humble origins as a *"bottle-washer"* demonstrated his great ability in politics and marked him out as different to the other Home Rule leaders.

Redmond, himself, speaking in the US during October 1910 twice described Devlin as "the real chief secretary in Ireland" (Sean McMahon, Wee Joe, The Life of Joe Devlin, p.125)

Devlin, who was more representative than Redmond and Dillon and who commanded the most sizeable popular base of the Home Rule movement was the man of the future who would be the most powerful figure in a Home Rule Ireland. If Home Rule had been achieved, and Redmond had died when he did, Devlin could have been the first Prime Minister of Ireland.

In October 1913, when the Home Rule crisis was escalating, the famous journalist, Lovat Fraser, was sent by *The Times* to see how things stood on the ground in Ireland. His mission was to judge where power lay between Nationalist Ireland and Unionist Ulster. But he also made a judgement of where power lay within Nationalist Ireland.

In the course of his tour he visited Limerick to hear Redmond, the Chairman of the Irish Parliamentary Party, speak. Fraser thought Redmond a worried man who was putting up a brave front in the face of Ulster Unionist opposition to his dream. But the interesting thing was how Fraser took Devlin to be the real substance of the Home Rule movement, even in far away Limerick:

> "His (Redmond's) speech may read like a paean of triumph, but there was no triumphant note in his voice and demeanour, only intense anxiety. Still, his declaration of defiance was absolutely resolute. I should say he has not the slightest intention of receding from his emphatic statement to-day; and if he had, then Devlin has not, and he must toe the line as Devlin directs. One thing struck me very much indeed. Devlin had a distinctly bigger reception than Redmond. He woke the people up more, although his speech was very brief... It was most instructive to mark his effect upon the people. He is evidently the coming man, and even here the Ancient Order of Hibernians was more in evidence to-day than the United Irish League... Dillon is regarded with much affection, but is no longer a great power, and did not sway the crowd much." (*Lovat Fraser's Tour of Ireland in 1913— An event within the Home Rule Conflict*, Athol Books, p.18)

The Reverend Robert O'Loughran of County Cork, wrote a few years later, in 1916, in a personal tribute to Redmond, that, "'wee Joe' as his friends call him, was the power behind the Redmond throne. At least until the Irish Rebellion, he was the most powerful man in Ireland." (*Redmond's Vindication*, p.66)

But not only was Devlin the most powerful individual within the Irish Party, he also made West Belfast the spearhead of the Home Rule movement.

Redmond might have been the Chairman of the Party and Dillon the great intellectual force but Devlin and his Northern men were the power and substance behind it. Redmond, who was always unsure of his position as Chairman of the Party, came to heavily rely on Devlin and his Hibernians to maintain Party discipline and quell 'Factionism'. Devlin had the measure of Redmond and knew that the nominal Leader had to pay the price to the Hibernians for the holding together of the Party and for his Chairmanship.

## The Future Is Imperial

Devlin's Hibernian power in Ireland first came to notice in relation to the opposition to the 1906 Liberal Government's proposed *Irish Council Bill* of 1907. The Irish Council Bill represented a retreat by the British Liberals from the Gladstonian pursuit of Irish Home Rule.

Gladstonian Liberalism had pledged itself to Irish Home Rule in 1886 through a Home Rule Bill for Ireland. In many ways the Liberal conversion to Irish Home Rule was a manifestation of the realisation that British rule could only persist in Ireland if hegemony could be established over Catholic Ireland in the era of democracy. That is why the conflict over Home Rule that brought the British State to the edge of disaster should be seen not as an internal Irish matter but as an argument within Imperialism itself about what was the most effective way of governing Ireland in the light of the constant widening of the franchise.

The democratisation process in the Union had prompted Gladstone's Home Rule Bill. Both British parties saw that continued British rule in Ireland depended on making concessions to the emerging democracy in Ireland and the growing nationalist movement that appeared in numbers at Westminster and with greater organisation under Parnell. The election produced a hung parliament and Parnell skilfully played the Liberals and Tories off against each other, before Gladstone came up with the Home Rule Bill.

But Gladstone's conversion to Home Rule badly split the Liberal Party and led to Joe Chamberlain taking his social reform Liberals over to the Tories to form the Unionist Party. The Home Rule Bill was voted down in the House of Commons as a consequence of this split.

After the Second Home Rule Bill of 1893 had been defeated by the House of Lords, Gladstone's Government decided not to make it an occasion for an appeal to the country and Lord Roseberry replaced Gladstone as Prime Minister.

Roseberry, a Liberal Imperialist, declared that Irish Home Rule could not come about until there was a majority for it in England — which he called the "predominant partner" in the Union. His young followers declared that a step by step approach to Home Rule would be preferable to a Home Rule

Bill. (These included Richard Haldane, future Minister for War; future Prime Minister Herbert Asquith; future Foreign Secretary Edward Grey; and Winston Churchill, the future Home Secretary, i.e., once he crossed benches to the Liberals.)

The Liberal Imperialists were reluctant Home Rulers saddled with the baggage of Gladstone. They were only too willing to discard it if possible. Rosebery called on the Liberal Party to realise the strength of association with the growing Imperialist sentiment of the nation and pointed to the liability of support for Irish Home Rule and other "obsolete" policies. He called for a "clean slate" with regard to Liberal policy on Ireland, which would involve the wiping away of the Gladstonian pledge to bring in a Home Rule Bill. And so there was nearly twenty years between the Second and Third Home Rule Bills for Ireland.

The Liberals returned in 1906 with their biggest parliamentary majority ever. They were led by the Gladstonian Campbell-Bannerman but would not touch Home Rule with a barge pole with the Liberal Imperialist coterie at the top of the party.

Chairman Redmond could do nothing about it. Until, that is, the Liberals achieved a famous settlement in South Africa, successfully incorporating the Boers into the Empire as loyal subjects and the Liberal argument over Irish self-government began to gather momentum again, albeit in the new context, as a dispute within Imperialism, rather than between Imperialism and Irish separatism.

The future was Imperial, and it was to this that the Irish Party began to reconcile itself under Redmond (For more on this aspect and its examination in detail see Pat Walsh, *The Rise And Fall of Imperial Ireland*, Athol Books).

## Devlin And The *Council Bill*

The Council Bill, similar to an earlier proposal made by the previous Unionist administration, was offered by the Liberals to the Irish Party as an alternative to Home Rule. It envisaged the setting up of an Irish Council in control of the great spending Departments of the British State in Ireland. It proposed the establishment of a representative, but non-legislative, all-Ireland administrative body — a kind of 32-County local government authority.

When the Bill had been introduced in Parliament Redmond, the Chairman of the Parliamentary Party showed an open mind toward it and said he would refer it to a Party Convention, when the final details of it were worked out. However, Redmond's welcome for it provoked a great outcry from the North and Devlin's men.

The main opposition to the Council Bill within the Irish Party was provided by the Ancient Order of Hibernians, led by Devlin. Two days after the introduction of the Bill, The Freeman's Journal, reported on May 10th that 8,000 Northern Hibernians had met at Lisnaskea, County Fermanagh, to show their opposition to the Bill and were calling out the Divisions of the Order to attend the National Convention in order to kill it. When the Convention took place, there were so many Hibernians present that the Party had great difficulty in getting its delegates into the Conference Hall.

Redmond initially had a mind to accept the Bill and try to work with it. And it appears that he intended, up until a very short time before the Convention assembled, to move acceptance of the measure in principle — without prejudice to the larger claim of future Home Rule. But he was persuaded otherwise by Devlin and the strength of the Hibernian opposition.

Devlin attributed Redmond's acceptance of the evolutionary approach to Home Rule to the conciliation process William O'Brien had adopted with Irish Protestants and the Unionist Party. O'Brien had seen a number of advantages in supporting the Irish Council Bill as he had supported the devolutionary scheme of the previous Unionist administration. His view was that if the Irish Party had taken up the Council Bill, it is unlikely that the House of Lords would have stopped it by Unionist objections. And, if an Irish Council had been established, the Irish Unionists would have had to function within it enhancing unity on the island.

The British Government had, despite everything it had done in Ireland, always treated Ireland as a single entity. The status of Ireland as a single political unit would thereby have been reasserted and enhanced in a separate administrative body with a representative element that would have progressively taken the place of Dublin Castle. And, if the functioning of the Council did not have the effect of eroding the opposition of Unionism, it would at least have increased the difficulty of British Governments treating Ireland as anything but a single political entity in any subsequent development.

O'Brien's position was that through participating in the Irish Council Irish Unionists would become used to acting in an institution which did administrative business with Catholics, and Catholics would have been able to familiarise themselves with the Protestants of Ulster in a practical environment that would help erode the national antagonism.

Redmond, who lacked confidence in his position, initially went with O'Brien but when he saw the power of Devlin's Hibernians he rapidly back-tracked to avoid another split.

## Devlin's Hibernians

The rejection of the Irish Council Bill was Belfast's first significant entry into national politics since the Union. It drew attention to the important force from the North that was growing in power and influence within the

Irish Party. The most vigorous and numerous sections of the Irish Party were composed of this new Hibernian element.

Devlin had been faced with a reunited Ancient Order of Hibernians (which had itself just recovered from a split) after he had seen off the Catholic Association in Belfast. It presented both a problem and a potentiality for Devlin, according to Michael Foy's thesis, 'The Ancient Order of Hibernians: an Irish Political-Religious Pressure Group 1884-1975' by "having a huge pool of potential members and, if it fell into the hands of people of ability, they might be able to build it up into a truly formidable organization."

Foy suggests that Devlin could have set out to crush the Order but because it was no threat to him, unlike the Catholic Association, he was tempted into an alternative: "If he could gain control of the A.O.H. and harness it to the United Irish League he might be able to supply the League in Ulster with the vital strength which it had been lacking up to then." (p. 46)

Devlin joined the AOH on the Falls Road in 1893. He saw the AOH, which had traditionally acted in a useful function as a semi-secret Catholic mutual assistance/defence force in Ulster, as a potential power base to expand his political influence into rural Ulster and beyond.

The United Irish League had not put down the roots in Ulster that it had in the rest of the country and Devlin calculated that the AOH would be a more effective vehicle for expanding his influence. It provided the activist membership (of around 10,000 in 1905 rising to 60,000 by 1909 and 100,000 in 1915) and the effective organisation that the UIL/Party was lacking. UIL Branches began to rapidly expand and increase with activists on Devlin's fusion of the Party with the Hibernians.

Devlin gained control of the Hibernians in July 1905 at their National Convention in Dublin and this marked the beginning of the knitting together of the AOH with the Irish Party.

A reading of the *Freeman's Journal* from about 1907 onwards reveals the growing power and influence of Devlin's Hibernians. Its pages show the extent of the Hibernian influence at Party meetings, marches, rallies, and Conventions and one can see the letters AOH scattered across the pages of *The Freeman* in the reporting of every sphere of purposeful Party activity.

The Hibernians began swallowing up the Nationalist MPs in Ulster, who found they could not survive if the Hibernians opposed them. From 1902 the Order had gained the right to send 4 delegates from each branch in a constituency to the conventions to select parliamentary candidates.

The AOH spread right out of Ulster and across Nationalist Ireland and it began to be used as a blunt instrument, which Devlin relied on to crush opposition in the constituencies, and to expand his personal influence in other parts of the country. It provided the means by which opponents could be intimidated, often violently, and Party Conventions conveniently 'packed'.

The AOH therefore became the main instrument in quashing the O'Brien resistance to the Home Rule/Liberal alliance that was the developing objective of the Irish Party leaders—Redmond, Dillon and Devlin. In this way Devlin made Redmond and Dillon dependent on the Hibernians and him if they were to be able to face down the substantial O'Brienite opposition, mainly centred in County Cork.

The ease at which the AOH spread through the Irish Party was not surprising, since the Party had become bereft of any organic political life in Ireland and something of an empty shell. This situation had developed partly because elections in most of the country were no contests (since the British State began to give up the ghost in contesting them) and the Irish Party leadership became largely concerned with affairs at Westminster and courting the Liberals.

But, it was very detrimental that Redmond, aiming for Home Rule to be enacted, allowed his Party to be infiltrated by a militant lay Catholic organisation which had no useful function in areas where Catholics did not require defence. That could only have had the effect of maximising Ulster Protestant resistance to Irish self-government by convincing them that a future Home Rule Ireland would be Hibernian in character.

Before Joe Devlin took it in hand, the Catholic Bishops had been very suspicious of the AOH, viewing it as a sort of Catholic freemasonry, which was secret and beyond their influence and control. Devlin significantly secured the support of his friend, Bishop Patrick O'Donnell of Raphoe, and he organised the removal of the Hierarchy's ban on the Hibernians in 1904 just in time for his take over of the organisation at its national convention in Dublin in 1905. Bishop O'Donnell was a powerful figure both in the Church and in politics, being the head of the Congested Districts Board, set up by Arthur Balfour as part of his policy of *'Killing Home Rule with Kindness'*, and a trustee of the United Irish League. He helped with drafting the new AOH Ritual.

The Catholic Church had a traditional distrust of secret societies but Bishop O'Donnell quickly woke up to the possibilities offered by the AOH. O'Donnell saw a militant lay Catholic society, which supplemented the spiritual control of the priesthood over its flock, by the social and political influence of a secret order over its members, to be a real asset for the Church in combating its various opponents and spreading its influence. And it meant that the Church could safeguard the position they had achieved under British rule in the new Home Rule Ireland.

By 1907 the Catholic Hierarchy were positioning themselves alongside Devlin and the Home Rule movement to ensure that if devolution came they would maintain and even expand their influence in the country and put a stop to any elements who might threaten that influence by seeking to establish greater separation from Britain. At the ordination of Charles

McHugh as Bishop of Derry in 1907 Cardinal Logue stated the Hierarchy's position vis a vis Home Rule:

"I have very strong views on the matter and... I think those who imagine we would make use of it as a lever to separate ourselves from the rest of the Empire are simply deceiving the people. All we want is what they have in Canada and Australia and South Africa, to have full control of our own affairs and the spending of our own money, which is at present shamefully wasted... it is a very ominous thing that we find the politicians of this country entering an alliance with socialism and secularism under the pretence of securing Home Rule for Ireland... Its policy is to banish God from the schools and from the hearts of the people" (IN 30.9.07).

Perhaps Logue's warning was prompted by the activities of Larkin and Connolly in Belfast that Summer during the Dock Strike or maybe it was Devlin's mustering of 15,000 Hibernians close to the arch-episcopal palace in Armagh a few days earlier that prompted the Cardinal.

Devlin's other great ally in the AOH was John D. Nugent of Keady, Co. Armagh, who led the Hibernians in Dublin and who was also on the Standing Committee of the League. Nugent was also the manager of the British Legal Assurance Company which attained rapid growth under his leadership. Nugent's expertise in this area was significant for the AOH in adopting a scheme of registration for the distribution of state funds. Foy notes that "Devlin and Nugent were not the sort of men to rely on verbal declarations of support... their object was to weave the Ancient Order of Hibernians into the U.I.L. structure so that escape would be very difficult indeed" (p.51).

## The Hibernians And The Party

The *History Of The Ancient Order Of Hibernians* was published by the Hibernians themselves in 1910 and Devlin wrote the Foreword. J.J. Bergin, the author, claimed that the AOH had 60,000 members, organised in 500 Divisions with 85 of them concentrated in the 'front line' in Co. Tyrone. In Ulster the Hibernians did in fact supersede the League as the primary nationalist organisation and at the Nationalist convention in February 1909, for instance, there were representatives from 135 UIL branches, and delegates from 132 AOH divisions.

The AOH was woven into the structure of the Party in a number of ways. Many Nationalist MPs for example, became members of the AOH. Prominent members included Devlin himself, The Chairman's brother Willie Redmond, Tom Kettle and Nugent. Significant numbers of UIL members on the county and borough councils set up by the *Local Government Act* of 1898 and on the public bodies, such as the Boards of Guardians, were Hibernians. The

Hibernians ran the electoral campaigns, supplying canvassers and checkers at polling stations and the AOH halls were used for political meetings and for distributing literature. As a result Party candidates became obliged and dependent on the AOH for the maintenance of their positions and careers.

Foy describes how the Order had members at every level in the Party — at the very top of the League structure on the Standing Committee where Devlin and Nugent were permanent fixtures, on the next level, the National Directory and at the National conventions, held under the auspices of the League, there was a rapid growth in the number of delegates from the Hibernians. Only two dozen AOH delegates attended the Party Convention of April 1903, but this expanded to 417 delegates at the Convention of February 1909. There were also Hibernians among the delegates from the other organisations represented. Considering the total number of delegates at Conventions usually ranged from 2,500 to 3,000, Hibernian strength was very significant (p.78).

Hibernians were encouraged strongly to join the League and some AOH chapters made membership of the League obligatory. Meetings of the AOH were held immediately before UIL meetings in the same Hibernian halls to encourage attendance. Nationalist parades emphasized the fusion of the AOH and the League with both organisations marching together behind Hibernian bands.

Foy also notes the other uses the Hibernians had for the Party. For instance, the AOH was a valuable source of finance. The Irish party was always short of money because the payment of salaries to MPs did not begin until 1911. So members of the Party had to be supported by financial assistance from party funds, and in 1904 the majority of Irish MPs were receiving payments. The AOH collections taken at division meetings for the UIL and fundraising events organised by the Order, such as dances, concerts, competitions, and donations made to the campaign funds of individual candidates at election time or to the Irish Parliamentary fund made up any shortfalls. Another source was the fees levied by the Order on divisions. For instance, in December 1907 the Board proposed a levy of 6d on each division as a contribution to Party funds.

Foy describes how the AOH was useful to the UIL as a disciplinary device. The Parnell split and the subsequent dissensions and recriminations had had a traumatic effect. When the split was healed, unity at all costs was the constant theme. Any individual or group who threatened to upset that unity could only expect to be vigorously and relentlessly pursued as a 'Factionist'. The UIL was already experienced at pressurising its opponents with methods which had been perfected in the days of the Land League but it now benefited from the additional support of the AOH in having an organisation doing the disciplinary work where the League was weak. The

AOH was prepared to do this work by shunning those people who went against the UIL (pp. 79-80).

The AOH, a feature of Northern Catholic solidarity against the Planter, became Redmond's indispensable instrument against the thing he feared most in the Party after the Parnell split—'Factionism'. Devlin's Hibernians thus facilitated Redmond's mindless discipline over the Party which ultimately led to disaster.


## Smashing Sinn Fein

In 1908 West Belfast sent its men south to help smash an emerging political rival to the Parliamentary Party, Sinn Fein, the 'Factionists' outside the Party.

The rise of Sinn Fein is sometimes seen as an irresistible process. But Arthur Griffith's Sinn Fein, which appeared on the political scene in 1905, practically vanished by 1911. The growth of Sinn Fein during 1907-8 was largely a protest against the Irish Party Leadership in placing their reliance on the British Liberals and in being badly let down by the absence of a Home Rule Bill. The post-1916 Sinn Fein was a very different IRB development.

From 1910 on, when Redmond was vigorously pursuing Home Rule in conjunction with the Liberals, Sinn Fein started to go into a swift decline. The likelihood of a Home Rule measure was, therefore, the political context of the rise and decline of Sinn Fein between 1905 and 1911.

The period 1907-9 was the most difficult for the Irish Party. Earlier, they opposed the Unionist Government, and the land struggle had occupied the people. When the Liberal Party took power in 1905/6 there was renewed hope of a Home Rule Bill. But when they failed to deliver and the Party rejected the Council Bill, a very despondent and purposelessness set in that was only seen out by the purposefulness of Joe Devlin's Hibernians.

Sinn Fein questioned the sole reliance of the Irish Party on the Westminster Parliament in achieving the national objective. It argued against the Parliamentary Party's policy on the basis that it was a betrayal of Ireland's case for nationhood in its recognition of the authority of the English Parliament to legislate for Ireland. Griffith saw the Westminster orientation as being damaging to the national interest by focusing attention on London and distracting attention from Ireland and Irish interests, and leading ultimately to Anglicization and West Britain.

Arthur Griffith's policy was self-sufficiency, self-reliance and the restoration of the Kingdom of Ireland, or Dual Monarchy (so-called because it would be acceptable for the king of England to be also the king of Ireland if the Irish people accepted it). It wasn't Republican and it wasn't physical force. Griffith urged passive resistance, an end to attendance of Irish members at Westminster and the formation of a National Assembly to rebuild Ireland's national standing vis-à-vis England.

The Sinn Fein policy had been formulated in Griffith's pamphlet, *The Resurrection Of Hungary*, in 1904. While Redmond and Devlin were beginning to cultivate the notion of applying the South African model to Ireland, within the British Empire, Griffith was advocating the model Austria applied to Hungary and increasingly to its other minorities in the Hapsburg Empire.

The fundamental Irish Parliamentary Party criticism of Sinn Fein was that it was no use embarking on a policy that Britain would not stand for, which would bring the country into inevitable conflict with England, when their argument could not be backed up with sufficient force.

One Irish Party MP, Charlie Dolan, who was impressed with Griffith's policy resigned his North Leitrim seat and decided to stand for Sinn Fein instead. Sinn Fein did not really want the election at this point and not in an area where its influence was minimal. But it was forced into the challenge. This was the first test for Sinn Fein against the Parliamentary Party.

Diarmuid Lynch, a member of the Irish Republican Brotherhood who campaigned for Sinn Fein, recalled:

> "It was a losing fight but a memorable one. On one occasion Alderman Tom Kelly and myself were assigned to a meeting at Kinlough, and had an exciting day. Not alone were the majority of the local people opposed to us but we had to contend with one of the Belfast gangs imported by Joe Devlin. Armed with long sticks they menaced throughout the meeting. The loud-voiced interference was so great the speakers could scarcely hear themselves; people who wished to hear us certainly could not. As we continued to speak eggs began to fly; the wall at the hotel in front of which our wagonette was drawn up was as 'decorated' as we were. On the return journey to Manorhamilton Headquarters our reception was unpleasant—to say the least. The Redmond-Devlinites beat us in Leitrim; their countrywide rout in 1918 was in the unforeseeable future" (The IRB and the Easter Rising, p.19).

Michael Foy has an account of the North Leitrim by-election of February 1908 and Devlin's West Belfast Hibernians' efforts on behalf of the Party's candidate, Francis Meehan. He describes how Dolan's campaign was "subjected to steady and organised harassment and disruption. Wherever he went, he was followed by squads of Hibernians, with the Belfast contingents particularly prominent, who heckled, shouted, jeered, and intimidated". Foy notes an example of this at Kinlough on 19th February. Here, on the day before, Meehan and his supporters had held a meeting with the understanding that Dolan could have a meeting the following day without interruption:

"However, a group of Meehan's supporters including the Belfast Hibernians arrived in Kinlough in advance of Dolan's party, and when the latter arrived it was faced with the sight of the Belfast party leading two bands up and down the village."

When Dolan's meeting began and he got up to speak he was met by "a torrent of groaning and yelling, drums were beaten and eggs were thrown at him and the rest of his party". Apparently Dolan, provoked, started shaking his fist at Meehan's supporters and shouted: "Constable, remove those men — West Belfast asses". But as Foy notes:

"This only encouraged the Belfast contingent to engage in singing songs, throwing more eggs and other objects including an old boot! Dolan, after shouting about the 'scum of Belfast' got down from the platform, made for the Belfast party and aimed an unsuccessful blow at their leader. At this point sticks were brandished, threats were issued, and fears began to grow that the police would be overpowered. A full scale riot was only prevented by Dolan agreeing to abandon the meeting."

Foy notes that the events in Kinlough were not untypical of what the Sinn Feiners had to put up with from Devlin's Hibernians.

The North Leitrim by-election was important on several counts:

"First, it had seen an impressive demonstration of the electoral muscle power of the Hibernians. Wherever Dolan went, there were sure to be Hibernians present to harass him and spoiler his meetings. It was a campaign of disruption carried through with great energy and managed with considerable skill."

After that the AOH was able to crow that "we have undoubtedly shown the power we possess" (pp.142-3).

It has been long forgotten that West Belfast's first electoral contribution to national politics was to help smash Sinn Fein.


## West Belfast Intervenes Again

A year later, in 1909, Catholic Belfast made its second, and most significant, intervention in national affairs by providing Redmond and Devlin with the muscle to see off William O'Brien at the notorious 'Baton Convention' of the Parliamentary Party. By that stage the leadership of the Parliamentary Party was determined to cleanse the Party of O'Brienite opposition to the alliance with the Liberal Government.

When in 1902 O'Brien began to advocate his policy of 'conference and conciliation' with Southern Unionists Devlin did not support him. Devlin feared a dilution of Home Rule in order to appease Unionists. Devlin, with

Dillon, also opposed the 1903 Land Act, which O'Brien championed, to facilitate the transference of land from the landlords to the people through a scheme of state funded land purchase.

O'Brien along with Tim Healy rejoined the Irish Party in 1908 mainly to try to prevent the Tories 1903 Land Purchase Act being undermined by the British Treasury after a movement in the international financial markets diminished the funds allocated by the British State for Irish land purchase. Redmond, Dillon, and Devlin went along with the Treasury reduction calculating that it would preserve the landlord bogey, which they took to be essential in preserving the national antagonism that they understood to be necessary for bolstering the Home Rule campaign.

The previous Unionist Government had introduced the Land Purchase Acts in an effort to 'Kill Home Rule with Kindness'. William O'Brien was a supporter of land purchase on the basis of its own merits in returning the land to the people who worked it. But he also saw it as building an all-Ireland unity on economic interest with the creation of an alliance around land purchase between Catholic and Protestant farmers against Landlordism. Dissensions had opened up within Ulster Unionism and this had possibilities for Nationalists in the political sphere, which O'Brien was keen to follow up on.

Whilst Landlordism was increasingly eradicated in much of the south-west by the 1903 Act and O'Brien's campaign for farmers to take up the scheme that enabled them to take out loans to buy out the Landowners, it was sabotaged in much of the rest of the country by Dillon and Redmond to preserve the land grievance in service of Nationalism.

The Party met at the Mansion House in Dublin in February 1909, and at the Conference, Redmond moved support for the adoption of the Finance Bill on the grounds that it would avoid a burden being placed on the Irish ratepayer. O'Brien aimed to counter with an amendment calling for the rejection of the Bill on the grounds that the abolition of Landlordism must not be stopped just to alleviate the British Treasury of a liability which was rightfully its own, and which it could not evade if the Party put up a united and determined resistance to it.

But when O'Brien got up to speak he was drowned out by Hibernian whistles, the stamping of feet and the beating of seats with sticks. Flanked by the Grand Master of the AOH, Devlin, and its Grand Chaplain, the Bishop of Raphoe, Redmond made no effort to get O'Brien a decent hearing, and instead let the Hibernians do their worst.

Joe Devlin's 500 Hibernians, delegates and stewards, some armed with clubs, were providing 'security' at the conference because two years early around 200 Sinn Feiners disrupted it and Devlin convinced Redmond that only his men could deal with the Sinn Feiners.

Not only was O'Brien prevented from addressing the Convention but anyone suspected of being from Cork, and consequently believed to be a supporter of O'Brien's, was prevented from reaching the platform by Devlin's West Belfast AOH men. O'Brien's associate Eugene Crean, MP, whilst attempting to have a word in O'Brien's ear was man-handled by the Hibernian 'security' and Devlin was alleged to have shouted, "Throw the fellow out!"

O'Brien had tried his best to prevent the Party becoming dominated by the Hibernians, whom he saw as an inevitably divisive force with regard to the Northern Protestants, confirming their cry that 'Home Rule would be Rome Rule'. But he failed and the Hibernians supplanted the United Ireland League within the Party and secured the supremacy Devlin desired. O'Brien then went off to set up the All-for-Ireland League, leaving the Party to Redmond, Dillon and Devlin's Hibernians.

That represented a point of no return for the Irish Party in which it was now gambling all-or-nothing on the Liberal alliance for Home Rule and making an accommodation with Unionism and Protestant Ireland impossible. The scene was set for the great confrontation over Home Rule that would involve not only Ireland but the British State and its parties heading for a monumental confrontation on how Ireland should be ruled in future.

The point of all this is that the ongoing development of the Northern Catholics in the first couple of decades of the Twentieth Century made it a most unsuitable community to be placed under a local administration of Ulster Protestants.

Of all the parts of the Irish nation it was the Belfast Catholics who were engaging most in purposeful activity within Ireland and in the wider UK State. They were also probably the least Republican community in the Nation at the time of Partition and the most enthusiastic about the Home Rule project under their leader, Joe Devlin. Yet, they were to be cut off from the foremost object of their desire, a self-governing Irish state within the Imperial State. And they were also to be cut off from the second best option: participation in the reform movement in Britain.

## Hibernian Patronage

It must be emphasized that whilst the AOH stood for Irish Home Rule it also stood for playing a full and active part at Westminster and in British Imperial affairs. Michael Foy notes that in 1912 Nugent described the AOH as, "a gigantic organisation capable not only of swaying the Irish Parliamentary Party but of having sufficient influence and power to dictate how the British Empire ought to be governed" (p.83).

Devlin had contributed greatly to its modern growth. He modernised the Order, gave it a political focus and secured clerical approval for it. He urbanised it in West Belfast, and registered it as a Friendly Society—thus enabling it to become a recognised body under Lloyd George's Insurance Scheme, which gave it the power of considerable patronage, as a distributor of State funds to the Irish working class.

On this significant development Foy notes that by 1905 the construction of a welfare state had not even begun and ill-health and death were things which individuals had to make their own arrangements for. Therefore a benevolent society like the AOH was attractive, because if misfortune hit a member the Order would pay benefits which would cushion the impact on the member and his family. There was a scale of benefits varying in accordance with the size of the payments made and any member wanting the full range of benefits could be covered by paying a weekly contribution of six pence half-penny or seven pence. For this sum the member and his family got in the event of illness free medical attendance and medicine, while the member themselves got a weekly allowance for the first three months of the illness and a further, reduced, allowance for the succeeding three months. If the member died his family got a mortality grant of £10 for his burial or if the member's wife died he got a grant of six pounds from the Order.

The attraction of the AOH as a Benefit Society was greatly increased by the Lloyd George National Insurance Act of 1911. The Act, in its application to Ireland, provided for the compulsory insurance of all workers between the ages of 16 and 70 earning less than £160 a year. These people were to be entitled to four main types of payment: Sanatorium Benefit; Sickness Benefit; Disablement Benefit and Maternity Benefit for the first time.

Significantly, the Liberal measure laid down that the contributions were not to be collected nor the Benefits paid by the State but instead the Act was to be operated through approved Friendly Societies sanctioned by the Insurance Commissioners. Since the insurance was to be compulsory, it was really essential therefore to become a member of an Approved Society. This meant a vast potential pool of new members created by the Act for the AOH when it was approved by the Insurance Commissioners. The AOH was quickly approved, and before the Act came into operation in Ireland, in July 1912, the Hibernians engaged in a great publicity campaign to attract new members. This resulted in a massive increase in membership and Nugent began to supervise the construction of a large Hibernian bureaucracy to cope with the expansion.

This process provided the Order with hundreds of jobs at its disposal to distribute. There had to be agents to look after the contributions and doctors employed by the Society to provide the sickness certificates for the employees. By 1915 the AOH had over 120,000 in its insured section, representing over one sixth of the total insurable population. It had eleven District Offices in Ireland and, including the central office staff, employed over 1,400 people.

As Foy notes: "It is little wonder, then, that in some parts of the country the AOH and the National Insurance Act were synonymous" (pp. 93-5).

This could be regarded as a system of patronage or corruption but what is certain is that it was a very substantial machine.

Although the Catholic Bishops opposed the extension of the National Insurance Act to Ireland, Devlin persuaded the Party to back it. That is another illustration of the power of Devlin and the Hibernians in being able to face down the Catholic Hierarchy.

Whilst Devlin's AOH proved a very divisive element in Irish politics during the lead-up to Home Rule, that is not to say that it would not have found a place in British political and social life if either Home Rule had been successful in an all-Ireland context, or if Partition had come about without 'Northern Ireland' (i.e. if the Six Counties had merely remained part of the UK with no Protestant Parliament in between).

## The Imperial Hibernians

The registration of the AOH as a Friendly Society under the Insurance Act indicated that it would have played an active part in the growth of the British welfare state — something that would have made a future detachment all the harder. This would probably have meant that both the AOH and Irish Party would have become absorbed in Labour politics with the other Irish communities in Britain — particularly since that is where Devlin gave thought to going politically after the Liberals fell apart after the Great War.

It also indicated that Ulster and Ireland were being structurally interwoven with Liberal Britain through Home Rule and this would undoubtedly have increased Joe Devlin's power both in Ireland and in Imperial affairs generally.

The administration by the AOH of the National Insurance scheme was part of a process that was making both Devlin and West Belfast more British and Imperial. John Redmond made a speech in 1909 in which he called the welfare provisions "*extravagant*" and something that, if a Home Rule Government had been in place, would not have been implemented. But the welfare provisions were undoubtedly a great boon to the Northern urban, working-class followers of Devlin.

Social reform and Imperialism went hand in hand in the UK State. The former was only possible because of the latter: So, being tied into the welfare reform provisions of the Imperial state, tended to tie West Belfast into Imperialism. If a Home Rule Ireland had occurred and a separatist element had gained momentum within the new Irish State, as Unionists predicted it would, Devlin's West Belfast would have represented a very substantial counter-force for the Imperial link.

It was ironic that Ulster Unionism would ultimately unravel such a substantial Imperial development within its midst.

Interestingly Devlin drew a comparison between the Insurance Act and Land Purchase, when the former came up for debate in Parliament during May 1909:

"The Old Age Pensions Act was one of the greatest proofs of humanitarian statesmanship that has been conceived in the last half century. It was a recognition by the State of its responsibilities not towards the professional or richest classes, who can defend their own interests, especially if they come from the North of Ireland; it was a recognition that the soldiers of labour, the workers and the toilers, have also some right to look to the State to safeguard their interests after they have served the State for 70 years... It is the first great act of restitution for which England has been responsible in her fiscal relations with our country. I am glad that the restitution has taken this form. I would rather see an old age pensioner receiving 5s. a week than an Ulster Unionist Member receiving 31 1/2 years purchase for his land. It is not only an act of justice, but it is a great act of social reform" (Hansard 13.5.09, col. 2056).

Land Purchase held the possibility of achieving some form of unity between Protestant and Catholic and preparing the way for Irish self-government, whilst the Insurance Act largely had the effect of binding and integrating Ireland into the British State. And Devlin was quite explicit in what he thought was the greatest act of British reform in Ireland.

## Imperialism And Home Rule

Joe Devlin seems to have become an enthusiastic Imperialist, like Redmond, as a result of the tours he made of Canada, Australia and New Zealand.

Around this time the Irish Party began to reconcile itself to the country being made into 'Imperial Ireland' and an active and constructive component of the British Empire. This development was taken up by the Irish Party leadership as an improvement over what had been done to the country in the previous centuries by England, and, indeed, since the Union of 1801. It was also seen as the only way to some form of self-government for the Irish in the context of the seeming permanence of and increasing British Imperial power in the world and the Liberal Party's own conversion to Imperialism.

Until 1909 the Liberal leadership, sitting on a large majority, avoided all commitment to Irish Home Rule and kept the Home Rulers at a safe distance. But then the Unionist-dominated House of Lords threw out the controversial Lloyd George Budget that threatened to tax the wealthy to pay for the National Insurance scheme, and resulted in a General Election that whittled away the Liberal majority and left the Irish Party with the balance of power in the House of Commons. The two British parties attempted to exclude the Irish influence on the British party conflict through a constitutional convention and then a second General Election in 1910 but to no avail.

Prime Minister Asquith, the reluctant Home Ruler, made a deal with Redmond for the Irish to support the Budget and House of Lords reform, removing its power of veto over legislation, in exchange for a Home Rule Bill.

But the abolition of the Lords' Veto removed a block on Home Rule that was simply replaced by other, more formidable, obstacles. An Ulster Army backed by a substantial part of the British political and military Establishments and half the House of Commons. Thus the fateful alliance between the Irish Party and the British Liberals led both up a blind alley to disaster.

In the subsequent conflict over Home Rule, Irish Nationalism and British Imperialism ceased to be mutually exclusive. The two were reconciled to the extent that they were seen as mutually beneficial by the Imperially-minded Home Rulers and the Home Rule-minded Liberals.


## The Ulster Opposition

But what about the traditional garrison in Ireland?

The Protestant ruling class of the British State in Ireland expected its power to continue and it remained committed to the sectarian system of politics which made it the predominant element, despite the democratisation under the Union that was eroding its power.

It rejected the possibility of joining with the Catholic majority in the formation of a new national development because of its anti-Catholicism, convincing itself that this form of politics, which had prevailed in England for the preceding three centuries, would last forever. It saw an increasingly assertive Catholic Nationalist movement confronting it and could not see that the assertion of Protestant power and the structure of governing and politics that it had maintained had itself produced such a development.

The Protestant ruling class never considered relinquishing its privileged position and becoming part of the new national development. If it had done so, it might have held an influential position within new national power structures in Ireland. But it did not do so and only the occasional individual jumped ship. Parnell did not become Home Rule leader as the representative of the Protestant community exercising hegemony over the new democracy. He was in that respect a mere individual that others in his social circle felt had betrayed them.

The Unionist response to the First Home Rule Bill in 1886 was an expression of outrage that a superior people should be subordinated to an inferior people on the basis of democratic head-counting, even though it was only a matter of local government that was being proposed. That and Anti-Papism remained the animating spirit of Ulster Unionism for the next century.

The Unionist opposition in Ulster to being placed under an Irish Home Rule parliament was not strategic or Imperial. It was intimate, of a local character, and traditional. It decided that it would not be governed, even in local affairs, by the native enemy which it had been its destiny to displace. It had failed to accomplish that destiny and would not suffer the indignity of having to suffer a form of native rule, even if it was the case that the natives were becoming accomplices in the business of Empire.

The measure of devolved government which the Home Rule Act of 1912 set out to establish in Ireland, within the Empire and within the United Kingdom, was to have very limited powers. It was subject to British sovereignty and was to perform its functions under the supervision of Whitehall.

But the Protestant minority declared against this proposal as it had against the previous two attempts at Home Rule and it began to organise politically and militarily to prevent it from being implemented, particularly in Ulster.

The alliance between British Liberalism and Irish Nationalism tended to mask the Ulster complication. The Liberal Government did not consider the exclusion of Protestant Ulster from the Home Rule Bill because of its dependence on the Irish Party.

But it was another question, entirely, for Irish Nationalists wishing to incorporate Ulster Protestants within a Home Rule state, what provision should be made for the complication of a distinct Protestant community in the North.

The Ulster Protestant community had opposed every movement to extend the franchise, to establish local Councils, to transfer to ordinary Irishmen any form of authority over national activity. And they had never before lived under the jurisdiction of the Catholic majority on the island. It was self-evident that such an innovation being proposed by British Liberalism would have been extremely traumatic for them, and it was essential that provision for their fears, however rational or irrational, should have been made.

The *Round Table*, an influential publication of Chatham House, in an article entitled *The Irish Crisis*, written in March 1914, touched on the fundamental problem Home Rule presented to Protestant Ulster in the way the Liberals were attempting to change the historical relationship the British State had with the two communities in Ireland:

"The pride of the Ulster Protestants, their power of action, their narrowness of mind, their religious bigotry, their absolute self-sufficiency—these are factors which will have to be dealt with, however unreasonable their present manifestation may seem to be... There may be too much arrogance and intolerance in the Ulster position, but neither Englishmen nor Scotsmen should forget that they are responsible for the history which planted the forebears of these Covenantors in the North-East of Ireland. It is enough that these men believe themselves to be arming to defend their fundamental rights of citizenship in the United Kingdom. They are not seeking to destroy the existing order of society... they are only seeking to preserve it from what they regard as a menace to established liberty... Until the end of the eighteenth century Ireland was governed in conformity with the views of the Protestant minority, backed by the physical force of England. The Liberal Party has now drifted into an attempt to settle Ireland on the converse of the same principle. It is no remedy of injustice to invert it."

The All-For-Ireland League, which gave priority to unity, recognised that provisions had to be made to make even this modest proposal for Irish devolution palatable for Ulster Protestants and that Devlin and his colleagues were proceeding on the road to ruin by grabbing at the chance for a Home Rule Bill in their opportunistic alliance with the Liberals.

William O'Brien and the All-For-Ireland League were of the belief that concessions should have been made to Ulster before its alliance with the Unionist Party had acquired substance and the Home Rule issue had become a central issue within British party politics.

But Redmond and Devlin persisted nonetheless in deluding themselves that the Ulster complication was something that could be conjured away with a Parliamentary majority.

## The Home Rule Conflict

The Redmondite faith that British Imperialism would universally go along with the new scheme for 'Imperial Ireland' should have been realised to be an illusion when it was found that there were two very different views in Britain as to the way Ireland should be pacified.

The conflict over Home Rule within the British State came about because British Unionism rejected the Liberal/Irish Party scheme for Imperial Ireland. It preferred to trust in the old garrison, the Protestant minority, to hold Ireland in perpetuity rather than rely on a democratisation of Imperial hegemony based on the conversion of the majority Catholic-Nationalists to Imperialism.

The Liberal proposal of a democratisation of Imperial rule in Ireland under Home Rule was unacceptable to Protestant Ulster, and the British Unionist Party backed it in whatever methods it decided to use to oppose it. The Leaders of British Unionism believed the Liberal leadership to be shameless opportunists who had no belief in Irish Home Rule but who were ripping up the British Constitution through an 'immoral bargain' with John

Redmond founded on mere parliamentary arithmetic.

A series of inflammatory statements by Unionist leaders sharpened the conflict over Home Rule to a level unprecedented in the party conflict of the British State. (The British democracy is effective and successful because it is arranged that there is very little of substance between the two major parties of State. The rule of the other party is tolerable on this basis. But in 1910-14 something of substance developed between the two parties due to the Liberal reliance on an external influence, Redmond's Irish Party.)

In June 1912 tensions were raised in Ulster when a group of Hibernians attacked a Presbyterian Sunday School outing in Castledawson. In response thousands of Catholic workers were expelled from the shipyards by angry Protestants.

In August 1912, after a Liberal Member had put down an amendment to the Home Rule Bill excluding the four North-Easter Counties, Churchill wrote a confidential letter to Redmond, warning him that Ulster was serious in using extra-parliamentary force against the Government and advising him to defuse the developing conflict and facilitate Home Rule by making an offer to Ulster on the lines of temporary exclusion of some of the North-East from a Dublin parliament (see Dennis Gwynn, *The History Of Partition*, pp. 48-9).

But Redmond ignored Churchill's advice and pressed on regardless in pursuit of the enactment of Home Rule.

Edward Carson and the Ulster Unionists were not advocates of Partition. They opposed Home Rule in the hope that their local opposition in North-East Ulster would defeat the implementation of the scheme right across Ireland, by making it unworkable. Just like the British Government, they accepted that Ireland was a Thirty-Two County political entity. But they believed that they had the right of veto upon the democratic claims of the rest of the Ireland's inhabitants and the island should remain an entity governed directly by a Protestant-dominated Parliament at Westminster.

However, at the start of the parliamentary session in January 1913 the Unionists decided they had to retreat, for tactical reasons, from their total opposition to Home Rule and put forward their first fall back position, a Nine-County Province of Ulster Partition amendment. This was not an attempt to express self-determination for 'Protestant Ulster'. Carson's proposal of excluding all nine Counties of Ulster was primarily a blocking device to prevent Home Rule entirely — on the basis that Redmond could never accept it. However, Ulster began to make provision for itself alone to be saved from the Home Rule government and the Ulster Unionist Standing Committee decided in the previous month to withdraw opposition to Home Rule in the event of Ulster being excluded.

When Carson put forward his Nine County exclusion resolution, Redmond said in the House of Commons: "no one who observes the current of popular opinion in this country can doubt for one instance that if this opposition from the North-East corner did not exist, Home Rule would go through tomorrow as an agreed Bill" (The History of Partition, p.53) .

But instead of accepting the Ulster complication as something that needed to be taken account of, and made provision for, Redmond dismissed it as a minor hurdle to be taken in the last lap toward Home Rule.


## Devlin And Ulster Resistance

Asquith's primary reason for deciding to reject the idea of inserting any special clause about Ulster in the Home Rule Bill was the Irish Party. He knew that Redmond would not consider it and his Government would fall if he attempted any form of separate treatment at that stage. So he decided to review the situation later on, when the extent and character of Ulster Unionist resistance was fully known, and then act accordingly.

The Irish Party was dismissive of the opposition to Home Rule and treated the Ulster Unionists with contempt, declaring they were an unrepresentative minority of the Ulster Protestant community. Redmond and Devlin advised Asquith that Ulster Unionism was insignificant and bogus. Devlin, who was taken as the authority on the subject—since he was from the Unionist heartland—continuously predicted that on the day Home Rule was passed there would be some rioting in Belfast and little else. Devlin's view of Ulster Unionism was that it was a "dying faction... fighting a losing battle, not for religious right, nor for Empire, but for that ascendancy which was passing from their grip forever and for whatever fat jobs they could obtain in England" (Irish News, 9.1.11).

Devlin, who had become engrossed in Imperial politics, saw Unionism's opposition to Irish Home Rule, very much in the context of what was happening in England, as a reactionary movement against Imperial democratisation: "we were at war with the class who were at war with us... privilege, ascendancy, and class were on the one side against freedom, democratic control, and the role of the people on the other" (IN 6.11.11).

There was, of course, no "Protestant Ascendancy" in Ulster. It was the actual physical presence of the society that developed from the Plantation that stood in Devlin's way. In the rest of the country the "Protestant Ascendancy" (i.e. the Landlord interest) was being eroded by this time but this was not the case in Ulster where no such thing existed. In Ulster a substantial Protestant community occupied the ground Devlin wanted for his Home Rule Ireland and it could not be wished away by pretending it was an obsolete remnant of aristocracy in an age of democracy.

Devlin's position *vis-à-vis* Ulster Unionism was summed up very neatly in this report of a speech of his made in January 1914:

> "Mr. Devlin described the Ulster opposition to Home Rule as sheer bluff, and it was a policy that failed to convince or intimidate anybody... the one and only agreed policy of the Unionists has been to keep on shouting that there will not be Home Rule. That policy... has failed everywhere and not least in Ulster itself, where the so-called Volunteer movement and the Provisional Government have been reduced to a miserable fiasco... the whole thing was a gigantic game of bluff, got up for the purpose of frightening the British people in order to stave off the fall of ascendancy in Ireland for a little longer. But the game did not work this time" (Freeman's Journal, 27.1.14).

And Devlin concluded that he "had every reason to believe that the vast majority of the people of Ulster, Protestant and Catholic were Home rulers".

The speeches made at the great Home Rule meeting held in Swords on 27th April 1913, were illustrative of the kind of things which Catholic Ireland was being told by its leaders about Ulster Unionism. It shows how the people of Ireland were deluded about the character of its resistance. John Dillon, J.D. Nugent (the National Secretary of the AOH), and Tom Kettle addressed it. Nugent of Devlin's AOH was reported by *The Freeman's Journal* of 28th April 1913 as saying;

> "He was proud to say that he belonged to North-East Ulster, and he agreed with those who said that when Home Rule was passed there would be war, but it would be a war between the Unionist lawyers in order to secure the jobs (cheers). It would be a war between these gentlemen to try and secure what they had in the past, the flesh-pots of power and influence in this country, and he could say that, so far as any revolt on the part of the people of North-East Ulster was concerned, that they need not fear in the least any revolt from the Orangemen of either Belfast or Derry. They need not fear that they would be called upon to raise either a wooden gun or a broken sword (laughter). There were quite enough Nationalists in North-East Ulster to look after themselves (cheers)."

On 20th February 1914, Devlin delivered a report to the British Cabinet which concluded:

> "We have exceptional sources of information in regard to the Ulster Volunteer movement, and we are convinced that its danger is grossly exaggerated. The main ground for this conviction is the fact that, in Belfast, the headquarters of the Carsonite movement, where the Catholic and Protestant Home Rulers would be among the first victims of any outbreak among the Orangemen, the Home Rulers regard the whole thing with absolute contempt, and are astonished that anybody outside Belfast should take it seriously." (Eamon Phoenix, *Northern Nationalism*, p. 10)

Therefore it was not taken at all seriously until too late.

# The 'County Option' Exclusion

Ulster Unionism, as Churchill predicted, chose to bring force into the equation of the Home Rule conflict and British politics. A 100,000-strong private army was established in Ulster, outside the authority of the Government, to make war on the Bill, if it ever was enacted and attempts made to implement it. In March 1914 this army, the UVF, was armed at Larne. The Government decided not to apply the law against the Unionist army that was being illegally armed and drilled because the Unionist Party was strengthening its position with British public opinion with its open defiance of Parliament in support of the minority in Ireland.

In November 1913 Lloyd George had proposed to the Cabinet the exclusion of Ulster from the Home Rule Bill. At that point Unionist Ulster had not shown the strength of their will in resisting Home Rule and Asquith pressed on.

But, when the Unionist opposition concentrated upon organising armed resistance in Ulster, Churchill and Lloyd George began to privately urge Asquith to make a concession to the minority, in order to localise the opposition and deprive the Unionist Party of its chosen ground for opposing Home Rule. The Liberals began to float the idea of dividing Ireland even for the purposes of only devolving a local government to Ireland.

The Irish leaders were very concerned about any sign of weakening in the Liberal ranks, feeling they had to maintain an immaculate pretence that Ulster's opposition to Home Rule was insignificant; that when the Home Rule Bill became law all would be well in the North; and that there was total confidence in the ranks of the Irish/Liberal alliance about it all. It was as if they had the belief that any doubt or second thought introduced into the process would be fatal.

In the early months of 1914 Redmond came under intense pressure from the Liberal Government to agree to a scheme, suggested by Lloyd George, that would give each of the nine Ulster Counties, and treating the towns of Belfast and Derry as separate entities, the option of voting themselves out of a Home Rule Parliament for six years.

The temporary exclusion scheme became known as the 'County Option'. Redmond had insisted that the excluded Counties would come under the Home Rule administration automatically after the 6 years, rather than by Act of Parliament. But it later became known that the Prime Minister secretly offered the exclusion of Six Counties to Bonar Law, with a plebiscite at the end of six years, in return for him dropping his demand for a British referendum.

Redmond described his offer as *"the extremist limit of concession"*, and said he would only be prepared to accept an amending Bill to the Home Rule legislation if the Unionists agreed to it. If they did not, he reserved the right to oppose it at its later readings in the House of Commons. He said in the Commons that, if it was rejected, it was the Government's duty to employ *"all the resources at its command"*.

A couple of things need to be said about this 'County Option' scheme which was rejected by Carson on the basis that it was only a *"stay of execution"* from Home Rule for North-East Ulster. Firstly, it would have resulted in a four-County exclusion at the most and a much smaller Catholic minority in the excluded area. Secondly, there was no suggestion of the establishment of a parliament in such a development.

If a comparison is made between the 1914 scheme and the scheme later presented to Redmond in 1916 it becomes clear how much the position of the Home Rulers deteriorated during the Great War, after the Unionists took control of the War Office and then of the British Government itself.


## Civil War Averted By World War

The temporary exclusion offer, far from settling the Ulster issue, had the effect of intensifying the conflict over Home Rule.

At Bradford in March, Winston Churchill, in a very aggressive speech, made references to the English Civil War and talked of meeting Ulster with force if she did not accept compromise. Churchill's speech demonstrated the feeling of bitterness and the level of intensity to which the conflict had developed between the Unionists and the Liberals and the inter-linking that had taken place between the issue of Irish Home Rule and other issues of political conflict in England.

The Unionist calculation was that the Liberal Leaders were bluffing over Irish Home Rule and would back down when serious resistance was put up. But the conflict began to develop a momentum of its own as the Liberal backbenchers, who were suspicious of their leadership over a number of matters, began to thoroughly and vigorously engage in it. The Liberal Leaders, who were also engaged in the planning of a war on Germany behind the backs of their own backbenchers and in conjunction with Unionists, found the Home Rule conflict a unifying force within the party and a useful distraction from the questions they were previously being asked about secret foreign commitments.

The Home Rule dispute led to a great intensification of the political conflict between the governing parties that was unprecedented in England.

On the same platform as Churchill in Bradford, Devlin made it clear that he was less happy about the exclusion offer and revealed it was a concession that had been forced on the Irish Party by the Government—a concession which should not have been made:

"I never believed in Civil War... I believe all the talk about Civil War, and all the much vaunted preparations for it, to be a sham, a fraud and a humbug, and the biggest and most audacious game of bluff ever attempted by a political party in any country... But there can be no doubt whatever that it has exercised influence in certain quarters where intimate and accurate knowledge of Ulster and of the real condition of affairs there is not to be expected. The Government, in my judgement, most unwisely, allowed pressure to be brought to bear on them to give way to this influence, and, as a result, the Premier's proposal, giving permission to certain counties in Ulster, to vote themselves by plebiscite out of the Home Rule settlement for a period of six years has been made... Demand for the exclusion of Ulster was not a demand made for the purpose of saving Protestant Ulster, but a demand made for the purpose of playing the Tory game of smashing Home Rule and destroying the Parliament Act. That is the real objective of the Tory Party (cheers) and that is why they had staked everything on the defeat of Home Rule. The dishonesty of the Unionist demand for concessions has been shown by the way in which they have received them (hear, hear)... We have gone to the utmost limit in order to conciliate them. We had strained the feelings of our people in Ireland, and particularly in Ulster, almost to breaking point" (FJ 16.3.14).

It was little wonder that Devlin was annoyed by Asquith's offer to Bonar Law. Earlier on in the Home Rule campaign he had told a large rally at Nenagh:

"There have been rumours started that the Home Rule Bill will pass with the four Ulster Counties of Antrim, Down, Armagh and Derry excluded from its operation. There is not a shadow of foundation for such a statement. Ulster and Ireland will stand or fall together. The Irish Party is a national, not a provincial or a county party, and they will accept no Home Rule Bill which does not include all Ulster, as well as for Munster, Leinster and Connaught" (FJ 16.9.12).

The Liberal Government's arm was paralysed by another event in the same month: the Officer Corps of the British Army in Ireland indicated that it would not allow the regular army to be used to enforce a Home Rule Act on Ulster. Some of the officers behind this 'Curragh Mutiny' were at that moment making secret arrangements for the War with Germany which the Government had in mind, and the Government therefore had to proceed cautiously and hush things up to prevent resignations and exposures. But without the British Army the Liberals were powerless to impose its will against Ulster.

The arming of Ulster and the support it achieved from a major party in the British State had significant effects for Devlin and the Parliamentary Party. In Ireland the blind faith in British Parliamentary politics was shaken and the precedent that was set by the formation and arming of the Ulster Volunteers was followed by the establishment of the Irish Volunteers as a counter to the Ulster militarism. The Irish Volunteers were established independently of Redmond but as they developed Redmond thought it advisable to establish control over them to keep them within the 'constitutional' ambit. There was opposition within the Irish Volunteers to Redmond's takeover but the bulk of the movement went along with the Irish Party.

This chain of events combined to set a pattern for the years to come. By bringing the gun into Irish politics and by over-ruling parliamentary democracy the Ulster and British Unionists taught the Irish, who had largely forgotten about such things under the Irish Parliamentary Party, that force was, unfortunately, still an indispensable element in any dealings with British Governments.

In Britain there developed an intensifying conflict between the Liberal and Unionist parties. A conference at Buckingham Palace called by the King failed to break the deadlock as the Unionists would not agree to any arrangement which did not include the possibility of Ulster remaining out of the Home Rule area, while the Nationalists would not agree to any arrangement which did include the possibility that part of Ulster would be excluded from their rule for an indefinite period. It seemed that nothing could prevent the situation approaching civil war. This scenario was only averted by the British decision to intervene in a European war in August 1914.

This event would have great repercussions for Ireland and for the Catholics of the North-East in particular. They had put their faith in the British Parliament and what their leaders had called *"the great English democracy"*. Their destiny of playing a prominent, if not predominant, part in a Home Rule Ireland within the Imperial State through Joe Devlin had been obstructed by the extra-parliamentary force of Unionist Ulster. Now their future was to be subject to the catastrophic fortunes of war.

After rejecting the O'Brien/All for Ireland League approach to the Protestants, Redmond and Devlin took the conflict with Ulster Unionism to the brink in the pursuit of Home Rule. After rejecting compromise and conciliation they would end up with nothing, or worse than nothing — not only Partition, but a form of local Protestant rule over the Northern Catholics that was unimagined at the time.

Out of the dream that seemed to be realisable was to emerge the most unimaginable of wildest nightmares for the Northern Catholics — 'Northern Ireland'.

# CHAPTER 2

# Great War

On 1st August 1914, as the European situation went into flux, and the Imperial Government pondered on whether to make the imminent European war into a world one through British intervention, the *Irish News* advised its readers:

> "The balance of argument and common-sense is wholly on the side of English non-intervention; but the English people and their statesmen settle these matters after their own peculiar fashion. Our primary concern is with Ireland; and we intimated yesterday how Irish interests can be most effectively guarded. Make the Volunteers into a great army without a moment's unnecessary delay."

But two days later John Redmond made his famous offer to England that was to have enormous repercussions for Ireland.

The *Irish News* editorial of 1st August seems to suggest that Northern Nationalism had a reluctance to engage in the War and, since Devlin was on the board of the paper, it can be assumed it was expressing his general viewpoint in the situation. It suggests that Devlin felt similarly to John Dillon in having deep reservations about it, if not opposition to it. Over the previous years Dillon, who had a keen interest in foreign affairs, and who unburdened his thoughts privately to C.P. Scott of the *Manchester Guardian* and publicly in Parliament, attempted to expose the secret diplomatic arrangements and military preparations the Imperial Government was making for its war on Germany whilst Edward Grey was denying all in Parliament.

But on the fateful day when Redmond abandoned his position as Chairman and hustled the Irish Party into support for war on Germany in his famous House of Commons intervention on August 3rd both Dillon and Devlin conceded and followed their Leader without objection.

## Devlin and Redmond's offer

Redmond offered the Irish Volunteers to the British Government "*to defend the coasts of Ireland*", which would free British soldiers in Ireland for continental warfare. He invited the Ulster Unionists to join him in this. He did not at this point offer Irish soldiers to Britain for use against Germany. However, the British Foreign Secretary declared Ireland to be "*the one bright spot*" and the Government politely ignored Redmond's actual offer.

The only information I have on Devlin's reaction to Redmond's offer is from F.J. Whitford's unpublished thesis on the Belfast Home Rule leader, in which he says:

"A legend has been created among some of Devlin's most fervent Belfast supporters that he disagreed with Redmond's unqualified offer of co-operation with Britain. All the available evidence refutes this. The cause of Belgium appealed to his heart and his head. His support of Redmond's policy was spontaneous and sincere" (p.95, the author cites a letter from 'Moloney' in 1956 as evidence of this 'refutation').

It is hard to judge this 'refutation' on the basis of a single letter whose contents are undisclosed to the reader. And it is quite possible that Devlin disagreed with Redmond's offer and then reconciled himself to the *fait accompli* delivered by Redmond in the Commons.

What is certain is that both Devlin and The *Irish News*, like the pre-War anti-war Liberals, took to warmongering with a vengeance when Redmond's policy lost its ambiguity at Woodenbridge and he proceeded to offer the Irish Volunteers to serve "wherever they were needed" by Britain—which was to mean from Belgium to Mesopotamia.

The Irish Party made a decisive contribution to this fateful decision of Liberal England and helped provide the necessary camouflage for it to wage an Imperialist Balance of Power War to destroy its commercial rival under the cover of a moral war. And that had great implications for the Irish Party in 1918.

The Irish participation in England's war to destroy its German rival was fundamentally bound up with the issue of Home Rule. Ireland went to war against *"Prussianism"* in August 1914 to establish the rights of small nations as a principle in future international affairs— particularly in relation to itself and England. The Home Rule leaders saw the Great War as a great opportunity to break out of the checkmate in the Home Rule conflict after Unionist resistance had paralysed the Liberal arm and brought the UK to the verge of civil war, and at the same time hasten the development of a unified Imperial Ireland on the basis of anti-German warmongering.

And so from September 1914 Redmondite Ireland enthusiastically threw itself into the Great War on Germany and whomever England chose to make war on—despite the refusal of the War Office, under Unionist influence, to facilitate it by organising the Redmondite Volunteers who enlisted into a distinct military detachment, as was done with the Ulster Volunteers.

The Home Rule Bill was placed on the Statute Book in September 1914 to aid recruiting efforts in Ireland. This was trumpeted by Redmond and Devlin as a great achievement, as if a Home Rule Ireland had really come into existence. Extravagant amounts of congratulatory telegrams were sent by Parliamentary Party supporters and the AOH, to add to the pretence, and were printed on whole pages of the *Freeman's Journal* of 21st September.

But the reality was that the Bill was suspended for re-consideration after the War, with no guarantee what Government would be in power or what the make-up of Parliament would be like then. If Redmond knew his British Constitution, he should have known that no British Government was bound by the acts of its predecessors. The probability was that he did, but did not want to spoil the moment: Ireland could prove its loyalty to Britain and seal the new relationship *"in letters of blood"*, as the telegrams of congratulations had it.

## A 'mere scrap of paper'?

But Sir Edward Carson and the leader of the Unionists, Bonar Law, announced their clear intention of preventing Home Rule in Ulster after the War. On 28th September Carson told a meeting that the Home Rule Bill was "nothing but a scrap of paper" and the Ulster Volunteers would "kick out anybody who tries to put it into force in Ulster" (IN 29.9.14).

Joe Devlin attempted to counter the impression that the Home Rule Bill was a dead letter in a speech he gave in the National Club in Berry Street, Belfast, on 9th October. Referring to the placing of the Home Rule Bill on the Statute Book Devlin said:

> "It represents a solemn treaty of peace and goodwill among the nations, and those who would attempt to treat it as a 'mere scrap of paper' would be essaying a moral infamy not less odious than the German Emperor committed in violating the neutrality of Belgium (hear, hear). But on one thing, I think, the Irish people can rest assured, and that is that in the face of the declaration of the Premier and of the Liberal and Tory leaders on the sacredness of treaties, and on the rights of small nationalities, there will be no disposition on the part of either of the great British Parties to perpetrate upon Ireland, when peace has been restored, an infamy which would be greater than that which they have denounced to the world as the justification for involving Great Britain in the greatest war of all time...
>
> "We know that the threats of civil war in Ulster indulged in by the Carsons and the Bonar Laws were largely, if not mainly, responsible for encouraging the German Emperor to declare war (hear, hear). We know how some of these men appealed to Germany to help them, and said that King George would no longer be their King if he gave Royal Assent to the Home Rule Bill. We know the efforts which the Irish Party and the Irish people have made for peace and unity to help the Empire in its hour of peril. And yet we find Carson and Bonar Law, the Privy Councillors of the King, coming to Belfast and proclaiming that once the war is over they will lead a rebellion in Ulster unless the terms they choose to dictate, are submitted to. There are,

however, signs already that the best and wisest among the Ulster Unionists are sick of Carsonism. But whatever happens, Carsonism is dead (applause), and the day when either Englishmen or Irishmen can be influenced or intimidated by it has gone for ever (applause). It represented nothing but the arrogance of brute force and ascendancy, inspired by hatred and guilty failure, and could have no permanent place in a civilised community. When the truce comes we shall be prepared to discuss terms with our Unionist friends in Ulster (hear, hear)" (FJ, 10.11.14; Devlin takes poetic licence in saying that the German Emperor declared war on Britain. It was the British King-Emperor who declared war on Germany).

Devlin believed that the Unionists had been morally disadvantaged by their pre-war arms dealings with the Kaiser, who had now become the personification of evil for British public opinion. He also believed that Nationalist Ireland had won the moral high ground over Ulster Unionism as a result of England having declared itself to be fighting a *"war for small nations"*. It was thought that because Ireland was the small nation most relevant to England, this fact placed the Irish Home Rule cause in a most advantageous position in Britain.

The Home Rule Bill had been checkmated by the forces of Unionism, which hitherto had been opposed to the causes of small nationalities. But now Unionism was involved in a war for small nations itself, and the moral high ground had gone to Irish Home Rule as a result. So, it was reasoned, the German entry into Belgium, and England's declaration of War, was, like South African war before it, a very fortuitous development.

These thoughts enabled Imperial Ireland to show its substance as it went to war with Germany, despite the Home Rule struggle still being unresolved, and this had the effect of accelerating, rather than holding it back in its Imperial development. It was all to reach a peak in April 1915 at the great Volunteer muster in Dublin on Easter Sunday and in the forgotten diplomatic mission to Paris by the Irish Party that helped to bring Italy into the War on the side of the *Entente* — an event that had important effects on the subsequent history of Europe.

But what if, when peace was restored, Britain was to welch on its *"solemn treaty"* with Ireland over Home Rule, and *"an infamy which would be greater than that which they have denounced to the world as the justification for involving Great Britain in the greatest war of all time"* was perpetuated on Ireland? What then?

## Imperial West Belfast

It is clear from a reading of The *Irish News* in this period that West Belfast was a very different place in 1914 than it came to be 60 years later. The past was, indeed, another country.

West Belfast had a small Republican grouping in 1914 centred around Dennis McCullough, a Falls man, who associated with Bulmer Hobson in the Dungannon Club, to produce The *United Irishman* newspaper. But the Republican presence was minuscule in comparison to Joe Devlin's great political machine and the Home Rule movement he commanded there.

When the split in the Volunteers occurred in September, 1914, after Redmond had pledged to support the British war effort, only about a hundred men stayed with Eoin MacNeill out of three and a half thousand in the city.

Then the Falls went into competition with the Shankill to raise recruits for the British Empire's Great War, continuing the Home Rule struggle at the level of proving loyalty.

Here are some extracts from the *Freeman's Journal* about the Volunteer meeting held in West Belfast on 25th October 1914, attended by Redmond and Devlin, which make very interesting reading indeed. They are reproduced at length to give the reader a flavour of what Redmond and Joe Devlin stood for and what West Belfast was like a century ago.

The *Freeman* set the scene in the following report:

"The visit of Mr. John E. Redmond to Belfast led to a series of most remarkable demonstrations... An elaborate scheme of decoration had been completed along the route of march, and today Divis street and the Falls road were bright with bunting, the houses being profusely decorated, and flags being even suspended between the tramway polls. Irish, British, Colonial, French, and Belgian flags figured amongst the decorations. Mr. Redmond was to have inspected the Volunteers in the park. The pouring rain, however, caused the abandonment of this part of the programme...

"In substitution of the parade and review it was arranged that Mr. Redmond should address indoor meetings, one of the boys of the Christian Brothers schools of the city who were to have marched over a thousand strong with the Volunteers, and another of the Volunteers themselves assembled in the Clonard Picture House. The Irish Leader's reception first by the Nationalist boys of Belfast, and next by the Volunteers, baffles description in its enthusiasm. The Clonard Picture House, spacious though it is, was found to be quite incapable of affording accommodation to the Volunteers, and an overflow meeting was held in the Clonard Catholic Boys Hall adjoining. It was estimated that about 4,000 Volunteers attended. The line of route to travel by Mr. Redmond's party along the Falls road was lined by Volunteers, and another body formed an escort for the party. Numbers carried rifles, and some had fixed bayonets... Vast crowds lined the footpaths and streets along the route notwithstanding the pouring rain, and cheered the Irish leader and his friends with intense enthusiasm as they passed along. A notable incident as indicating the changed feeling which the passing of the Home Rule Bill has brought about was the singing of 'God Save the King' by the crowd in the Clonard Picture House while awaiting Mr. Redmond's arrival" (FJ 26.10.14).

Redmond and Devlin addressed a gathering of a thousand boys at St. Mary's Christian Brothers School in Divis Street, where the Irish Leader gave a tribute to the Brothers. Joe Devlin then addressed the boys from his old school and said he felt disappointed that they could not march with the Volunteers, due to the weather:

"I can only say that I hope that when the Irish National Volunteers within the next few months will have their thousand or fifteen hundred uniforms, and when they will march, armed and equipped, to the review which we shall then be able to hold, I promise Brother Craven and the boys that you will then get the opportunity which has been denied to us today (cheers)..."

The party then proceeded to the Clonard Picture House where Redmond addressed the Belfast Volunteers:

"I have recently inspected large bodies of Volunteers in other parts of the country, and I have invariably said the same thing that I say to you here now: A force of this character, an armed force may be either a very great blessing or a great curse to a country. If it is inspired by a proper spirit of discipline, if it is made up of men who are earnest... if it is animated with real military spirit of obedience to superior authority... then it is certain to be a blessing to the country in which it exists (cheers). When I speak of obedience to lawful authority, let me explain what I mean: It is part of the constitution of this country now that Ireland must be governed by a freely elected Parliament of the Irish people (cheers), and that that Government must be carried out by an Executive consisting of Irish Ministers responsible only to that Irish Parliament (hear, hear). Now that is what I mean by lawfully constituted authority, and when that Government comes into force the National Volunteers of Ireland must be absolutely at the disposal of that Irish Government and must yield to it absolute and unquestioning obedience (loud cheers). What was said by a great poet about the soldier of the ordinary army will be true absolutely to you: 'Theirs not to reason why; Theirs but to do or die.'

"Until that lawfully constituted authority comes into working order... I say the obedience and the loyalty of the Volunteers must be given to those who approach nearest to the actual Government of Ireland; that is to those who stand today as the elected representatives of the Irish people (cheers). In that way, and in that way only, can a volunteer force of this character be a blessing to this country (cheers)... Those who range themselves under unauthorised and irresponsible men, men with no record in the National movement behind them (hear, hear)— in that case, most undoubtedly, an armed force such as yours would prove itself a danger and a curse to the country (hear, hear).

"Well, I am glad to know that everywhere I have gone in Ireland I have found the right spirit of discipline, and the right spirit of obedience to the lawful authority—(A voice 'You will get it in West Belfast') (cheers) and here in Belfast I am delighted to know that is the spirit of the entire Volunteer force (cheers). The manhood of Ireland has sprung to arms for the purpose of defending Ireland and Irish rights, and let me say to you quite candidly what I have said elsewhere, that when I speak of defending Ireland and Ireland's rights, I do not mean only defending Ireland and Ireland's rights within the shores of Ireland (cheers). Our country is not being attacked within her shores; Irish rights and liberties are not being menaced within the four shores of Ireland at this moment... at the same time let us be honest with one another, and admit that at this moment an attack on Ireland is being made on the shores of the Continent of Europe (loud cheers), and if the manhood of Ireland rose up here, and uniformed and drilled, and armed itself, and refused to strike a blow in defence of Ireland where the real fighting is going on, believe me, our country would be covered with disgrace, and, for my part, I don't see how any longer we could go on speaking of that fighting race (hear, hear)...

"In addition to the reservists who have gone from the ranks of the Volunteers in thousands to the front... something like 35,000 recruits have already gone to the Colours within the last two months from all parts of Ireland, and from the Catholic and Nationalist part of Ulster just as much as from the other parts...

"I am speaking the truth when I say of the Irish race, as a whole, that they would feel covered with humiliation if, when this war was over, they had to admit that their rights and liberties had been saved by the sacrifices of other men while Irishmen remained safe at home and took no risk (loud cheers, and a voice 'We will go to the war', and "The Irish Brigade')...

"I will come again (cheers), a little later on when you have all got your uniforms and when every one of you has a rifle (loud cheers), when you have had your rifle range practice and when every man of you is a good shot (cheers). I will come again then, and meantime I ask you to do your work in steady, soldier like fashion. This is no child's play... You have got to show that this is a serious business, that you have gone into it seriously, that you mean to turn yourselves into efficient soldiers... (loud and prolonged cheers)."

Redmond and Devlin were trying to create some of the English military character in West Belfast, which would be useful in enduring mass slaughter dutifully and loyally without question. In this they failed utterly. Irish society had a much bigger problem with indulging itself in mass killing and dying than English society, which had by this time centuries of militaristic culture and experience in it. And, as it was increasingly exposed to carnage, it started to draw back from its Imperial mission.

The *Freeman's Journal* reported further on Redmond's address to another meeting of the Volunteers in the Catholic Boys Hall, Clonard, where over a thousand had assembled, unable to gain admission to the Picture House: "A piper's band played National airs during the interval" and "Hundreds of rifles were piled up in front of the platform. The scene when Mr. Redmond arrived was of the most enthusiastic character".

Redmond told his audience:

"I am glad to see that I am surrounded by these rifles. I know these rifles... I have submitted these rifles to the highest expert authority in the British Empire. Only the other day one of the greatest living soldiers— a general in high command in the British Empire, and a good Irishman into the bargain— examined one of these rifles for me, and he told me that... these rifles were every bit as good a weapon as the modern British rifle (applause). They have a range of nearly two miles. They have a magazine carrying five cartridges and one in the barrel. The same exactly as the most modern British service rifle. These very rifles were used in the Italian army in the war against Tripoli two years ago, and I know that tens of thousands of them have been used in the fighting in Belgium by the Belgian troops the other day (applause). These are magnificent weapons...

"I hope the day will never come when you will have to fire them in battle, at any rate in this country. I am sure that day will never come. At any rate it is well for all of you to learn the art, the business of the soldier, so that those of you who remain in Ireland may be efficient to guard our liberties, and that those of you who make up your minds to go abroad and to take some share in fighting the battle of liberty on the Continent may be in a position to be efficiently trained that much quicker than if you had never learned any rifle practice at all (applause). I am afraid if I do not put a rein upon myself I may go on longer than I ought..."

The Italian rifles that Redmond enthused about, known as "gas pipes", proved to be of little military use. They were probably old Carcona rifles used in Africa and lost in the Italian defeat at Adowa and then sold on by the Ethiopians.

Redmond's lecture on guns shows the comparative undevelopment of military knowledge in Catholic Ireland in contrast to its fulsome development in Protestant Ulster. So this is really the origin of the military art in Catholic West Belfast. And it came about entirely under the ambit of 'constitutional' Nationalism and within the British Imperial sphere of influence.

The West Belfast recruiting rally was a tremendous success. In the early stages of the War, while the Liberal Government conducted it, the Catholic community in Belfast supplied more recruits, proportionately, to the British Army for its war on Germany than the Protestant community did. As The Freeman's Journal noted:

"From Belfast alone 3,515 National Volunteers have enlisted— a decidedly larger proportion of the Roman Catholic population than the 10,112 enlisting Ulster Volunteers formed of the Protestant population; not that it is the slightest reflection on the devotion of the Belfast Unionists to have come in a good second in this honourable competition" (8.12.14).

Out of the Catholic population of Belfast, Devlin was able to raise five full regiments for the British army to fight in France. There was probably nowhere in Catholic Ireland which took to the Imperial spirit so much as Joe Devlin's West Belfast and no community that gave such service to the Empire.

## The Home Rule 'dead letter'

As Redmond and Devlin recruited in Catholic Belfast on the basis that Home Rule was a reality and Irishmen should do their bit for the Empire in return, events in Britain started to undermine the Parliamentary Party and make Home Rule a dead letter on the Statute Book.

The Redmondites failed to appreciate the character of the Great War that Britain was going to fight, which led to a decisive alteration of power within the British State away from Home Rule. Redmond, Devlin and Dillon, like their Liberal allies in Government, believed that this would be a traditional British war, primarily using the senior service, the Royal Navy and the small expeditionary force R.B. Haldane had assembled and seen off to the continent in August 1914. Most of the fighting would be done, as usual, by the continental allies—this time France and Russia—and it would all be over by Christmas, or maybe in the new year of 1915.

It can be read in the speeches of Dillon, the reluctant warmonger, that the Home Rulers were gambling on a quick British victory giving a triumphant Liberal Government and its militarily-trained and battle-hardened Irish Volunteers the edge in the Home Rule struggle after the War.

But it didn't turn out like that. The War Office was already the preserve of the Unionists, including the Curragh Mutineers. General Kitchener, the hero of numerous colonial wars, was appointed War Minister on the spur of the moment by popular demand. And Kitchener was convinced it was a big land war that needed to be fought to destroy the German Army rather than a traditional sea one.

Kitchener was also one of those anti-Irish Unionists born in Ireland and he would have nothing to do with creating an 'Irish army', that would fight the battle for Home Rule after the War, within his Imperial army. All he wanted was Irish cannon-fodder and his association with Redmond was based purely on the ability of the Irish Leader to procure fodder for his great army. So while the UVF got their own division the Irish had to pretend they had theirs as they were inter-mingled with various other elements of cannon-fodder in Kitchener's army.

And then Britain revealed that it had other ambitions in the world apart from saving the world from "*Prussianism*". It went to War with the Turks to grab parts of the Ottoman Empire, sending Irish soldiers, who had volunteered to save "*Little Catholic Belgium*", to die at Gallipoli.

The Germans did not help John Redmond either. They proved a much harder nut to crack than the Liberal Government imagined and this put the Unionists in their element, insisting that what was needed was conscription, and complaining, justifiably, of the Asquith Government's reluctance to conscript in waging a war to save 'civilisation.'

There was another assembly of Volunteers in Belfast during March 1915. The *Freeman's Journal* of 8th March described it under the main headlines: *"Review Of Belfast Volunteers by Mr. Dillon, Mr. Devlin and Col. Moore. 'We Shall Never Consent To Divide This Island Or This Nation'."* Subsidiary headlines declared: *"Uniformed Men With Rifles And Bayonets. Belfast's Fighting Spirit At Home And Abroad. Mr. Devlin's Appeal For Volunteers. Church Parade In Historic Edifice. How The Cause Of Ireland Was Saved."*

The main difference between the Volunteer muster held in West Belfast during March 1915 and the earlier one in October 1914 was the increased emphasis on the necessity of physical force in Irish politics. The message that was put across in the speeches of March 1915 was that Northern Catholics would have to volunteer to ensure that the democratic will of Ireland and Britain would be respected and would not be over-ridden by Unionist force. Devlin and Dillon were telling West Belfast Catholics that they would have to counter the military manifestations of Protestant Ulster and, however reluctantly, step outside the normal sphere of constitutional politics, if democracy and "solemn treaties" were going to be respected.

That was because the Home Rulers had begun to worry that they had been sold a pup when the Home Rule Bill was placed on the Statute Book. They had expected, naively, that with the Bill on the Statute Book and the Irish Volunteers organised and trained by Britain into an Irish army, giving their blood for the Empire, and with the War being over, that things would work out in their favour.

The *Freeman* described the Volunteer Assembly of March 1915 as follows:

"Mr. John Dillon, MP, was an honoured visitor amongst the nationalists of Belfast today. The occasion of his visit was principally to participate in the function of a review of the Irish National Volunteers of the city... the scene in Celtic Park at the imposing muster of the Belfast regiment of the Volunteers was a most impressive and significant one... A most impressive ceremony marked the opening of the proceedings of the day, when a Requiem Mass was celebrated in Saint Mary's church at half-past ten for the repose of the souls of the Irish soldiers or soldiers of Irish descent who had perished in the war. It was attended by the entire body of the Belfast Volunteers in uniform, and the scene in the church was altogether a memorable and imposing one."

At the conclusion of the inspection Joe Devlin gave a short speech:

"I think we have reason to rejoice at the power and strength of the National Volunteer movement in the city of Belfast (cheers). Already from our ranks there have gone 1,500 reservists and 1,500 recruits to fight the battle of human liberty on the plains of France and Belgium (cheers). And, wherever these men go, or wherever duty calls them, they will be sure to show the virile and fighting spirit of Ulster and Belfast Nationalism (cheers)... let it be understood the purpose for which we exist: we are here to maintain the liberties we have won and to keep upon the Statute Book of England the Home Rule Act which we have won after 30 years of constitutional agitation (cheers)..."

Devlin also made it clear to the men leaving for the Front that the Great War was not a parting gift from Home Rule Ireland to the Empire. It was just the start of a new relationship between Ireland and the Empire in which the Irish were going to become a more activist component of Imperial power in the world:

"They were not only going to fight for their own liberty, and the liberty of these Islands, but for a grand and gallant little nation—Belgium... They intended not only to maintain their National Rights, but to claim a full and increasing share in the work and glory of the Empire, which the blood and brains of Irishmen have done so much to create, and which Irishmen to-day were so powerfully helping to save and to consolidate" (FJ, 13.3.15).

This expression of enthusiastic Imperialism by Devlin should be borne in mind if it is ever imagined that Home Rule was meant to be the first instalment in an evolutionary separatism by Redmondite Ireland. That fact is central in understanding what happened to West Belfast in subsequent years.

## Volunteering against Partition

John Dillon's speech is worth reproducing to provide an understanding of how recruiting by the Parliamentary Party was assuming a more desperate character by early 1915. It also shows the basis on which the men of West Belfast were being encouraged to fight for the Empire—in order to prevent Partition, in which they would be stranded on the wrong side of any border. And a reading of it will inform the reader why disillusion was to set in so quickly after the Great War:

"For the moment, the Great War has suspended politics... in Ireland, and with the practical common sense of Belfast Nationalism, which has so often in the past taught a lessen to the South of Ireland, you have realised what was the most urgent duty that lay upon true Nationalists who mean business in the National cause. The National Volunteers of Belfast have not been content with drilling here in Belfast on Irish soil. They have set an example to the rest of Ireland by sending their best and bravest in hundreds to prepare to go to the front, to fight in Flanders and in France for the liberty of Europe, and they have recognised that when the war is over, and when we shall commence to resume the thread of Irish politics, that section of the Irish nation which has done best on the battlefields of France will be the strongest in the struggle which may then be thrust upon us (cheers)...

"Today, as Mr. Devlin had said, England and the Empire are fighting on the side of freedom (cheers). England occupies a great position before the world (cheers). She has come forward as the champion of small nationalities and of oppressed peoples; but how could she have assumed that position, how could she have dared the public opinion of the world if she had not placed upon the Statute Book the Home Rule measure, and if she had not given liberty to South Africa, following our policy and our advice in that respect? (Cheers)... That is why England is able to take her stand in the proud position she occupies, and because she has had the courage to do these things she is able to go before Europe and say: 'I am the champion of human liberty' (cheers)...

"We have, as I have already said, assembled in no spirit of contention or hostility to our fellow countrymen, but we have assembled to get ready for any struggle that may be forced upon us, and from this Celtic Park today we tell all whom it may concern that, while we are willing to travel far on the road to conciliation, always on the condition that other parties enter on to that road to meet us, and come some of that road to meet us, we will never consent— and I say it here in the face of you, the Volunteers of Belfast, who may yet have to make good my words—we shall never consent to divide this island or this nation (cheers), and we shall never consent to allow any section, clique, or faction to rule the people of Ireland (loud cheers)."

There is a reference to this aspect of recruiting in Belfast in the diaries of C.P. Scott, the famous Editor of the Liberal *Manchester Guardian*. Scott was told the following at the end of November 1914 by T.P. O'Connor, the Irish Party MP in Liverpool, who was a close friend of Devlin:

"As to recruiting in Ireland they could only look for a moderate success. Great numbers of Irish, it must be remembered, were already in the Army. Devlin was the only man who was having a real success and could deliver the goods. He did it by pointing out to the Nationalists in Ulster that the Covenanters had gone and would come back trained soldiers and, if they wanted to hold their own against them, they must get trained too. In the south and west the Sinn Feiners told the peasants that they were only asked to enlist in order that they might be conveniently killed off" (Trevor Wilson, *The Political Diaries of C.P. Scott, 1911-1928*, p.114).

The speeches of Devlin and Dillon are important in explaining the traumatic effects that the Catholics of the North suffered after Britain's behaviour between 1918 and 1922.

The Northern Catholics were being led to believe by Devlin, Dillon and Redmond that they could expect to be an integral and valued part of the Empire in the future. They were being encouraged to think of the British State as their friend and as the guarantor of their liberties; they were being encouraged to kill and die for the Empire because its cause in the Great War was the cause of Ireland; they were being told that they had a Government in waiting with an army in tow that could be expected to enforce the will of that future Government in Ireland on the Ulster Unionists; they were being assured that only by enlisting, fighting and dying for the Empire was a united Home Rule Ireland possible.

The Northern Catholics were therefore being given great responsibility for, and pretensions of status, in the promised land of a Home Rule Ireland. And they were going to feel badly let down if these predictions did not come to pass.

## Dublin 1915 and 1916

As *The Freeman* noted, the Volunteer muster in Belfast in October 1914 was meant as a preliminary to the great assembly of the Irish Home Rule army that took place in Dublin at Easter 1915. The latter event has been forgotten about in Irish history books. It involved the marching of 30,000 men watched by 100,000 spectators in what the London *Times* called the greatest military manifestation in Irish history. And yet it was consigned to oblivion after a much smaller army took to the same field a year later.

Belfast was as prominent in Dublin at Easter 1915 as it was absent at Easter 1916. The *Freeman's Journal*, in devoting three pages to describing the progress of the Volunteers along the quays of Dublin to the Phoenix Park, noted that:

> "Belfast furnished the most imposing corps in the review. Fully armed and in uniform, they swung along with splendid entrain. The efficiency they displayed could not well be surpassed by regular troops. Having reached their station they deployed in line of company with absolute precision and rhythm of movement, and the display drew once again the admiration of all who saw them" (FJ 5.4.15).

But the Belfast contingent of the Home Rule army was marching into oblivion.

In the following months things got considerably worse for the Home Rulers. The Irish, like the Liberals, were against conscription and this put them at a great disadvantage when Britain's Great War started to go wrong and compulsion was shown to be necessary if it was to be won. As a result of the Liberal dithering in their conduct of the war, the Unionists forced their way into the Government with Asquith, in mid-1915 in a War Coalition.

Home Rule was shown to be a dead letter on the Statute Book with the formation of the War Coalition with Carson and Bonar Law in the Cabinet (Redmond was invited but refused). Although the Government was outliving its five-year electoral mandate, elections were suspended and then the Home Rule 'Act' itself was suspended for another year, without protest from the Irish Party.

Shortly after the Unionist *coup* senior Catholic clerics and local Nationalists met in Omagh, County Tyrone, for a conference which aimed to oppose any further Irish Party agreement to an exclusion of Ulster from Home Rule. From this time recruiting to the British Army in Fermanagh and Tyrone began to dry up for the Redmondites.

On 3rd June 1915, Michael Fogarty, Bishop of Killaloe, formerly a supporter of the Irish Parliamentary Party and their policy to obtain Home Rule, wrote to Redmond:

> "The English have got all they wanted from Ireland, and don't care two pence about her feelings. Such is our reward for her profuse loyalism and recruiting. The people are full of indignation, but are powerless...
>
> "As far as Ireland is concerned, there is little to choose between Carsonism and Kaiserism, of the two the latter is a lesser evil: and it almost makes me cry to think of the Irish Brigade fighting not for Ireland but for Carson and what he stands for — Orange ascendancy here.
>
> "Home Rule is dead and buried and Ireland is without a national party or national press. The *Freeman* is but a Government organ and the national party but an imperial instrument. What the future holds in store for us God knows — I suppose conscription with a bloody feud between people and soldiers. I never thought that Asquith would have consented to this humiliation and ruin of Irish feeling. There is a great revulsion of feeling in Ireland" (as quoted in *Conflict of Nationality in Modern Ireland*, A.C. Hepburn, pp. 91-2).

The War Coalition bankrupted the Irish Party's sole remaining political strategy which was geared around the playing off of one English Party against another. Redmond had placed all his eggs in the one Liberal basket and the destiny of Home Rule with it. Parnell had kept up a relationship with the Fenians to reinforce 'constitutional' pressure on Britain, but Redmond had forced a rupture with the Fenians in the hope of convincing Britain of his total, loyal, unconditional constitutionality. And the Liberal allies, in whom Redmond had placed all his trust, had gone into alliance with the Unionists.

Political opinion had begun to shift, but Redmond and Devlin could not see it because they had agreed to the suspension of elections.

# Connolly and Devlin

Militarism had been brought into Irish politics by the formation and arming of the Unionist Army in Ulster. As a result of Redmond's decision to support the Imperial War effort and the campaign of recruiting for it carried out by Devlin and the other Home Rule leaders, the spirit of militarism and warfare abounded in Ireland for the first time since the 17th Century. The military art was something that was no longer external to Irish society, practised in far away fields by economic conscripts. Ireland was alive to the sound of war and warmongering well before the Rising in Dublin at Easter 1916.

James Connolly wrote the following in *The Worker's Republic* of 28th August 1915, in an article headed, *Wee Joe Devlin*:

"That great, that heroic figure, Wee Joe Devlin, at the recent Convention of the Ancient Order of Hibernians (Board of Erin), told how his society had rallied to the Empire in its day of difficulty—that difficulty for which all good Irish Nationalists were wont to pray... As I think of the hundreds of good men I have known, fathers of families, husbands, sons with aged parents, etc., who have been enticed to leave their homes and dear ones and march out to battle for an Empire that never kept faith with the Irish race, and think that it was Wee Joe's influence that led them to their folly, I think things that the Defence of the Realm Acts will not permit me to print.

"Belfast opponents of Joe Devlin usually refer to him sarcastically as the 'Wee Bottlewasher,' alluding to his position before he climbed into power. The sarcasm is pointless. A Bottlewasher was an honest occupation, but a recruiting sergeant luring to their death the men who trusted him and voted him into power is—ah well, let us remember the Defence of the Realm Act.

"The present writer cannot ride up the Falls Road in his own motor car, the penny tram has to do him. But thank God, there are no fresh made graves in Flanders or the Dardanelles filled by the mangled corpses of men whom he coaxed or bullied into leaving their homes and families. And that consolation counts more to the peace of his soul than would the possession of a motor car, or the companionship of grossly overfed boon companions of the Bottlewasher—or of the bottle.

"There are widows in Belfast today whose husbands would still be with them if they had taken my advice; there are orphans in Belfast today whose fathers would still be able to work for them and love them if they had taken my advice; there are stricken mothers and fathers in Belfast today whose sons would still be smiling and happy at the family hearth today if my advice had been listened to. And I am confidant that it will not be long before these widows, orphans and bereaved parents with every sob and sigh will breathe a curse upon the conscienceless politician to whose advice they did listen.

"You can fool all the people some of the time, you can fool some of the people all of the time, but you cannot fool all of the people all of the time.

"What is true of my attitude in Belfast is true of our attitude in Dublin and all over Ireland wherever our voice and influence could reach.

"We saved the lives of thousands, held together thousands of homes, and amid all the welter and turmoil of a gigantic and unparalleled national betrayal we presented to the world the spectacle of the organised Irish working class standing steadfastly by the highest ideals of freedom, so that the flag of Labour became one with the standard of national liberty."

In Dublin at Easter 1916 Connolly played a prominent part in the protest in arms against all of this and the rule of the unelected British Government. It was suppressed after a few days with the bringing up of big guns and the indiscriminate shelling of the city by the Royal Navy.

It has been called a lunatic *"blood sacrifice"* in recent years by those who wish to commemorate the much larger and pointless blood sacrifice that Kitchener was organising with Redmond's cannon-fodder in his vast war of attrition against the Germans on the Western Front and the Turks at Gallipoli.

The *Irish News* described the Easter Rising in Dublin 1916 as a failed German plot conducted by agents of the Hun. In its editorial on 1st May it said: "Happily the Irish people were not duped. We say nothing of the unhappy instruments of Teutonic duplicity who have fought Germany's battle in the capital of this country."

## Redmond's chance

Here is Denis Gwynn's explanation of how the Easter Rising provided the Irish Party with a last chance to influence things and salvage Home Rule when things were running away from them with the formation of the War Coalition. But there was a heavy price for the Northern Catholics to pay:

"The parliamentary methods which Parnell had evolved in the early eighties were never designed for dealing with a Coalition Government in England. They had assumed always that the party system would continue in English politics, and that the strength of the Nationalist Party would depend upon playing off one party against the other. Once they combined, the power of the Nationalists vanished...

"Redmond's... chance came quite unexpectedly as a result of the Dublin rising in Easter Week 1916, when the war—which had done so much to defeat his hopes suddenly produced new and powerful factors in favour of an immediate settlement. It had seemed inevitable until then that the Home Rule Act could not possibly become operative until the war was over. But the revulsion of feeling which followed upon General Maxwell's military administration in Ireland created an overwhelming pressure from the United States in support of an immediate settlement. America was still neutral, and more sympathetic towards Germany than towards the Allies. The sanguinary suppression of the Dublin rising had produced a new wave of fierce anti-English feeling in the United States, after several years during which Irish-American influences had virtually ceased to count. Demands for an immediate settlement poured into Whitehall, and Asquith undertook a personal visit to Dublin to explore the possibilities...

"Long experience had convinced the Nationalist leaders that Lloyd George required the closest watching in negotiation. His quick enthusiasms, and his equally quick changes of attitude, were well known; but his personal ambition counted for much. In the situation which had arisen he had the strongest reasons for accomplishing a settlement by consent, and the presence of so many Unionists in the Coalition was a guarantee that there would be no serious resistance if the Ulster question could be settled.

"That Carson and his friends might go into opposition was always probable, but they would be subjected to great pressure to give their assent. Discussions took place in which Redmond made his position absolutely clear. He was willing to accept a strictly temporary exclusion of the six counties, on the clear understanding that the whole settlement would be reviewed by an Imperial Conference when the war ended. As a guarantee that the exclusion of six counties would be only temporary, he insisted that the Irish members must be retained at Westminster in full numbers until the final settlement after the war.

"These terms were put before Lloyd George by Redmond, Dillon and Devlin, and accepted by him as the absolute basis of future discussions. Redmond's papers include a memorandum made by him at the time, in which he records that Lloyd George not only accepted the terms but declared that he would stake his own political life upon pushing the agreement through, if the Nationalists could obtain the assent of their own followers in the six counties. On that basis Devlin went to Ulster to explain the position, and at a fully representative Nationalist conference in Belfast, Redmond and Devlin both announced that they would retire from public life at once if the proposals were not accepted.

"...Signs of trouble arose quickly when the consent of the Ulster Nationalists had been obtained, and when Carson also had got the consent of the Ulster Unionist Council to the proposals. What the Nationalist leaders did not know was that Lloyd George had discussed different terms with them and with the Orangemen. The Orangemen's consent had been obtained on a basis of permanent exclusion, while the Nationalists had stipulated absolutely that the exclusion must be temporary. After weeks of delay Redmond was informed that the basis to which he had agreed could not be adopted, and Lloyd George threw in his lot with the majority of the Cabinet. The whole negotiation broke down..."   ('John Redmond and English Politicians', *Studies* Vol. 21, No. 81, March, 1932, pp. 20-36)

# Black Friday at St. Mary's Hall

The "*fully representative Nationalist conference in Belfast*" was held in St. Mary's Hall in Belfast, on the 23rd June 1916. It was composed of Nationalist MPs, Councillors, and representatives from the AOH and the Irish National Foresters.

By threatening to resign Redmond and Devlin secured a majority of 475 to 265 for a qualified version of temporary Six-County exclusion from Home Rule. Those Six Counties were to remain as an integral part of the United Kingdom, with Ireland as a whole continuing to be represented at Westminster.

Before the St. Mary's Hall conference the Northern Catholic Bishops had made their opposition to this proposal known and the Nationalists of western Ulster told the leadership of the Irish Party that they had overstepped the limit on concessions, fixed at the time of the Buckingham Palace conference with the so-called 'County option'. A number of senior clergy and Nationalist representatives then met in conference in Omagh and publicly rejected any exclusion. Eamon Phoenix describes this conference as highly significant for the subsequent transformation of Nationalist politics by providing focused opposition to the Irish Party, and a future local leadership of a reconstituted Sinn Fein in western Ulster (*Northern Nationalism*, p. 26).

Opposition was expressed by parish priests, Nationalist councillors and even Hibernians in the West. The Bishop of Derry in a well-publicised letter said it would be better to stay in the Union for another 50 years than accept the proposals. He drew attention to Carson's claim that exclusion would place Ulster in "an impregnable position".

Bishop McHugh also pinpointed an ominous development that potentially lurked behind the exclusion proposals, namely the setting up of a northern administration under the Ulster Unionists.

The proposal was declared "too ridiculous for consideration" by the *Irish News* (14.6.16).

But Devlin convinced the 1800 representative section of his Belfast supporters on 17th June to back the exclusion proposals as the best basis for eventual unity, declaring there was to be no permanent Partition and no Six County Government. Devlin then carried its acceptance with the AOH.

At the Northern Nationalist Conference in St. Mary's Hall, Redmond said that if the scheme were rejected by Nationalists: "the constitutional party would expire... and with it the last hope of Home Rule coming into operation in any shape or form" (IN 24.6.16).

This threat demonstrated the desperation of the Home Rulers. They were prepared to countenance Partition, which would involve surrendering a principle which could not be recaptured. However much they wanted to believe that the proposals were only 'temporary' in nature in order to salvage

Home Rule, they must have seen, as practical politicians, that, if the Unionists got Partition temporarily as a fact, their hand would be strengthened in refusing to budge from that fact when '*time*' was called on it.

This is where the Liberal Alliance had ended up — if Home Rule was not quickly forthcoming, then they knew the Party was finished, and yet to have Home Rule, in order to save the Party in the rest of the country, they had to agree to the exclusion of most of Ulster.

Although the Conference voted in favour of accepting a temporary exclusion of the Six Counties there was a split between Antrim and Down on the one hand, which fell in behind Redmond and Devlin, and Tyrone, Fermanagh and Derry which were against the concession.

Eamon Phoenix says that Black Friday at St Mary's Hall:

> "continued to exercise an influence on the Northern nationalist political scene and revealed a broad dichotomy in the body politic between a pragmatic east Ulster wing, strongly identified with Joe Devlin, and a stridently and anti-partition west Ulster alignment with its base in... Tyrone, Fermanagh and Derry City. It was the attempt by the latter to displace the old Party locally that enabled Sinn Fein to make drastic inroads into the 6 counties during 1917 to 18. The effect of this division on Northern nationalism was to prove particularly enduring, and largely conditioned the framework of anti-partitionist politics within the north-east until at least 1928. Thus the split in Northern nationalism in June 1918 bequeathed a bitter legacy" (*Northern Nationalism*, p.35) .

One immediate effect of the conference was the formation of an Irish Nation League in western Ulster by F.J. O'Connor and the anti-exclusionists. The League represented a Nationalist revolt against the Party and proceeded to function as a kind of transition between 'constitutional' Nationalism and Republicanism in the North. Kevin O'Shiel, who later became a Sinn Feiner and represented Collins in the Six Counties, saw it as giving 'constitutional-ism' its last chance and the INL formed a relationship with the All-For-Ireland League in Cork. It helped to draw off some of the more active elements that would have been drawn to the Parliamentary Party and merged with Sinn Fein in 1917, providing the bulk of the Republican leadership in Ulster afterwards. One Priest described it as a form of purgatory, "a place or state of punishment, where some Parliamentarians suffered for a time before they joined Sinn Fein" (Irish Independent 15.10.17).

But the Irish Nation League never succeeded in breaking out of Tyrone, Fermanagh and Derry and into the Devlinite strongholds of the east despite the active support of the clergy in these Counties. The Irish Party held together due to the Unionist threat that gave the 'factionist' label a strong resilience.

The convention of June 1916 was a watershed in the history of northern nationalist politics according to Eamon Phoenix. As a result of the exclusion proposals and its decision the Nationalist organisation began to disintegrate. The weakening of support for the Party among local branches of the A.O.H. and the clergy shown in the by-elections of 1918 cleared the way for the displacement of the Party in large parts of Ulster by Sinn Féin (p. 43).

Stephen Gwynn later wrote:

"That day really finished the constitutional party and overthrew Redmond's power. We had incurred the very great odium of accepting even temporary partition—and a partition which, owing to this arbitrary extension of area, could not be justified on any ground of principle; we had involved with us many men who voted for that acceptance on the faith of Redmond's assurance that the Government were bound by their written word; and now we were thrown over" (*John Redmond's Last Years*, p. 239).

## Turning of the Tide

The Parliamentary Party managed to hold two seats in South Armagh and East Tyrone in 1917-18 (which were to become very Republican areas a half century later), despite the rising tide of the new republican Sinn Fein with its electoral victories in the south.

*Sinn Fein* was a new Irish Party after the Rising. It was not the *Sinn Fein* that Devlin helped crush in 1908. It took the name of that party and absorbed it but it now included a strong Irish Republican Brotherhood element with a programme for the establishment of independent Government in Ireland.

Dillon called the South Armagh seat "the most favourable seat for us in Ireland" and the Sinn Fein challenge there was depicted as a Republican "invasion of Ulster" (Michael Laffan, *The Resurrection of Ireland*, p. 123). After playing a part in the Sinn Feiners' defeat, Devlin's Belfast men then set off to Waterford to play a prominent role in the defence of John Redmond's seat, whose death left his son contesting it successfully for the Party in March 1918. Willie Redmond's taking of his father's seat in Waterford meant he surrendered his own seat in East Tyrone for another contest between the Party and Sinn Fein.

Seamus O'Connor, a young Sinn Feiner, who found himself in East Tyrone in the early spring of 1918 at the time of the election, described in his memoirs the continuing power of the Devlinites he encountered:

"The AOH were inclined to prevent meetings by a constant barrage of interruptions and other rougher methods, so that volunteers were formed and marched to the meetings ostensibly for protection, and to ensure that the speakers were left speak. At this election was greatly enlarged the innovation of bringing in Irish Volunteers from places in the south for the purpose of protection and perhaps also as propaganda during the campaign... It was looking for trouble to be caught alone wearing a Sinn Fein badge...

"I remember, one market day in the Diamond (Square) in Dungannon, a Sinn Fein meeting was held in front of the Hotel. There were a couple of hundred of us lined up at the outside fringe to give a sort of protection from a huge crowd of AOH supporters who kept up a barrage of shouting and throwing stones, potatoes and eggs (which they were buying at 6 pence each) at the speakers. Most of the windows of the hotel were broken.

The Countess Markievicz in a trench coat was one of the speakers. She was hit several times with potatoes and eggs and once, when she got hit by a nasty shot of a stone, she exclaimed, in what to me was her peculiar accent, 'I care no more for your stones than I cared for the bullets of Easter Week'...

"That election was won by the AOH candidate by a substantial majority." (*Tomorrow was Another Day*, pp.43-4).

In the two by-elections the Hibernians were prominent in their use of force against Republicans. The other factor in the Northern victories for Devlin's supporters was the fear that the abstentionist policy of Sinn Fein would reduce the opposition at Westminster to Partition. Partition remained the greatest threat to Northern Catholics— overriding all other considerations in the North-East.

So the most important factor in the victories of the Irish Party was the belief in the North that unity was essential—particularly in relation to the forthcoming *Irish Convention* which, it was hoped, would prevent Partition.

The calling of the Convention in June 1917, like the previous British initiative of 1916, had much to do with the desire to gain more Irish cannon-fodder for the Western Front. Lloyd George, in the previous month, had proposed as the basis of a settlement the immediate enactment of Home Rule, excluding the six North-Easterly counties with the status of the excluded area being assessed five years later. Failing agreement on this, an Irish Convention was called.

During the Convention Redmond managed to achieve the separation of the Southern Unionists from the Ulster Unionists by agreeing to all-Ireland Home Rule with control over customs remaining with Britain, provided this was given legislative effect at once. Redmond's calculation was that his agreement to this limited form of Home Rule, which gained the support of the Southern Unionists, would make it difficult for the Ulster Unionists to resist, given that it meant a settlement and Irish soldiers for the Front. However, the Catholic Bishops and Devlin scuppered the Redmond amendment and he had to withdraw it for fear of splitting the Nationalist forces. This was the end for Redmond's authority over the Parliamentary Party and he died soon afterwards.

The Convention proposal had also been useful in convincing the US that Britain was adhering to the character of the War President Wilson had trumpeted in his Fourteen Points, increasing the likelihood that the

Doughboys would reinforce the crumbling Allied lines in France as quickly as possible.

The seriousness of the situation in France, when Germany made a great effort during April 1918 to win the war before American numbers arrived, led to the introduction of the Irish Conscription Act in Parliament. (British Conscription had been introduced in 1916.) This Act was coupled with the announcement of the Government intention to introduce a Home Rule Act, with the threat of resignation if it were not passed by the House of Lords.

Sinn Fein organised a campaign of resistance to the attempt to conscript in Ireland and the Irish Party joined the campaign. With the result that Lord Curzon announced the suspension of both Conscription and Home Rule for Ireland.

This represented a final moral collapse of the Parliamentary Party. For four years it had declared that the Great War Britain was fighting and Ireland was participating in on its behalf was a 'war for civilisation', a war of good versus absolute evil that could not be ended, despite the appeals of Pope Benedict, until evil was finally vanquished and democracy saved. And yet it would not countenance Conscription, something that was surely an absolute essential in such a situation of possible Armageddon.

By not supporting Conscription, and not remaining true to the recruiting propaganda it had churned out for four years, and in following the 'Pro-Germans' of Sinn Fein, it was, in effect signalling that it had been conned by Britain and it had conned the Irish people in the process. It was, in effect, morally bankrupt.

But that was only the start of it. The following two years made it clear that victorious Britain, whom 200,000 Irish had been recruited for by Redmond and Devlin, was not about to honour its "Sacred Treaty" with the Irish or anyone else. The Home Rule Bill had been passed on paper but it soon became clear that it was only "a scrap of paper".

And Partition, which Redmond and Devlin promised their Northern recruits they would prevent by coming forward and fighting and dying for the Empire, had become a very likely outcome of the Great War.

A great disillusion was about to set in.

CHAPTER THREE

# Great Disillusion

In November 1918 a joint manifesto was issued by the British Prime Minister Lloyd George and Unionist leader Bonar Law just before a snap General Election, called to capitalize on the winning of the Great War. In this the Unionist-dominated Government made its position clear: Britain would not accept Irish separation from Britain and Ulster would not be placed within any future Home Rule Ireland.

In the election Sinn Fein stood on the basis of an independent Irish State as opposed to Home Rule and it put up its President, Eamon De Valera, against Joe Devlin in his West Belfast constituency to show that it was serious about seeking to take the Hibernian heartland.

Devlin apparently sank into a state of depression upon the announcement of the General Election and he played no part in supporting the Party outside his city. John Dillon noted what a blow this was, to no longer have the Belfastmen to support the Party around the country. It seemed to be that Devlin had no wish to involve himself in the impending disaster.

Dillon seems to have also been stricken by the belief that the end was nigh. He had failed to implement a new policy when he took over from John Redmond, despite the fact that in 1918 it had become clear that a gigantic deception had been practised on Ireland in 1914 and the War had been an Imperialist War, waged for the kind of Balance of Power motives that Dillon had exposed in his questioning in the British Parliament prior to 1914.

But instead of seizing the moral high ground, the disillusioned Dillon just carried on in the purposeless Redmondite groove towards oblivion. No wonder Devlin would have nothing to do with fighting the lost cause in the rest of the country.

## Devlin versus De Valera

Devlin's speech accepting nomination for the Falls in the General Election gives a flavour of what he purposefully stood for and what West Belfast was voting for in 1918:

> "Did any man in his senses believe in the practicality of establishing an independent Republic of Ireland? ('Never') Then were they expected, though they did not believe in it, to go out and shout for it? He would shout for nothing he did not believe in. (Applause) He did not stand for an Irish Republic. The thing was absolutely impossible...

"Germany was defeated... Belfastmen had done a part in raising the standard of freedom for small nationalities... And when those gallant soldiers came back again it was they and their gallant sacrifices that would free another small nationality at home. (Loud applause) They were told by their opponents that if the policy of an Irish Republic failed they could fall back upon another idea, namely the Peace Conference...

"Their opponents suggested that in the event of the failure of the Peace Conference idea they had another suggestion, and it was abstention from Parliament... Labour was claiming its share of representatives and Labour would go to Parliament... during the seventeen years he had been a Member of Parliament the only notice England ever took of Ireland was when the Irish Members were active in the House of Commons. Were they then to have a section of the Irish people setting up a toy Parliament in Dublin with no power to enforce its decrees, and its acts no more than florid, picturesque resolutions of a Sinn Fein club, and to have all this horrible burlesque going on along with the tragedy of an Ireland broken, disunited, and handed over to the mercy of the ascendancy party — was that all Sinn Fein had to offer to those who had been fighting for reform and freedom for 30 years..?

"They had been doing great work in Ireland for the past 25 years but they wanted to see the rich harvest reaped... They wanted to end the industrial and economic policy which sweated women and children... They wanted to establish an eight-hour universal day for all workers... They wanted to lift the shadow of unemployment from the homes of the poor, they wanted the slums destroyed and clean and healthy homes created for the people. There were countless reforms that had to be carried out. They were going to be carried out in England... were they in Ireland going to wait until there was established an Irish Republic before they should share in these benefits?..

"Mr. de Valera knew nothing about Belfast.... Probably if he did know Belfast he also would feel deeply on this question, and would come to the conclusion that Belfast and Ulster workers could not afford to wait on urgent reforms. (Hear, hear.)..." (IN 14.10.18)

De Valera sent Sean T. O'Kelly to Belfast to campaign on his behalf. Speaking at a meeting in St. Mary's Hall O'Kelly clearly laid out the difference in policy between the Republicans and the Devlinites saying it was Sinn Fein's intention to "clear the English Government and everything it stood for bag and baggage out of the country" (IN 28.11.18).

This *"bag and baggage"* phrase was familiar to its audience who would have heard it used by Gladstone in relation to his aim of driving the Moslem Turks from the Balkans. According to the *Irish News*, however, Republicans had considerable difficulty campaigning against Devlin as their rallies were broken up by local people and O'Kelly returned South convinced Sinn Fein would be defeated.

The *Irish News* published the names and addresses of Devlin's 8,000 nominees over several editions in the first couple of weeks of December, 1918.

## Devlin alone

Sinn Fein, standing on a platform of abstentionism from Westminster and an independent Republic, swept aside Devlin's party in the 1918 Election winning 73 of the 105 seats in Ireland. The Parliamentary Party was reduced to a mere half a dozen seats in Ulster and that thanks to an electoral pact with Sinn Fein to prevent Unionists taking seats on a split Nationalist vote.

The *Irish News* marked the demise of the Parliamentary Party and its replacement by Sinn Fein in the following editorial:

> "There will be no desire to-day on the part of Irish Nationalists to question a patent fact, to ignore it, or to 'explain it away'.
>
> "By large majorities... an overwhelming preponderance of the Irish Nationalist people have declared their conviction that the leaders of the Sinn Fein Party will succeed in establishing an Irish Republic by refusing to attend the British Parliament and appealing to the peace conference.
>
> "... when the 73 exponents of the Sinn Fein policy have been deliberately returned by the people as against 6 of the Party founded by Parnell in 1880, no one can think of contending against the stern logic of figures and the unchallengeable conclusions of accomplished facts... The country as a whole has made its choice. After fifteen years of persistence and unscrupulous effort, the enemies of the 'Parnell Movement' have succeeded in their object. The 'Elder Statesmen' of the nation have been dismissed...
>
> "Ireland has handed over control of its National destinies to the Sinn Feiners now elected because the masses of the people believed that the object of Sinn Fein policy can be practically realised...
>
> "If the Peace Conference separates without establishing the Irish Republic, what can the 73 Sinn Feiners in Dublin do?... The employment of Force, or the mere suggestion of it, will mean another Insurrection. If we are heading for another Insurrection, let the facts be clearly understood...
>
> "There is an alternative, of course: the 73 Sinn Fein representatives of Ireland may cross the Irish Sea and join the little group of Nationalists who will be battling as best they can in defence of their country's interests at Westminster. But every Sinn Fein representative was elected because the people believed that Abstention from Parliament was essential and that the country had failed to win its liberty because Irish men went to the British House of Commons.
>
> "... The country that recorded the momentous decision on 14 December, broke with the past, and set aside a Movement that had rescued it from serfdom and despair, now awaits its dividends from the promoters of the venture: and Ireland's Cause is ours now, and shall be ours in all the time to come, no matter what befalls..." (30.12.18).

There are two points to be made here. The newspaper of Northern Nationalists doubted that Sinn Fein could deliver on the Republic, believing its stance would inevitably lead to trouble as Britain ignored it, and wished it would instead return to the methods of the Irish Parliamentary Party.

There was a great pretending done by Devlin and the *Irish News* that Sinn Fein's abstentionist policy left Ireland open to Westminster doing what it would with Ireland. And when the 1920 Act that Partitioned the country was passed it was inferred that 80 or so Irish MPs would have made all the difference in opposing it.

But that was nonsense. The British political spectrum had formed itself into a mighty Coalition to deal with the problem of Ireland (and other problems it had accumulated in winning its Great War) in the way it saw fit. The Unionist Government headed by Lloyd George had a massive majority in the House of Commons. The days when the Irish Parliamentary Party could play the parties of state off against each other and bring them to the brink of civil war were long gone. And the British democracy was determined to get Ireland out of the way, in one way or another, before that could ever happen again.

Secondly, The *Irish News* was absolutely certain, beyond doubt, that the Irish people had spoken and put their trust in Sinn Fein, rejecting the Irish Party and its approach. That clearly marks it out from the recent trend in Irish history writing questioning the nature and extent of the result of the 1918 Election and the comprehensive Sinn Fein victory it represented. There is nothing here to suggest that Sinn Fein misled the Irish people into voting for it or they *really* voted for something else whilst apparently voting Republican.

Devlin in his victory speech, after he had defeated De Valera by 8,488 votes to 3,245, emphasized that West Belfast was different to the rest of the country, both in character and in turning back the Sinn Fein tide:

> "We have fought them and we have beaten them...
>
> "They may gain support elsewhere; they will not gain it here... They attacked us; we met them and we have thrashed them at the polls and given to all Ireland a symbol and proof of our unshaken fidelity to the old principles and the old cause...
>
> "Freedom will not wait — (cheers) — Any more than Labour will wait. Both will go together to an everlasting triumph." (IN 16.12.18)

There is in Devlin's speech recognition that Belfast was special — with a Labour interest akin to that of the great British cities, different from elsewhere on the island.

In the *Irish News* editorials over the following months there is a strong disdain for Sinn Fein on the basis of comments made by some Dublin publications mocking Devlin's working-class female supporters (the mill girls). It is clear that one of the attractions for Devlin and West Belfast of Home Rule was that it would have kept the city attached to the emerging

British Labour movement and its representation at Westminster (where it was to become the Official Opposition).

The fact was that Belfast was a part of Britain, particularly in its economic life, like no other region of Ireland, could not have but left its imprint on Nationalist politics in the city, as represented by Devlin. Belfast was closely bound up with adjacent parts of Britain like Glasgow and Liverpool and had many similarities economically, socially and with regard to religious antagonisms

But it had one crucial difference. What made Belfast different from Glasgow and Liverpool was the fact that British politics had failed to get a grip in Ireland, even in the city that most resembled Britain. Devlin had come up through the Home Rule movement that threatened the prospect of one religion ruling another. This was not a consequence of the character of the Home Rule movement *per se* (although it had been accentuated by the rise to prominence of the Hibernian element in the Home Rule Party). It was a fact of life resulting from the failure of British party politics to root itself in political life in Ireland after the Union of Parliaments. This failure was caused chiefly by the sectarian (anti-Catholic) consensus of British politics as a whole during the generation following the Union.

The complex character of Devlin, and of Catholic Belfast—as an integral part of the British economy, becoming increasingly involved in the conflicts within British politics and society, seeing the Empire as its opportunity rather than its oppressor—found a complementing in the demand for Imperial Home Rule, which suited the peculiarities of Belfast like no other part of the country.

In the bulk of the country Home Rule was a concession made by Nationalists to the impossibility of getting independence from Britain. But this was not the case in Belfast or for Devlin. In many respects Imperial Home Rule was the ultimate objective and in many ways preferable to the fuller Nationalist demand that had the potential to upset the complex relationship Catholic Belfast had with both its Protestant neighbours and with Britain. Imperial Home Rule was the best of both worlds for Devlin. But it was gone.

Devlin's acceptance speech still looked forward to a Home Rule future for his city, rather than a Republican one:

"A golden opportunity presents itself. The world has changed. Out of the tragic events of the last four years has sprung up a new spirit... I invite the Protestant toilers to join with their Catholic fellow-countrymen in a great organised battle against reaction and Toryism... we are out to unite Orange and Green, Protestant and Catholic, mill-worker and engineer—all men and women who believe that humanity was not made to be crucified on the cross of a bad industrial and economic system... I lift tonight the flag of a new Ulster" (IN 29.12.18).

Devlin persisted in arguing that Sinn Fein had made a grave miscalculation in abstaining from the Westminster Parliament, as in the following speech at the annual AOH Our Lady's Day demonstration at Hagardstown, Co. Louth on 15th August 1919 where he revealed his and the Hibernians' continued attachment to the British State and its politics:

> "The House of Commons is the heart of the Commonwealth, and the best public platform in the world... the power of taxation, of legislation for Ireland still remained with the House of Commons, and I believe it is our duty to go there, if for no other purpose than to defend and safeguard the interests of Ireland in so far as they are affected by legislation or administration" (IN 16.8.19).

Devlin also continued to immerse himself in the politics of the British State at Westminster, speaking regularly on a wide range of issues and new social legislation. He served on the Old Age Pensions Committee, where he wrote the Minority Report. This, of course, was during the period when a crucial conflict was developing in Ireland to decide whether it should be governed by the British administration or by the party elected in Ireland to govern it.

Devlin's policy has to be seen in the context of his acceptance at St. Mary's Hall a couple of years previously of the exclusion of some of North-East Ireland on at least a temporary basis. In the context of this it might have been possible for Devlin, with the strength of his personal following in Belfast and the AOH in Eastern Ulster, to come to an accommodation with Protestant Ulster within a number of Counties that remained in the UK, continuing to participate within Imperial politics at Westminster.

Whatever the practicality of this policy in that context, it was made impractical by the British Government's reaction to the result of the 1918 General Election in the rest of the country.

## What now?

The Sinn Fein MPs elected on a programme of establishing Irish independence met in Assembly in Dublin in January 1919. The Assembly declared itself the Irish Parliament, declared independence from Britain and elected an Irish Government. It then set about establishing functional departments of state to make good its intentions. This was not going to be a *"toy parliament"* or *"Sinn Fein debating club"* as Devlin believed.

However Devlin was right about what would happen next: The British Government declared the Irish Government illegal and moved to repress it by force.

That is the context of Devlin's speech to the British Parliament in February

1919. There he asked the Members, as a remaining fragment of a once great Party, which had served as the representative legitimating factor in Westminster's authority in Ireland, what they were going to do now that Ireland had voted for its independence.

Devlin's speech was made during the debate on the King's Speech on 19th February at the opening of Parliament in the aftermath of the 1918 Election—in which the Irish Parliamentary Party had been destroyed outside of Ulster. In his speech Devlin openly confronted the British Parliament, asking the Government benches a series of pertinent questions about what it was now going to do after the mess it had made of his country. Devlin was asking the smug majority of Unionist Members, who had helped to destroy the Irish Parliamentary Party, on what basis Britain was now going to administer Ireland. He said:

> "I have risen for the purpose of asking the Prime Minister, if he were here, or the Leader of the House, if he were here, or the Chief Secretary for Ireland, if he were here, or any responsible Minister, high or low, great or small, this question: What is the meaning of this passage in the King's Speech:
>
>> "'The position in Ireland causes me great anxiety, but I earnestly hope that conditions may soon sufficiently improve to make it possible to provide a durable settlement of this difficult problem'.
>
> "That is a very enigmatical sentence. It is characteristically Lloyd-Georgian. Why was that paragraph put in the Speech of the King, unless we had some explanation of it from the Prime Minister? I waited here and listened to his reply to the two rather meek and humble speeches from the two leaders of the Opposition. I waited here and listened with interest to get some explanation as to what that passage meant. I wanted to know from him what is the position in Ireland?, what is the Government in Ireland?, who are the Government in Ireland?, what is going on in Ireland?, and what you propose to do with Ireland? Do not imagine by your pledge-breaking, by your false promises, by your criminal treatment of Ireland, that you have rid yourselves of your responsibility when you engage in a conspiracy, which is successful, of driving the constitutional representatives of Ireland out of public life. For nearly forty years this party, of which there are only a few of us left, laboured by constitutional means to win the great constitutional end of a great constitutional party, namely the right of our people to govern themselves on their own soil. We won that great reform by the constitutional judgment of the electorate of this country. We won it because it was a just cause, and because it was sanctioned by public opinion. We won it because it had the moral sanction of the Colonies. We won it because mankind in every English-speaking country in the world was in its favour. Yet the Gentlemen who from these benches are now lecturing labour upon their extreme courses, are the very Gentlemen who destroyed the possibility of that solution and have cast Ireland again into the melting-pot of agitation and discontent.

"For my part, representing nobody here but my constituents, not speaking for Ireland... I am here to demand from this Government what they are going to do about Ireland, and I ask that an answer be given to that question... Yet the Government sit helpless and hopeless, giving no guidance to the House of Commons—this new, fresh, magnificent, democratic assembly that has come here without principles, but merely to cross the 't's' and dot the 'i's' of the Prime Minister. These men know nothing about Ireland. They have heard nothing of our debates. They have not followed these controversies. They are entitled to get guidance from the Government... Are you going to carry out your promises and keep your pledges, and carry out the purpose for which you said you went into this War. I want an answer to that question.

"There are only two courses for this Government to adopt. The first is either to give Ireland representation at the Peace Conference or to give her the right to self-determination. Are you afraid to let Ireland state her case at the Peace Conference?... President Wilson not once, I think, but twenty times has stated that the purposes for which this war was won was to secure freedom for small nationalities, and the right for every people to determine its own destiny... The Prime Minister accepted every declaration of President Wilson. He iterated and reiterated that he was in full sympathy and accord with all that President Wilson said on the inspiring purposes of the War. It was for this that countless men went out from Ireland...

"We are here to see that blood has not been shed in vain... Give Ireland her fair representation at the Peace Conference or give her the right to self-determination. You yourselves have proposed no solution. Therefore we are entitled to demand that either one or other of the two solutions which we have presented should be accepted by the House, or, if they are rejected, we should be told the reason why." (Hansard 12.2.19, see full speech in Joe Devlin, *What Now*, Introduction by Brendan Clifford, Athol Books, pp.18-9.)

No reply was made to Devlin from the Government benches. They just sat there feeling pleased with themselves, presumably believing that having won their Great War they could do as they pleased, wherever they pleased.

Devlin must have found the House of Commons a very different and more hostile place than what it was before the Great War. His own party had melted away and his former allies in the great Liberal Party had been decimated and were few on the opposition benches. The opponents of Home Rule overflowed on the Government side sitting behind a mighty coalition of Unionists and Lloyd George, whom the Tories put up with because he had won the war and was useful in sorting out the peace.

He complained that this first democratically-elected House of Commons had "sprung into existence in a moment of public panic and was therefore "not a democratic assembly". It may have been the case that the electors had chosen their representatives in an atmosphere of 'Hanging the Kaiser' and a great desire to punish the evil they had put down. But it was the most democratic parliament ever elected in the UK since the electorate had been tripled by the 1918 reform.

The problem for Devlin was that it was no longer *"the great English democracy"* that the Home Rulers had pressed their struggle on before the War. It was a much greater democracy that was not necessarily enhanced in its ability to govern by the extension of the franchise.


## The Great War Radicalizing

Devlin realised that the simple demand for the bringing of the Home Rule Bill into operation could not be sustained into 1919, even in the North. This was due to both the radicalising effect of the British War propaganda with regard to 'self-determination' and the unfolding events in the South after Whitehall decided to repress the democratic will of the Irish electorate.

The war that was developing in Ireland during early 1919 resulted from the decision of the Westminster Parliament to take no heed of the decision of the 1918 election in Ireland and attempt to govern Ireland as if nothing had happened. Military rule was imposed to enforce British government in Ireland over the populace who had voted otherwise.

The calculation of the British Government was that if a firm hand was applied to the situation the Irish would see sense once again, as they had in the past, once they had been shown what's what.

However, in 1919 the Irish did not respond as they had in the past to the firm hand. They took the British Government by surprise in standing by their electoral verdict. They set themselves the task which the British, along with the remaining remnants of the Parliamentary Party, took to be utopian. Their electoral stance was shown to be not just Irish bluster. So there was war.

The new determination of the Irish, that took Britain so unawares, was definitely to do with the effect that Britain's Great War had upon them, both through the war propaganda and battle-hardening.

One of the factors that had undermined Devlin's position, along with his party, was the British championing of the principle of 'self-determination' as enunciated by President Wilson. The Irish Party had been based on the sound belief that the British Constitution would not allow the Irish such a thing and that anyone who proposed such a thing was being preposterous and engaging in dangerous fantasies.

Prior to the Great War there was not a hope in hell that Britain was going to recognise this principle in relation to Ireland. That indeed was the whole logic of the Irish Parliamentary Party's existence and approach, and of its criticism of any separatists that might periodically emerge. The British would never allow 'self-determination' in Ireland, and sufficient Irish military power could never be mustered to compel it. Therefore all that could be hoped for was a measure of devolution—Home Rule—within the British state. That is the reason why the Irish Parliamentary Party went to Westminster, swore an Oath of Loyalty to the Crown, and confined itself to the strategy of manipulating the Parliamentary arithmetic.

But in 1918 a whole new situation emerged with the New World Order on show in Paris and the overwhelming vote for Sinn Fein in the Irish part of the British General Election.

## The problem of 'self-determination'

This is a subject that has been curiously neglected by Irish historians, who seem to have taken it to be of the 'natural order of things' that the British Government, which was supposedly fighting for *"the freedom of small nations"*, and establishing a great number of new states across Europe and the Near East where none had previously existed, would, in 1918, not respect the democratic decision of a people closer to home for 'self-determination'.

This acceptance of British power in Ireland as being in the 'natural order of things', and therefore legitimate, is essentially an adaption to the British mindset. The British State legitimately does what it wants in the world. Those who challenge it are in conflict with the nature of things. They are troublemakers and are wrong.

The vast majority of people in Ireland expected some British respect for the General Election result in Ireland. Why else would they have voted so overwhelmingly for Sinn Fein? To emphasize the point the newly established Dáil Eireann then took the trouble to appeal to the victors at Versailles on the basis of Woodrow Wilson's 14 Points relating to self-determination and the democratic propaganda of the Allies.

R.M Henry, in the conclusion to his informative 1918 book *The Evolution of Sinn Fein*, describes very effectively how England, by means of its hypocritical double-standards in the Great War, undermined the legitimation of its government of Ireland that the Home Rule Party gave it, and lost Ireland:

> "The months before the European war broke out saw Nationalist Ireland practically unanimous in its support of the Home Rule legislation of the Liberal Government, ready to be reckoned as a part of the British Empire, prepared to acknowledge the supremacy of the Imperial Parliament, content with an Irish Parliament charged only with the control of a number of matters of domestic concern. Though the policy of the Home Rule Act had been definitely and deliberately adopted by the English electorate, it was defeated by threats of armed resistance on the part of a minority of Irishmen, backed

by promises of support from a minority of Englishmen, and by the refusal of the Liberal Government either to vindicate its own constitutional authority or to appeal to the country to do so for it. The Government put itself in the position of seeming to prefer in England the conciliation of its enemies to the satisfaction of its friends, and in Ireland to acknowledge the claim of a minority to veto the legitimate expectations of the majority. Occupying this position at home, it plunged into a war in Europe to vindicate 'international morality' and 'the rights of small nations', as a protest against the doctrine that the force of arms is superior to the force of justice and law. The month after the war ended saw Nationalist Ireland still claiming and still denied (in obedience to the same obstructing forces) the right of self-determination; but the self-determination sought was no longer that in which before the war it had been content to acquiesce. It held that the war, which it had done something to win, had secured to the weaker nationalities (if the public and reiterated professions of the victors were not meant deliberately to deceive the world as to their intentions) the right to their own national existence, independent of the claims and interests of the stronger nations by whom they had been subjugated. It held that during the war the rights, the interests, the feelings and the liberty of Ireland had been treated by the English Government with so much indifference and disdain as to make the future subordination of Ireland to English domination a prospect distasteful to Irishmen and a position injurious to Irish interests. It revived the claim of Ireland to independence, declaring that it was justified in the light of history and by the common consent of Europe and America, and as a first step in the assertion of that claim refused for the first time since the Act of Union to send representatives to sit in the English Parliament" (pp. 279-80).

Lionel Curtis, who was on the Liberal wing of British Imperialism, in his *Round Table* article of June 1921, gives something of the feeling of the British Establishment about the democratic propaganda which was utilised to win the Great War on Germany but was never meant to have been taken in earnest, lest it cause great problems after the War in Ireland:

"The tide of war had now turned against Germany; and as the prospect of peace came in sight President Wilson multiplied apophthegms. The stricken world swallowed them wholesale. Rich and luscious as honey, they offered nothing to bite on, and when kept for future application they lost the appearance of clarity and turned opaque. 'Shall strong nations be free to wrong weak nations and make them subject to their purpose and interest?' And again: 'All who sit at the peace table must be ready to pay the price, and the price is impartial justice, no matter whose interest is crossed'. British statesmen hastened to declare that all the problems of the war were soluble in the alcohol of 'self-determination', which was... merely the English version of Sinn Fein. It was also a solvent upon which Lenin was consciously counting for the disintegration of civilized society. The effect of the formula is attested on all sides in Ireland. On November 5 (1918) the Irish Party proposed a motion calling on the Government to settle the Irish question in accordance with Wilsonian principles. It was voted out, the Government declaring that Ireland was a domestic question, and that no outside interference would be tolerated."

The first manifestation of the British double-standard was when the Irish were refused entry to the Peace Conference despite a resolution passed in the US Senate in support of their presence.

A minority of people in Ireland believed that Britain, even in this brave new world of small nations and self-determination it had trumpeted, would ignore the Irish decision and Ireland would have to show that it was in earnest before it was shown respect. They were a minority but they were the ones who were proved right.

Devlin still believed that Sinn Fein was full of idealist nonsense and a Republic could never come about because the Sinn Feiners did not have the substance to press home their position and Britain would never allow it.

His view was proved to be half-right, or right in the end, alternatively.

But in the era of self-determination the result of the 1918 Election posed problems for Britain it did not have before in Ireland. For one thing, with the Sinn Fein victory there was a clear and unambiguous mandate for Irish independence registered by the Irish people, instead of the legitimizing of Imperial hegemony that was a product of Parliamentary Party dominance.

Britain began to see that the new era self-determination needed to be combated to make it tolerable for the Imperial interest. What was clear and unambiguous needed to be made unclear and ambiguous.

The two approaches Britain took to this involved the appliance of force— to put doubt in the minds of those who had expressed a will for self-determination in one way that it was impossible and they would need to think again and express their 'self-determination' in a more limited way. And secondly, it was important to remove the all-Ireland self-determination of the 1918 Election, by breaking up the island to create a new 'self-determination' that could be used to obstruct and impede the overall one.

## Devlin's plea to Britain

In Ulster the Protestant population supported military rule and the enforcement of arbitrary British authority across the country and the Catholic population supported those who stood by the decision of the election of 1918.

While the two communities in the North were effectively at war with each other as a consequence of the general war in the country over the question of independent government in Ireland that the British were attempting to overrule by military rule, there was little overt conflict between them in 1919. Both seemed to accept that the thing would be decided between Sinn Fein and the British Government in the bulk of the country. And the Northern Unionists were probably expecting a walk-over.

Republicans, who were a minor, though growing part of the Nationalist community in the North, saw themselves as part of this general conflict and the North as part of the battlefield through 1919. And the *Irish News*, also, could not help being affected by the new situation—even if it wanted to continue the Home Rule struggle of former years, rather than the new conflict that had emerged after Britain's decision to defy the Irish democratic verdict.

In the North the Protestant complication and the strength of the personal following of Devlin inclined Catholic Belfast to uphold the position that the rest of the country was discarding as a relic of pre-war affairs in the Brave New World. But there was a distinct movement toward a maximising of the demand for Irish autonomy in the direction of 'self-determination' even amongst the Devlinites.

Five months after his questioning of the Government about what they were going to do about Ireland Devlin went back to the British Parliament, to a debate on the Peace Treaty in July 1919, to press the case for Irish self-determination. For four years the Irish people had been barraged by British war propaganda, some of it delivered by Devlin himself, in which it was said that a British victory would bring about a New World Order in which democracy and the rights of small nations would flourish. Thousands of Devlin's constituents had gone off to fight for this and many had paid the ultimate price for it. And they were now expecting something in return.

Here are some extracts from the MP for West Belfast's intervention, which is worth quoting at length to capture the essence of the Irish demand in relation to what Britain was supposedly standing for in the world but was acting very differently in Ireland:

> "Mr. DEVLIN: I am glad to find that not only have we had a war for high and noble ideals, but that now that we have triumphed in that War those ideals are not to be forgotten in time of peace... I rejoice that now that the War is over we are given an opportunity to find out for ourselves whether the noble precepts that we have written on our banners are to materialise... For my part I have never hesitated to believe and to act up to the spirit of the belief that this was a war for freedom, and in the early stages of this War I joined with my leader and my party in rendering such service as was possible under the circumstances for an Irishman to give in order to strengthen the Allied Forces, and to enable them to meet that Prussian tyranny and that military system that was waging war upon democracy and freedom in Europe.
>
> "I rejoice now that the War is over that we on these benches, the few of us who remain, have been vindicated, and as we thought it was a War for liberty for the world we trusted to find that it would be a War for liberty for

Ireland. In the course of the propaganda which has been carried on throughout the Allied nations and in no country more than in England, we have had many declarations as to what the issues were that were involved in this world conflict. I do not know of any man who has more clearly and more completely stated those issues than President Wilson...

"What were the issues of this War, and what was the purpose that brought America into the War? In bringing America in upon these issues, President Wilson declared that he acted in union and spirit with all the Allied leaders. This is what he said... The issues are these: shall the military power of any nation or group of nations be suffered to determine the fortunes of people over whom they have no right to rule except the right of force? Shall strong nations be free to wrong weak nations, and make them subject to their purposes and interests?...

"I rejoice that the Prime Minister has done us the honour of being here in the House this afternoon.... I want to put a question to him now. I want to ask him, now that he has succeeded: Are we to understand that this principle which President Wilson has laid down is to be applied to Ireland—namely: That the military power of no nation or group of nations shall be suffered to determine the fortunes of peoples over whom they have no right to rule except the right of force. Ireland is being governed to-day by no rule but the rule of force. The right of the people to determine their own destiny is a thing that no member of the present British Cabinet would laugh at. Therefore, I want a clear and definite statement from the right hon. Gentleman upon that point.

"President Wilson further goes on to say: Shall peoples be ruled and dominated, even in their own internal affairs, by arbitrary and irresponsible force or by their own will and choice? There is no rule in Ireland to-day except rule by arbitrary and irresponsible force, and there is no free will and choice in the determination of the destinies of her people. Shall there be a common standard of right and privilege for all peoples and nations, or shall the strong do as they will and the weak suffer without redress? Shall the assertion of right be haphazard and by casual alliance, or shall there be a common concert to oblige the observance of common rights?...

"President Wilson... delivers a most powerful impeachment of the present system of government in Ireland... You have an Army of Occupation there of from 60,000 to 70,000 soldiers governing the people against their will... Is not that a sorry tribute to the ideals for which you went into the War? If you decline to allow these people to be the masters of their own destiny, to conceive the plans and the systems of government best suited to their own genius and to their national power; if you insist that you will impose upon them a form of government that is against their will; and if, in order to prevent their free will operating, you keep an Army of Occupation in the country, then, I say, that is not an impeachment of Ireland, but it is an impeachment of the system of government that is imposed upon Ireland.

"This question of Ireland has ceased to be a purely domestic problem... The widespread influence of Ireland to-day has assumed such proportions that, if the question is not solved, it will be bad for the world, and if it is solved it will be good for the world... Cannot this England that has made so wonderful a sacrifice for its own liberty and for the liberty of the world, this England to which I, speaking here as an Irishman, must pay the tribute of saying that during the last five years its superb patience and enduring courage and self-sacrifice has been one of the wonders of the world, this England that has risen so high in the fight for human freedom for the world, rise now to the same noble height in dealing with the little sister island almost at its door? It is not that you are dealing only with a little island almost at your door; you are dealing with something else; you are dealing with a race persecuted, downtrodden, landlord-ridden, robbed, plundered. {Laughter}

"This hilarity may well come from Gentlemen who know nothing of Ireland... Follow my argument if you have intelligence enough to do so. I have no doubt that your predecessors sneered at some Members of Parliament who stood, as I stand here in this House to-day, to put the Irish situation before British Members. But when a speaker was sneered at the facts remained. It was a great English newspaper that amid the horrors of the famine period, when the emigrant ships were carrying millions of the race away to foreign lands and when the children of this persecuted race could find no place for them in the homeland to which they were passionately attached, declared, 'The Irish are going, and going with a vengeance', and I have no doubt that intelligent Conservatives cheered that sentiment in this House. What was this Irish race that left Ireland amid the hilarious cries of the Tory newspapers and their Tory friends in Parliament? They were the men whose descendants to-day in America, in England, in Australia, in New Zealand, in Canada, and in South Africa... Therefore, when you come to deal with the Irish question, you are not only dealing with four and a half millions of the Irish upon the soil of Ireland, but you are dealing with a great world-wide race, exercising a powerful... influence...

"This question, then, is not a domestic question; it is a world question. There sits the Prime Minister congratulated, and rightly congratulated, upon his services in solving all those problems at the end of a bitter and horrible war. Surely he is not going to admit, after his experiences during the last five years, after he has had upon his shoulders this colossal and almost impossible task of adjusting the countless difficulties that arose in the Peace Conference, that he is not capable of dealing with a question at his door! If he wants the root foundation upon which to build it dealing with that question, he will find it in the declared principles of President Wilson which I have ventured to read to the House. We have not only the declared principles of President Wilson before America went into the War, but we have the declaration of General Smuts after the War was over and when this Peace Treaty was concluded.

"Will hon. Gentlemen sneer at General Smuts? I would ask them not only to listen respectfully to his words, but also to remember who he was and mentally to examine the analogy that there is between his case and the case of the late Mr. John Redmond. He said in a recent parting declaration which he issued to the people of this country: Most pressing of all constitutional problems is the Irish question. It has become a chronic wound, the septic effects of which are spreading into our whole system, and through its influence upon America it is now beginning to poison our most vital foreign relations. Unless the Irish question is settled on the great principles which form the basis of this Empire, this Empire must cease to exist. That is a very strong declaration. It has added weight coming straight from the source from which it comes, because who has played a nobler part in the great trials and vicissitudes of the last four years than General Smuts? He led an Army as violently opposed to you as the Irish are to-day... You conceded to the nation for which he fought the widest and noblest form of liberty, and when in the hour of your Imperial danger you sounded the bugle for men to rally to your flag he came and he rallied his forces to your support; he contributed the men of his race... and he became one of the most striking and one of the noblest figures of the fight of the last four or five years. Is this man not to be listened to? Is America not to be listened to?...

"May I point out to the right hon. Gentleman that, as I understand it, there is only one difficulty, and that is the question of Ulster? I take it that if that difficulty were met he would be prepared to give Ireland the widest form of freedom given to any other part of the Empire... He has not altogether been without the Ulster question in other countries at the Peace Conference. When he had the map of Europe before him, when he was partitioning out the various lands, and saying how they should be settled, were there no Ulsters? The right hon. Gentleman often must have found in Paris as great difficulties as he has done in Belfast. There were Germans in Poland... there was a very large German population in Bohemia; all these things had to be settled. I do not know how they were settled; perhaps the right hon. Gentleman will tell us how..."

"If he finds he cannot settle it, if he finds it even beyond him, I will tell him there is a simple way in which it can be solved—a very simple way, and that is upon the declared declaration of President Wilson and others associated with us in this War. 'Let every people determine their own destinies for themselves—every nation', I should say. {An HON. MEMBER: "Let Ulster!"} Ulster is only a part of a nation. I am an Ulsterman myself, and that is why I am so egotistical. Ulster is only part of the nation, and it must be prepared to make some sacrifices... when you come to the records, not only of how almost countless men rushed to the Colours at the commencement of hostilities, you find nothing so wonderfully splendid as the endurance and courage of the Catholic Nationalist soldiers... from my own Constituency" (*Hansard* 21.7.19, Col. 994-1002).

## The Ulster complication

Devlin's case against arbitrary rule in Ireland was eloquently put and contained many of the old Redmondite arguments blended into the brave new world of Wilsonian *"self-determination"*. It was unanswerable as a debating case for Irish self-determination. But it had one weakness and Lloyd George seized upon it, ignoring everything else Devlin said.

"The PRIME MINISTER:... My hon. Friend appealed to the Government to apply the principles of President Wilson to the case of Ireland, and he asked me a question, whether I was prepared to do so? I will answer that question if he will answer me another... Will he apply those principles to the whole of Ireland? Because as he himself realises — no one knows better — that is the supreme obstacle in the way of settlement he talked about forcing authority upon a free people by arms. In principle it is the same thing whether you force 1,500,000 of people or 3,000,000 of people. It is the same principle, and he must know that that is the difficulty. The real difficulty is that you cannot, if he will allow me to say so, get his countrymen to face the facts. They are not satisfied with getting self-determination for themselves without depriving others of the right of self-determination. I tried to apply the principles of President Wilson to Ireland. It was suggested to me that a Convention of Irishmen should be summoned. I thought it was a very good idea. I said... 'Let them settle it themselves'... Here was an opportunity for Ireland to determine its own fate."

There was then a series of exchanges between the MP for West Belfast and the Prime Minister:

"Mr. DEVLIN: Of course the right hon. Gentleman recognises that I cannot follow him in his intellectual strategy; but will he permit me to say... that the principles of President Wilson can be applied by taking a referendum of the country. I imagine that if you want to test the will of the people you do so by a declaration of the people by their votes. That is my idea of self-determination.

"The PRIME MINISTER: My hon. Friend knows very well that a referendum is a question of area. If, for instance, the area were the United Kingdom would my hon. Friend accept it? Of course he would not.

"Mr. DEVLIN: No; but my right hon. Friend has put a question to me. That is the right of nations to determine their own destiny. Ireland is a nation.

"HON. MEMBERS; No, no!

"Mr. DEVLIN: The right hon. Gentleman has put a question to me, and, I say that Ireland is one country. I think the right hon. Gentleman has stated that himself more than once. The way to determine the opinion of that country, that nation, is to take a plebiscite or a referendum.

"The PRIME MINISTER: I really have not time to go into this matter of dialectics. It is much too serious for that. To come to the real practical difficulty; it is that Ireland is not a nation. My hon. Friend believes it in his heart, but when ever you come to try to settle it you discover that Ireland is not a nation. The mere fact that it is one island is no proof that it is one nation. Great Britain is one island... The mere fact that Ireland is one island is no proof that it is one nation, or that Great Britain, an island, is one nation. There are the Scottish, and the little nation to which I belong. That is the difficulty—the difficulty I have stated. It is a difference in temperament, religion, tradition, and in everything that constitutes the fundamental essentials of nations. If they can bridge over that difficulty I do not believe there is any other difficulty, but until you do that it is no use talking about the principle of self- determination. My hon. Friend insists upon laying down conditions, and he says there must be a referendum, but it must be for the area which he determines. We have had exactly the same difficulties in the case of Danzig. You could have carved out an area there which would have handed Danzig and Marienbad to Poland. You could have handed over whole territories which were purely German to Poland, if you had only made the area according to the wishes of certain sections of the Poles, but it would have only created difficulties which might have ended in grave trouble for Poland itself. That is what I am afraid of for Ireland, and until Irishmen have made up their minds definitely to face that difficulty, I should despair of any settlement which would commend itself—

"Mr. HARBISON: Were there not two nations in 1782?

"The PRIME MINISTER: Certainly there were, and a permanently Protestant Parliament, and I am just giving my hon. Friend the reasons why it is no use quoting the principles of President Wilson, and saying, "Will you apply them to Ireland?" I shall be perfectly prepared to apply them to Ireland if they are applied to the whole of Ireland... There is no feud between the nations of Great Britain—I am talking of the feud between the Celtic race in Ireland, the Celtic Catholic population of Ireland, and Great Britain. {An HON. MEMBER: 'It is the same in South Africa!'} Yes, but South Africa is a thousand miles away, and my hon. Friend must know that there is a very great difference between the settlement of a problem a thousand miles away and a settlement between a country which is at our own door, and which is part of the organisation of these Islands. That is my answer to my hon. Friend. {An HON. MEMBER: 'The further away you get the more justice you give!'}" (*Hansard* 21.7.19, Col. 1051-4).

If Lloyd George's best example of his successful application of the principle of 'self-determination' was how he settled the Danzig question, then history would not be kind to him. It was the Danzig question that led directly to the Second World War—or, to put it more accurately, it was Britain's use of the Danzig issue that enabled it to launch a Second World War on Germany.

Devlin also had a case with regard to 'Ulster' in relation to what Britain was doing in Europe. As the *Irish News* had said in an editorial the previous year:

"The 'Ulster' pretence deludes no one. 'Ulster' has been nothing better all along than a despised instrument in the hands of those unscrupulous English political tricksters. Bohemia has an 'Ulster'—a powerful German population numbering two-fifths of the country's people—yet Bohemia's absolute independence has been recognised. Alsace and Lorraine are not to be independent; they are to be returned to France; yet three-fourths of the people in these provinces think and speak in German, and a still bigger population of them are Germanic in race and blood—perhaps in sympathy. The population of the new Kingdom—or Republic—of Poland will include from 35 to 40 per cent. of Germans and Austrians; yet its independence and its territorial integrity have been recognised and will be asserted" (6.11.18).

The creation of many independent states with large and concentrated regional minorities by Britain in 1919 must have given Devlin the impression that the British Government could do similarly in Ireland if it so chose. It certainly had nothing in principle against interpreting 'self-determination' in this way.

But, of course, these 'self-determinations' all had various strategic purposes for Britain connected with the desire to create buffer states between Germany and Bolshevik Russia. And as the nameless Hon. Member said to the Government: "The further away you get the more justice you give!'"

There is a strange sentence at the start of Devlin's reply to Lloyd George. It is this: "*Of course the right hon. Gentleman recognises that I cannot follow him in his intellectual strategy.*"

The only sense I can make of this is that Devlin was unprepared to argue the point with the Prime Minister that part of Ulster had a right to self-determination as a separate nation if the rest of Ireland was granted the same right. Devlin was only willing to assert the belief that Ireland was a nation, and only one nation, deserving of self-determination as a single unit.

Lloyd George was bluffing (or stalling—one can never be quite sure with Lloyd George). And the only thing Devlin had to do to call his bluff was to agree to a right to self-determination of the parts of Ulster that saw themselves as British if the Prime Minister was prepared to concede the right to the bulk of the island to self-determination.

Of course, if Devlin had done this he would have been making the "*sacrifice*" rather than 'Ulster'. And he just couldn't bring himself to do it.

## One Nation or Two?

An *Irish News* editorial produced a few months later at the time Lloyd George unveiled his Partitionist Government of Ireland Bill is very pertinent to all this.

It was headlined '*Father O'Flanagan's Partition Scheme*'—a reference to the Sinn Fein Vice-President's view of 1916 that there were two Irish Nations and that Nationalists had better take account of that fact if they were to successfully establish a single state on the island. Here is the *Irish News*:

"Lloyd George was generous; he found an Irish father for the Partitionisation plan; his speech might have been an utter failure... had he not commandeered the Rev. Michael O'Flanagan to the Partitionist front and turned the batteries of Sinn Fein's Vice-President against the principle of Irish National Unity with so much effect that the most phlegmatic Saxon became impressed... The case for Partition was made out for the English Prime Minister by the Rev. Father O'Flanagan. If the Vice-President of Sinn Fein had not written and published the fatal letter of June, 1916, which was recited against Irish nationhood at Westminster with such remarkable effect last night, the necessity for discussing and rejecting the scheme propounded by the Prime Minister might never have arisen. Father O'Flanagan wrote and published that letter two months after the Dublin Insurrection had been quelled in the blood of its leaders; he wrote and published his eloquent exposition of Ireland's 'dual nationhood' at the moment when the leaders of the Irish National Parliamentary Party were making a desperate attempt to rescue the country from chaos and ruin by framing a temporary arrangement under which peace and the possibility of constructive national work might be secured pending the end of the war. Mr. John Redmond and his colleagues never for a moment contemplated the permanent division of Ireland into two fragments, nor did the idea of acknowledging the existence of 'two nations' in this island ever enter their minds. They were negotiating on the basis of a strictly temporary arrangement when Father O'Flanagan's letter appeared. Thereafter, Lord Lansdowne and his friends in the House of Lords insisted on making the tentative arrangement permanent and binding for all time. The words in which Mr. John Redmond rejected the heresy of Permanent Partition may now be recalled...

"Mr. Redmond spoke as follows: — 'We took the position of saying that in the middle of the war he could not expect the Parliament of the country seriously to take up the final and permanent settlement of these proposals, and when the right hon. Gentleman, the Secretary of State for War, Mr. Lloyd George, put this proposition before us it was presented to us merely as a temporary war measure. I do not believe that for one moment he ever thought that this proposal was to contain a permanent settlement of any of these great problems. It was put before us as a temporary emergency or war measure, not to settle any of these great problems, which could not be settled in existing circumstances, but merely to bridge over the period between now and the permanent settlement. As such it was accepted by us, and as such it was submitted to our followers; and I repeat today... we cannot consent, and no fair-minded man can expect us to consent, now to vary that agreement by making the whole future of these Ulster counties the subject of a permanent and enduring settlement such as Lord Lansdowne demanded in his speech'.

"During the same debate Mr. Devlin declared, even more emphatically, that he 'would never agree to the permanent exclusion of Ulster'. That was the position taken up by the Irish Nationalist representatives of 1916 when the question of an arrangement to end with the war was under discussion.

Nothing has occurred since then to alter the convictions which inspired those vigorous and uncompromising repudiations of the destructive 'two nations' theory; but three and a half years later Mr. Lloyd George comes before the British Parliament, the Irish nation, and the world with an elaborate scheme for permanently disrupting the country; and he commends that scheme to Nationalist Ireland and to the Irish race on the authority of the Rev. Father O'Flanagan...

"Ireland is to be split, with all possible scientific accuracy, into two sections divided by alleged racial and existing religious dissonances... no Irish nationalists attended to listen to the Prime Minister's long explanation of his reasons for adopting Father O'Flanagan's full theory. We do not suppose he will ever seek to put into practice; if he does he will fail" (23.12.19),

The context of the Fr. O'Flanagan letter was Asquith's offer to Redmond in 1916 and its acceptance by Devlin and the conference of Nationalist representatives on Black Friday at St. Mary's Hall.

Three days before the conference a letter written by Fr. O'Flanagan was published in the *Freeman's Journal* urging acceptance of Asquith's proposal for temporary exclusion of six Counties.

Father O'Flanagan's "*two nation heresy*" went as follows:

"We can point out that Ireland is a nation with a definite geographical boundary... National and geographical boundaries scarcely ever coincide; geography would make one nation of Spain and Portugal history has made two nations of them. Geography did its best to make one nation of Norway and Sweden; history has succeeded in making two nations of them. If a man were to contrast the political map of Europe out of its physical map he would find himself groping in the dark. Geography has worked hard to make one nation out of Ireland; history has worked against it. The island of Ireland and the national unit of Ireland simply do not coincide. In the last analysis the test of nationality is the wish of the people... The Unionists of Ulster have never transferred their love and allegiance to Ireland. They may be Irelanders, using Ireland as a geographical term, but they are not Irish in the national sense...

"We claim the right to decide what is to be our nation. We refuse them the same right. After three hundred years England has begun to despair of making us love her by force. And so we are anxious to start where England left off. And we are going to compel Antrim and Down to love us by force" (FJ 20.6.16).

Father O'Flanagan had the courage to recognise the complication that confronted Nationalist Ireland if it wished to build a single state on the island. That complication was there long before Father O'Flanagan recognised it and would have been there even if he had never acknowledged its existence. However, The *Irish News* wished to pretend that it would not have existed and it would not have come to the attention of the British Statesmen, who wished to make something of it, if it were not for Father O'Flanagan's Two Irish Nations.

Father O'Flanagan's suggestion of the existence of Two Irish Nations was subjected to the same misrepresentation at the moment of his letter as it was in 1919 and has been ever since. He was arguing that Ireland had an inalienable right to independence and that should be immediately recognised by Britain. Having conceded that right it was then up to Nationalist Ireland to obtain the consent of those who felt themselves to be part of the second Irish Nation to be a part of an Irish State.

Fr. O'Flanagan understood nationality to lie with the subject, rather than being an external imposition. If anyone wishes to know another's nationality, wrote O'Flanagan, the ultimate test is "Ask him" (*The Leader* 12.8.16, and also see Denis Carroll, *They Have Fooled You Again—Michael O'Flanagan, Priest, Republican, Social Critic*, for a biography of the Gaelic Leaguer; contributor to *The Catholic Bulletin* and *An Phoblacht*; Vice-President of Sinn Fein from 1917 and President of Sinn Fein, 1933-5; advocate for the separation of Church and State; and defender of the Spanish Republic against Fascism).

Fr. O'Flanagan was not "*Partitionist*" and was not arguing that Ireland should be dismembered. He was in favour of a united Ireland and wanted to bring it about through recognition of the facts of the matter that were preventing it.

Father O'Flanagan made explicit recognition of the Two Irish Nations in order to try to overcome the complication in Ulster. That was a prerequisite for a functional policy on the issue. Redmond and Devlin would never take the necessary first step of recognising the national difference and as a result they never had a functional policy on Partition. And it was their policy rather than O'Flanagan's that tended to be passed down to Sinn Fein.

The Devlinite *Irish News* persisted on making the point that Sinn Fein's 1918 election victory was responsible for the Partition of Ireland. But it was against Redmond and Devlin's Home Rule proposal that the Ulster Protestants signed the Covenant, set up and armed the Ulster Volunteer Force, that the Curragh mutiny occurred and that civil war was promised through "*the full grammar of anarchy*" by British Unionism.

It was in reaction to the threat of Home Rule that Ulster Protestants most revealed that they believed themselves to be another nation.

If Devlin did not know that some form of exclusion was inevitable by this time he was living in a land of make-believe. He, himself, had countenanced it and carried it among those affected, against substantial opposition, at St. Mary's Hall, while wishfully thinking that this would have no bearing on the situation after the War.

And yet the *Irish News* believed the formal agreement of Ireland's representatives to Partition, however temporarily they might have believed it to be, would have less effect than a letter from a member of a small party without a single MP.

One can only conclude it must have been that Devlin could not face being the man who agreed to the Partition of his country. He would *"never accept it"*, even though he must have known he had no means in preventing it and he would also probably work with it.

Because Devlin would not admit to the Protestant complication that made Two Nations in Ireland, he was open to Lloyd George's counter-argument that Ireland was not a Nation itself and did not come under the Wilson Principles because it could not as a single unit agree what it wanted.

Of course, Lloyd George was just making a debating point that hid Britain's real reason for not allowing 'self-determination' to Ireland — that the Irish wanted more than Britain was willing to concede to it and it just would not allow self-determination to Ireland in the first place. And he was using the 'Ulster' complication (and Fr. O'Flanagan) to obscure the issue.

But he was able to do this because of the position of Devlin and the *Irish News* whereas he would not have been able to do so if Fr. O'Flanagan's understanding had been widespread within the Nationalist movement.

In the end Devlinite politics amounted to this: wanting to maintain Ireland as a single unit, with national recognition through a local parliament, within the U.K. and Empire. But that was something that proved to be unrealisable between 1912 and 1918 and it was definitely an impossibility by 1919.

And what did Joe Devlin matter to Britain by 1919? It had wrecked his party and left him washed up on the back benches of its parliament — an inconsequential remnant of the lost world of Imperial Ireland, who would be thanked now and again for the recruiting work he did in the War.

Lloyd George was a clever politician — one of the cleverest. He must have realised that the inability of Nationalist Ireland to deal with the Ulster complication could be utilised in the Imperial interest in dealing with the demand for self-determination that he must show he was addressing. And, if this was the case with Devlin, even more would it be the case with Sinn Fein, who stood for a greater demand than the Parliamentary Party ever did. Just as 'Ulster' had defeated Devlin it also had future possibilities for leverage over the Republicans as long as they persisted in their desire for having it. Because knowing someone's desire for something that can be kept from them is a sure way to manipulating them.

## 1919 — Imperial Retreat

In a speech in Belfast on 1st August 1919 to welcome home the survivors of the 16th ('Irish') Division, Devlin said that the Ulster and the 'Irish' Divisions "had fought shoulder to shoulder against the common foe at the front and he hoped that friendship and comradeship would grow and be perpetuated in Ireland when the war was over".

Marx once said that history repeats itself, first as tragedy and then as farce. When he talked of farce he could have been talking of the resurrection in the modern era of this type of sentiment to encourage 'peace and reconciliation' in 'Northern Ireland'. It was all said by Devlin 90 years ago and history tells us what the Northern Catholics got from it.

His words to the surviving Irish volunteers of the British Army, whom he had personally recruited, are an epitaph to Redmondism and the great fraud of the Great War perpetuated on them:

> "No conscription was necessary to force them into the army. They were told by their great leader, John Redmond, that their war was Ireland's war, that it was a fight for Belgium and small nationalities. They believed that they were fighting, not alone for small nations and for humanity, but in a special degree for Ireland... {Ireland} kept her faith, but faith has not been kept with her... That such a system of government that operates today should stand is an outrage upon the principles for which men fought and died" (Phoenix, *Northern Nationalism*, pp. 67-8).

The Devlinites in the North were coming under pressure because, nearly a year after the Armistice, there was no sign of the Home Rule Act that they had claimed lay on the British Statute Book—supposedly ready and waiting for the end of the War. The Home Rule Party had recruited hundreds of thousands to fight for the Empire on the understanding that Ireland had already been granted its Home Rule Parliament and it was only the Suspensory Act—that was due to run out at the war's end—that was preventing its implementation.

The *Irish News* had to resort to the excuse that the Suspensory Act still stood and Home Rule had not come about because the War was not quite over—yet. The Ottomans/Turks had not signed up to a 'peace treaty' in 1919 so Britain was still technically at War—despite the Armistice. And the *Irish News* used the argument that the Home Rule Act on the Statute Book was "a great achievement" since the British Government could not repeal the accomplished fact of Home Rule until a satisfactory settlement was produced. And this was now essential, due to US pressure on Britain:

> "The Irish demand is plain enough... A measure based on the principles of 'dominion self-government' and embracing all that 'dominion self-government' implies. The only feasible alternative that commends itself to Ireland now is Self-Determination. Anyone who thinks of a settlement in any other terms forgets that a World War has been fought, and the world's ideas altered beyond recognition since 1914" (IN 9.10.19).

There is a definite indication here that the Devlinite scepticism about Sinn Fein is changing. The Republic might still be seen as an unattainable wonderland, but as the Republicans showed their mettle in the face of British pressure the *Irish News*, reflecting its constituency in the North, began to move its demand further on than Home Rule.

## No Armistice Here!

The rapid disillusionment of the Northern Catholics with the Imperial Government and all things Imperial was evident in the *Irish News'* reaction to the first ever Armistice Day. It is a sobering statement that should be placed against latter-day Poppycock. The heading of its editorial was 'NO ARMISTICE HERE!':

"Tuesday next, November 11th, being the first anniversary of the Armistice between Germany and the Allied Powers, we are all royally requested to stand stock still as Lots wife in the desert... and devote 'the brief space of two minutes' to pious meditation on the end of the Great War. But how can a man, woman, or child in Ireland fulfil the royal behest without self-conscious hypocrisy. The war on the French and Belgian front was ended at 'the 11th hour of the 11th day of the 11th month', 1918. Hostilities on the Irish front are conducted by the Government with more virulence than ever a year after the date of the Continental Armistice. 'I believe' wrote the King in the document published yesterday, 'that my people in every part of the Empire fervently wish to perpetuate the memory of that Great Deliverance and of those who laid down their lives to achieve it'. Amongst those who died to defeat the Germans were scores of thousands of Irish Nationalists. But many Nationalist soldiers, who fought as gallantly as their comrades who died, have returned; and we doubt whether there is one amongst the survivors to whom the appeal from Buckingham Palace will not come as a mockery and taunt. Those Irish soldiers went out to the fields of slaughter freely, not as conscripts but as enthusiastic volunteers, to fight and shed their blood for the 'rights and liberties of small nations'. Thousands of the bravest of them fell. The thousands who escaped came home to find their own small nation betrayed, crushed under a juggernaut of Coercion, denied the slightest gleam of the rights and liberties secured by their valour and self-sacrifice for the Poles and Esthonians, Croats, Czecho-Slovaks and Jugo-Slavs, overridden by an Ascendancy whose rampant intolerance has increased rather than diminished since the 17th century, and not only debarred from political freedom but threatened with economic destruction.

"We know from the reports of their meetings published in our columns how the Veterans of the Great War feel in Belfast and the North of Ireland; we have seen it stated recently on the authority of an English correspondent that the men who fought the Germans to the last gasp and who returned to the South and West of Ireland are now members of the Sinn Fein organisation and active drill-masters amongst the Irish Volunteers. This statement may be misleading, or exaggerated, or accurate: in any case it is certain that not an Irish Nationalist ex-soldier in this country or Great Britain thinks of his experiences and the net result of his work on Europe's battlefields with any other feeling than bitterness deep and enduring.

"We are asked to stand still 'so that the thoughts of everyone may be concentrated on reverent remembrance of the Glorious Dead'. The two minutes of profound stillness will be given to thoughts of what William H. Redmond and Thomas M. Kettle would say had they lived to see the Ireland of their love in the position to which British statesmanship has brought it a year after the last shots were exchanged between Germany and the Allies...

"No matter how the anniversary of the Armistice in Europe may be celebrated in free countries, the battle on the Irish front proceeds without suggestion of Armistice from Whitehall or Dublin Castle..." (IN 8.11.19)>

Elsewhere, in the same edition, the *Irish News* published the thoughts of *"an Irish ex-soldier"* who "pictures the thoughts of all Nationalists" regarding the Armistice commemorations of the Great War in Britain and Ireland. It is extraordinary in repudiating Joe Devlin's position that "they were right then and they are right now". The former soldier wrote:

"There is no armistice or no peace for Ireland. Thousands of Irish Nationalists who fought through the Great War will breathe a prayer for their comrades dead today; they will also mutter a curse that they ever left the home shores....

"Death might have been easier... but they lived, and came home—to suffer more. One thousand of them walk their native Belfast streets to-day—turned from the workshops and the foundries—told to 'go elsewhere' out of 'loyal' Belfast if they want to exercise the right to work.

"That is their reward; and mighty England doesn't care, for England's hour of need has passed. And what of Willie Redmond and Tom Kettle and all the rest?... They died for Ireland... we will give them all a thought to-day. Perhaps it is better that they did not live to see the evil which British treachery has wrought."

Disillusion was becoming widespread, even amongst the great believers in good British intentions in Ireland and the world. But it was not as yet complete. The real nightmare was just about to become a reality.

CHAPTER FOUR

# Origins

This chapter examines the origins of 'Northern Ireland' in the 1920 *Better Government of Ireland Act* and its modification under the 'Treaty' of 1921. It is about how 'Northern Ireland' came about and what went into the making of its perverse character mainly concentrating on the British architects and their motivations in creating the Six County political entity.

However, it also looks at the effects this had on Ulster Unionism which became detached from British Unionism as a consequence of Imperial policy and how this created the Protestant predicament that, in turn, created the Catholic predicament in 'Northern Ireland'.

There are two fundamental facts that have determined the character of Catholic politics in the Six Counties—Partition and the establishment of 'Northern Ireland'. Most of the time these two things are regarded as one and the same thing. However, by running them together as if they are inseparable, Catholic political life in Ulster over the last century has become incomprehensible.

Ireland was partitioned by setting up a Six County Government in 1921 which had the choice of joining with the rest of the island or keeping separate from it. Then after a 'Treaty' was made setting up the rest of the island as the Irish Free State with greater power than was provided for by the 1920 Act, 'Northern Ireland' was allowed to become part of it or secede from it. There was little doubt what the Six County Government would choose, but that really wasn't the point of the pretence.

For many years after Partition, Anti-Partitionist accounts were the staple of Irish political history writing. These traditional Nationalist accounts ran complaints against the Six County entity together with Anti-Partitionism to maximise the case against the Border. That was understandable. Partition was taken to be a great injustice to Catholic Ireland and in constructing a case against it Nationalists naturally concentrated on the thing that most gave Partition a bad name—'Northern Ireland' itself.

What is less understandable is the position of the new historians of 'revisionist' Ireland. They run Partition and the establishment of 'Northern Ireland' together in the pretence that 'Northern Ireland' was a state. That pretence served a political purpose—to deflect attention away from the actual architects of 'Northern Ireland' by excluding the possibility that Partition might have taken place without the construction of the perverse political entity known as 'Northern Ireland'.

Far from being a new thoughtful analysis of what the problem in the North is, revisionism is a mystification of history in the interest of the devious concoction of 'Northern Ireland'.

## The Unionist retreat to Ulster

'Northern Ireland' originated in the British Government's 1920 'Better Government of Ireland Act'. So it is worth asking how it came about and why?

The British Prime Minister, Lloyd George, stated in the House of Commons, in October 1919, that he viewed the Irish situation in terms of three "*basic facts*": three-quarters of Ireland was in 'rebellion' against the Crown and the Government (i.e. it had voted in a democratic election to leave the U.K. and form a Republic); Ulster was loyal and couldn't be placed under a parliament of these people; and the British State would fight separation from the Empire as vigorously as the United States had fought Southern secession in its civil war. What emerged from these "basic facts" was the 1920 Act.

The British Cabinet decided in September 1919 to replace the suspended Home Rule Act with new legislation, which became fancifully known as the 'Better Government of Ireland Bill', and then the 1920 Government of Ireland Act.

At that point Ireland was standing firm behind its elected representatives and refusing to defer to the firm hand Britain was applying to make it change its mind. And on two further occasions after the General Election of December 1918, during the course of the Home Rule Bill through the British Parliament, Ireland publicly declared its National democratic will: In the Municipal Elections of January 1920 when 77% of the towns and cities returned majorities in favour of an Independent Ireland: and in the County Council Elections of June 1920 when 81% of the County areas declared in favour of an Irish Republic" (see *Irish Bulletin*, Volume 2, 14.6.20, Athol Books edition, p.619)

So the thing that had been held from the Irish for decades, Home Rule, was to be conceded now that the Irish had broadened their demand to independence.

By November 1919 it had become clear to Devlin that Britain's 'settlement' of the Irish issue was going to involve the proposal to establish two parliaments in Ireland, one for 'Ulster' and the other for the rest of the island. The only thing Devlin was unsure of was the size of 'Ulster'.

It had been made clear by the Committee set up by Lloyd George under Walter Long (a hard-line Unionist) to determine the new Irish policy that some action had to be taken with regard to Ireland: "that in view of the situation in Ireland itself, of public opinion in Great Britain and still more of public opinion in the Dominions and in the United States of America they cannot recommend the policy of repealing or of postponing the Home Rule Act of 1914" (CAB 27/68/4-10).

It would not, of course, have been politic to mention the verdict of the Irish people at the 1918 Election and the persistence of the Irish in continuing in their determination to have independence even in the face of the force applied to them over the previous year.

No matter how much the anti-Home Rule Unionists wished to 'repeal' the Home Rule Bill they could not, due to the change in the political situation that was produced by the victory of Sinn Fein in Ireland, and the growing power of the US and consequently the influence of Irish America on the situation.

In replacing the 1914 'Act' with a new policy there were two principles followed by the Walter Long Committee. The Bill would not let Ireland secede from Crown authority and 'Ulster' would not be placed under the jurisdiction of any Southern authority established within the Empire.

Most significantly, in its First Report made in October 1919, it rejected the policy of Ulster exclusion from an Irish Home Rule Parliament either by a 'clean cut' or by 'county option' plebiscite. Plebiscites were the means by which Britain settled a number of territorial disputes involving claims made to territory by different nationalities after the Great War, but they were ruled out in this case. 'Ulster' was to have a parliament despite not wanting one:

> "The proposal will certainly deeply affect Ulster. But if the withdrawal of British rule and the establishment of a local legislature in Ulster is necessary in order to heal the feud which has estranged Ireland and Great Britain for so many decades, and which is now seriously imperilling the relations of Great Britain both with the rest of Empire and with the United States of America, the sacrifice which Ulster will be called upon to make in assuming control of its own local affairs is one which the Imperial Government and Parliament is clearly entitled to ask its people to make" (CAB 27/69/).

There was no explanation of how an Orange parliament in Belfast was going to "*heal the feud which has estranged Ireland and Great Britain*". All the indications were that it would prolong it for generations if this was done. So there must have been an ulterior motive for establishing a parliament in 'Ulster' that no one wanted. And that is confirmed by the use of the word "sacrifice" in the report.

It was even made clear in a Memorandum to the report that the authors knew that "the Sinn Feiners will reject the offer with contempt and that the Ulstermen will not welcome it" (CAB 27/68/11). Lord Birkenhead, a former Die-hard, signed up with fingers crossed and declared in his own Appendix to the Report that:

"I assent to this proposed Bill as affording an ingenious strengthening of our tactical position before the world. I am absolutely satisfied that the Sinn Feiners will refuse it. Otherwise in the present state of Ireland I could not even be a party to making the offer..." (CAB 27/68/11).

So the policy was not the policy that was desired or that which would have been implemented if things were as they had been before the War, and its only merit lay in satisfying America and preventing the Irish democracy from obtaining what it had actually voted for.

When the Report came to the British Cabinet in November there was some disquiet that "Ulster has hitherto always taken the standpoint that its citizens were entitled to be in all respects on the same footing as citizens of Great Britain and under this scheme they would be subject to a different scheme" (CAB 23/18/36). But the "disquiet" was simply noted and the new scheme was approved nonetheless.

The initial scheme wished to create an Ulster parliament of the whole nine Counties to "balance the religions". But this scheme left the Ulster Unionists insecure about their majority and it was agreed that the territory assigned could be whittled down to a six County version giving a two-thirds to one-third Protestant majority if the Ulster Unionists desired, as the price for their "*sacrifice*".

In the cabinet debate Balfour proposed that Home Rule should be granted to the bulk of the island with the six North-East Counties remaining an integral part of the UK. But the Cabinet ruled this out immediately on the basis that ultimately a united Ireland was desired with the closest possible ties to Great Britain. Simple Partition would be counter-productive for the British objective of controlling the destiny of the whole island.

This was the first indication of the underlying strategic purpose of an 'Ulster' Parliament that over-ruled all democratic sentiment in Ireland — whether Nationalist or Unionist. The idea being that the Six Counties would be the lost, but achievable, prize that Nationalist Ireland could obtain on good behaviour. And at the same time a smokescreen of 'self-determination' would be created to placate Irish-America.

The *Times* of the 12th November 1920, commenting on the Government of Ireland Bill, left its readers in no doubt that this was a settlement imposed by force against the democratic will. It said that the British Government, "are now engaged in an effort to scourge the Irish into obedience, leaving, as sole alternative to resistance, the acceptance of the present Bill, although such acceptance must involve the sacrifice by Irish men of their true political ideas".

The 1920 Act was produced without reference to those it affected in Ireland. Even as it was being produced, it was clear to its proposers that it would be rejected by the representatives of the people of most of Ireland.

But it was continued with regardless in order to establish 'Northern Ireland'.

What is clear from all this is that the 1920 Act (and 'Treaty' of 1921) was not a recognition of reality on the part of Westminster in relation to Ireland. This was actually an adjustment to Imperial policy in order to re-subordinate the island after the events of the previous decade had made the pre-war position no longer sustainable.

The creation of 'Northern Ireland' was no *"compromise"* on Britain's part to the *"conflicting demands of the Irish parties"*, as we are led to believe. It was purely a product of the Whitehall imagination to suit Imperial interests.

The proof of the pudding in this is that another possibility was open to the British Government, on the lines proposed by Arthur Balfour. This true recognition of reality would have involved letting the bulk of the island go whilst allowing for the two and a bit north-easterly Counties to remain an integral part of the UK, without imposing a sub-government that nobody wanted, upon it.

But this was ruled out at the outset.

## 'Internationalism' and 'Little Nationalism'

So why did Britain establish the peculiar and perverse political entity called 'Northern Ireland'?

The policy that created 'Northern Ireland' and determined its character was the result of things that are overlooked. To understand the character of 'Northern Ireland' we need to understand why Britain chose to bring about the particular settlement of 1920-1 that created the strange political entity in the North-East.

A good place to start is with British Unionism, since it was here that the movement in British policy is most pronounced both in terms of change and in the influence it exerted resulting in 'Northern Ireland'.

The British Unionists, in signing the 'Treaty' in 1921, went far beyond what the Liberals were willing to concede to Ireland in 1914. They actually helped establish an Irish State in 1921/2, providing arms and the other requisites of power to Sinn Fein when they had vigorously opposed installing the Irish Parliamentary Party in a merely devolved assembly only a few years earlier. So why did they do it?

Unionism in its prime, under Arthur Balfour's policy of *'Killing Home Rule with Kindness'*, sought to counter the Irish National movement through the better government of Ireland. The better government of Ireland was a real attempt to provide Ireland with good government, unlike the *Better Government of Ireland Bill* that was cobbled together in 1920 and which had little to do with governing Ireland for the better.

There are not many Unionist criticisms of the 1920 Act and the 'Treaty' that modified it—despite it going against everything the Unionists were saying about the 1912 Home Rule Bill. But there is one I have come across. It is in the Introduction to a minor book published in 1922, *A Journey in Ireland* by Wilfred Ewart, Captain, Late Special Reserve, Scots Guards. The Introduction is by Major, The Earl Winterton, M.P. then Under-Secretary of State for India and a prominent Unionist supporter of the Anti-Home Rule campaign in England before the Great War. Winterton, writing after the 1920 Act had been adjusted by the Anglo-Irish 'Treaty' of 1921, regretted that:

> "The problem of the inter-relationship of England and Ireland for the last four years has been made even more complicated than it naturally is, by external and world conditions. As everyone knows, the Allied statesmen of 1918 and 1919 ran two horses and refused, in racing parlance, to declare to win with either. Those horses were 'Internationalism' as represented by the League of Nations, and 'Little Nationalism' as represented by self-determination. Both horses have had a rare gallop in Ireland. 'Internationalism' demanded that the British Government should justify or attempt to justify before the world its action and attitude in what is really a domestic quarrel. 'Little Nationalism' demanded that two states should be set up in an island, which judged by every standard except that of the Balkans, is barely large enough for one. The resultant progeny, to change the metaphor, would have been of a character comic in the extreme, if Irish perversity had not made it so grim a tragedy of lost lives and ruined homes. A perusal of Mr. Ewart's book strengthens the conviction that the Irish Agreement, at least, offers a chance of conditions a shade less intolerable than those that prevailed before it was reached" (pp. viii-ix).

Winterton had been very much a "*die in the last ditch Unionist*" before the Great War changed everything utterly for England. In his memoirs, *Orders of the Day*, he recalled being one of the "many young Conservative M.P.s who were ready to support Ulster in the physical sense and took effective means to that end. The number of us was greater, and the extent to which we were committed larger, than was known at the time or has been disclosed since. For instance, I formed what would now be described as a Commando which was ready to give physical assistance to the Ulster Volunteers" (p.38).

Earl Winterton's 1922 position was very much that of a Unionist reconciling the pre-War position to what had to be done after the situation had been drastically altered by Britain's bungling of its Great War on Germany. That was what Winterton meant when he said that "the problem of the inter-relationship of England and Ireland for the last four years has been made even more complicated than it naturally is, by external and world conditions".

The complication of "*Internationalism*"—something England could ignore to its heart content before it decided to embark on its Great War—was the first thing that went into the creation of 'Northern Ireland' as part of Britain's overall settlement of Ireland.

The 1920 Act (and then the 'Treaty') came about because Britain was no longer a free agent in world affairs after its Great War had gone badly wrong. It had indeed won its War, but only in the end with the American infusion. That diminished Britain's freedom of action in relation to what it could do with Ireland afterwards.

The US had remained neutral in the Great War until 1916 so when it joined the conflict it had to pretend that it was fighting a different war than the one it had abstained from previously—the Imperialist one. So it made out that the character of the War Germany was fighting, rather than the War itself, had brought it into the conflict and as a result of the US entry the character of the Allies' Great War had also changed from an Imperialist one to one of democratic principle—formulated in President Wilson's Fourteen Points.

Britain humoured President Wilson's Fourteen Points by treating them as war propaganda to disorganise the enemy—and disorganise the enemy they did with great effect. The League of Nations was set up to institutionalise these Principles. However, Britain quickly took the League as a vehicle to utilise America in a new Balance of Power operation against its former allies, and to use in governing the less pleasant parts of the world it had acquired in the course of its war. Also Britain was facilitated in establishing the buffers it needed for strategic purposes—saving it money and trouble in the world. However, there was a crucial vote in the United State's Senate on 19th November 1919, which put up conditions before the US ratified the League of Nations, and ultimately the US steered clear of the *"entangling alliances"*, consequent upon the Peace Conference, and from the League of Nations, that England wanted to tie it into. The US determined to be nobody's pawn in the world, by rejecting Versailles and the League in March 1920. But Britain, despite disappointment at this, still needed American quiescence in its post-War plans.

The appearance of the US on the world stage and President Wilson's Fourteen Points ensured that Britain had to take its 'war *for small nations'* propaganda somewhat in earnest after the War and make a gesture towards respecting the principle of *'self-determination'* that it had rejected within its own sphere before the War—'not in my Empire!' as it would have said.

Furthermore, as a result of the war Britain was in deep financial hock to the Americans. It was also worried about a challenge on the seas from the American Navy (which, if it were expanded, would threaten British control of the world market through the Royal Navy's century-long dominances).

In addition, the Irish in America had grown greatly in numbers since the forced mass migration of the Famine of 1847-8 and were now an important consideration in British dealings with Ireland. The Boer War measures, which Britain could once have applied to the Irish, could not have been applied in these new conditions. Irish America would have been outraged by blockhouses, concentration camps and a new conquest. So Britain took a different approach to Ireland in from 1919-21.

The Irish problem assumed an acute character just as Britain needed better relations with the United States in order to preserve its position of primacy. As Winterton, said "its condition was a disgrace to civilisation, and an outrage upon humanity". And, now that America had helped win the War and taken a place alongside England in the world, it had earned the right to determine what *"civilisation"* constituted, what a *"disgrace"* and *"an outrage upon humanity"* to it was. No longer was that in Britain's gift alone—hence the *"complication"* . Britain's freedom of action in what it could do in Ireland was now restricted.

Thus the 1920 Bill ran right through the whole course of the US Presidential election, to convey the impression to America that Britain was doing right by Ireland.

The proposal to establish the two Parliaments in Ireland, connected by the Council of Ireland, was the device meant to achieve the satisfying of the US. It did not look like blatant Partition. It could be presented as giving autonomy to the whole of Ireland and 'self-determination' to both Ulster and the rest of the country. It would give the appearance of the British Government acting benevolently as an independent arbiter of conflicting national rights, whilst ensuring in practice that Ireland was safe for the Union and Empire.

As Earl Winterton said, 'Northern Ireland' was the *"progeny"* or genetic offspring of this complication, as was 'Southern Ireland'. The difference was that 'Southern Ireland' was aborted later in favour of the Irish Free State.

The second aspect of this *"progeny"* was what Winterton called *"Little Nationalism"*.

In 1919 Britain constructed many new states in Europe, applying the standard of historic political territory, combined with current national opinion (through plebiscites), to the construction of the borders of these states. In many instances the factor of historic territory was given priority over national claims. This procedure resulted in the formation of composite states, like Czechoslovakia and Yugoslavia, in which there were large dissenting national minorities, and a bloated Poland which also contained other ethnic groups.

The drastic constitutional innovation of breaking up the Kingdom of Ireland was something that Whitehall could not devise as a systematically thought-out project. Many deceived themselves about what they were doing when they were doing it. Indeed, in Westminster 90 per cent of MPs chose to be absent when the measure was turned into Law, despite the near civil war that the issue had caused between them before the Great War.

Earl Winterton quite rightly saw the construction of two 'states' in Ireland as absurd and ridiculous — just as Joe Devlin did. The place was barely big enough for one, as he said. But the problem was that a single Irish state was only allowable if it were in Union with Britain: An independent united Irish state was impermissible — so there had to be division into two entities.

It is always tempting to view the actions of the British establishment as extraordinarily devious and astute. And this notion is particularly likely from an Irish Republican (or socialist Republican) viewpoint. But Britain's *Government of Ireland Act 1920* cannot be seen in this way. It should be viewed as an act of political trickery, improvised in the context of the shambles Britain made of the world it was left master of in 1918-19, after it had won its fraudulent *"war for civilisation"* and *"self-determination"*.

The Partition of Ireland was one of a series of disastrous decisions which undermined the Empire at the moment of its greatest power. It was not something that was at all inevitable. It stank of the miserable expediency, cost-cutting and decline in Imperial will that characterized Imperial policy after it had exhausted itself after winning its Great War. And so Partitionist Ireland took its place in the world with Iraq — which was constructed by Britain at the same time and with the same characteristics of reckless Imperial behaviour.

## Devlin and the 1920 Act

When Lloyd George unveiled his proposals in Parliament on 22nd December 1919, the remnants of the Irish Parliamentary Party boycotted the event. The argument Lloyd George used to justify the Partition proposal was disingenuous. He claimed that "if Ireland got 'self-determination' then Ulster was also deserving of self-determination". He said these words as British military forces were denying Ireland the self-determination which had been expressed in the 1918 Election, and his Government was declaring *'proscribed'* and liable to arrest those returned by the people in a British General Election.

It was also clear that the Act had nothing to do with *'self-determination"*, since it went against the wishes of Nationalists to be part of an independent Republic and of the Unionists to remain an integral part of the Union.

The 1920 Act proposed separate Parliaments for six of the Counties of Ulster and for the other twenty-six Counties of the rest of the island, with powers to create a Council of representatives of both Parliaments. The powers of the Irish Parliaments were less than those granted in the 1914 Home Rule Act. The supremacy of the Westminster Parliament was preserved. Irish representation at Westminster was to be cut to 42 members. (Ireland came to be 'over represented' in the Westminster Parliament when the Famine/Holocaust decimated the Irish population and the British Government, maybe due to sensitivity about this, 'forgot' to adjust its parliamentary seats accordingly.) The Imperial Parliament would control all matters concerning the Crown, peace and war, treaties on foreign relations, navy, air force and army, customs and excise, trade and merchant shipping. And there was an oath of allegiance to the King.

The immediate consequence of the 1920 Act, however, for Northern Catholics was Britain's revolutionary act of Partitioning the island and establishing a pseudo-state in its North-East corner.

The *Irish News* was so horrified it was reluctant to take the Bill as a serious attempt at a settlement at all. Its editorial, *'Playing with Fire'* said:

> "It is not only possible, but certain, that the Prime Minister and his Tory colleagues put forward their crude proposals for no other end than to utilise them in America and the Dominions to Ireland's detriment. But would Irish national interests be advanced any way, at home or in the eyes of the 'watching world', if we emulated Ministerial hypocrisy and devoted ourselves to a miserable 'battle of wits' with Messrs. Lloyd George and Bonar Law by pretending to take this humbug seriously and discussing it as if we could be induced to accept an Act of the British Parliament drafted on dissectional principles?...
>
> "If the possibility of dividing Ireland into 'separate entities' — of splitting a nation into two fragments on principles never adopted by statesmen in any other country — was once accepted, we might come to a 'fair discussion' of the methods by which the surgical operation could be effected. But we hold that the operation would be fatal — that even the attempt would prove disastrous" (24.12.19).

Three days later, under the editorial heading *'Two Parliaments... A Miserable Failure'* , the paper described the meagre thing Ireland was being offered by the British Government:

> "Lloyd George offers us the familiar combination of the bludgeon and the olive branch... The olive branch fulfils our worst expectations... The Long Committee's plan... proposes to set up two State Legislatures, one, for a homogeneous Ulster and the other for the rest of Ireland, with a Council of Ireland consisting of delegations of equal strength from each. Almost every power that the Irish people is firmly resolved to possess in its own hands is reserved to the Imperial Parliament... the control of all vital national affairs — the control of customs and excise, income tax, external trade — remains at Westminster. Even the meagre powers which the Council of Ireland might exercise are contingent upon the assent of the Ulster Legislature.
>
> "Did we believe that there was in Mr. Lloyd George's scheme any hope of peace for our unhappy country, we should be ready to assent it as a possible basis of settlement...
>
> "In a word the scheme is of no value because it is unreal. It is a paper constitution drafted for an imaginary country. The utopia with which Mr

Lloyd George desires to bless with the system of government which his own imagination, aided by Mr. Long's Committee, has produced is a dream country inhabited by people with no history, with no passion, with no memory. But the country with which he has in reality to deal is one where today passion has turned into frenzy, history has become an obsession, and memory is charged with the bitterness of years of misgovernment and misunderstanding. It is a country in which the sanction of law has become meaningless and in which the hands of the assassin takes the place of the hand of friendship...

"Here, once again, is our concrete suggestion. Instead of an arrangement of two State Parliaments with a nerveless, powerless and shadowy Council, let the government give Ireland the powers of a Dominion, and let it leave Ulster and the rest of Ireland to determine in a Constitutional Assembly their relations to each other. Ireland is tired, and the world is fast becoming tired, of the perpetual dictatorship of Sir Edward Carson" (27.12.19).

On 13th February 1920 Devlin, who was considering attending Westminster for the Second Reading of the Bill, wrote to his oldest and most significant ally, Bishop O'Donnell of Raphoe, about his concerns in the event of a Northern parliament coming into the Brave New World:

"This will mean the worst form of partition and, of course, permanent partition. Once they have their own parliament with all the machinery of government and administration, I am afraid that anything like subsequent union will be impossible. I propose, if an opportunity is offered, to attack the Bill, and to do so from an Ulster point of view, giving reasons why we Catholics and Nationalists could not, under any circumstances, consent to be placed under the domination of a parliament so skilfully established as to make it impossible for us to be ever other than a permanent minority, with all the sufferings and tyranny of the present day continued, only in a worse form" (Phoenix, *Northern Nationalism*, p.76).

Devlin and the remaining fragments of the Parliamentary Party wondered about the purpose of this Northern Parliament that nobody wanted and which could only mean greater disaster for Catholics left under its jurisdiction than mere Partition.

C.P. Scott, the Liberal Home Ruler, wrote to John Dillon on May 30th with his own thoughts on the matter:

"As you say, the present Bill has no relation to the needs of the situation. Its real objects, so far as I can make out, are, first to get rid of the Home Rule Act, and secondly to entrench the six counties against Nationalist Ireland. Its effect, one fears, will not be to make a solution easier but to make it harder, by creating a fresh and powerful obstacle. Why not take Carson at his word and simply leave the six counties as part of the United Kingdom and establish one Parliament for the rest of Ireland?"

At the end of March 1920 Devlin went to Westminster and spoke against the Partition proposal included in the Bill. During the debate Bonar Law taunted Devlin with having agreed to the exclusion of the six north-eastern Counties back in 1916. This prompted Devlin to write a letter, on 2nd April 1920, to Bishop O'Donnell explaining his position, which Eamon Phoenix has in his book. It is interesting in revealing Devlin's opposition to a Northern Parliament which had led him to agree the 1916 proposals for exclusion of the Six Counties:

> "It was impressed upon me during the controversy about partition, and indeed it strongly influenced my action years ago, that in the absence of any agreement about the six counties, a parliament would be set up in Ulster, and I considered that it would be the greatest and last of all calamities...You will, therefore, understand, that in consenting at the time {1916} to the proposals...I thought they would avert the setting-up of an Ulster parliament, and, at the same time, create a condition of things that would force Ulster to take the initiative in bringing about ultimate unity. Indeed, Sir Edward Carson has stated repeatedly in the smoking room of the House of Commons that, if these proposals had been agreed to, Ireland would now be united. At all events, by agreeing to them at the time, setting up a parliament for the twenty-six counties, keeping Ulster under the control of the Imperial Parliament, with 100 Irish members, 85 of whom would have been Nationalists, still having the same power over governmental and administrative matters for Ulster as formerly, and recognising that the whole scheme would have been unworkable, my visualisation is that they would have been glad to come to the parliament of the twenty-six Counties to plead for union. On the other hand, if once a parliament were established in Ulster, with all its governmental and administrative machinery, and all the vested interests that were bound to be created in consequence of its establishment, it would mean a permanent arrangement. For that reason, I believed that what could be done ought to have been done at the time to prevent such a parliament being brought into existence" (*Northern Nationalism*, p.82).

The Partition that seemed to be abhorrent in 1916 now seemed to look all the better after 'Northern Ireland' was threatened in the new Bill.

The Catholic Bishops were outraged by the Partition proposal and the idea of setting up a parliament in Belfast. They were unhappy at the response of the Irish Parliamentary Party which didn't seem to know whether to go to Westminster and oppose it or ignore it altogether—presumably because, while Devlin was predicting dire consequences for Northern Catholics in private, the *Irish News* was treating the proposal as preposterous in public editorials.

Bishop McHugh attacked the proposals in an open letter in which he warned that Catholic Ulster would "never submit to a Belfast parliament" and "become hewers of wood and drawers of water for Sir Edward Carson".

The Northern Bishops took the view that the only form of partition that ever had any semblance of justification was the 'County Option' proposed under the 1914 amending Bill. The Bishops and "a large section of opinion in the western part of the 6 counties, was prepared to accept a partition based upon the exclusion of the four counties with Unionist majorities", according to Phoenix (*Northern Nationalism*, p.79)

But, despite Devlin's protestations, as Phoenix notes, there was still a disinclination amongst Northern Nationalists to take the Partition scheme and its Parliament seriously during early 1920. The *Irish News*, for instance, called it "a vanishing scheme" in its edition of 24th February.

## The Issue of Partition

Joe Devlin and Nationalist Ireland generally were disinclined to believe Britain was serious about the Partition that was being proposed because of the attitude it had historically taken to Ireland.

Ulster Unionist publications of the mid-19th Century had often complained of the British policy of always treating Ireland as a single indivisible entity, arguing that their different social and economic structure required different laws and a different administration from the rest of the country. But Westminster had paid no heed to these expressions of superiority. It was as the Kingdom of Ireland that Ireland entered the Union in 1800, and it was as the Kingdom of Ireland that it was governed by Britain until 1920.

The Home Rule Bill was framed in accordance with the historical British view of treating Ireland as a whole ever since its original conquest. All the senior Liberals indicated their belief in this in the Commons during the early exchanges over Home Rule. Asquith said on 11th June 1912: "You can no more split Ireland into parts than you can split England or Scotland into parts... You have, in Ireland, a greater fundamental unity of race, temperament and tradition". Lloyd George, who later as Prime Minister was responsible for the Partition of Ireland, said on 13th June:

"Take all the great questions through years of controversy... Ireland has been treated as a whole, as a separate unit, and there has never been a demand from any county in Ireland or from any part of Ireland or from any party in Ireland that Ulster should be treated separately" (cited in Frank Gallagher, *The Indivisible Island*, pp. 91-2)

This position was universally held in British politics. The biographer of the Unionist leader, Bonar Law, for instance, noted:

"The Home Rule issue from 1886 to 1912 was invariably discussed on the assumption that partition was impracticable and that, whatever solution was ultimately adopted, it must embrace the whole of the island" (Robert

Blake, *The Unknown Prime Minister: The Life and Times of Andrew Bonar Law*, p.124)

Ireland was until 1920 treated as a single constitutional and political entity by Britain and it continued to be governed as a unit by the British administration in Dublin Castle. The Castle Administration never made any preparations for breaking up Ireland as a constitutional unit. It was governed differently from Britain, but the region of the Unionist minority came under the same administration as the region of the Home Rule majority, throughout the long conflict over Home Rule between the 1870s and 1914.

But in 1918, when the first General Election of the democratic era resulted in Ireland electing a massive majority of Sinn Fein representatives on an independence programme, the British set aside the election result and began the movement to break Ireland up into two constitutional entities—still governed differently from Britain.

The Partition of Ireland was not based, therefore, on a benevolent attempt on the part of Britain to prevent 'civil war' in Ireland. It was rather, part of a wider British design to undermine the putting into operation of the election result of 1918 and to continue the holding of as much of Ireland as possible through other means when 'consent' to its rule was evaporating in the bulk of the country.

Britain didn't Partition Ireland for some altruistic purpose of recognising two conflicting sets of national rights. It just so happened that one set of these 'national rights' coincide with its own selfish Imperial interests and was thereafter utilised as a cover to respect the requirements of 'self-determination' in the Brave New World.

A central feature of the Partitionist arrangement, which was presented as a means to protect a Protestant minority that comprised less than a quarter of the population of Ireland, was the creation of a Catholic minority under permanent Protestant government, which would comprise more than a third of the new Six County entity.

It is sometimes said that Partition was inevitable. But no event in history is inevitable. Britain determined the future Ireland through a conscious act of statesmanship in 1920-1.

Revisionist historians would now tell us that Partition was just Britain recognising reality and Lloyd George never intended it to be permanent. But when the Government of Ireland Act failed, all that became permanent was what was meant to be temporary—the Six Counties and its Parliament.

The 1920 *Government of Ireland Act* was a very limited form of Home Rule, with an ingenious device to prevent it developing beyond the limits Britain desired. The two new entities to be established in Ireland were to have a Council of Ireland with the small Six County construct having a veto over any slightly extended powers which could be later conceded by the

Westminster Parliament. The fundamental idea was to block the road to effective Irish self-government. But it failed because Britain could not impose it on the bulk of the country.

What had encouraged Northern Nationalists in this view were the results of the local government elections in June 1920. Across the island candidates supportive of Irish independence gained control of the vast majority of the County Councils switched allegiance from the British Government to the Irish. In the 58 Rural District Councils of Ulster there were now 34 Councils returned with a majority of Nationalists and Republicans, and only 20 returned with a majority of Unionists. The seats on the four remaining Councils were evenly divided between the Republican-Nationalists and the Unionists. So less than two-fifths of the Rural public bodies were now in favour of the Union with England, whereas nearly three-fifths demanded full self-determination for Ireland. Republican-Nationalists wrested control of Derry city from the Unionists and had captured around half of the town councils in Ulster.

The 'pivot counties' of Fermanagh and Tyrone were also taken from the Unionists. This was despite the fact that Whitehall had directed its Local Government Board to re-gerrymander Tyrone, which it did, forming the county into five 4-membered constituencies, ensuring that a minority of 42% Unionists received the same representation as a Nationalist majority of 58%.

This had come about after the Westminster Parliament decided that Proportional Representation should be suddenly operative in Ireland. The move was made to head off the capture of the local Councils by Sinn Fein and Dublin Castle decided to scrap the entire system of electing local governing bodies in favour of a complete scheme of Proportional Representation.

Through these elections Nationalists believed that the "*myth of a homogeneous Protestant Ulster*", on which the Partition proposal was based, had been exposed for all to see and Partition dealt a fatal blow.

This was followed up in June 1920 when anti-Partitionist Councils in Fermanagh, Tyrone and Derry City recognised the Irish Government, and the IRA began to expand its campaign into the areas earmarked for an 'Ulster' parliament in which the popular will had demonstrated itself to be anti-Partition. The elections also saw Sinn Fein over-taking the Irish Parliamentary Party across Ulster, outside of Devlin's Belfast stronghold.

## An Armistice Day gift

In the Summer of 1920 the Unionists got the message that it was going to be their responsibility to crush the Irish Nationalist minority in the area that was being designated to them, which had been fenced off from the rest of the battlefield, where British military rule was dealing directly with resistance.

The result was what the *Irish News* called, the "officially-sanctioned anti-Catholic pogroms in Belfast", in which nearly 100 people died and 8,500 were expelled from their employment (including 1000 Catholic ex-servicemen in the shipyards). There were also substantial attacks mounted on Catholics in Derry and in Lisburn (where practically the entire Catholic population was ethnically cleansed after the shooting of an RIC Inspector). The pogrom may have been a limited attempt to create what otherwise did not exist, the 'homogeneous Ulster' of British statement. It was evident that it had not been undertaken merely as a reprisal for the death of Colonel Smyth. In Derry, Belfast, Bangor, Banbridge, and other places there was no attempt to single out for victims those who were known to be Republicans. Joe Devlin's working women's hostel in Bangor was clearly not an attack on 'Sinn Feiners' and there was a systematic serving of notices on Catholics warning them to clear out of Unionist quarters.

This was, in effect, the devolution pogrom war to establish the authority of the new ethnic elite over the new minority, as a prelude to the establishment of 'Northern Ireland'.

Hugh Martin, correspondent of the English Liberal *Daily News*, published an account of the events of September 1920 that would be now termed 'ethnic cleansing' in the area earmarked for Ulster Unionist rule:

"The war on Catholics was being systematically and ruthlessly pressed. The entire Catholic population of Lisburn and Banbridge, about 1,000 in each case, had been successfully 'evacuated' — that was the military term universally employed — and the Orange army was dealing section by section, night by night, with Belfast. 2,000 men, women and children had been evacuated from the Ballymacarret district, and on the night of my arrival the attack upon the Catholics of the Crumlin Road district began 'according to plan' as the saying goes. For this was no mere faction fight. There can be no doubt that it was a deliberate and organised attempt, not by any means the first in history, to drive the Catholic Irish out of North-East Ulster, and the machinery that was being used was very largely the machinery of the Carsonite army of 1914...

"As the Catholic Irish in Belfast number close to 100,000 and the so-called Protestants were but poorly armed, there could, of course, be no question of extermination. But the Catholic population might be largely reduced by emigration and rendered economically impotent...

"Refugees were pouring into Belfast by road and rail, though the city had its own problems to face. Since the early days of the German invasion of Belgium, when I witnessed the civil evacuation of Alost and the flight from Ostend, I had seen nothing more pathetic than the Irish migration. Over 150 families, numbering 750 people in all, were dealt with in a single day at one of the Catholic receiving centres, St. Mary's Hall, and it was to the credit of the afflicted Catholic population of the city that every family found a refuge before nightfall" (*Ireland in Insurrection*, p.167)

It was ironic that the Belfast Catholics who had been recruited into the British Army by the Home Rulers and their Liberal allies through the tales of what was being done by the Germans in Belgium should return home to find their own homeland had become another 'Belgium' under the auspices of those they had fought for.

At the Final Reading of the Government of Ireland Bill, Devlin reminded Lloyd George of these events in 'Ulster' that should have shown the Prime Minister why the establishment of a Parliament there would not lead to *"better government"*:

> "I know beforehand what is going to be done with us and, therefore, it is well we should make our preparations for that long fight which, I suppose we will have to wage in order to be allowed to live. The Right Honourable gentleman has not put a single clause in his Bill to safeguard the interests of our people. Will the House believe that we are 100,000 Catholics in a population of 400,000? It is a story of weeping women, hungry children, homeless in England, homeless in Ireland. If that is what we get when they have not their parliament, what may we expect when they have that weapon, with wealth and power strongly entrenched? What will we get when they are armed with Britain's rifles, when they have cast round them the Imperial garb, what mercy, what pity, much less justice or liberty will be conceded to us then? That is what I have to say about the Ulster parliament" (IN 12.11.20)

But Lloyd George pressed on regardless and Westminster enacted 'Northern Ireland'.

When the Government of Ireland Bill was passed on the second Armistice Day, the *Irish News* headline was *'An Armistice Day Gift'* — which the paper said came:

> "... in the shape of an infamous Bill for severing the country into sections — a Bill which Mr. Devlin characterized with absolute exactness when he said that –
>
>> 'Nobody believed in it; Nobody supported it; Nobody asked for it: and Nobody but the Government would stand by it' ...
>
> "Only 235 Members of that British Parliament — not fully one third of the total number — thought it worthwhile to register their votes in the final division fraught with consequences of the direst import to Ireland, and to Great Britain...
>
> "Parliamentary Government in England is a thing of the past. After yesterday's pitiable and tragic exhibition of cynical ineptitude and callous stupidity on the part of the 'Mother of Parliaments' the field should be clear for a fair fight between advocates of 'Sovietism' and the Ascendancy who have already established on the ruins of the 'Parliamentary System' a Despotism that lacks nothing but 'official recognition' and a name" (IN 12.11.20).

The British democracy had organised itself through Coalition to nullify the *"great English Democracy"* that the Irish Party had put its faith in and made itself completely impervious to Irish influence. Through this Parliamentary device it was now solving the 'Irish problem' to its own satisfaction without reference to Ireland.

In its 'London Letter' the *Irish News* noted that the Bill was the biggest and most important in the Government's Legislative programme and purported to be "a final solution" of "the problem that has vexed and defied British Statesmanship for centuries". Yet hardly anyone was there and there was not a good word to say for it, even from the Prime Minister.

The Government would have been expected to justify the Bill as a necessary recognition of the political division in Ireland. However, it did nothing of the sort. In the muted debate the British Prime Minister and every other Government speaker, including hardened anti-Home Rule Unionists, stressed Ireland's fundamental unity and described the institutions established by the Bill as the speediest instruments to bring about the re-establishment of this unity. The message was that Partition was a temporary expedient due to the conflict over Home Rule but the final solution lay in undoing Partition and "a United Ireland within the Empire" as the Chief Secretary for Ireland put it. (See *Hansard*, 29.3.22, Col. 944.)

In the Official Summary of the Act (p.8) there was the threat that, if the people of Ireland refused to work the new institutions, they would be placed under Crown Colony Government—a form of administration reserved for the most 'uncivilized' and used by the British Empire in parts of Africa for the 'lesser breeds without the law' who were felt incapable of self-government.

And between the Second and Third Readings of the Bill the special corps, who became known as the Black and Tans, arrived in Ireland to show the British Government meant business.

It must have been a great anti-climax for the Devlinites and remaining Redmondites to see the great arena of their past struggle, where the two British Parties of State had been brought nearly to civil war over Irish Home Rule, dish the issue with little more than a whimper from Mr. Asquith, the former leader of a once great party that had been destroyed in the course of pursuing Home Rule and waging a Great War.

All the great parliamentary struggles of the Irish Party had been for little or nought as the British political system arranged itself to establish a new relationship with Ireland to suit its new interests without regard for what it was condemning the people of the Six Counties to.

# Great War disillusionment

The great disillusionment with the Great War for small nations was very evident when Remembrance events concentrated Devlinite minds on the War Ireland had fought for the Empire only to be rewarded with Partition and 'Northern Ireland'.

On Armistice Day 1920 the *Irish News* editorial was headed, *'After 24 Months'*, and said:

"An 'optimistic' harangue was delivered by Mr. Lloyd George at the London Guildhall on Tuesday night. Most things were going well with the world, he declared and where 'troubles' still prevailed, progress was being made ... The Prime Minister spoke practically on the eve of the 'solemn celebrations' of the second anniversary of the Armistice which are to be held today... The body of an unknown soldier is to be buried within Westminster Abbey this morning with the pomp and ceremony surpassing that associated with the interment of Kings. It may be... that the body thus honoured is that of an Irish Nationalist soldier. It is unknown and unidentifiable. But if the identity of the heroic dead could be revealed, and if it were announced that he was the son of an Irish Nationalist father and mother, would not the Irish parents of the man who fought and fell in defence of the 'rights and liberties of small nations'—as he thought he would fight when he went forth in the battle—raise their voices in wrathful protest, and repudiate and forbid the 'honours' paid to their son's moldering corpse by the sovereign, rulers, and statesmen of England?

"That is the spirit created in Nationalist Ireland by Mr. Lloyd George and his masters and sycophants 24 months after the Armistice. This country was peaceful—even hopeful—on November 11, 1918. Amidst all the self-glorification in England today, the shadow of her tragic failure in Ireland stands, stern and sinister, between her and the respect of the world. Two years have passed since the Armistice... and Ireland is as Belgium was in November 1918.

"There is no real peace; not in Europe, or in Asia or in Africa. Germany is dissatisfied. She would strike again tomorrow if she could. France hates Germany... she distrusts England; she sees no safety for herself but in a permanent assertion of her military power. Russia is a cauldron of tortured humanity. Poland has been turned into a militarist state in bankruptcy. England holds Mesopotamia by the sword; she is breaking faith with Egypt again; her position in India is more perilous than she cares to confess. America has cut off political association with militarist Europe by the most decisive vote in her electoral history. The League of Nations has become a sham and mockery. Men who died that freedom and peace might bless the world forever gave their lives in vain. They won the War; they failed to win Peace: and after-dinner optimism has made no impression on the grim and too-solid fact" (IN 11.11.20).

This is an aspect of Northern Catholic politics that has not interested historians. It is significant in that for four years the *Irish News* had told its readers that Great Britain could do no wrong in the world. It was fighting a war for civilisation and democracy against barbarism and autocracy and that justified the sacrifice of Irish lives wherever England chose to sacrifice them. And it reported Devlin as saying that Ireland was going to have a great future helping to expand and strengthen the Empire as one of its integral parts.

But now that Britain had won that war of good over evil and it was greater than ever, it had disgraced itself, turned the world it had at its feet into in a mess and it could do no right as master of it.

In an editorial of 18th November headed *'Self-Determination'*, the *Irish News* set out its post-Imperial view. It argued that, despite the fact that Germany would never have been beaten if it were not for the United States, and President Wilson had declared the War to be for the glorious objectives of *"freedom"* and *"National Self-determination"* in July 1918, "dishonest" and "unscrupulous" Britain had managed to subvert these War aims everywhere in the world:

> "Self-determination was denied to shattered Germanic Austria by the guilty makers of the Treaty of Versailles. A million Austrians have perished of Famine and the diseases induced by Famine within the past eighteen months. That country might prosper as a constituent State of the German Republic. It is condemned to perpetual Famine, to exhaustion, to death, by the criminal exigencies of the 'statesmanship' for which Mr. Lloyd George and his government stand before the world" (IN 18.11.20)

Not only did the *Irish News* draw attention to the hunger blockade of the Royal Navy, that starved to death and killed by disease millions of civilians in central Europe after the Armistice but also to the mischief it was doing elsewhere in the world. The same editorial pointed to how England had gone back on a declaration by Lord Milner that Egypt would determine its own future, and instead re-established its Protectorate over the country and military rule. It also mentioned the Anglo-Persian Treaty which was being forced on Persia, and its "young and stolid fool named the Shah", to rob the country of its oil resources.

Also highlighted was the plight of Iraq, which came into the world at the same time as 'Northern Ireland' born unto the same 'Mother of Parliaments':

> "Mesopotamia was deluded into the war on a specific promise of Independence. It is to be a mere 'Dependency' with a shadowy and elusive pretence of liberty—like Egypt and Persia. Nearly 10,000 Mesopotamians have been killed or wounded already in the effort to 'conciliate them' and convince them that a British Protectorate is the most beneficent of the blessings bestowed on mankind."

Finally, the same editorial noted that Britain's Greek Allies had also been told that they had no right to Self-determination when they challenged

Britain's influence by insisting in voting Venizélos out of office and inviting King Constantine to return.

The *Irish News* concluded: "West and East, the English Government are Freedom's uncompromising foes. And England cannot divest itself of responsibility for its government".

Disillusionment with the Empire that Joe Devlin had championed on the recruiting platforms and its so-called 'war for small nations' was nearly complete in Catholic Belfast.

It took half a century of being subjected to the government of 'Northern Ireland' for West Belfast to become the motor force behind a war to undo the political consequences of the failure of the Redmondite Home Rule campaign. And revisionist Ireland has reserved a special antipathy toward it as a result, associating the people of the area with an inherent militarism derived from an alleged long tradition of militant Republicanism.

This view was naturally reinforced from the Republican position during the post-1969 conflict, because Republicans, with the interest of having to keep a War going over two decades, were keen to stress the Republican history of West Belfast to the exclusion of its other history—despite the fact that the Republican history of the city was a very small part of the story in comparison to its Imperial history.

The transition of West Belfast from Imperial Home Rule to Sinn Fein was very, very slow—taking over half a century—and it left many remnants.

The transition happened largely through painful experience of 'Northern Ireland' itself, rather than through the propagation of Republican sentiment. The Catholics who enlisted to fight for the Empire in 1914 came back with honours and were treated like dirt by a new administration which rejected what they had gone off to fight for. They naturally resented this humiliation, but they still retained an attachment to the Empire they had served. They enthusiastically engaged in Imperial victory parades as part of the Empire, commemorated their dead and participated in Remembrance events, even if they had to do it separately from Unionists.

And it wasn't the hostility of Republicans that made them cease these activities but the actions of their former comrades in arms, and of the State they had fought for.

## Resisting Partition

In November 1920, with the imminent passing of the Government of Ireland Bill, the *Irish News* began to wake up to the reality of what was confronting the Catholic community and called on them to resist Partition with greater cohesion. In the editorial headed *'Ulster Nationalists'* it said:

"A handful of Tories at Westminster will resume today the manipulation of the Bill under which, when it passes to the British Statute Book, the cities of Belfast and Derry and the counties of Antrim, Down, Armagh, Derry, Fermanagh and Tyrone will be severed, as with a legislative axe, from Ireland and handed over to the control of a bogus parliament of the Ascendancy...

"The men of north-east Ulster must fight their own battle. If they do not show their determination to resist this fatal imposition, they need not look for help from any other quarter. 'Southern Ireland' has a desperate struggle and ghastly problems of her own on her hands. Her people will help us— only if we help ourselves. We have no aid to get from America or England, France or Spain. 'Now's the day, now's the hour' for preparation. Lacking unity in thought and cohesion in action, the passing of the Partition Bill will find 500,000 nationalists helpless before a merciless Ascendancy. Sporadic, frantic useless attempts at resistance or opposition will only provide excuses for strengthening the chain and riveting every link more firmly on nationalist limbs. The people of the 6 Counties and two boroughs can save themselves, and Ulster—and all Ireland: but they will 'sell the pass' if they sit still, and dream of something like a miracle to be wrought in their favour, until it is too late to move" (IN 8.11.20)

This editorial marked a new realism on the part of Northern Nationalists, casting aside the notion that Partition was an impossibility—a notion which was still being held in Dublin. A few days later a large conclave of Nationalists, including both Sinn Fein and the Parliamentary Party met in Omagh and pledged their determination to resist by every possible means the Partition of the country.

In early 1921 it began to sink in that Northern Nationalists were going to be cut off from the rest of the Nation and trapped under a Parliament of Ulster Unionists. The *Irish News* still tried to convince itself that the reality would never come and Partition would fail but it was clueless about how it could be prevented.

In the South, too, the Sinn Fein leadership began to take the threat of Partition more seriously and moved to decide what attitude should be taken to the elections to the new Northern Parliament which were being held by the British at the same time as those for its Southern equivalent. Michael Collins suggested that Sinn Fein should contest the elections on an all-Ireland basis treating them as elections to the Irish Parliament rather than the two British ones in Ireland and Sinn Fein in the North should ignore the Partition Act and carry on with their colleagues in the south of Ireland as a national body, as in the Dail.

Collins' view was that a Northern entity, separate from the rest of the Nation, must not be accepted or allowed to settle down and gain permanency and he suggested using the Anti-Partitionist Councils in Fermanagh and Tyrone to whittle the Partitioned area down to four Counties. He hoped to turn the North entirely Sinn Fein and remove the complication of Hibernian candidates. In this he was encouraged by Bishop MacRory's view that the Nationalists should give Sinn Fein a clear run.

However, Devlin announced his intention to mobilise his forces against the "simulacrum of a Parliament" and engage in "united national action" against it (IN 2.2.21).

This led to secret talks between Devlin and De Valera in Dublin. Devlin was confronted with the choice of co-operating with Sinn Fein in a division of seats contested on an abstentionist basis or going it alone with half a dozen followers into the Belfast Parliament.

A deal was done and the electoral pact was endorsed by an 800-strong Nationalist conference in Belfast on April 4th which bound Devlin and the remnants of the Parliamentary Party to the Republican programme of self-determination and abstention from the new 'Northern Ireland' Parliament. As part of this pact an equal number of candidates were fielded by the two parties in the Six County area. But the Devlinites struggled to field candidates in Tyrone, Armagh and parts of Down. Out of the 21 it was allowed by the pact Devlin's party could only come up with 13.

Here was the first indication of how Nationalist politics would operate in the new Six County entity as Catholics moved freely between 'constitutional' and Republican forms to secure the maximum political advantage as the situation changed.

## The 'Northern Ireland' Parliament

Joe Devlin launched his campaign in the Falls with 'A Thrilling Call to Arms', according to the Irish News. In his speech he had some pertinent things to say about the new Parliament:

"Why are we forced into this electoral contest? It is because there has been passed by the English Parliament what is known as the Government of Ireland Act. Ireland asked for one Parliament; England, generous and magnanimous gave us two (Laughter). For one hundred years we have fought for one Constitution; England has forced upon us a dual Constitution. This is a Parliament which was asked for by nobody, was not sought for by anybody or any party, and was not voted on by any Irish representative, Orange or Green. This is an arrangement, a trick, an English Dodge, a piece of characteristic political expediency on the part of English ministers, not to satisfy Ireland, not to bring the Irish people into one great common Constitution, but to raise a barrier between North and South... to create a permanent division where there ought to be unity... We asked for one Parliament, we seek one Parliament, we desire one Parliament; we will not have two Parliaments! (Cheers) — For if they go on with this Ulster Parliament it will be our duty and our right to smash it and to make it impossible (Loud Cheers). This is not a Parliament for a nation, it is not a Parliament for a province; it is only a parliament for about half a province...

"... it will be nothing but a collection of pampered politicians, of unsuccessful placemen, of political puppets who have played their part too long on the political stage in Ulster. (Hear, hear). We want a real Parliament, representative of the whole genius, character, civic spirit, and capacity of our people, and not a mere hotch-potch parliamentary rump -call it what you will—a thing for which no man, be his creed or his politics what they may—NO MAN WITH DIGNITY COULD ACCEPT, AND NO MAN WITH SELF-RESPECT COULD ENTER. (Cheers).

"Well, now, having received this Parliament, having left this legacy of 25 years of hatred in Ulster, the master-architect who constructed this superstructure has fled from the scene of operations. (A Voice: 'he's on the run' and laughter). Sir Edward Carson has created the mess, and he has left Sir James Craig to clear it up (Laughter).

"Did any of you ever read the speeches? (Cries of 'no'). They are not the speeches of triumphant generals taking a parliamentary Citadel. They are not the speeches of triumphant constitutional warriors; they are not the speeches of men going forth to great privileges with their spirits raised and their hearts inspired. No, their speeches are wails from beginning to end, regrets and explanations, doleful prophesies; the whole thing is a caricature from beginning to end.

"They have neither a platform, a programme, nor a policy for the people whom they desired to send in to that Parliament. And amidst it all, Sir Edward Carson has left them (Laughter). Sir Edward is wise. He may regret this Parliament's existence if it comes into existence, but they will regret it far more. (Cheers). Sir Edward Carson knew what he was doing when he left Belfast and accepted the office of a higher legal Lordship in London...

"What is this parliament going to do? I have waited for months and months to know what their programme was, what had they to offer to the people as compensation for this attempt to destroy the sanctity of Irish unity.... by isolating Ulster; by cutting off the Six Counties and placing their people in a little pen in the north east corner—segregating the people and leaving them neither Irish nor English, but the mere creatures of this conspiracy against the people's liberty and national unity" (IN, 13.5.21).

Devlin was right to mock the imposition of two parliaments on Ireland when it had been denied a single one for the best part of a century. It seemed a ludicrous experiment by the 'Mother of Parliaments'.

In his speech to the people of West Belfast Devlin sneered at the political pygmies that he was left with and who were standing against him to fill the unwanted Parliament. He was the giant amongst the pygmies who was coming from a real Parliament and being asked to enter a simulacrum, and he knew it.

In some ways what happened to Joe Devlin personified what happened to the community he came from. Before the Great War he was one of the three most powerful men in the Home Rule Party and many saw him as the most influential force in Ireland. Indeed the Liberal *'Review of Reviews'* had wondered in March 1911: "Can the Empire spare this man to the narrow, parish-pump politics of a single nation? Why narrow his field and to Ireland give up what was meant for mankind".

But the Empire, a decade later, did not just give up Joe Devlin to "the narrow, parish-pump politics of a single nation". It cut him off from the Nation, as well as from the Empire that could not spare him, and put him into the narrowest of confinement, in 'Northern Ireland', "a parliament for half a province", of a provincial backwater.

The quarantining of North-Eastern Ulster from the body politic of the U.K. was an act of the utmost Imperial selfishness.

North-Eastern Ulster was the only part of Ireland where the British party-system had taken root after the Act of Union. The Whigs and Tories combined in opposition to the Home Rule Bill in 1886, but the two strains remained discernible even in 1919, and there had in addition been a strong Labour development in working class Belfast which included Devlin.

If there had been a simple Partition of Ireland in 1919, with the Declaration of Independence being accepted for most of the country, or at least being negotiated with, and three or four Counties simply being part of the British political system, Hibernians and Unionists would in all probability have found natural niches for themselves in the political life of the State. But Eastern Ulster, the part of the country most suited for participation in the politics of the British state, was the only part of Ireland ever excluded from the politics of the British State. And the only strong survival of 'constitutional' Nationalism in Ireland was left without a constitutional outlet.

'Wee Joe' was a giant in Ireland, a great force in Liberal England and in the Empire, who had been indispensable to recruiting Irishmen to the British Empire's ranks in the Great War. But the creation of 'Northern Ireland' cut him down to a pygmy amongst pygmies. He lost all power and influence outside his constituency in Ireland, he became a broken fragment of a once great force at Westminster and he became a forgotten man in the Empire/ Commonwealth. And this must have contributed greatly to his personal decline as a man.

The election result gave some indication of what lay in store for Northern Catholics in the Belfast Parliament. Although Nationalist candidates polled a third of the votes, they ended up with only 12 seats (6 Sinn Fein and 6 Nationalists) against 40 successful Unionists. Devlin's optimistic prediction of 15-20 seats was way off the mark.

## A painful transition

On 7th June 1921 the new Parliament assembled formally in Belfast City Hall and it was opened by the King on 22nd June. The King gave a conciliatory speech that was aimed at drawing Sinn Fein into negotiations.

The Dáil had rejected the 1920 Act as a basis of settlement, as the British Government knew it would. The British intention was that there should also be a Parliament and Government of 'Southern Ireland' parallel with those of 'Northern Ireland'. But in the Irish election of May 1921 the Nationalist electorate returned Sinn Fein to every seat. Not a single supporter of the Act was elected outside of the undemocratic University seats. In fact, not a single supporter of the Act contested a seat against Sinn Fein in the democratic constituencies. But Britain still refused to concede independence to the Twenty-Six Counties where there was a clear democratic will for it.

In the North-East, in the new 'democracy' Britain created under its simulacrum Parliament, the Catholic community was subject to a brutal-isation to knock them in to acceptance of the situation.

In June 1921 Devlin pointed to one of the most extreme manifestations of this in a debate in the House of Commons: The abduction and murder of Catholics, many ex-soldiers of the Great War, by elements within the new Unionist security apparatus. Devlin described the murder of three Catholic men who were taken from their beds during curfew, abducted, tortured and killed. The first was Alexander McBride and the second, William Kerr:

"The deceased was a member of the Ancient Order of Hibernians, of which I am President, and was a member of the Foresters. His brother is a regimental sergeant-major in the Machine Gun Corps in Mesopotamia, and was to have arrived home this week. He himself, probably, was one of the soldiers who went out to fight in the War, on the appeal that I made to the Ancient Order of Hibernians and to other citizens who helped in that War, and were repaid in the form in which this man has been repaid.

"Let me come to the third case, that of Malachy Halfpenny... Armed men numbering about 14 or 15 arrived at the house in what was described by neighbours as a blue-gray motor lorry about 1.15 a.m., which is within the curfew hours when no civilian is allowed to walk the streets. One of the men knocked at the door, and the deceased's mother went to the window and asked if they were the military. She received no reply to the question, but was ordered to open the door. This she did, and one of the men came into the house and asked if that was where Halfpenny lived, and she replied in the affirmative. Others came into the house and rushed past Mrs. Halfpenny upstairs to deceased's bedroom where he was asleep. They dragged him out and down the stairs in his night attire. He asked the men to let him put on some clothes, but they refused. The mother and sister rushed between the men and their victim. One of the men produced a revolver and threatened to shoot both mother and sister. The family appealed to the men to release deceased, but in vain. The deceased man resisted, and it was stated his arms were twisted as he was dragged to the motor. He was put into the motor which drove off, and the people in the street heard shots a few minutes afterwards. The family were distracted, and they entertained the worst fears, and after curfew hours a search was made. Even the neighbours of this man who watched this ghastly tragedy, who were the witnesses of this spectacle of the glory of your rule, were not permitted to go out during curfew hours to try and get the remains of this poor murdered lad—an ex-soldier—who was dragged out by your servants and murdered in this cruel and merciless fashion. Who was this young boy? He was a young fellow like the others, in the prime and fullness and glory and flower of youth. I will give you his record. He was 22 years of age and he served for 3½ years in the Army with the Royal Field Artillery. He joined the Army when he was 16½ years of age, and he served in France.

"He was twice gassed, and on being demobilised he returned to the General Post Office, where he was a postman. Four brothers of his have served or are serving in your Army. One of them was killed in France on the same date and at the very spot where my lamented colleague, Major William Redmond, lost his life, and the other three brothers also fought in France and were also wounded. This is the boy, who in the dead of night, in the name of British law, with your authority, in pursuance of your policy, and for the preservation of order as we understand it in modern conditions, was put to death. There was the end of this young and inspiring career. This poor lad did not know what the pleasures of youth were, for he spent the most glorious days of his young life fighting your battles in France, and he died your victim in the presence of his mother and his sisters. That is the British rule we are called upon to respect and in honour of which we are asked to sing 'Rule Britannia' upon every platform in these islands...

"What is my case? My case is that on three different occasions innocent men have been either taken out of their homes and shot, or else shot in their homes, by forces of the Crown, and there never has been the slightest attempt to bring the perpetrators to justice...

"If this young fellow of 22, this ex-soldier who joined at 16½ years, did join the Sinn Fein or Republican Army—I do not know whether he did or not; there is no allegation that he did, and as a matter of fact, I think it is stated that he belonged to the organisation to which I am attached—but supposing he did, what a commentary on your rule. Countless ex-soldiers who went out and fought with superb courage, men of the 16th Division, who played a magnificent and gallant and fruitful part in that War, have come back and joined the Sinn Fein movement, because you have driven them into it, as you have driven those of us who are not soldiers, but mere politicians, to exasperation and despair by all these things that are being done in Ireland" (Hansard, 14.6.21, cols. 343-5).

This was a characteristic terror policy used later by colonials in places like Kenya in which people were abducted, tortured and done to death in horrendous ways—to put the fear of God into the rest of the community.

What was at issue between Catholics and Protestants in the North was not the same conflict that had been developing in the rest of the country, but involved the terrorizing and humiliation of Catholics by the local Protestant administration in the name and interest of the Empire. But the Protestant administration was not the defence of the Empire against the Catholics, who had shown themselves quite amenable to the Empire, but a kind of obstacle raised between the Empire and Catholics who had rallied to Devlin's call back in 1914. 'Northern Ireland' was created as a kind of glacis (killing ground outside the citadel) of Britain.

The fact that the men Devlin had sent to kill and be killed for Home Rule and the Empire were the victims of it must have had a shattering effect on the Belfast Catholic community who had supported the Imperial Home Rulers.

## The Police State

Because the British Government decided to farm out the responsibility for suppressing resistance to its military rule to a local stratum in Ulster, it needed to construct a repressive state apparatus from the Ulster Volunteers and the 'well disposed' citizens that had been conducting the pogrom against the Catholic community.

The creation of this local military force was handy in relation to Imperial responsibilities. In the course of winning its Great War against 'Prussian expansionism' Britain conquered large new territories which it then proceeded to add to its Empire. But in doing so it over-stretched itself both economically and territorially. It paid such a price in blood and treasure to beat the Germans and Ottomans, and in expanding itself, that it could not govern the new additions to its Empire, along with the older problem areas that it had exacerbated. It needed troops to subject the Egyptians, Iraqis, Indians, Persians and Turks as well as dealing with the Irish.

The creation of the Special Constabulary in October 1920, manned by Ulster Protestants who were unwilling to do Imperial policing duty whilst Ireland was in flux, released soldiers to other parts of the country and Empire where they were needed to suppress the democratic will.

One of the more interesting statistics about the war in the North is the low level of British casualties there, which amounted to a handful amongst the 600 or so people killed between 1920 and 1922. With the handing over of security to local forces, coupled with the Truce and 'Treaty', the IRA was forced to wage its war almost exclusively on the local Unionist security forces.

The Northern statelet's repressive apparatus was constructed and developed between late 1920 and 1922 with the active or passive support of the British political and military Establishment. The Unionists' military advisors, using their personal connections were able to by-pass unfriendly Westminster Departments to build up and arm their paramilitary forces. The British military, which was trying to re-establish "law and order" in the

South, were not too concerned about the illegalities, murder and mayhem going on in the North-East. That was not surprising, since the officers who had mutinied at the Curragh in support of the Ulster Volunteers in 1914 were now the High Command of the British Army with Sir Henry Wilson, Chief of the Imperial General Staff, on hand for the Ulster Unionist cause.

The Ulster Volunteer Force became part of the security forces in the Ulster Special Constabulary and its 30,000 illegal guns were "decommissioned" by being commissioned into the Unionist statelet's paramilitary state apparatus.

It was essential for the successful functioning of the new political entity that the Catholics be made to lie down at the outset in order that they could be policed by the Protestant community through the state apparatus assigned to it. Within a few months of taking power the sub-government at Stormont gave itself Special Powers to deal with the emergency. These powers included the right to arbitrary arrest suspects, send to trial, search without warrant, intern without trial, ban political assembly or organisation and dictate where a citizen could live. They were of such remarkable character that they were envied as far away as Apartheid South Africa and they were renewed year by year until 1933 when they were made permanent. They became part of the ordinary law and were added to in 1951 when the Public Order Act was passed. 'Northern Ireland' was thus in a permanent state of emergency in relation to one of the most law-abiding communities in the world.

The security apparatus of the subordinate government was a qualitatively different phenomenon from what it replaced. The old RIC, which was a colonial police force designed for the general pacification of Ireland, had been viewed as too even-handed in its policing by Ulster Unionists. It maintained the peace between the two communities in periods of tension, and because it was not scared to treat Protestant rioters in the same manner as Catholics it was accused of bias by the Unionists.

It was replaced by an entirely different animal made up of the new RUC and Special Constabulary in which the Catholic element was squeezed out to make room for the loyal men who knew who their enemy was and what to do with them.

An editorial in the *Irish News* of 8th November 1920, headed *'The Future Police"*, revealed how on that date the Belfast constabulary was made up of a 50/50 Protestant to Catholic membership. However, at the Second Reading of the 1920 Bill, Carson suggested the disbandment of the R.I.C. and its replacement by two police forces attached to the proposed new Parliaments.

A Government amendment empowered either Parliament to take over its police as soon as it 'desired' or 'was in a position to do so'. And the Unionists began to enrol 'Special Constables' even before their Parliament was up and running according to the *Irish News*:

"These 'Special Constables' will ultimately—and before many months—replace the Catholic members of the R.I.C. When this 'force' are fairly disbanded, there will be no 'desire' to 'take over' men whose religious belief has been indicated... it will be disguised behind an intimation that the Ascendancy 'Parliament' of the coming time is 'not in a position to do so'.

"Sir Edward Carson... and many others have talked about the 'non-political' and 'non-sectarian' character of the new 'force'. All were welcome to join its gentle ranks; Catholics and Nationalists were invited... to enrolment. We cautioned the Nationalists of Ulster that association with the project would be fatal—that anyone amongst them connecting himself with it would find reason to regret his short-sightedness. Indeed, nothing but an incurable tendency to toadyism could account for the action of a professing Nationalist who identified himself with this scheme for the establishment of a 'Standing Army' under the control of the Ascendancy...

"The 'R.I.C'. as presently constituted will disappear from 'Carsonia'; their functions will be 'taken over' by the lodgemen who will make 'the province ring' and resound to the old watchword—No Surrender" (IN, 8.11.20).

So, while the Unionists were intent on excluding the Catholics from the police, the *Irish News* was caught in a bind—if Nationalists joined the security apparatus of the Partitionist entity they would be legitimising it. So the *Irish News* was all in favour of Catholics excluding themselves.

During the height of the British counter-insurgency operations in Ireland in 1921 around 80,000 soldiers and police policed a population of 4,500,000. In 1922 the Northern sub-Government was employing nearly the same number of armed men, 70,000, to police a population of 1,200,000—a ratio of 1 to every 17 inhabitants (and these forces were effectively policing less than 450,000 Catholics—or 1 to 6). The Northern statelet was a police state.

(The 'A' Class of Specials was subsequently dissolved but the 'B' Specials were retained to police the Catholics. In 1955, when 'Northern Ireland' had not faced any substantial threat for over three decades, there were still 1 policeman—R.U.C. and Specials—for every 48 adults in the population—or 1 for every 18 or so Catholics—according to the Ministry of Home Affairs in Belfast.)

These figures are contained in a book by G.B. Kenna, *Facts and Figures of the Belfast Pogrom 1920-22* (pp.96-7), in which the author comments:

"... Sir James Craig is not satisfied with the progress made by this instrument of diabolic efficiency. In a recent speech he asserted that their police system was so devised as to enable the entire body of 'loyal' men in Ulster to arm themselves. In other words he was aiming at the arming of the whole Protestant population against their Catholic neighbours. English policy in Ulster at least made a pretence of 'keeping the ring', to use the elegant expression used by Lord Fitzalan at the opening of the Belfast Parliament. The Belfast Government makes no pretence about its aims. It has no use for any cant about 'keeping the ring'.

"It has deliberately unchained forces whose one simple object is the extermination of the Catholic population in the 6 Counties. The rioting mob, the snipers, the murder gang, and the Special Constabulary are not so many distinct institutions of Belfast life; they are all parts of the same organism; or, rather, they are one and the same set of forces operating in different ways. Owing to the ingenious system of A., B. and C. Specials, individuals can operate in some or all of the four above-mentioned capacities within the space of a few hours. And it is a mere truism to state the fact, of which everyone in Belfast is aware, that the Specials supply with arms and ammunition the mobs, the snipers, and the murder gangs in whose activities the Specials take a very prominent part" (pp.98-9)

*Facts and Figures* was an eyewitness account of the violence that accompanied the beginnings of 'Northern Ireland' under its subordinate Government and Parliament. 'G.B. Kenna' was a pseudonym of Father John Hassan, the curate in St. Mary's Church, Chapel Lane. The book was apparently withdrawn soon after publication in 1922 by the Free State Government in one of the first indications that Collins' policy in the North was being abandoned.

Fr. Hassan noticed the change in atmosphere in Belfast from the summer of 1920 onwards as the 'Northern Ireland' entity was being mooted. On 12th July Carson had given a very provocative speech at Finaghy where he said that the British could not be relied upon to defend Ulster from the Sinn Fein threat and he was sick of words. It was time for action to be taken. There was then a series of inflammatory letters printed in the Belfast Newsletter professing to show that the rapid growth of Catholics in north-east Ulster (the 'peaceful penetration') was a serious menace to the survival of Protestants and hinting at the remedy (These are included in an appendix). Fr. Hassan showed that the actual Catholic population of Ulster had declined in both absolute and relative terms from 51% to 44% over the previous half-century and in Belfast from 34% to 24%.

Fr. Hassan commented:

"There was no camouflage regarding Sinn Fein here, but a call to battle of Protestant against Catholic in Belfast, and, we suppose, in every other place where they were in a sufficient majority. The publication of such shameless letters appealing to the lowest instincts of bigotry, in staid newspapers claiming to be respectable, was surely very significant". These ran parallel with "speeches of extremists all over Ulster delivered on the Twelfth of July platforms urging undying conflict with the Church of Rome, and calling on the Protestants to prepare to protect themselves against an imminent danger" (p.17)

Fr. Hassan's book records the names of 455 individuals killed in the Belfast from July 1920 until June 1922, including 267 Catholics and 185 Protestants. (The Protestant figure included security force members and was inflated by a sizeable degree by those killed by the British military whilst attacking Catholic areas.) Over 2000 were wounded in the period.

A strong feature of Fr. Hassan's book is the desire to show that the Unionist pogromists were often men who had stayed at home during the Great War whilst their victims were in many cases Catholic ex-servicemen who had fought for the Empire in the Great War:

> "These Catholic workmen were also ex-soldiers of the British Army who had seen service on many fronts during the European War. Their attackers had probably, many of them, never been in the army, having been among the stay-at-homes who had earned bloated wages on Government work, and who, feeling secure in their indispensability, had clamoured for the application of Conscription knowing that it would not affect themselves" (p.114).

Along with this there are periodic comparisons made between the pogroms against Catholics in Belfast and Ottoman massacres of Armenians during the Great War—a characteristic of British War propaganda at the time. These aspects say a lot about the persistence of the Imperial understanding of the world among Belfast Catholics. This was not an exercise in propaganda for the Republican cause but the plea of a community that felt badly let down by those it had served and placed its faith in.

James Kelly, of the *Irish News,* remembering the experience of the hand over of 'security' from Britain to the Ulster Unionists during 1922 in West Belfast, later wrote:

> "We all sensed the feelings of despair and abandonment which prevailed at the time. A sinister British brasshat, the saturnine Sir Henry Wilson, the jack-booted intriguer of the 1914 war, arrived in Belfast as military adviser to the new northern unionist administration led by Sir James Craig. He devised the so-called 'block-house system' of repression under which the Specials entered the Catholic areas to dominate the largely defenceless population and bring them into submission to the new Orange rulers. There was little resistance when these undisciplined forces, armed to the teeth, moved in to seize St. Mary's Hall and other strong-points throughout West Belfast...
>
> "The open hostility of these swaggering louts was soon manifest as they flaunted their guns threateningly at every opportunity. Innocent people felt intimidated by their murderous reputation... Once a month, on paynight, a minor reign of terror descended on the district... About 8 pm, after several hours boozing, the Specials issued forth, swinging their rifles and into their Lancias and caged armoured cars for a night of fun 'shooting up' the area and teaching the Fenians a lesson. Speeding along Beechmount Avenue they fired volley after volley up the long streets where neighbours gossiped and children played. As they fired at random, women and children ran in terror or dropped down out of sight in the little gardens. Door after door slammed shut and in spite of the bright summer evenings nobody risked

going out, even though the official curfew hour was not due until 10 pm.

"About this time British troops, who had maintained a semblance of fair play and decency in the sectarian confrontations, were withdrawn to barracks, a strange decision by some sinister influence at the top. It seemed that the powers-that-be in London were letting the Specials loose to cow the minority population. The disaster of the vicious and stupid civil war in the south had played neatly into their hands...

"Britain was washing its hands of the Six Ulster counties, abandoning its responsibility to a bigoted new regime, a one-party state which had chosen the weapons of repression and discrimination to bolster up its seizure of power" (B*onfires on the Hillside,* pp. 16-7).

That was the experience that filled the memory of generations of Belfast Catholics. It remained there in 1969 and informed their actions at that time.

## Carson and 'Carsonia'

The *Irish News* christened the new Six County political entity '*Carsonia*'. But this was a very inappropriate name for it since the Unionist Leader had not wanted a sub-Government. Devlin was unfair to Carson in describing him as "the master-architect who constructed this super—structure". But he was correct in saying that Carson rapidly fled the scene of the crime, after the deed was done.

Back in March 1920, the British Chancellor, Austen Chamberlain, and the Unionist Leader, Bonar Law, warned Ulster Unionists that if the Government of Ireland Bill did not go into law, establishing a Parliament of 'Northern Ireland', the old Home Rule Bill, which was still "on the Statute Book" would cease to be suspended and would have to come into law. This was supposedly because the Ottoman Sultan was about to sign the last of the Peace Treaties, with Istanbul occupied and the Royal Navy's guns trained on his Palace. The War would then be officially over (see Hansard 29th and 30th March, Cols. 980 and 1122).

This had the effect of neutralising Ulster Unionist opposition to the Bill since the only way they could escape John Redmond's old Bill was in accepting Lloyd George's new one.

Sir Edward Carson made it clear when he abstained in the vote over the *Government of Ireland Act* in May 1920 in the House of Lords that 'Northern Ireland' was set up against the wishes of Protestant Ulster:

"It has been said over and over again, 'you want to oppress the Catholic minority, you want to get a Protestant Ascendancy over there'. We have never asked to govern any Catholic. We are perfectly satisfied that all of them, Protestant and Catholic, should be governed from this Parliament and we have always said that it was the fact that this Parliament was aloof entirely from these racial distinctions and religious distinctions, which was the strongest foundation for the Government of Ulster. Therefore, not only have we never asked to get an opportunity of dealing in a hostile way with the minority, but we have sought from beginning to end of this controversy to be left alone and go hand in hand with Great Britain as one nation with Great Britain ... No, sir, I urge even now at this hour that the proper course is that Ulster should remain as she is and that you should govern her, as you are governing her now, from here; there is very little difficulty about it, and that you should above all things have it as a place of your own with feelings toward you exactly like your own people, and from which, if these eventualities occur, you will have a jumping off place from which you can carry on all the necessary operations because to my mind, it is utterly idle to suppose, and indeed it has been said so over and over again, that this country can ever afford or will attempt to try a complete separation of Ireland from Great Britain" (Hansard, col. 1292, 18 May, 1920)

Carson, in opposing Home Rule institutions for 'Northern Ireland' was suggesting the use of 'Ulster' as a base for the future reconquest of Ireland if necessary and desirable. But he was also conceding that the game was up for any opposition to the establishment of 'Northern Ireland' as he had been told behind the scenes that the Imperial interest demanded Ulster make *"a great sacrifice"*.

And so Unionist Ulster, having rejected the Home Rule Bill for Ireland by force, had Home Rule thrust upon it by Britain as the price of avoiding Irish Home Rule.

Previously, on 23rd December, 1919 Carson had told Westminster that Ulster did not want a Parliament but it was prepared to make 'any sacrifice' called for by the Empire:

"Ulster has never asked for a separate Parliament. Ulster's claim has always been of this simple character: 'We have thrived under the Union; we are in sympathy with you, we are a part of yourselves. We are prepared to make any sacrifice that you make, and will be prepared to bear any burden that is equally put upon us with other parts of the UK. In these circumstances keep us with you' ... keep Ulster in this united Parliament. I cannot understand why we should ask them to take a parliament which they have never demanded and which they do not want... What is gained by a second parliament in Ireland?... I have never heard discussed in Ulster the question of a second parliament."

Carson's offer of *"any sacrifice"* was taken up by Westminster, even though it was meant as an alternative to accepting the imposition of a separate parliament in Belfast. And Unionists sacrificed their primary objective of being an integral part of the UK state, so that the State could handle the rest of Ireland in the future on a leash.

Carson led the Ulster resistance against the British Liberal Government but abandoned it in the moment of its triumph because what it had got was not what he had aimed to get—quite apart from the question of territory, 32, 9 or 6 Counties. And as a result he retired from politics in protest at the betrayal of the Union by the British Unionist Party and fled the scene.

Carson probably realised that the Imperial scheme for Ulster could only do harm to the Unionism left in Ireland in the long run. While Unionists in the North were allowed their 'British connection' on the understanding that they would no longer be an integral part of the U.K. Carson sensed that this would make them less British every day. And, in becoming less British and more 'Ulsterish', they would increasingly antagonise the Catholics, who they were to control. And this would make them even more anti-Irish and so on, forever, Amen.

Of course, that was the price that the Ulster Protestants had to pay for maintaining the connection with England. In some recompense Westminster gave them some control over their destiny in an era when the British State began to lose the run of itself—as it did after its defeat by Ataturk at Chanak. And for about forty years the Unionists managed to minimise the effects of their detachment by minimizing politics in their semi-detached annex of the British State.

## Imperial rather than British

In the days of Carson Ulster Unionism was a component of the great British Unionist Party. The two are sometimes confused but there should be no confusing them. One was a national party, made up of the 'natural party of government' in the British State, the Conservatives, and Joseph Chamberlain's social reform Liberals. The other proved to be merely an ethnicist defence grouping of a provincial backwater of the Empire.

In 1914, being a Unionist meant being the driving force behind 'the greatest Empire the world had ever seen', that spread across the world and which was 'civilising it' i.e. remaking it in its own image. Within British Unionism Protestant Ulster was an active participant in the Empire, at the height of its powers, and the Ulster Protestants were one of the foremost peoples of its expansion across the world in the form of 'Greater Britain'.

Joseph Chamberlain himself conferred upon the Irish Protestants the title of "*a great governing race*"—an immense privilege in the era when there was a strict racial hierarchy in the world . It was a position that John Redmond could only look up to with envy, and aspire to. And, if the correspondence of the British Statesmen that made the settlement in Ireland is anything to go by, it is clear that in 1920 they still believed the Irish to be a second-class people unfit for exercising governing powers.

In 1914 the Ulster Protestants were one of the master peoples of 'Greater Britain', and therefore of the world. But in 1921 they were the first victims of the collapse of the great Imperial vision. The world order which gave certainty to their lives fell apart in the same moment that the leaders of the Empire made a deal with the leaders of the "murder gang" and the inferior people on their island.

The settlement of 1920-1 had a disastrous effect on the Ulster Protestants because their link with the Motherland was largely Imperial rather than British. Cutting Protestant Ulster off from Britain by devolution changed the character of the link to Britain and brought out the worst in them.

The Ulster Protestants were descendants of the Scots and the English, but that did not make them British in any essential fashion. Britain was not really a nation in any case — it was really a State more than anything else — a great multi-national state with a mission.

The Ulster Protestants played little part in the great events of the British State from 1832. They built ships for the Royal Navy and did the Imperial work with relish in various parts of the world but they had no organic link with the life of the UK State. When the Ulster Protestants were part of the British State so was the rest of Ireland. And later when the greater part of Ireland left the British State the part of Ireland that remained formally part of the British State found itself excluded from its most important political framework.

Protestant Ulster was changed substantially by its Great Revival of 1859 and it turned itself into something quite different afterwards — distinct and original — from what it had been before. 1859 represented a true watershed in its social development. The Ulster which gave rise to the United Irish movement had begun to be eroded politically by the Act of Union, which many of the United Irishmen supported. But all dispute was rendered obsolete by the shifting of ground in the great popular upsurge of enthusiasm in 1859, which many saw as pure 'hysteria'. Frank Frankfort Moore, author of *The Truth about Ulster*, and himself a fundamentalist Protestant, has a section about it in his Anti-Home Rule book in which he looks down his nose at the goings on in the North Antrim villages, but then concedes that it changed everything. Protestant Ulster became a product of the Great Revival as its politics became narrowed into a form of Covenanting and it developed its largely apolitical character.

The Ulster sense of affinity with Britain was primarily Imperial. The Ulster Protestants were certainly British in the British Empire sense and were an enthusiastic part of 'Greater Britain' — but Home Rule Ireland also aspired to become so under John Redmond and Joe Devlin in the years leading up to 1914. Ulster just would not have it, sensing that this would erode its difference, and its edge, over the Catholics within Imperial politics.

The British political system of Whigs and Tories in the 19th Century might have shaped Protestant Ulster and made it British if it had continued. But it only lasted for about a generation after 1832 before dissolving under the influence of Gladstone's First Home Rule Bill (1886), back into the mode of communal politics in which Ulster had lived for a century and a half before the 1830s. And so, for all its Union Jacks, Ulster was not British in one of the most important dimensions of British 'national' life. It was not British politically, and being British was largely a matter of politics in the modern era.

All of this had great ramifications in the placing of the Northern Catholics under the Ulster Protestants after what Britain did to them in 1920-1.

## The Protestant predicament

This book is about the Catholic predicament in 'Northern Ireland' but the Protestant predicament cannot be ignored since it has so much bearing on the situation of the Catholics who were forced into a position of subjugation under those who were damaged by the Imperial innovation in its Irish policy.

One consequence of 1920-1 was that every British Government became under suspicion of wanting to do to the loyal people of Ulster what James II tried to do to the Protestant settlement besieged in Derry in 1689—and every compromising leader that had thoughts of alleviating the position of the Catholics became a Lundy. Protestant Ulster thus reverted back to being a community under siege—even though this was a state of mind much more than a physical fact. And it became a kind of residue of 'Greater Britain', hanging onto the illusions of the crumbling Empire through the ideology of Empire Loyalism that in England began to be seen as increasingly distasteful.

Ulster did not feel the pain of the arrangements on the island made between 1920 and 1921 as Carson, the Dublin Unionist, did. The Ulster Unionists were, if anything, rather proud that they had become a semi-detached statelet of the Imperial family of nations, and they felt little loss at being excluded from the new democracy of what they grandiosely called "the mainland". The culture of Ulster Unionism pre-dated and had little to do with democracy as an actual mode of government. It saw in democracy only the threat of being engulfed numerically by the lower-quality natives and it was happy to support military rule in Ireland after the 1918 Election to make sure democracy did not triumph. And after 1922 it was equally content to be excluded from the politics of governing the State, and to occupy its own wee apolitical niche in its outpost of Empire.

The Ulster Unionist Council had no experience of statecraft and no aptitude for it, and it never saw its business as making sure that the Partition settlement in the North was democratically viable. Its duty was "no surrender" and "not an inch". It was not greatly concerned about democracy, which it used only as an opportunist slogan to justify its separateness from the major part of the democracy on the island. Its only concern was that it should not be subjected to government by a democracy of inferior Papists. And that fundamental demand was secured for it by Partition.

But the condition on which Britain enacted Partition for it was that it should conduct a Home Rule Government of 'Northern Ireland' outside the political system of the State.

It might be argued that the Unionists did not know what they were getting. But Whitehall undoubtedly knew what it was giving them and what it was for.

There is an argument that Partition, in the form that it took, proved to be actually more detrimental to Protestant Ulster than it did to the Catholics. Both communities became stranded fragments—one cut from the British State of its choosing and the other cut off both from this state and the Irish Nation, of which it formed part, and its state.

The Northern Catholics were placed in a predicament within 'Northern Ireland' but they continued to live a rich life of their own within their ideals, holding onto the hope that their day would surely come. But the day of the Ulster Unionist had gone with the withdrawal of Britain from Ulster. Life was now to be of a much more modest insular and mundane character. Having been once part of a great world-wide Master Race the Ulster Protestant was now constricted and curtailed into a singular function of merely mastering the local natives. Such were the limits of its new Imperial duties under orders from Headquarters in London.

What the Ulster Protestants had desired was to simply settle down as a normal part of the British State. But British policy did not allow it. British policy said they must either govern Catholics, or else be governed by them and come under what they saw as Rome Rule. Faced with that choice they agreed to govern the large body of Catholics in their assigned territory, on a communal basis, in a separate devolved Government, outside the ambit of the democratic political system of the State.

One other aspect of events entrenched the Ulster Unionist attachment to devolutionism—the Anglo-Irish 'Treaty' of 1921. The 'Treaty' was a formal amendment to the *Government of Ireland Act* of 1920 in British Law. It had the effect of unbalancing the 1920 proposals for the creation of two more or less equal jurisdictions in Ireland—'Northern' and 'Southern' Ireland. This worried the Ulster Unionists who saw a much more substantial state entity being established in the South than they had got in the North and it potentially 'negotiating' with Westminster on a higher level to what Belfast was capable of. It led them to see their devolved Parliament as some kind of defence mechanism against British intrigue in relation to the whole island and as an insurance against being absorbed by the rest of the island if the Imperial mind changed again.

# The 'supreme sacrifice' of Ulster Unionism

Professor Ronan Fanning, in a highly-acclaimed book, makes the following statement about the new British policy of 1920-1:

> "The harsh truth for Unionists was that they no longer were of use but had become an embarrassment because the Irish garrison protective of British strategic interests in earlier centuries had become redundant" (*Fatal Path, British Government and the Irish Revolution, 1919-22*, p.216)

That statement might have been true if the Liberal scheme for Home Rule had gone through in 1914 and John Redmond had become Prime Minister of Imperial Ireland. But Imperial Ireland collapsed under what the British State did to it. What happened between 1914 and 1925 surely proved that Ulster Unionism had not become *"redundant"* within *"British strategic interests"* on Ireland. The Ulster Protestants had, in fact, been ear-marked for a different purpose within a wider strategic interest and they were far from being "an embarrassment" to Britain.

In February 1922, after British Unionists had faced down Ulster Unionist opposition to the Boundary Commission provision in the Anglo-Irish 'Treaty', the *Irish News* noticed something significant had happened in the relationship between British and Ulster Unionism. It elaborated this understanding in its editorial, '*Keep Moving Forward*':

> "While they were of use to British politicians—while they served the purposes of an English Party—they were persons of note and importance. But the bulk of the Tory Party in Great Britain have decided to abandon Ireland as a political asset.
>
> "Tories thrived as 'Unionists' from 1886 until 1920. They opposed the Irish demand for Self-Government; they maintained that all Ireland should be held within the links of the chain forged by Pitt and Castlereagh.
>
> "It was a definite policy. By adhering to it the Conservative Party held the Government of Great Britain in their hands... from 1886 until 1892; from 1895 until 1906; and again, in alliance with Mr. Lloyd George and the Coalition-Liberals, they secured a huge Parliamentary majority in 1918. The war altered many things—nearly everything except the 'politics' of the N.E. Ulster Ascendancy section...
>
> "Therefore, Unionism as a political policy was a Paying Proposition. English Conservatives found it profitable to exploit Ulster...
>
> "The Partition of Ireland Bill was a brutal and monstrous plan for the destruction of the Irish nation; but its appearance at Westminster marked the end of Unionism as a policy and of the Unionists as a Party in the British State.
>
> "The term 'Unionist' has no more significance now, and no closer relation to actual fact than 'Guelph' or 'Ghibeline'.
>
> "The legend of Ulster was exploded—blown to smithereens...
>
> "England has no further use for them... But though Mr. Churchill... and

his fellows need the N. Eastern Irish Tories no more... it still serves the purposes of the British Government to keep Irishmen divided; they hope N.E. Ulster will serve as a sort of drag while the negotiations are over and the Settlement is completed" (18.2.22)

'Ulster' had fulfilled one role for the British State in Ireland and now it was about to assume a different one.

The Ulster Unionists were told privately they must have a Home Rule set up of their own so that a deal could be made with some elements in Sinn Fein in order to divide the Republican forces. These elements in Sinn Fein they were assured would be forced to accept the Crown, having been assured that if they did the concoction in 'Northern Ireland', established in 1921, would be made unviable.

In strategic terms Ulster Unionism agreed to make the 'supreme sacrifice' and accept semi-detachment from Britain so that the Imperial Government could make a 'Treaty' with the rebels, in order that the independence movement could be disorganised and weakened, enabling Britain to retain its hegemony over the whole island.

The extent of that sacrifice was obscured by the ideology connected with *'our wee Ulster'* and the real debilitating extent of it did not become apparent until decades later.

## The Six Counties and the 'Treaty'

That brings us to what 'Northern Ireland' was for in relation to the rest of the island.

Lloyd George established 'Northern Ireland' as a negotiating position to be used against the Irish independence movement. He established it as a reality and then encouraged Sinn Fein to believe that Partition was negotiable, to encourage it to conference and make it amenable to concession on independence to regain the lost Six Counties.

The problem that confronted Britain was that the Republican Army that defended and made good the elected Irish Government did not break up under British military power. So, after a couple of years of a war that it showed no sign of winning, the British Government tried a new policy of Truce leading to negotiations. The war in Ireland was doing Britain no good in the world and it had the choice of either escalating it to the massive proportions necessary for victory or trying to do a deal with the 'rebels', that would concede to them less than they had pledged themselves to, in return for their submission to Crown authority.

In June 1921, with the Northern Parliament opened, 'Ulster' was out of the way for Britain, to be utilised in relation to an overall settlement with the Irish independence movement.

Lloyd George had withheld services from 'Northern Ireland', to give the impression that 'Northern Ireland' could, at this late stage, be aborted. And, while the 'Treaty' negotiations were proceeding, the British encouraged the Irish delegates to believe that they would help to whittle away Northern Ireland, if the Irish signed the document called the 'Treaty'. But, no sooner had the ink dried on the 'Treaty', than all the British will to take responsibility for the Unionist statelet evaporated. Churchill, Chamberlain and Balfour were already highly supportive of Craig's administration and Lloyd George, who opposed (or pretended to oppose) some aspects of Unionist behaviour in Cabinet, did nothing—presumably because of his dependence on Bonar Law to remain in power.

Towards the end of the 'Treaty' negotiations Lloyd George informed the King that he could sign the Order in Council to transfer services to 'Northern Ireland' and complete Partition.

Then the negotiations were brought to a close by the British in presenting the Irish delegation, headed by Arthur Griffith and Michael Collins, with a document. They were told to sign it, without consulting the President, De Valera, or the rest of the Irish Government in Dublin, or face *"immediate and terrible war"*.

The understanding of this was that Britain was prepared to use the methods it had quelled Boer resistance to its authority a couple of decades before—blockhouse, relocations and concentration camps—as well as blockade and the new air power, if the delegates did not sign, and be it on their consciences.

Imperial pressure succeeded and the result was the Anglo-Irish 'Treaty' of December 1921.

Captain Henry Harrison, a former Redmondite (or more accurately, a surviving Redmondite after Redmondism had been discredited by Britain's treatment of it), made the following perceptive comment about the signatures of Collins and Griffith on the 'Treaty' with regard to Partition and the proviso for a Boundary Commission under Article XII of it:

> "Partition was, of course, wholly unacceptable. And assent to partition would have been an unjustifiable surrender to the threat of 'immediate and terrible war' which appears to have been used as inducement to them to sign. The envoys, on their side, maintained that partition could not endure in view of the proviso for a redelimitation of the boundary, if Northern Ireland exercised its option to remain in the British Parliament. They pointed to the wording of the proviso which conformed to the recent precedents providing for the recasting of frontiers in Central Europe in accordance with the doctrine of self-determination. They argued with much force that such a redelimitation in Northern Ireland would reduce the already truncated province of Ulster

to such diminished proportions as would virtually ensure its prompt reunion with the parent Ireland on all practical grounds. Nay more, they asserted firmly, that their view was based on assurances as to the meaning of Article XII given to them privately by British negotiators as an inducement to sign. There is no reason whatever to doubt the truth of the latter statement — which, indeed, has received a good deal of independent confirmation...

"Collins and Griffith...cannot, perhaps, be acquitted of imprudence in relying upon informal and unrecorded assurances. In negotiation at the sword's point it is always wise to insist that the written document which is to be executed should clearly specify in unambiguous language the terms upon which reliance is placed — and to place no reliance upon any oral assurances which the opponent is unwilling to embody in the express terms of the written document. And this is especially so in the case of envoys negotiating in a representative capacity, whose private engagements cannot possibly be enforced against their principal" (*Ulster and the British Empire*, pp. 46-7).

The British Government succeeded in getting the Irish delegation, led by Collins and Griffith, to sign the 'Treaty' confining Ireland to Dominion status within the Empire and ending the Irish Republic established in 1918. The statelet of 'Northern Ireland' remained in being, but Lloyd George led Collins to believe, in getting his signature on the 'Treaty' as a whole, that the financial position of Ulster — which was to continue to pay an Imperial contribution as an inducement to join the South — and a Border Commission, would undermine it and whittle down its territory to the extent that it would prove unviable.

Collins, therefore, rather than accepting Partition — as some later historians have alleged — saw the 'Treaty' as reopening the question of the status of the Six Counties from the *fait accompli* of the 1920 Act.

Collins and Griffith were convinced by what Britain was doing in Europe that a Boundary Commission would presumably whittle the artificial construction in the North-East down to nothing, as the historic position overrode the issue of local sentiment very quickly.

The chief governmental effect of the 'Treaty' was to unbalance the 1920 Act by replacing one of the two Home Rule Parliaments with a Parliament with the full trappings of state. That in turn had a political effect as Collins attempted to use his new trappings of state in the South, provided to him by the Imperial power, against the remaining Home Rule parliament in the North — but more of this aspect in the next chapter.

# CHAPTER FIVE

# Enter Collins

What became the Catholic predicament in 'Northern Ireland' was largely created by external influences on the community. The primary influence was what the British Government did in Ireland between 1920 with the Government of Ireland Act and 1921 with the 'Treaty' examined in the last chapter. A secondary influence was what the Provisional Government of the Irish Free State, under Michael Collins, established in the Twenty-Six Counties within the political framework of the 'Treaty' and then did with it in the North from 1922 up until its abandonment of the Six County Catholics in 1925.

For about a year, between mid-1921 and mid-1922, the Northern Catholic community, which had previously been Devlinite and Home Rule in orientation, came under the hegemony of the new National force, Sinn Fein. This was almost entirely due to the success of Republican Ireland in resisting British attempts to subdue it. By forcing Britain to the conference table and promising a way out of the predicament the Northern Catholics had found themselves in Sinn Fein momentarily swept aside Devlin's forces.

Having signed the 'Treaty' Collins believed he could undo what had happened in the North and he put his considerable energies into this. But Britain is immensely skilled and resourceful in these matters knowing how to turn set-backs around. And what happened in the show-down between Collins and the British was nothing short of catastrophic for the Six County Catholics.

## Collins in Armagh

The first indication that Michael Collins was going to play a significant part in the destiny of Northern Catholics came in a highly-publicised visit to Armagh on 4th September 1921 during the Truce.

Collins addressed what the *Irish News* called a "vast assemblage" of nationalists from Armagh, Tyrone, Down, Monaghan and Belfast, including a large contingent of IRA volunteers. The content of Collins' speech is noteworthy for a number of reasons. Here are some of the things Collins, "the Commander in Chief of Republican forces", said to rally the Northern Catholic community behind him:

"For the first time in more than two centuries England had dealt with them as an equal. She could never go back on that (Applause). They had called them murderers; they had made a Truce with them. If indeed they were murderers... what would the nations of the world think of a country which had made a Truce with murderers? If they were not murderers, then they had recognised them as an army; and what would the nations of the world think of a country that executed the members of a recognised army?...

"Their last effort before the Truce was designed to do what they did in Germany. They sent out their aeroplanes over the battle fronts in Ireland and dropped leaflets to wean the people from the Army and to wean all local commanders from the high command. The Irish people, the Irish Army, were proof against that insidious effort. It was not Germans they had to deal with in that (Applause). The Irish people had been fooled too often; they had believed the fair promises of England too often, and they had passed away from that sad belief. Their false promises had no magic spell to cast over them now. They had seen the last of them. They had to deal with them now openly as one nation with another nation, and they had to deal with men who understood essentials, who would not be fooled by any of their promises..."

During the Truce the IRA was accorded recognition by the British military and the Specials were ordered to stand down. Eoin O'Duffy (who also spoke at Armagh, delivering a more menacing speech than Collins which promised to "show the lead" to Unionists) established the IRA Headquarters in St Mary's Hall in the city centre of Belfast and the IRA began to formally constitute its Northern divisions. O'Duffy's establishment of IRA Headquarters in St. Mary's Hall symbolized the passing of power from the Devlinites to Republicans in the North. The presence of Republican H.Q. in the centre of the Unionist city must have represented a huge provocation. Only the year before General O'Duffy occupied it the RIC were refusing the GAA its use because of the fear of 'seditious speeches'.

Just before Collins' visit to Armagh O'Duffy had mobilised the Belfast IRA to defend the Catholic York Street area from a large Unionist attack. Seven of the attackers were killed by O'Duffy's men. Another successful defence of the Short Strand a few months later showed that O'Duffy and Collins meant business in the North and sent the Unionist Cabinet into hysterics.

The IRA expanded drastically in the North as recruits flooded in. Large-scale IRA training camps were established in County Down and North Antrim and other areas. Dan Breen and other senior officers, now free from the threat of capture, came up to train the new volunteers in guerrilla warfare for the unfinished business North of the Border.

When the Republic's Bureau of Military History collected accounts from veterans of the War of Independence during the 1940s and 1950s, it came up against a problem with the Northern IRA men who deposited their statements. The Bureau defined the end of the War of Independence as beginning with the Truce with the British, but for the Northerners the War of Independence continued on into 1922, and escalated. And for many in the North it only began with the Truce.

There was no Truce in the North as the War intensified there. It could be said that there was a Truce between Collins and the British in the North but in no respect was this just a Northern war between Republicans and Unionists in the Six Counties, disconnected from a War of Independence that went before. It was also Collins' War and therefore rightly forms part of the War of Independence and should not be written out of it. It was, of course, the part of the War of Independence that was a complete and utter failure. But that is beside the point when attempts are being made to forget it.

## Half right Collins

As Collins noted the Truce was a major event in the life of the Imperial State. It was the first act of appeasement forced upon it when it was supposed to be the greatest Empire the world had ever known, at the pinnacle of its power, after seeing off Germany and establishing its Carthaginian peace. Having had *"murder by the throat"* until fairly recently, it came to terms with *"the murder gang"*.

The British had out-manoeuvred the undefeated German Army by turning the Armistice into surrender but it was not going to do the same with the Republican Army in Ireland, according to Collins.

But Collins was only half right when he said that*"England had dealt with them as an equal"*. Or more accurately, he was right about the Truce but he was about to be very wrong about the next phase of Imperial engagement with the Irish—the 'Treaty' and its aftermath.

The British did not negotiate with the Irish as the elected Government of their country, as one Government to another, on equal terms. To the British, Collins and his comrades were still rebels to be brought under the authority of the Crown.

The 'Treaty' that Collins signed was not a Treaty as such. Treaties are signed between recognised sovereign authorities and Britain never recognised the Dail as having any legitimate standing. Under the 'Treaty' signed by Collins, the Irish had to meet as the Parliament of Southern Ireland under the Government of Ireland Act. They then were required to form themselves into a Provisional Government on British authority. They were allowed to establish a new Army, armed by Britain, with the understanding that it would repress those who disagreed with the 'Treaty' and made any attempt to restore the Republic.

Collins was right about the Germans. Their gullible Social Democrat leaders were over-awed by the Wilsonian propaganda and their resistance collapsed—although their army remained unbeaten. The Irish, who did not have the army the Germans possessed, had developed a cynicism about British promises and were not to be gulled like the innocent-minded Germans. So they had to be dealt with in another way.

## The still-born child with no name

When he took the platform again in Armagh, Collins began by ridiculing the notion that a Six County political entity could even come into existence— even though, in fact, it already existed in substantial form. Collins said:

> "They would expect him to say something not about Ulster. No; about something for which there was no name. No historical claim existed to help them to give it a name. No; there was no historical or geographical justification for the division of Ulster, and there was no practical justification for giving the ancient name of Ulster to the few counties that were causing the trouble to-day. There they remain without a name, and they need not be named. The still-born child was not given a name".

A confident Collins then gave his audience the impression that the Six Counties and its Parliament were doomed in the face of inevitable British betrayal and increasing Nationalist resistance that he was going to lead:

> "England was handing out Parliaments—a veritable patent medicine which would cure everything. The North-East wished to remain in the Union—it got a Parliament. They wanted to bring Ireland out of the Union—they also got a Parliament. But let him return to this Northern Parliament. James Craig had... said that he accepted the elections to this Parliament as an expression of self-determination... and if he accepted the principle that government must rest on the consent of the governed, where then could the case be made out for the inclusion of Fermanagh and Tyrone in the Northern Parliament?...
> "It was obvious that an artificial excuse was being made of the existence of the Northern Parliament to keep Ireland asunder... There, then, was a clear indication of the purpose of the Northern Parliament. There again was England using the Orangemen for her own interests, and the interests of the Orangemen had never been the same as those of England. The Orangemen had been used as a tool to preventing up to the present what is now inevitable. The moment was near where they would no longer be used as a tool; when they would, in fact, stand in the way of an agreement with Ireland, which had now become essential to British interests. Then they would be thrown aside, and they would find their eyes turned to an England which no longer wanted them. Grattan told their forefathers: 'If you are not Irishmen, you are

139

nothing'. We want them to join with us as Irishmen to come into the Irish Nation while they can still come in with their heads up; to come in to take their share in the government of their own country...

"Are they really going to accept the status of an English shire, and pay their six shillings in the pound income tax while Ireland pays one shilling or less? Are they really going to remain sitting in their Parliament in its doomed building, erected on such unsound foundations? That is more dangerous to those who are within than those who are without...

"Our proposal is as I have said, that they should come in. We can afford to give them even more than justice. We can afford to be generous (Applause). That is our message to the North, and it is meant for those who are opposed to us rather than for those who are with us. But to those who are with us I can say no matter what happens, no matter what the future may bring, we shall not desert them. The Parliament in its doomed building does not, or cannot, control its unruly enemies, and already that doomed building is shaking. I rejoice to see that already this impossible combination in the North-East is breaking up. Tyrone and Fermanagh have fallen away; they come to us for the protection which we are bestowing elsewhere throughout this land.

"I would remind my listeners here that in this county was fought the Battle of the Yellow Ford between the English under Bagnall and the Irish under O'Neill and O'Donnell. At that Battle the English met with the greatest reverse they had ever experienced since they set foot in Ireland. May I hope, may we all hope, that Armagh will have the honour also of bringing their final overthrow by following Tyrone and Fermanagh as a result of this gathering today" (IN 5.9.21).

Perhaps Lloyd George was informed of this speech. The British Prime Minister had a special talent in getting people he was dealing with to believe what they wanted to hear when he was talking to them. Collins was hooked, there is no doubt.

During the period of the Truce the Six County entity, under construction, was subordinated to the Imperial Government's larger Irish policy. The 1920 Act was suspended and no major powers were transferred from Westminster to the 'Northern Ireland' Government', to encourage Sinn Fein into signing the 'Treaty'. Perhaps that was a sign of the betrayal at the final hour to those who wanted to believe it?

For Northern Catholics the Truce, Collins' confidence at Armagh and the promised negotiations between Sinn Fein and Britain all went to provide an unexpected fresh hope of deliverance from the Six County construction. After the humiliating experience the community had suffered in supporting Devlin's party and its policy, Sinn Fein had re-opened the Partition issue and promised to extricate Catholics from the intolerable situation in which they had found themselves.

## Overcoming the Devlinites

During the Truce Sinn Fein were able to get on top of the Devlinites in Belfast for the first time through the Republican success of forcing the British to the conference table. Seamus Woods, the Belfast IRA O/C, noted the change in support from Belfast Catholics "believing for the moment that we had been victorious and that the Specials and UVF were beaten... practically all flooded to our standard" (Phoenix, *Northern Nationalism*, p.141).

Whole Branches of the United Irish League and Ancient Order of Hibernians ceased to exist or simply became Sinn Fein branches taking the Hibernian Halls with them.

Prior to 1916 the Devlinite Home Rulers had held the political ascendancy in 'Ulster'. Between 1916 and 1921 the Six Counties had been divided into the largely Devlinite east and the largely Sinn Fein west. Sinn Fein ascendancy across the Six Counties over the 'constitutional' Nationalists would last in the North-East for about one year, from June 1921-June 1922, and it become bound up largely with the fortunes of one man, Michael Collins.

Nationalist hopes were raised by an optimistic assessment that the ending of Partition would be a precondition of a settlement on the Irish side. However the publication of the British settlement proposals presented to De Valera on 20th July ended this brief optimism. A form of Dominion status was proposed by the British but with full recognition of the existing powers and privileges of the Parliament of 'Northern Ireland' which could not be abrogated except by its own consent. The child was born and it had a name.

Eamon Phoenix notes:

"A difference of emphasis or perspective existed between the Dáil leadership and the Northern Catholic minority. For the nationalists, as one of their few authentic spokesman in the Dail, Sean MacEntee, has asserted 'partition was the one supreme issue'; indeed, MacEntee, himself a Belfast Catholic and son of a Nationalist city councillor, later recorded that he 'would have voted for the 'Treaty' in January 1922 but for the inclusion of partition'. The bulk of Sinn Fein supporters in the north-east were prepared to compromise on the issue of national status if it would ensure unity. The Sinn Fein leaders in the South, however, accorded national status an importance at least as great as 'essential unity' and, as time went on, the latter tended to become obscured by the twin issues of crown and Empire" (*Northern Nationalism*, pp.145-6).

In the lead-up to the negotiations, a large number of deputations of Northern Nationalists from every part of the Six Counties descended on the Dail, concerned at the prospect of Partition continuing after a settlement between Sinn Fein and the British, in contradiction of what Collins had told them in Armagh. However, Sinn Fein's Cahir Healy's suggestion that the plenipotentiaries be advised on the Partition issue during the negotiations by Northerners was taken as a slur on the negotiators. Devlin, who was in London at the time, with his experience of past negotiations with Lloyd George, was also ignored by the delegation sent from Dublin.

This was an early manifestation of Dublin excluding the North from all influence on National affairs, even on those that directly concerned and affected Northern Catholics.


## Northern Catholics and the 'Treaty'

In London the Irish plenipotentiaries initially requested that the British tell the Unionists that the alternative to the acceptance of a united Ireland should be a subordinate parliament for a reduced Northern area, under the jurisdiction of an all Ireland Parliament. The reasoning was that if the Unionists were threatened with plebiscites and a drastic reduction of their area by the British Government they might be made more amenable to the all Ireland solution.

However, Lloyd George, through a process of trickery involving side-deals, tied Griffith into the British alternative of a Boundary Commission to delimit the area of 'Northern Ireland', which would remain outside an Irish State. In this way the Partition issue was removed by Lloyd George from the 'Treaty' negotiations while the Irish delegation was pinned down to the British position on Crown and Empire.

That is not to say that Partition resulted from inferior Irish negotiating power in London. 'Northern Ireland' was a nearly done thing when the 'Treaty' was being 'negotiated', awaiting the British grant of services to turn it into the finished product. It was a nearly thing to give the Irish hope that it might not, in fact, come to pass after all, and therefore to encourage some amenability on them. But all it required was a couple of signatures to have the great degree of Imperial power it could count on behind it.

That the Irish could have negotiated 'Northern Ireland' away in London is a fantasy.

When Lloyd George was able to be sure that he had the Irish delegation hooked into his negotiating position he decided to transfer responsibility for law and order and Local Government to the 'Northern Ireland' Ministry of Home Affairs, investing the Unionist administration with executive power to make 'Northern Ireland' the finished article. He did this in November, even before the signing of the 'Treaty'.

In response to this, Tyrone County Council and eight smaller bodies repudiated the Northern Government's authority and pledged allegiance to the Dáil, resulting in the RIC taking charge of the Council offices in Omagh.

Despite the Partition aspect, the *Irish News* supported the 'Treaty' and hoped that opposition to it would not gain wider support. It particularly felt that the British threat of *"immediate and terrible war"* , made to those who signed the 'Treaty', would be particularly felt by those stranded in the Six County area:

> "The nation will neither be stampeded, confused, disunited, or discouraged at this supreme hour by the opposition of one man, or group of men, to the decision reached and registered by the plenipotentiaries... The alternative to this course is so horribly obvious that we need not describe it" (9.12.21).

The *Irish News* had been reassured that Dublin knew what it was doing after a large delegation of Northern Nationalists, including Republicans and Devlinites, concerned at the implications for them of the 'Treaty', were met by Eoin MacNeill, two days before, at the Mansion House in Dublin. MacNeill assured them that although Partition was "a real danger it was an artificial one" and "It had not got the strength of permanency" (PRONI, 2991/B2).

MacNeill asked the Northern Nationalists to adopt a practical programme of passive resistance to the Northern Government's authority, involving non-recognition of the Northern courts and non-payment of taxes. He informed the Northerners that the cornerstone of this policy would be the support of Dublin for the non-recognition of the educational authority of the Belfast Parliament. Northern Catholic schools and teachers would not accept finance from Belfast but would be financed by Dublin.

With the signing of the 'Treaty', the view of the *Irish News* was that peace and stability in the South would provide the best possible conditions within which the Twenty-Six County State could establish itself and exert an influence that would wear away the Border in the years to come. Its pro-'Treaty' position was almost universal across the North from both Devlinites and Sinn Feiners, who wished for the establishment of a Government in Dublin that would work in the North's interests and use its power of state to undermine the authority of the Northern administration.

When Dáil Éireann voted to support the 'Treaty' in early January 1922 the *Irish News* was supportive of the decision:

> "The debates were exhaustive; they had practically exhausted the patience of the Irish nation. But that point need not be laboured now. At the close there was a majority of 7 for the 'Treaty': 64 votes to 57. We doubt if one T.D. of the 57 would be re-elected in an Irish constituency if it were possible to hold an election... The 64 who voted for the Resolution of Approval represented 90 per cent of all the Irish people...
> "Now, what next?

"Mr. De Valera seems determined to defy the majority... He will fight Ireland, not the British Government...

"Messrs. Griffith, Collins, Duggan, Barton and Duffy... hammered out a Treaty; they signed it... and now Dáil Éireann has accepted the result of their labours by a competent majority, while its acceptance by more than 90 per cent of the people who elected Dáil Éireann is not really disputed.

"Therefore, the path is clear for the establishment of a Provisional Government forthwith.

"When those members for constituencies in Southern Ireland who represent over 90 per cent of the people have assembled in response to the stipulated summons, the constitution of a Provisional Government can be undertaken and completed. Then that Provisional Government can assume control over the 26 Irish Counties.

"The sooner these steps are taken... the better by far for the country and the Irish people... If the men who carried a majority in Dáil Éireann into the Division Lobby in favour of the Anglo-Irish Peace Treaty hesitate, now, they are lost; and hopeless anarchy culminating in destruction and ignominious failure will be the nation's lot for years to come.

"But we should not have said 'the nation', for those people of those six excluded counties whose devotion to Irish Nationality stood a thousand tests never applied elsewhere, and who look across the boundaries of the Irish Free State at the squabbles and the 'quibbles' and the charges and allegations that have tortured the community for a month, can do nothing more than face the terrible realities of their own position, though they do not hold themselves divorced from the Irish Nation.

"We want it to be understood clearly that the Nationalists of the Six Counties approve the verdict delivered on Saturday night; they regret the majority was not 107, not merely 7. Of all the specious arguments against the Peace Treaty employed during the months of December and January, the most impertinent and cruel was the pretence that the Nationalists of 'Northern Ireland' would be sacrificed if the Treaty was made operative.

"The Nationalists of 'Northern Ireland' had been 'sacrificed' ever since the day when it was made possible for the British Parliament to pass the Partition Act of 1920. That was done in 1918, not 1921" (IN 9.1.22).


The last sentence was a dig at Sinn Fein. The Devlinite *Irish News* held the Republican victory in 1918 responsible for the 1920 Act. Of course, Partition had been in the air long before that and it was Devlin and the Party who, in producing the Unionist resistance to Home Rule, had done most to place it on the agenda, between 1912 and 1918.

The view that 90 per cent of the Irish people were in favour of the 'Treaty' was undoubtedly an exaggeration. But the editorial would have been representative of the Northern Catholic view of the 'Treaty' especially in its dismissal of the opposition to it as *"quibbles"* in comparison to what had been already done to the Northern Catholics through Partition. The debating points presented to the Dáil regarding the rights and wrongs of the 'Treaty' were viewed as meaningless in the North, particularly since consideration of Partition had been almost entirely absent in the debates — in recognition that all were opposed to it with equal hostility but also that there was no alternative policy about ending it.

A few weeks later the leader of the Twenty Six Counties, Michael Collins, signed a Pact with the leader of the Six Counties, James Craig. The *Irish News* called the Pact *"a Treaty"* and welcomed it:

> "That Treaty's bearing on the position of the Nationalists who live in the Six Counties should be calmly and carefully considered. When 'two Governments' agree 'to endeavour to devise a more suitable system than the Council of Ireland for dealing with the problems affecting all Ireland', it is quite evident that a new situation has been created for the 450,000 Nationalists of the North-East" (24.1.22).

The problem for Northern Catholics was that Collins had a very different purpose in signing the Pact with Craig than the *Irish News* imagined.

As for other Northern Nationalists, the Pact brought great confusion over what Collins was actually trying to do. Different approaches were adopted in Belfast, Derry, Fermanagh and Tyrone about how they should act in the circumstances, in support of Collins' political maneouverings. But they were unable to read Collins' mind on recognising or not-recognising the Unionist administration as the best way of undermining it and divisions began to emerge in the confusion, both within Sinn Fein and right across the Nationalist spectrum.

## Collins and the North

At this point it is worth considering Michael Collins' policy with regard to the North because it was to have a significant effect on Northern Nationalists in 1922 and for decades to come.

The one thing that can be said in Collins' favour is that he seems to have been the only Southern leader to think about the necessity of having a Northern policy: Most simply engaged in wishful thinking about ending Partition.

Before the Truce and 'Treaty', Collins had come up with the idea of dealing with the North by whittling down the Six Counties until it became unviable. He proposed doing this by supporting the Anti-Partitionist Councils in the North that had raised the Tricolour in defiance of Stormont to make their areas ungovernable by the new administration.

Collins' views on the North were later included in *The Path to Freedom* collection of his thoughts:

"The decision of the boundary commission, arranged for in Clause Twelve (of the Treaty), would be certain to deprive 'Ulster' of Fermanagh and Tyrone. Shorn of those counties, she would shrink into insignificance. The burdens and financial restrictions of the Partition Act will remain on North-East Ulster if she decides to stay out. No lightening of these burdens or restrictions can be effected by the English parliament without the consent of Ireland. Thus, union is certain. The only question for Northeast Ulster is—How soon?" (p.80).

That might seem an over optimistic reading of the situation. But Collins had great faith in his own abilities. Under Article XII of the 'Treaty', if the Six Counties opted out of an all-Ireland Dominion a Commission was to be established that would redraw the boundaries between the Irish Free State and 'Northern Ireland', "in accordance with the wishes of the inhabitants".

Collins, in agreeing to the 'Treaty', had been led to believe that the Boundary Commission would reduce the area allocated to 'Northern Ireland' to unviable proportions. Lloyd George at the same time, however, had privately told Craig that it would only transfer pockets of Protestants and Catholics to the other side of a slightly amended borderline to benefit Unionists.

But Griffith and Collins convinced the Nationalists in Fermanagh and Tyrone that Article XII would compel Craig to choose between entering an all-Ireland unit or suffering a reduction of up to a third of the Six Counties.

It was widely understood that the Irish delegates would never have signed the 'Treaty' without such an assurance and Lloyd George said in Parliament, on 14th December 1921, that Fermanagh and Tyrone were probably unsustainable within 'Northern Ireland' because the majority in these Counties wanted to live under a Southern jurisdiction (Hansard, 14 December, col. 40). Churchill suggested the same in very careful language a few months later when he said that Britain had agreed to the Boundary concession when it was "sore-pressed with burdens, with threats, with menaces in every quarter of the world" that made agreeing to this part of the 'Treaty' a necessity. The only alternative, he said, was "the re-conquest of Ireland at enormous expense in money and men" (Hansard, 16th February, cols. 1271-2).

So Article XII and the Boundary Commission was, in fact, a holding operation on Britain's part to be dished when circumstances changed.

The Sinn Fein assertions about the Commission were reinforced by the attacks Ulster Unionists made in Parliament on Article XII arguing that, if it was carried out properly, and large border areas lost, 'Northern Ireland' might indeed be unsustainable for them to govern.

On 4th February Collins issued a statement to the press in which he claimed: "majorities must rule, and... on that principle we secure immense anti-partition areas" (Ronan Fanning, *Fatal Path*, p.319). Collins then attempted to undermine the Unionist regime by a combination of force and political pressure, waging a campaign of military and civil subversion in the North in the early part of 1922.

## Collins takes control

The Northern Catholics supported the Free State after the 'Treaty'. It was said by Devlin and the *Irish News* that the 'Treaty' had recognised Partition. So it would have been logical on the basis of this argument for Northern Nationalism to be Anti-Treaty. However, aside from a minority of Republicans, the vast majority of Northern Catholics, including the large majority of Republicans, were pro-Treaty and Free State.

This did not mean that they agreed with the 'Treaty' or had any strong position in the debate and conflict that was raging in the South over it. The important thing in the North was who would help them overcome their predicament in 'Northern Ireland' and what outcome in the South would enable it to provide them with the greatest assistance in that.

Opposition to the 'Treaty' in the South, which endangered Collins' policy, was therefore seen as both anti-National and ultimately Partitionist in the North.

Michael Collins sold the 'Treaty' to Northern Nationalists as a means of undoing the 1920 Act which had cut them off from the rest of the Nation: The Free State was to be the base of operations against the Unionist regime; the new Dublin Government, which was on intimate terms with Whitehall, would influence British policy towards the Ulster Unionists; and then, finally there was the Boundary Commission, which, Collins had secured in the 'Treaty', would whittle away 'Northern Ireland' by awarding predominantly Nationalist areas to the Free State, making the rest of it unviable.

That was the Collins plan for the deliverance of the North.

The first thing Collins did upon signing the 'Treaty' was to assume the leadership of the Northern Catholics. The signing of the Pact with James Craig was the opening move in this. Collins had no intention of making peace in Ulster through this Pact in January 1922. It was part of his campaign of subversion of 'Northern Ireland'. In it Collins promised to end the Boycott of Belfast goods established by the Dáil in September 1920 as a response to "the war of extermination" that was being waged against Catholics in the city, in return for Craig seeing his way to restore the employment in the shipyard those Catholic workers who had been expelled by Loyalists.

Collins must have known full well that this was not in the gift of Craig when, with the Great War over and the demand for ships collapsing, the shipyard had to lay off workers. And he angered many Belfast Nationalists by calling off the Boycott without consulting them. Collins also made a deal with Craig to sort out the forthcoming Boundary issue between them. This unilateral decision more than anything else showed Northern Catholics that he was taking them in hand and going to decide their future in a personal capacity.

Collins then moved to take direct control of the Northern IRA. The IRA, while maintaining a central command structure in its GHQ staff, had remained a fragmented and local-orientated force, based on geographical divisions. Collins got Eoin O'Duffy to establish a new Northern Command through an 'Ulster Council', making the IRA in the North the united instrument of his policy. This comprised the six O/Cs of the six most Northerly Divisions of the Army. The 'Ulster Council' was headed by Collins himself and it was conducted under the auspices of the IRB — indicating that its work would be conspiracy, even though open government had by this time been attained. One of the first things it did was to begin paying the salaries of all Northern IRA officers, securing their personal loyalty to Collins.

The work of the IRA 'Ulster Council' was, according to a document from the Ernest Blythe papers, "directed towards preventing the Northern Government from functioning effectively to consolidate the area which had been allocated to it under the Government of Ireland Act of 1920" (UCDAD, P24/554).

The IRA in the North had seen itself as part of the all-Ireland struggle coming from the 1918 Election result. But it had had to operate in a more hostile environment than other areas of the country, due to the Unionist presence and the Hibernian influence in its own community. It also suffered from a lack of weapons. From mid-1920 it became, by necessity, engaged in defensive work, particularly in Belfast. Because of these considerations Robert Lynch claims that "the creation of IRA Divisions in Ulster in the Spring of 1921... signaled the birth of the Northern IRA itself" (*The Northern IRA and the early years of Partition, 1920-22*, p.47).

This meant that the Northern IRA was a blank slate for Collins. There had been a great increase in IRA membership and training in the North during the Truce with the British, and Collins decided to use his new men in a Spring offensive by providing them with the necessary weaponry and support from the South.

The split in the IRA over the 'Treaty' in the South had not been reproduced within the Northern IRA. In fact, during the Truce period the major conflict within Nationalism in the North was between the Hibernians, put out by Lloyd George's recognition of Sinn Fein, and the newly confident Republicans. Many instances of violence and even deaths occurred in the conflict around possession of Hibernian Halls. But there was no conflict about the 'Treaty'. Nearly all Northerners were 'opposed' to the 'Treaty' because of Partition and supportive of it at the same time in their backing of Collins and his promise to undermine it.

Eoin O'Duffy, a close friend of Collins and unofficial leader of the IRA in the North since 1921, told a meeting of Northern IRA officers in Clones, that the 'Treaty' was "only a trick" on Collins' part to rearm the IRA for the final push on the North. (This was according to Ernie O'Malley and Frank Aiken, see Robert Lynch, *The Northern IRA and the Early Years of Partition, 1920-22*, p.97).

## The Collins zig-zag

The Collins strategy, operated through the 'Ulster Council', was to alternatively escalate and de-escalate IRA activity in the North, as Collins saw fit in order to exert pressure on the Unionists. It seemed a contradiction but it was a policy of zig-zag. IRA activity was to be increased to demonstrate power and then decreased at the time when negotiations were desired to obtain concessions from the Unionists.

In early February 1922, just a few weeks after the Pact with Craig, the escalation began with Collins telling Craig he intended taking half the territory of the Six Counties into the Free State through the Boundary Commission and then ordering an attempt to kidnap 100 Unionists from Border areas. These were to be held as hostages for the release of IRA men captured in the North, who were under sentence of death. Over 40 prominent Unionists were successfully abducted in the Border raids that Collins' men made, and much destruction was caused along the Border. The Pact with Craig ended.

The *Irish News* was appalled at this and, while condemning the Unionist Government for not reprieving the IRA men until the last minute, was very hostile to the actions taken from the South:

"When stupid obstinacy and undisciplined hot-headedness collide the consequences are bound to be unpleasant, if not disastrous. The fact has been demonstrated tragically on numerous occasions in Irish history, and the raids reported to-day furnish yet another striking instance... The recklessness of the adventure and the official wrongheadedness which provoked it are equally deserving of the severest reprehension...

"The Provisional Government, as we expected, has taken the first opportunity to vindicate its authority in regard to this unpleasant business by proceeding at once to secure the release of those who were seized...

"The possibilities of any complications involving an extension of disorder must be minimized by thoughtful men on all sides, who will take the lessons of the episode to heart... Conditions in Belfast, we regret to observe, are taking a turn for the worse.... The large issues at stake are ripening for settlement: they will not be settled the sooner by magnifying every regrettable incident into a casus belli" (9.2.22).

The *Irish News* did not suspect that it was Collins, himself, who was behind the *"reckless adventures"* that were resulting in things in Belfast *"taking a turn for the worse"*. On 13th February 1922, after the Clones incident, its editorial *'Honos Habet Onus'* noted that "the Provisional Government's efforts were hampered on all sides from the very outset... by restless and dissatisfied groups and malevolent individuals in many parts of Ireland".

The *Irish News* believed that governmental responsibility was absent in the South. And it was very worried about the predictable repercussions for Northern Catholics:

> "What 450,000 Nationalists of Fermanagh and Tyrone, Armagh and Down, Derry and Antrim may fairly ask themselves—if they cannot address the question to any Government—is: How are their present interests to be served or their future fate affected by a continuance of this exchange of shots, and deaths, and 'raids', and 'reprisals' along the border line from Carlingford to Derry?...
>
> "We are not terrified by threats of vengeance against Nationalists in Antrim and Belfast... 'Reprisals' failed in Munster, Leinster and Connaught; they would fail—more terribly, perhaps—in the North... Honus habet onus: Honour is laden with responsibility. We are confident yet that those who have assumed responsibility will acquit themselves so well that all the people will honour them in the time to come."

The Collins campaign in the North continued into March and April with raids, shootings, burnings of Unionist Big Houses and the capture of several barracks and their garrisons in Pomeroy, Co. Tyrone and Maghera, Co. Derry. But it had significant repercussions for Catholics in Belfast who began to pay dearly for Collins' escalation. Nearly half of all Catholics who died in communal violence between 1920 and 1922 perished in the first half of 1922. This was the period of the Weaver Street massacre of children, which occurred after the killing and abduction of Specials by the IRA in Clones, the slaughter of the McMahon family and the Arnon Street killings.

On 15th March Dawson Bates, Minister for Home Affairs in the Northern Government, made what the *Irish News* called a "wild speech" stating that the Northern Government was at war with the IRA and would begin using the Special Powers Act to effect. This signaled that the Unionists would no longer regard the Truce between the British and IRA as operable.

On the day following St Patrick's Day the Specials raided St Mary's Hall in Belfast and captured weapons and a huge amount of intelligence documents containing the names of nearly every senior IRA man in the Six

Counties. This did incalculable damage to the IRA in the North. Collins must have believed that the IRA would be safe from the Unionist authorities to have authorised the storage of these in such a vulnerable location. There were protests from Dublin at the Unionist breaking of the Truce with this raid. The assumption must have been in Dublin that the Truce with the British would keep the IRA HQ safe from the Unionists.The occupation of St Mary's Hall was the symbolic moment when the Unionists reasserted their authority over West Belfast and Collins was powerless to prevent it.

Collins denied all knowledge of the Border raids he organised. He wrote a letter to *The Times*, published on the 24th March, expressing outrage that he could be accused of such things. He also denied all knowledge of the raids to the Sinn Fein President, Griffith, while his IRB clique continued to plan and organise mayhem within the Six Counties.

At the same time Collins concluded another pact with Craig in late March which boasted in its first clause: "Peace is today declared..." This was the headline in the *Irish News* editorial of 31st March that saw it to be a new beginning in amicable relations on the island:

> "In this co-operation between Irishmen, hitherto hostile and feud-ridden, for the achievement of great and beneficent objects rests the whole country's best and surest hope of redemption... Seven Irishmen—four representing the Twenty-six Counties and three representing the Six—signed a document on March 30th which began with the splendid announcement: 'Peace is declared to-day'.
>
> "The statement reads like an unexpected avowal, that a miracle has been performed...
>
> "The seeds of peace had been planted in the hearts of the masses of the people... we must cherish and nourish the new plant, guard it and tend it, and cultivate it until it becomes the very finest flowering of national unity and solidarity that the world has yet known... Mr. Collins, Sir James Craig, and their colleagues followed the road of Truth; it is our business now to make perfect the Peace they found and handed over to the people."

Collins ordered the IRA to scale down its activity after the Pact. The immediate purpose of the Pact was to get Craig to stop the escalating killing and intimidation of Catholics in Belfast by official and unofficial Unionist forces that Collins' own military sallies into the North had sparked off.

But, having signed the Peace Pact, which was widely welcomed in the Northern Catholic community, Collins then set up a Northeast Advisory Committee, which had the remit of using the agreement as a means to apply pressure on the Unionist Government and wring concessions from it. Collins, through the Pact with Craig, also kept pressing the British Government for public enquiries concerning atrocities against Catholics in the North and for prison releases of Republicans.

The Northern Government was only recognised by Collins in order to undermine it. And when it became apparent that the Pact was not producing what Collins wanted of it, a combined IRA offensive against the North was decided upon by the 'Ulster Council' on 21st April 1922.

## The view from the North

A journey through the *Irish News* between May 1922 and the outbreak of the Treaty War (aka "Civil War") at the end of June shows the effect of Collins' actions on the Northern Nationalist community.

The first editorial, *'The Path of Blood?'*, was written at the time of the Kilkenny standoff between the Republican Army occupying the town and troops sent by the Provisional Government to dislodge them (it was subsequently, as in a similar event in Limerick, resolved without war).

After Sinn Fein had divided on the 'Treaty', a pro-'Treaty' Dail Government was elected with Griffith succeeding De Valera as its President. Under the 'Treaty' a Provisional Government, led by Collins, was established to administer the transfer of power from the British to the Free State and administer the 'Treaty'. There were therefore two pro-'Treaty' Governments existing side by side between January 1922 and the start of the 'Treaty' War at the end of June. Theoretically the Provisional Government was responsible to the Provisional Parliament, under the 'Treaty', but in effect it was only really responsible to the London Government that had established it.

The Army Convention of March 1922 was boycotted by the Treatyites and this formalised the split over the 'Treaty' within the military. It elected a new Army Executive from those attending the convention who were all Anti-Treaty and recognised only the Dail, not Griffith's Government. From January 1922 local IRA units took over vacated British Army barracks and there were ineffective attempts by the Provisional Government to assert its authority over the bulk of the IRA that opposed the 'Treaty'. On April 13th, acting on the orders of the new Army Executive, Rory (called Roderick by the *Irish News)* O'Connor took over the Four Courts complex in Dublin as the Republican military headquarters, as well as several other buildings in Dublin.

Here is how the *Irish News* saw the developing split over the 'Treaty':

"The Truce of July 1921 was a victory for Ireland; the Treaty of December 1921 was a 'crowning victory'... the path to freedom for five-sixths of Ireland had been cleared at last, and the certainty of complete national reunion on terms to which only a minority of hopeless incorrigibles might take exception was practically assured.

"Mr. Erskine Childers and Mr. De Valera barred the way; before many days they had a host of reckless partisans at their side; then the writing of the bitterest chapter in Ireland's history was begun. That chapter has not been completed...

"We refuse to believe—and events at Kilkenny justify the refusal—that the hearts of these young Irishmen who have been deluded or dragged into this horrible warfare against their brothers are in the evil work planned for them by the Childers, De Valeras, and Roderick O'Connors of Dublin city. They are foolish to the verge of criminality; they are engaged in an enterprise that once is irreligious, unpatriotic, and ruinous...The young men of the South and West will refuse to wade through Irish blood along the path marked out by a sinister Englishman..." (3.5.22).

The *"sinister Englishman"* referred to by the *Irish News* was not Winston Churchill, who was seeing that the 'Treaty' was being adhered to, but Erskine Childers, who was opposing it. Childers was viewed with suspicion as an Englishman wanting to do harm to Ireland. He had been a militarist British Imperialist who fought in the Empire's expansionary African war on the Boers a couple of decades previously and who wrote a volume of Leo Amery's famous *'The Times History of the Boer War'*.

The symbiosis between Liberal Imperialism and Irish Nationalism that occurred between the South African War and Britain's Great War was demonstrated most dramatically in the person of Childers. Childers changed from being a Unionist to a Liberal Imperialist. And, in becoming a Liberal Imperialist, he became an Irish Home Ruler. He wrote, according to A.V. Dicey, the best defence of Irish Home Rule in his book *'The Framework of Home Rule'*, which was published in 1911. In July 1914 he ran guns for the Irish Volunteers in conjunction with some other Anglo-Irish gentlemen and ladies before going off to fight Germany for the British Empire a few weeks later—a War he had prepared England for through his popular best-seller, *The Riddle of the Sands*.

Childers seems to have been propelled toward more separatist National-ism by the cheating of Ireland of Home Rule by British Unionism. He followed the logic of the argument he presented in his 1911 book *The Framework of Home Rule* and went over to Sinn Fein, being in charge for a time of *The Irish Bulletin,* the official fact-sheet of the War of Independence. He went Anti-Treaty Sinn Fein after viewing the 'Treaty' negotiations at first hand as Secretary-General to the Irish plenipotentiaries, opposite his former school friend, Lionel Curtis, on the British side.

Childers was not a *"sinister Englishman"*—he was an earnest Englishman who became an Irishman as the Empire went on a drastic and destructive change of course, leaving a man of principle behind it.

The *Irish News* also kept up a view of De Valera as an *"extremist"* when, in fact, he was a moderate in the Republican movement. It was just that the

'Treaty' did not meet his moderate requirements and his compromise, Document No. 2, was unacceptable to the British because it threatened, if accepted, to hold the Irish national movement together.

Holding De Valera responsible for the 'Civil War' was ill-judged. Dev was on the political side of the Republican movement. It was Collins who was very much the Army man and the intransigent—until he put his signature to the 'Treaty', without consulting De Valera. De Valera did not have the influence to determine how the Army would behave. He estimated that not enough had been got by Collins in the 'Treaty' to carry the Army with him. And he was proved correct, despite Collins' best efforts to obscure it through his hyper-activity with regard to the North in the six months following the signing of the 'Treaty'.

De Valera had made a statement on 22nd August 1921 to a closed session of the Dáil in which he said that he was opposed to the coercion of Ulster and he made the same point clear in his correspondence to Lloyd George that same month. Instead, he said, he would be willing to accept individual Counties voting themselves out of an Irish state, if the British conceded a full Republic to the rest of the country. That, of course, would have led to the inclusion of Fermanagh and Tyrone in the Irish state.

De Valera initially proposed renegotiating the 'Treaty' to make it more acceptable to those who opposed it. But making the 'Treaty' palatable to those who opposed it was not a British objective. The objective was to engineer a split that would lead to conflict within the independence movement and hopefully war over the 'Treaty'.

Document No. 2, which De Valera presented to the Dáil on 15th December 1921, as a compromise in relation to the 'Treaty', mirrored the relevant articles of the 'Treaty' in relation to Partition. De Valera told the private session: "The difficulty is not the Ulster question... As far as we are concerned this is a fight between Ireland and England. I want to eliminate the Ulster question out of it... We will take the same things as agreed on there" (Ronan Fanning, *Fatal Path*, p.314).

The war to subvert the Six Counties was Collins' war, not De Valera's, as the *Irish News* mistakenly believed.

The IRA was dividing over the 'Treaty' in the South. Most of the IRA, and practically half the country, saw the signing of the 'Treaty' as more significant than Collins saw it—as a mere tactical retreat within which it was possible to conspire to recover what had been actually signed away in the 'Treaty'.

For many, particularly in the Republican Army, the signing of the 'Treaty' represented the surrender of the Republic and the negation of the Irish people's democratic decision in 1918. The bulk of the Army considered itself duty-bound by its Oath to the Republic and it would not easily take another Oath in contradiction to the one taken.

The *Irish News* did not pretend that the issue between those in favour of working within the 'Treaty' and those who could not bring themselves to do so was anything to do with 'democracy' as it has been latterly presented. It saw the issue in terms of stability and instability with stability in the South being preferable to instability for Northern Catholics.

But the 'Treaty' was not something that Britain imposed on the Irish national movement to stabilize it.

Collins sold the 'Treaty' as a *"stepping stone"* to freedom and could not bring himself to be honest about the power politics involved i.e. that he had signed it under duress. If he had done so—as Lenin did in relation to the signing of the Brest-Litovsk Treaty—he might have held the Republican forces together. As it was, they could not bring themselves to adopt Collins' conspiratorial approach as an easy substitute for democratic principle.

In this period there seemed to be two successful approaches to dictated treaties—Lenin's one of honest surrender to terms that preserved the power of the Soviet Union within a smaller territory and Ataturk's approach of smashing the Treaty imposed on the Turks at Sèvres. Collins approach fell between the two stools and divided his forces—which, of course, was the chief objective of those who imposed the Treaty in the first place.

## Partition versus Republic?

To Northerners the main issue was Partition and how to overcome it. The developing 'split' in the national movement, upon which the North depended for its deliverance from the Six Counties, seemed irresponsible and reckless.

From the Northern Catholic perspective the Oath of Allegiance and the relationship with the British Empire were issues of secondary importance and not worth destroying the National forces for. This position was partly because the bulk of the North, including the *Irish News,* was never Republican and so such things were meaningless to it. And, since it was Devlinite and the 'Treaty' was an advance on Home Rule, it was seen as a gift-horse that should not be looked at in the mouth. But it was also to do with the calculation that, without help from the South, the Northern Catholics would be helpless in relation to the Imperial and local Unionist forces that could be employed against them.

This fear was reflected in the *Irish News* editorial on the next day, *'Meaning of Civil War':*

"What does Civil War mean?

"Civil war means absolute destruction for Ireland—for the Irish race and nation at home.

"This country is not the England of the War of the Roses, or the England of 1641-52, or the vast American Republic of 1861-65. Civil wars have desolated countries and ruined nations time after time in the course of the world's history... England and America were free countries when the Plantagenets fought for the English throne... and when Abraham Lincoln and the North battled for vital constitutional and moral issues against Jefferson Davis and the South...

"English statesmen have left the people of Twenty-Six Irish counties a perfect liberty to frame their own Constitution, rule themselves, provide for their own Army, arrange their industrial and commercial affairs as they choose, fashion their own administrative and educational systems—in fact, to exercise every practical privilege and power that a free nation is endowed with. Alternatively, these British statesmen have left the country of the Twenty-Six counties a perfect liberty to murder one another wholesale...

"These are the simple alternatives before the majority of the Irish people. England will not interfere in the Twenty-Six counties. England's forces will be on the side of the armed and dominant majority if any mad and criminal attempt is made to carry the torch of Civil war into the Six counties" (4.5.22).


There is some understanding in this editorial that the developing *"Civil War"* in Ireland was not a civil war at all. A civil war is a war within a state to determine what a state should be. That is what the situations of "England of the War of the Roses, or the England of 1641-52, or the vast American Republic of 1861-65" were. Yorkists and Lancastrians, Royalists and Puritans, Yankee Unionists and Confederates were all free agents with disputes about the governing of their respective states that could be only resolved by war.

The parties to the Irish "Civil War" were in agreement about what an Irish State should be—an independent Republic separate from the British Empire—and they had all voted and fought for that State. What they disagreed about was whether they should or should not submit to a British ultimatum, under the threat of "immediate and terrible war", that it must be something different. What separated those who were willing to accept the 'Treaty' from those who could not was that actual question—British interference. There was no pretence that Britain had left Ireland "at perfect liberty" to form its own democracy from the side of the Republican forces that accepted the 'Treaty'. They simply judged it was better for the country to accept the British threat and attempt to work within it rather than reject the 'Treaty' imposition in favour of a conflict with the British Empire at that point.

The *Irish News* view that *"English statesmen have left the people of Twenty-Six Irish counties a perfect liberty to frame their own Constitution, rule themselves, provide for their own Army... in fact, to exercise every practical privilege and power that a free nation is endowed with"* was wishful thinking. It was proved to be false almost immediately when Collins tried to foist a Republican-style Constitution on the British. He was told to go back to his drawing board and start again and come back with one that corresponded with what he had signed up to in the 'Treaty'. And he did — leading to further division in the National forces.

Everything that was done in Ireland from December 1921 was done under duress — under the threat of a British war similar to that which had been waged on the Boers, with a Blockade, Blockhouses and Concentration Camps that had decimated the civilian population. The election held in June 1922 that secured a majority for the 'Treaty' was just one of the events that occurred in this context, as was the shelling of the Four Courts itself, a couple of weeks later, that actually began the 'Civil War'.

There was a fine balance to be achieved by Britain in its new plan for Ireland between placating the Northern Unionists and cultivating the Southern Free State as an instrument of Imperial interest. Lionel Curtis, who was British Secretary at the 'Treaty' negotiations and who worked closely with Churchill in seeing that it was implemented by the Free State, wrote an anonymous article in the *Round Table* of June 1922, entitled *'Ireland at the Crossroads'* in which he described this balancing act:

"There are Ulstermen, not a few, in whom it is impossible to distinguish the expectation from the hope that the Treaty will fail and the South founder in chaos. Their dearest wish and their confident prophecies would be equally satisfied on the day which saw the British Government recommitted to the government of Ireland. After seven centuries of failure their remedy for disorder and disaffection is still that of British bayonets. This group has now a powerful representative in Sir Henry Wilson... As Chief of Staff he has surveyed the weaknesses of the Empire and he has confessed himself conscious of a mission in Ulster to save 'our rocking Empire' by methods which the Imperial Government has, in his opinion, foolishly if not criminally, deserted in Egypt and India. His influence is seen in the presence of a 'military advisor' at the elbow of the Ulster government, and in the stress which is laid upon the perfecting of its quasi-military defences.

"It is the British Government which supplies the rifles on either side of the border. It is a position which might at any moment test the judgement of the British Cabinet in the highest degree. From Ulster it calls for the continued and increasing exercise of patience and restraint and a willingness, in spite of all, to meet the South upon any matter on which it reasonably can be met.

"Ulster's representatives were not a party to the Treaty. It has had from Ulster neither consent nor approval. It is within the power of Ulster, if she wished, to take action that would wreck the settlement... We need not argue here whether or not Ulster's interests would be truly served by such a course.

The position is that with the strong approval of the whole Commonwealth, Great Britain stands committed to the Treaty. The high stake of the Treaty is peace with and in Ireland, with all that means to the unity of the Commonwealth and its standing in the world. In that stake Ulster is interested in common with every other community that claims to put the interests of the Commonwealth first... The venture challenges Ulster peculiarly... It requires her to see the Treaty as the Commonwealth sees it and to give it some confidence as an instrument of conciliation in Southern Ireland. If Sir James Craig proves himself in the coming months the leader of Imperial vision that we have already reason to think him, Ulster will not refuse in the most crucial stage of the Treaty policy, in which the question of Irish unity or the boundary question will fall to be decided, to take some risks for a plan which is not her own..

"For the rest, Great Britain has sown the seed at last with a sure hand in a straight furrow and must abide the harvest. The limit of our power to help it is to avoid shortcuts that will trample the growth. It is Nature's provision that the young shoot bears the worst of the weather. There are storms in Ireland to threaten the yield. Their gathering is seen with anxious eyes. But good husbandry knows the seasoning virtue of the wind and the clouds and will not yet give way to despondency."

Britain was, through force of circumstance, nurturing the growth of a new system in Ireland. That new system aimed at clawing back the position that had been lost in the previous few years and putting Imperial hegemony over Ireland on a whole new footing. The new position necessitated a more indirect system of influence that involved careful cultivation at the outset, when it was taking root and was most prone to failing.

"*It is the British Government which supplies the rifles on either side of the border*" noted Curtis. And that was the means by which it cultivated things in the direction it wanted and nurtured them to fruition.

## Exclusion of the North

In the middle of May the *Irish News* produced the following editorial, *'Peace? And Turmoil'*. The context of this were the peace negotiations that led to the Collins-De Valera Pact of 19th May. This Pact involved the forming of a National Coalition Panel to fight the forthcoming elections demanded by the British, as a way to bring the Anti-Treatyites back into the Government. The Pact proposed that, if the new Government, which was to include 5 Pro-Treaty and 4 Anti-Treaty members, could not reach an agreement on the Treaty, another election would be forthcoming.

It appears that Collins did not consult with Griffith on the Pact and Griffith was furious at what he saw as an unjustified concession to De Valera. (However, in public statements just before the election, Collins appeared to repudiate the Pact.) The tone of the *Irish News* shows that it took the Griffith position.

The Pact was aimed at demonstrating the desire of both De Valera and Collins to avoid *"Civil War"*. But with the Collins repudiation of it on election day, presumably on British orders, the Pact only delayed the war about the 'Treaty' for a fortnight. The *Irish News* commented:

"Time must test the value of the Agreements signed by Messrs. M. Collins and E. De Valera on Saturday... the Agreement is a Compromise; many people in Ireland will regard it as a lop-sided Compromise.

"A 'National Coalition Panel' for the June elections will be presented to the voters through the agency of the Sinn Fein organisation. The members of the Provisional Government and their opponents—or perhaps the members of the Dáil Cabinet—will pick candidates for the constituencies—the number for each party being their present strength in the Dáil...

"Let it be taken for granted that the next Dáil will be composed almost entirely of the membership of the body that has kept Ireland in a state of something far worse than suspense during the past five months...

"The Republicans have agreed to abandon Civil War; the Treatyites have practically yielded for the time being the vital principle for which they had contended all along—the Irish people's right to give a verdict at the polling booths on the main issue. The question of the Armies will probably be determined by the new coalition. Time and events will tell their tale. Those who hope for the best of the worst of circumstances in the Twenty Six counties can console themselves with the thought that Civil War will not be waged next month.

"But there are other and extremely serious circumstances that must be taken up at once in Dublin. Mr. Griffith's... resolution provided for the holding of elections on June 16th in 4 Irish borough constituencies... and 24 Irish election areas specified and boundaried in the British 'Government of Ireland Act, 1920'.

"No reference was made in either of Mr. Griffith's resolutions to the 4 Irish borough constituencies of Belfast and the 5 Irish electoral areas called Northern Ireland by the authors of the same British Act.

"Dáil Éireann adopted Mr. Griffith's resolutions unanimously, and with enthusiasm, last Saturday. Therefore that part of Ireland known as 'Northern Ireland', embracing Belfast and Six Counties, has been definitely excluded from the sphere of Dáil Éireann's operations and from the purview of the new government of the Twenty-Six Counties.

"The 'exclusion' is an act of Dáil Éireann as an assembly. It binds the new Coalition Government. And, under these circumstances, the organised series of 'raids' throughout parts of N-E Ulster last weekend—the attacks on police barracks and post offices, the burnings of private houses, be these castles or cottages, and the midnight warfare generally were not conducted under the auspices of any authority recognised in any part of Ireland..."

The Collins-De Valera Pact dominated news in the South but the formal exclusion of the North by the Free State went practically unnoticed. Collins position of early 1921—that Sinn Fein in the North should "ignore the Partition Act and carry on with their colleagues in the south of Ireland as a national body, in fact as the Dáil"—had been abandoned under the 'Treaty' and the increasing pressure being mounted on him by the supplier of his rifles in Whitehall.

## Pawns in Collins' game

The other context of this editorial was the launching of the joint IRA offensive in the North, which was directed by Collins but which the *Irish News* was greatly perplexed about:

> "Those who 'raided' in the Counties of Down and Antrim on Friday night and Saturday morning had no more care in their hearts for the lives and the fate of the Nationalists of north-east Ulster than had the band of agent-provocateurs to whose plans and deeds attention was directed recently.
>
> "The Nationalists of the Six Counties are 'pawns' in a game.
>
> "But whose game? Who are playing these hideous pranks with the very existence of 450,000 men, women and children in the Six Counties?
>
> "A stern repudiation and condemnation of crimes so deplorable in every respect and aspect is due from the Provisional Government of the Free State. If these things are done in the name of Sinn Fein—and we doubt it—it behoves the accredited leaders of Sinn Fein to disassociate themselves and their movement from the doers without delay. 'The rule of the gun' has already been denounced by the Belfast branches of the movement.
>
> "Horrors multiply all around us. The campaign of extermination against Nationalists is pursued relentlessly—and the Belfast Government are doing nothing to stay it. Self-defence is a God-given right. But the Nationalists of the North-East must keep their hands clean" (22.5.22).

The *Irish News* raises a valid point about the invasion of the North by the combined IRAs under Collins' direction. If the Free State Government is recognizing, through its obedience to British requirements for it to formally submit to Partition, on whose authority is it attacking the Six Counties and getting Northern Catholics killed in great numbers in Unionist reprisals?

The answer to that was the Irish Republican Brotherhood's.

The IRB was the revolutionary nucleus of the independence struggle, organising the Easter Rising and reorganizing Sinn Fein after it on Republican lines. Some, like De Valera, left it, believing its purpose to have been fulfilled by making the pursuance of the Republic possible in an open and constitutional way, through remade Sinn Fein and the 1918 Election mandate. But Collins and other Brothers did not see its mission as being as yet accomplished or its usefulness exhausted.

The 'Treaty' had split the IRB, but the Brothers continued to observe its constitution. There was a large Treatyite majority on the Supreme Council and Collins proceeded to utilise it for political purposes. At the same time, Anti-Treaty IRB men like Liam Lynch continued to see in it a possible instrument for reconciliation.

Most important, Collins' IRB considered itself the true Government of Ireland rather than the Dail or the Provisional Government. These were two temporary incidentals to be worked within as far as the IRB was concerned. For Collins the great advantage of the IRB was that the Republic could be concealed within it for a later date whilst he proceeded with the 'Treaty' for the eyes of the British. In February 1922 the IRB's Supreme Council passed Resolution 27 which, while accepting the fact of the present governmental structure of the Free State, declared itself to be "the sole government of the Irish Republic, until Ireland's complete independence is achieved, and a permanent Republican Government is established, and the Supreme Council shall be unquestioned by its members" (Sean MacEoin papers, UCDAD, P151/1941).

It was through the IRB that Collins and Liam Lynch, the chief Anti-Treaty Republican commander, had got together on the joint invasion plan. Collins used the IRB (his personal Government outside the two other pro-Treaty ones which included Richard Mulcahy, Minister of Defence in the Dail Government) to secretly organise the offensive with O'Duffy and Mulcahy from his side and Lynch, O'Connor and Joe McKelvey from those opposed to the 'Treaty'. The policy decided upon was that the Northern Divisions should be reinforced by men and material from other areas, and that it should strike vigorously in the North in a widespread and concerted way.

The Republican Army Executive that had occupied and was defying Collins in the Four Courts agreed to send men from Anti-Treaty units of the IRA in Cork and Kerry up to Donegal, under the leadership of Seán Lehane, one of the best officers from Tom Barry's column. A number of veteran officers and a large quantity of men were sent from Cork and Kerry with instructions to lead the war in the North, on and inside the Border. They visited the Four Courts on the way up where they were briefed by Liam Lynch on their mission. In early April these forces crossed the Border and mounted a large attack on the Specials' base at Garrison.

Arms were supplied for the Northern offensive by a simple arrangement between both IRAs. Weapons left by the British forces in the hands of the Pro-Treaty IRA were given to the Anti-Treaty IRA in exchange for their arms, which did not contain British serial numbers. The Anti-Treaty weapons were dispatched northwards while Lynch received the British weapons in exchange from Collins. This fact became public and was aired in the Southern press by O'Duffy when there was some disagreement over the fairness of the swaps (*Irish Independent* 26.4.22). The British General, Neville Macready was certainly aware of it by the end of April (Ryle Dwyer, *Michael Collins and the Civil War*, p.176).

Collins was able to order his army to co-operate, despite opposition he might have encountered within the Provisional or Dail Governments because it remained his personal fiefdom through the 'Treaty'. The British, in refusing to permit a Minister and Ministry of Defence in the Provisional Government, presumably for reasons of de-legitimation or perhaps because they wanted the military to remain as Collins' sole instrument, had left the army in his personal hands. (In the rest of the Free State governmental apparatus the same Minister acted for the Dail and Provisional Governments.) Because the British would not allow a Minister for Defence in the Provisional Government, Collins maintained extraordinary control over the pro-Treaty IRA, which was the Free State's army, independent of the Provisional Government. Collins now used this provision against its authors by transferring arms between the pro- and anti-Treaty sections of the IRA and arming the Northern units without governmental sanction.

The plan visualized the formation of Northern Flying Columns, led largely by experienced Southern officers and men whose members would remain on continuous active service and who would be paid and funded by the Free State Government. By late June, the Free State Chief of Staff, Eoin O'Duffy, estimated that 700 Munster Republicans had arrived in Donegal, in addition to several hundred anti-Treaty members of Charlie Daly's old division from Tyrone and Derry. Thousands of rifles, machine guns, grenades, land mines and ammunition crossed the Border for the offensive. The IRA in the North was never so well armed and reinforced.

In mid-May Commandant Tom Barry arrived at the Border to address the Corkmen before the start of the offensive. The plan, as the Anti-Treaty fighters saw it, was to smash the Northern Government by military means. Collins insisted that the British be left alone, as he did not want to compromise his strained relationship with Whitehall.

Collins invasion of the North, using the three Northern and two Midland Divisions of his army, along with Anti-Treaty fighters, began on 18th May. The Third Northern Division opened this up with a concerted campaign of arson and destruction across the Eastern half of Ulster involving attacks on police barracks, business premises, railway lines and stately homes. In the most provocative incident, the Unionist M.P. W.J. Twaddell was assassinated in Belfast.

The coordinated and expansive nature of these attacks unleashed a great backlash against the Catholic community in Belfast over the weekend of May 20th-21st.

The *Irish News* could not understand why the Southerners were indulging in this activity, which it saw as both provocative and inevitably doomed to failure. The Unionist community in the North could only see it as an IRA invasion of 'Northern Ireland'.

The *Irish News* concluded that: "The Nationalists of the Six Counties are 'pawns' in a game".

"But whose game?" it asked. The only answer was Collins' game.

## A weakness for intrigue and conspiracy

Collins attempted to maintain a distance from his offensive and denied responsibility for it, putting the blame on 'irregulars'.

As the Donegal Republican Peadar O'Donnell noted, Collins had a "weakness for intrigue and conspiracy" (*The Gates Flew Open,* p.31). Furthermore he had enormous faith in his own ability. But he was unable to cope with the situation which his own action in London on 6th December 1921 had brought about.

His power had been conferred on him by the British, he found himself increasingly supported by the power of money, by British guns and by the old establishment that he had himself undermined in his war against the British. He had become increasingly boxed in by Whitehall and his room for manoeuvre was being gradually constricted down to one direction—the implementation of the 'Treaty' he signed and the making of war on his former comrades.

The invasion of the North was a last desperate throw of the dice by Collins to engage his former comrades in something that would distract them from the inevitable he was being forced towards. Perhaps Collins, being an instinctive conspirator, even thought it would be a good thing to have some of his most experienced and vigorous opponents out of the way, up North, if (or when) the bit came to the bit. And they were all too likely to go along with something that was dear to their hearts in unified activity against the detested 'Treaty'.

But, of course, this was no good at all for the Northern Catholics. It sharpened the antagonism between the Nationalist and Unionist communities at the outset of the Six County's existence, strengthening the Unionist view of the Northern Catholics inside the territory of their statelet as a Fifth Column for Southern espionage and subversion. And the folk memory of what was done to the Catholics by the Unionists in reprisal for Collins military activities left a lasting memory that had repercussions half a century later in 1969.

# A perplexing situation

Towards the end of May the *Irish News* editorial described *'The Situation'* as it saw it:

> "Representatives of the Irish Free State and members of the British Cabinet are once more conferring in London. We shall not anticipate the result of this Conference...
>
> "In the Six Counties we are entitled to remind present and future members of the public bodies in the Free State that those leaders and elected representatives of the Irish majority who brought about the 'split' of last January will be justly held responsible in the coming time for much, if not most, of the appalling mischief that is being wrought in the Six Counties since that 'split' began.
>
> "Had the Irish people and their leaders outside North-East Ulster set themselves to the work of reaping the harvest of their victory, it is quite probable that a great part of the way towards a complete and final settlement of the 'Irish Question' within Ireland would have been travelled before the present date.
>
> "But some leaders and a few people in Dublin preferred the 'split' to the certainty of a great national settlement; they gave Sir Henry Wilson his opportunity; they filled despairing diehards in Ireland and England with fresh hope; they helped directly and materially to bring 450,000 Ulster Nationalists to the pass in which these Nationalists find themselves today.
>
> "And all this should be told to the people in plain words before 16 June" (27.5.22).

The 16th of June was the date scheduled for the vote on the 'Treaty' in the Twenty-Six Counties.

The *Irish News* fundamentally misread the situation from its Northern vantage point. It was really De Valera who wanted an agreement with England that would be a final settlement and Collins who signed an agreement in the form of the 'Treaty' that he was determined to break as the opportunity arose. Collins' intention was to undermine the 'Treaty', once he had accumulated sufficient power by apparently submitting to it. But the juggler who was juggling a number of balls gradually began to lose control and everything eventually came crashing down on him.

The Southern electorate gave a split verdict on the 'Treaty' on 16th June, with the threat of war with the Empire producing a majority for the advocates of accepting the 'Treaty'. This election, which has been claimed as having given a clear mandate for the 'Treaty' as opposed to the Republic, did nothing of the sort. It endorsed the 'Treaty' only on the basis that the majority of the electorate preferred it to *"a war with the British Empire"*.

But in the North different issues pertained and what was going on in the South was all very perplexing indeed.

CHAPTER SIX

# Exit Collins

The period from the launch of the combined IRA offensive in the North to the collapse of the Boundary Commission had a hugely demoralising effect on Northern Republicans and the Catholic community in general in the Six Counties. After Collins' promises at Armagh in 1921, great hope had been built up, in at least some sections of the community, particularly those living near the Border, that some form of deliverance was at hand.

That hope diminished with the events of May 1922 and was dashed with the exit of Collins from the scene. But it was Collins himself who began to subvert his own policy and the hope it gave to the Northern Catholics as he came under increasing pressure from those who supplied his guns at Whitehall with which to enforce the Treaty he had signed.

In his book *Myth and the Irish State*, John Regan suggests that this was part of a wider movement within Twenty-Six County nationalism, characterised by excluding Northern influence from the national movement, failing to challenge Partition militarily, acquiescing behind closed doors to Six County exclusion, and ignoring the North in the Treaty debates, "delineated in these non-events, silences, and bold contradictions of stated intents", to connive at Partition in order to save the Southern State (p.61).

Be that as it may, the *"stated intents"* and behaviour of Michael Collins, particularly in the subversion of his own policy, was to have catastrophic effects on Six County Nationalists and Republicanism in particular.

Regan's book, however, does not see the role of Michael Collins in making things immeasurably worse for Northern Catholics through his activity in relation to the Treaty. It does not understand 'Northern Ireland', what it was, and the problem it presented to nationalist Ireland.

## Subverting the policy

The disastrous effect of Collins' activity on the North was due to his sudden subversion of his own policy in deference to having to implement the 'Treaty' he had earlier signed up to.

Having drawn many of the most active Republican fighters to the North, Collins, presumably under increasing British pressure, decided to subvert the Northern offensive himself, resulting in it going off at half-cock.

The 2nd Northern Division went into action in the Six Counties but found the two Pro-Treaty Border Divisions mysteriously failing to act in support of it. Collins held back the Pro-Treaty IRA in Longford and Monaghan, presumably in preparation for his impending war on the opponents of the 'Treaty' in the South. Ernest Blythe (Pro-Treaty) hinted at this in a memo: "... a decision appears to have been taken that there would be no fighting on the Border or around it which... meant that there were no 'offensive' operations carried out by the 1st Northern or 1st Midland or 5th Northern" (Lynch, *The Northern IRA and the Early Years of Partition, 1920-22*, p.141).

The 3rd Northern Division began its offensive in Down only to find itself confronted with large amounts of Specials coming from Newry, who were supposed to have been engaged by Frank Aiken's men. O'Duffy was contacted to order the 4th Northern Division into action but it failed to take the field. The 4th Northern Division under Frank Aiken, which had assembled in large numbers throughout Armagh and South Down, called off its offensive and began, instead, settling accounts with local Unionists. The IRA units in Belfast, Down and North Antrim were isolated and mopped up by the Specials.

Although Frank Aiken had been ordered to stand down his men and to cancel the offensive, Collins neglected to inform the 2nd and 3rd Northern Divisions which covered the bulk of the Six Counties outside of Armagh and Fermanagh.

Kieran Glennon, the grand-son of a Belfast IRA Officer who joined the Free State Army, in a recent book says this about the mysterious activity on Collins' part:

"This indicates that GHQ was giving, not just mixed messages, but directly contradictory orders to the different divisions. This cannot have been an accident... The non-participation of these divisions (1st and 5th Northern and 1st Midland) has never been adequately explained, but it may well be that because they were some of the few divisions of the IRA whose loyalties Collins, Mulcahy and O'Duffy could depend on, they were loath to commit them prematurely when they might still be needed in the south. The whole operation was later shrouded in mystery..." (*From Pogrom to Civil War, Tom Glennon and the Belfast IRA*, p.125).

As Glennon notes, it seems that documents and notes referring to these orders were regarded as so sensitive they were later destroyed — even though the rest of Aiken's correspondence largely remains intact.

## Why Collins subverted himself

The reasons for Collins' behaviour remain unclear. But they can be understood. Having promised the Northern Catholics at Armagh that he would deliver them, he found himself increasingly boxed in by the British over the implementation of the 'Treaty'. On April 12th Churchill had sent a personal letter ("man to man") to Michael Collins, reminding him that the alternative to him fully implementing the 'Treaty' he had signed was "a state of war with the British Empire". In this letter Churchill showed his awareness that arms he had supplied to Collins for repressing opposition to the 'Treaty' had fallen into those very same "bad hands". He warned Collins against seeking an accommodation with those opposed to the 'Treaty', saying that any such move would be interpreted as opposition to the 'Treaty'. Churchill urged him to rally as wide a range of forces behind him to defend the 'Treaty' State and move against its opponents.

This letter, as John Regan notes, was not made public until 1929, in edited form, and not released to the public until 1976. It has been ignored by the new breed of revisionists, like Tom Garvin, wishing to construct a democratic 'myth' around the 'Treaty' State, and a consensus around not mentioning it developed among historians that Regan rightly condemns (*Myth and the Irish State*, pp. 227-8).

Dr. Regan is concerned with "how an event central to the origin of a state can be denied in scholarly research, and the denial... then go almost unnoticed" (p.229). And it certainly is the case that Churchill's letter arrived with Collins at the very moment he was going ahead with his Northern offensive and just before he decided to subvert it. Although the British made many threats of renewed war and reconquest of Ireland against the Southern administration, the Churchill letter of April 1922 can be reasonably taken to be a seminal event in Collins' subsequent actions and a disaster for the Northern IRA.

The implementation of the 'Treaty' threatened a war in the South within the National forces. There is little doubt that Collins saw the possibility of avoiding such a war in the south by waging a war in the North, binding those who were for and against the 'Treaty' together. And this policy also had its attractions for the Anti-Treaty Republicans who did not want war with Collins.

The policy also had the advantage of diverting the energies of many of the most experienced Anti-Treaty Republicans from the South-West, where the Independence War had been won, into the Northern offensive. If the bit came to the bit Collins probably thought he could deal with the Dublin Brigade himself.

Glennon puts forward his own view of how Collins began to abandon his original objectives in favour of other ones, in the face of increasing problems brought about by the British insistence that he should implement the 'Treaty':

"Collins original views began to change rapidly under the influence of unfolding events. As the army unity talks broke down and the May truce lapsed, the military position of the Free State government was becoming increasingly vulnerable as they could only count on the support of a minority of the experienced fighting men; he needed to buy time to continue building up the new Free State Army. What better way to do so than to allow his opponents to be distracted by continuing to prepare for the forthcoming offensive while he arranged for his own forces to gradually disengage from the process? In addition, his two most senior military advisors—Mulcahy as Minister for Defence and also former IRA chief of staff and O'Duffy as current chief of staff and also former truce liaison officer for the North— would have known, both from their experience of the Northern IRA and also from the size and degree of organisation of the enemy forces within the North, that the whole concept was impractical and futile from a military point of view...

"The three southern-based pro-Treaty divisions (1st and 5th Northern, 1st Midland) were told to hold back..."

The general uprising in the North planned for May, 1922 was thus suddenly called off, although not all areas were informed. The Brigades loyal to Collins were informed and preserved themselves whilst others, including the Northerners were not and headed for disaster.

Glennon comments that the Northerners "were being encouraged to proceed with a plan that could only end disastrously. Were the Northern IRA now becoming expendable pawns which, however much Collins may have regretted it, had to be sacrificed to maintain his precarious position of the south?" (pp.178-9).

A report sent at the time by James McCoy, the Adjutant of the 3rd Northern Division, reveals how Collins' subversion of his own offensive affected the IRA in the North:

"The enemy soon felt the operations were not general and concentrating in great numbers in our area, they realised that it was not difficult to cope with the situation. They now believe that they have beaten the IRA, completely in Antrim and Down...

"There is a feeling among the civil population that we are not recognised by GHQ and that our orders came from the Executive {Anti-Treaty IRA. PW}. Most of the priests are under this impression and some of them in fact have said from the pulpit that they will not give absolution to anyone who is a member of a secret Military Organisation... They have refused to hear Fianna boys' confessions.

"The people who supported us feel they have been abandoned by Dáil Éireann, for our position is more unbearable than it was in June 1921. Then the fight was a national one and our suffering was in common with all Ireland. Today the people feel that all their suffering has been in vain and cannot see any hope for the future.

"The people who did not support us are only too glad of the opportunity of assisting the enemy, and practically all over the Division the Police

Barracks are stormed with letters giving all available information against the IRA and its supporters. We have captured some letters… In some cases they regret they did not give this information two years ago" (Mulcahy Papers, UCDAD, P7/B/287).

The catastrophe of 'Northern Ireland' for Northern Catholics had occurred in June 1921 but the Nationalist position within the Six Counties had actually been made worse by the actions of Collins, from his speech at Armagh to his decision to enforce the 'Treaty' by war. The denial of the Northern Republicans had a big effect within the wider Catholic community in the North in delegitimizing the IRA in the Six Counties and placing them with the 'irregulars', whom the community saw as a destabilising and malevolent element in relation to their predicament. Not only did Republican morale collapse, but the community's solidarity and cohesiveness began to fragment in reaction to the erratic behaviour of Dublin.

## Border Warfare

As a result of these conflicting orders, the IRA in the West of the Six Counties was greatly exposed to enemy action and began to collapse and retreat into Donegal. The remnants of the 2nd Northern Division, retreating before Unionist forces, had regrouped at Pettigo just over the Border on the Southern side. They were attacked by a large force of Specials who crossed Lough Erne in a steamer. The Free State Army and IRA got the better of the Unionists and forced the Specials back into Pettigo before the British were forced to directly intervene to defend the Border which they had meant to be defended by the Unionists. The British failed to break the stubborn Free State/ IRA resistance until they brought in heavy artillery and began shelling Pettigo. Fifteen Free State soldiers were killed, dozens were wounded and captured.

Whitehall had allowed Collins to play at war against its local militia but when the Treatyite/Republican forces had threatened its Northern construction the local facade was discarded and the substance of the army of the state unleashed.

This is how the *Irish News* saw the incident at Belleek/Pettigo in its editorial, *'The Border 'Warfare'*:

"Conditions in at least two salients on the Border are indistinguishable from civil war.

"Men have been firing on one another from both sides of the 'imaginary line' in the Counties of Louth and Armagh; the situation in Pettigo has already inspired a host of romanticists to imaginative literary efforts that would astonish Walter Scott, or Charles Lever, or Mrs. M.T. Pender, or any past chronicler in fiction of battles, feints, stratagems, and surprises…

"What is to be gained by these proceedings on the confines of Louth and Armagh, Donegal and Fermanagh, and Derry and Donegal? Sir Henry Wilson and Sir James Craig know.

"They are pursuing a clear-cut policy directed to the achievement of a well-defined object. They have framed their plans to prove to Great Britain and to the world outside it that peace cannot be restored in Ireland until the Act of Union has been re-enacted and the re-conquest of the country completed...

"'Warfare' on the Border helps to convey the desired impression; so do outrages in Belfast; therefore those who lend themselves to the Border 'warfare' are playing the game of the die-hard strategists—consciously or unconsciously...

"In the Six Counties 450,000 Nationalists are in a position of peril and difficulty tenfold greater than that which confronted them on the day the Treaty was signed... If the leaders of the people of the Twenty-Six Counties had handled their own affairs with average strength and courage, the Nationalists of the North-East would not have been condemned to the tortures of the past six months.

"What is to happen now? We have been insisting since September that the real issue before five-sixths of Ireland was frank acceptance or blunt rejection of this Treaty. The people's minds were violently deflected from that plain issue... Now we will probably see the big issue decided—for good or ill" (3.6.22).

In late May Churchill summoned Collins to Whitehall to discuss the implementation of the 'Treaty'. It was made clear to him that this was an offer he could not refuse. Sir Henry Wilson was advising the Northern Government that, with the reconciliation between Collins and De Valera in the Pact between them, a Republic was being organised behind the backs of the British Government and Ulster. Further evidence for this was the massing of Republican forces, both pro- and anti-Treaty on the Donegal border. As a result Craig notified the press that the Boundary Commission would not take place (IT 24.5.22). This jeopardized Collins' position and the 'Treaty' overall and Churchill was now determined to make Collins fully implement the 'Treaty'. He was told to shove his draft Republican Constitution and enforce an Imperial one on the opposition.

In a much publicised statement on the Irish situation made to the House of Commons on 31st May, with Collins attending in the public gallery, the Colonial Secretary emphasised the choice that was being imposed on Ireland through the 'Treaty' and which he was insisting be carried out:

"The Irish people would thus have been free to reject or accept our offer with their eyes open. Had they rejected it and returned a Parliament pledged to set up a Republic, an issue would immediately have been raised comparable to that which arose in the American Civil War between the States of the American Union and the seceding Confederate States" (Hansard, 31 May 1922 vol. 154 cc.2125).

Churchill made it clear that, if the Pact was implemented during the election, and if those anti-Treaty men who were part of the panel did not sign up to the Imperial Constitution when it was produced, Britain would regard it as a breach of the 'Treaty', meaning war.

Churchill maintained the fiction in his Commons statement that Collins had nothing to do with the offensive in the North and said that the Provisional Government had assured him that the forces massing on the Donegal border were entirely 'irregulars'. But privately the Colonial Secretary warned Collins about the situation in Belleek/Pettigo and told him that he had been rumbled on his pretence that the force consisted only of 'irregulars'. Churchill advised Collins that, if he invaded Six County territory, he would be met by the full force of the British Army.

The readiness of the British to back up the Unionists with the required military force should have shown Collins that a military assault on the North was futile. But Collins continued to encourage Anti-Treaty fighters to go North and the Northern IRA to believe that he was mounting an offensive in Ulster to destroy the 'Northern Ireland' construct.

Collins was apparently angry at Churchill's military intervention at Belleek/Pettigo and protested to Whitehall. Why? Was Collins led to believe by the British that they were, after the 'Treaty', no longer an element in the conflict in Ireland? Did Collins presume that it was only the Unionist Government that he needed to defeat to end Partition?

That must have been the case. It also explains why Collins' war in the North was directed almost exclusively at local Unionist forces. He seems to have, as a matter of policy, avoided attacking the British, the prime targets of Republicans in all their campaigns, to avoid coming into conflict with them.

After the British assault at Pettigo the Republicans in the area expected a follow-up attack from the British. The British approached the Republicans under a flag of truce, urging them to stay out of Tyrone and Derry. The British Army confined themselves to holding the line of the River Foyle. They then watched puzzled as the Republicans were suddenly and unexpectedly attacked by their former comrades in the Free State army, not realising that Churchill had had a word in Collins' ear.

## The 'Treaty' War

On June 22nd Sir Henry Wilson, former Chief of the Imperial General Staff and security advisor to the 'Northern Ireland' Government, was assassinated in London by two IRA men, who were captured at the scene. Collins had blamed Wilson for what happened at Pettigo/Belleek and was apparently going to have him pay with his life for it.

The assassination, it seems, was carried out on orders from Collins, perhaps as another conspiratorial attempt to maintain Army unity, and in the belief that Lloyd George would not have minded seeing the back of Wilson either—which he didn't. Collins expressed responsibility for it to General Sweeney on the following day, according to Ernie O'Malley (O'Malley papers, UCDAD, P17b/97).

The British Government, however, had no intention of blaming their instrument in Dublin for Sir Henry's assassination and blamed the Republican leadership in the Four Courts complex, ordering Collins to dislodge them or they would do it themselves. The British had regarded the results of the June 16th election as a mandate for the Provisional Government to move on the occupiers of the Four Courts and the killing of Wilson helped bring things to a head.

The British had treated Collins with great patience in the first half of 1922 because he was indispensable to them. He was the strongman, on the lines of General Botha, who was the most likely to carry off the new policy they had in mind for Ireland. A number of English periodicals commented that he, and not Redmond, was the real 'Irish Botha', having a successful guerrilla military background against the British instead of just being a man who served out his life in the House of Commons. And so Collins was left on a long leash despite the knowledge of his subversive behaviour in the North because he was the best hope for establishing the new regime, indispensable to the overall policy, in the South.

Having tolerated Collins' duplicity and shenanigans for six months in the interests of bedding in the new Imperial settlement in Ireland, Churchill brought his activities to a halt with an order to make war on the Republicans or face a resumption of British control.

The attack on the Four Courts occurred on June 27th, after Collins gave the occupiers an ultimatum to evacuate. On the night before Collins' assault that began the Treaty War, Sean Lehane and other officers leaving for Donegal to join Collins joint-offensive in the North were led to believe that an accommodation had been reached that had prevented a 'Civil War'. The agreement, they were told, that was reached revolved around a common policy of war in the Six Counties that would re-unify the national forces. They left believing this to be the case.

After three days of shelling with heavy artillery, on loan from the British to take the Four Courts, Rory O'Connor, and the other Army Executive members who had occupied it since April, surrendered. The Four Courts were then destroyed by a massive explosion of mines lying on lorries awaiting transportation to Donegal for use in the Six Counties.

Here is the *Irish News* editorial during this event entitled, *'The Crime of War'*:

172

"News from Dublin comes slowly. The struggle for possession of the buildings seized on Friday and Saturday by Mr. De Valera and his supporters in O'Connell Street was raging last evening...

"Mr. Michael Collins said late last week... that 'he believed the present disorder in the South of Ireland was not the cause but the result of the outbreaks in Belfast'.

"Controversy on the issue is futile — at this juncture. The series of 'outbreaks' in Belfast that were inaugurated on July 21, 1921, could not have been inspired by the present disorders in the South of Ireland; but one of the parties to the present conflict in the South has been exploiting the sufferings of the Catholics in the North-East for its own partisan ends, and the policy and performances of that party in the South have helped materially to make a horrible situation more difficult and ghastly for the Nationalists of the North-East...

"Mr. Collins opinion as to the origin of the Irish Civil War can be discussed later on. His statement made to another journalist last week is definite. He said:

"'There can be no question of forcing Ulster into union with the Twenty-Six Counties. I am absolutely against all coercion of that kind. If Ulster is to join us, it must be voluntarily. Union is our final goal: that is all.'

"When circumstances made possible the passing of an English Parliamentary Act severing the Six Counties from the Twenty-Six, no one who did not willfully blind himself to facts could have regarded reunion by force as anything better than a foolish and impractical vision.

"The mischief was done: it could have been averted; but it was not averted because the means to avert it were not available. It was done; and it can only be undone by means and methods wholly disassociated from the idea of force. Mr. Collins knows the facts of the situation; the policy of Northern Nationalists must be based on his plain statement" (4.7.22).

When the *Irish News* said that *"one of the parties to the present conflict in the South has been exploiting the sufferings of the Catholics in the North-East for its own partisan ends, and the policy and performances of that party in the South have helped materially to make a horrible situation more difficult and ghastly for the Nationalists of the North-East"*, it was entirely mistaken about which one.

## Collapse of the Northern IRA

The withdrawal of support from the South gave the Unionist Government the opportunity to see off the IRA within its territory.

In the first instance, the Northern Government responded to the IRA offensive by confining its forces to barracks. But, when a lull set in caused by the countermanding order made by Collins that resulted in the offensive running out of steam, the Specials went into action. After the Treaty War was embarked upon by Collins's forces in the South the Unionists initiated massive raids against the IRA. Within five weeks the offensive had been broken and by August the Northern IRA was beaten—this time for generations.

At the same time the launch of the Treaty War led to Collins abandoning military affairs in the Six Counties. Despite the fact that British forces continued to occupy positions within Free State territory, after the battle of Pettigo/Belleek, the Free State forces were switched to putting down the Anti-Treaty men.

The outbreak of the 'Civil War' in the South had a great demoralising effect in the North. Seamus Woods, O/C of the 3rd Northern Division (covering Antrim and East Down), wrote a plea for help from Belfast to the Chief of Staff Mulcahy at the end of July:

> "The people who supported us feel they have been abandoned by Dail Eireann, for our position today is more unbearable than it was in June 1921. Then the fight was a national one and our suffering was in common with all Ireland's. Today the people feel that all their suffering has been in vain and cannot see any hope for the future.
>
> "The people who did not support us are only too glad of the opportunity of assisting the enemy and practically all over the Division the police barracks are stormed with letters giving all available information against the IRA and their supporters... the Divisional Staff feel they cannot carry on under the circumstances, nor can we in justice have the volunteers and people support us any longer when there is not a definite policy for the whole six County area and our position as a unit of the IRA on the GHQ defined" (Mulcahy Papers, UCDAD, P7/B/77).

At a meeting in Dublin shortly afterwards Woods reported to Michael Collins, Mulcahy, O'Duffy and other senior GHQ officers that "... in a whole divisional area there is a feeling to recognise the Northern Government. The National spirit among the people is practically dead at the moment" (Mulcahy Papers, UCDAD, P7/B/79).

After some discussion Woods was led to believe that it had been decided that the Northern IRA should regroup south of the border, with a view to resuming the offensive in the North in the future. Collins concluded the meeting with a pledge that the North would not be forgotten: "I now propose to call off hostilities in the North and use the political arm against Craig so long as it is of use. If that fails the Treaty can go to hell and we can all start again" (Tim Pat Coogan, *Michael Collins*, p. 383).

Collins neglected to tell Woods and his fellow Northern IRA officers that on the previous day the Provisional Government had established the North East Policy Committee of Five in order to develop and adopt a 'Peace Policy' toward the Unionist Government.

# Dublin's turnabout on the North

The Committee agreed to a new policy with regard to the North, as set out in a paper by Ernest Blythe, a Northern Protestant Republican with the most realistic view of things with regard to Northern Protestants. This paper urged a policy toward the anti-Treatyites of "attacking them all along the line" and a complete change of policy in relation to the North, from one of aggression to one of conciliation. It is worth reproducing as a criticism of the Collins policy, to show how much that policy was attributable to Collins alone, and to show the great *volte face* that the Free State was about to embark on in relation to the North:

"There is no prospect of bringing about the unification of Ireland within any reasonable period of time by attacking the North East, its forces or Government. Military operations on regular lines are out of the question because the certainty of active British support ensures that the Six County Government will be able to repulse any attack we can make. Guerrilla operations within the Six Counties can have none of the success which attended our operations against the British. The fact that the Protestant population (in most places the majority) will everywhere be actively against our men makes that impossible. The continuance of guerrilla warfare on any considerable scale can only mean within a couple of years the total extirpation of the Catholic population of the North East. The events of the past few months make that evident. We cannot even hope that a condition of turmoil in the Six Counties will bring about or hasten a financial crisis which will make their Government ready to throw up the sponge. As long as we, or people supposed to act with our approval, assail the authority of the Northern Government so long will the British Government continue to lend them financial support. As soon as possible all military operations on the part of our supporters in or against the North East should be brought to end.

"Economic pressure against the North East, gives no greater promise of satisfactory results than military action... Nothing that we can do by way of boycott—the economic weapon heretofore in use—will bring the Orange party to reason... A state of turmoil moreover will mean the continuous expulsion of Catholics... The use and threat of arms must be ruled out of the dispute, because there is no form of economic pressure open to us which would be of any avail against a war-fever.

"The hope of getting the Six Counties back if they opt out depends therefore on the abandonment of all thought of force on our part and on the cessation of any relations with, or any encouragement of any section in the North who refuse to acknowledge the right and authority of the Northern Government...

"If the relations between the two Governments were perfectly amicable, if we did not reveal any desire to use coercive measures and if we did not attempt to undermine the authority of the Northern Government in its own territory, then it is certain that in the course of time National unification would come to be regarded as a wise and economical thing, by the majority in the Six Counties... the idea that we can get unification without effort, because the Northern territory will prove too small to support a Government is utterly fallacious. The Northern Government will be left to stand on its own legs only when peaceful conditions have been established. Under peaceful conditions there is no reason why the Six County Government should not swallow its pride, economise, and live within its means. There are many Governments controlling less territory and ruling fewer people.

"The line to be taken now and the one logical and defensible line is a full acceptance of the Treaty. This undoubtedly means recognition of the Northern Government and implies that we shall influence all those within the Six Counties who look to us for guidance, to acknowledge its authority and refrain from any attempt to prevent it working. Pending the Boundary Arbitration the Northern Government is entitled to claim obedience in the whole of the Six Counties and we are bound by the Treaty to encourage obedience to it.

"On the other hand the Treaty gives us a clear claim to at least two and a half counties of the Six and we must make it clear that just as we shall give all it binds us to give so we shall use every means to secure the last title of what the Treaty entitles us to. Fears have been expressed that the Belfast people may in the interval before the Boundary Arbitration dig themselves in what may be called the disputed area. The truth is that they can only dig themselves in if we help them by producing a state of turmoil and disorder. The events of the past few months have done much towards fixing the border where we cannot consent to its being fixed. It is full time to mend our hand. We shall in no way strengthen the Northern claim to hold all they have by taking our stand definitely on the Treaty. On the contrary we shall put ourselves right in the eyes of an impartial arbitrator... A fuller acceptance of the terms of the Treaty than we have yet agreed to is the only way of bringing about a better British attitude in regard to the Catholics of the North. We must do our bit if we expect them to do theirs.

"In order to prepare the way for a state of feeling which may lead to the unity of Ireland it is necessary that we should immediately change our policy in regard to various minor matters:

"(a)   Payment of {Catholic} teachers in the Six Counties should immediately be stopped. From the point of view of finance, educational efficiency, and public morality it is indefensible...

(b)   We should stop all relations with {nationalist} local bodies in the Six Counties and should try to arrange that those which have been suppressed should be restored on condition of recognising the Northern Government.

(c)   Catholic members of the Northern Parliament who have no personal objection to the oath of allegiance should be urged to take their seats.

(d)   Ample precautions should be taken to prevent border incidents from our side. And any offenders caught by us should be definitely handed over to the Northern authorities...

(e)    As it is quite evident that the Catholics of the Six Counties cannot by use of arms protect themselves we should on receiving satisfactory assurances from the British, urge them to disarm.

(f)    Prisoners in the North should be requested to give bail and to recognise the courts.

(g)    The 'Outrage' propaganda should be dropped in the Twenty Six Counties. It can have no effect but to make certain of our people see red which will never do us any good... Much of it, particularly in regard to prisons is, like all prison propaganda, false.

(h)    All kinds of minor nagging should cease.

"When we adopt a new policy towards the North we shall be accused of letting down the Northern Catholics and shall be asked if the Pogromists are to be allowed to have their own way unhindered. The answer is obvious. The belligerent policy has been shown to be useless for protecting the Catholics or stopping the pogroms. There is of course the risk that the peaceful policy will not succeed. But it has a chance where the other has no chance" (Blythe Papers, UCDAD, P24/70).

This was recognition that Collins' policy had been a delusion and was bankrupt. The British hadn't gone away and weren't about to. The policy of force had failed. Economic measures were ineffective. Recognition of the Northern regime which had been discouraged was now to be encouraged.

The decision of Collins' committee was communicated to him as he left for his last tour of West Cork. It will never be known whether Collins intended to follow it or whether he planned a last, final zig-zag. But with Collins removed from the scene his colleagues in the Free State followed it.

The decision was not, however, communicated to the Northern IRA, who were still led to believe they were going to be trained in the South for another day.

## Abandonment of the Northern IRA

After the death of Collins, when assistance to the Northern IRA from his fellow Treatyites began to dry up, Seamus Woods wrote to General Mulcahy seeking clarification of the new situation. It, again, is worth reproducing at length, to show the effect the latest fluctuation in policy had on Collins' former instrument in the North:

"...As, I am inclined to believe, the attitude of the present Government towards its followers in the Six Counties, is not that of the late General Collins, I am writing this memo., with a view to ascertaining from you what exactly the position of my Division is now, and is likely to be in the future relative to G.H.Q., and I would also like to know through you what policy the Government has for its followers in the Divisional area.

"When the Treaty was signed in December last we were given to understand by Gen. O'Duffy that although the Six Counties did not benefit as much as the rest of Ireland by it, it was the best that could possibly be got at the time, and it was the intention of the Dail members and the members of G.H.Q. Staff who supported it, to work and try to overcome the Treaty position with regard to Ulster.

"During the three months following the signing of the Treaty I am satisfied that G.H.Q. did their best to assist the Army in the Six Counties, and when the split came in March I recommended to the Officers and men to stand with G.H.Q., as I considered that by so doing we were giving the people who supported the Treaty a better chance of overcoming the position in the North.

"After the outbreak of hostilities between G.H.Q. and the Executive there was the danger that the position in Ulster would be more or less overlooked and allowed to drift, and in order to have a definition of our position and of the policy of the Government here, I asked for a meeting of the senior Officers of the Six County area G.H.Q. Staff.

"Before that meeting was held I sent you a memo. dealing with the events in the Division from the time I took over Command and outlining the position generally at the end of July, as regards the morale and tactics of the enemy; the morale of our troops and the morale of the Catholic population; and their attitude towards the I.R.A.

"On August 2nd. the meeting was held and the late Commander-in-Chief presided. At that meeting the situation in the Six Counties was discussed at great length, with a view to improving our organisation and training, and deciding on a policy to be adopted by our people in the North and which would have the sanction of the Government in Dublin. The late C-in-C. outlined the Policy we were to adopt — one of non-recognition of the Northern Government and passive resistance to its functioning. At the same time, from the Military point of view we were to avoid as far as possible coming into direct conflict with the armed forces of the Northern Government, and any action on our part would be purely protective.

"The late C-in-C. made it clear to us that the Government in Dublin intended to deal with the Ulster situation in a very definite way, and as far as this Division was concerned, every Officer present felt greatly encouraged to carry on the work when we had a definite policy to pursue and an assurance that the Government here would stand by us.

"After the death of the late General Collins it was encouraging to us to see that the Government were determined to carry out his policy. I took it that this meant his Policy regarding Ulster also.

"A new situation has now arisen. F. McArdle was up a fortnight ago with the President regarding the course of action to be adopted by our people in connection with the signing of a declaration of loyalty to H.M. the King and the Northern Govt. which that Government is imposing on certain people, and I expect through time will impose on every citizen in the Six County area. McArdle informed me that the President brought the matter before a meeting of the Cabinet and the decision was that the Government in Dublin had no objection to our people signing this. Owing to the position that has arisen in the rest of Ireland I take it the Government feel that they are not equal to the task of overcoming the Treaty position with regard to Ulster. If it is their intention to recognise the Northern Government, it is well that they should be acquainted with the present position in Ulster, and also have an idea of what the future of Ulster is likely to be as we visualise it...

"Recognition of the Northern Government, of course, will mean the breaking up of our Division. None of the Divisional, Brigade, or Battalion Officers could remain in the area except under war conditions, and that only for a short time, and even under guarantees from the Northern Government, if such will be arranged, these men would not be safe from unofficial murder-gangs. With the departure of these officers it would not be possible to maintain the I.R.A. Organisation, which is the only Irish Organisation in the Six Counties at the present time. The breaking up of this Organisation is the first step to making Partition permanent. If this must come, then there is very little hope of organising in Ulster on Gaelic lines for a long time..." (Mulcahy Papers, UCDAD, P7/B/77).

At the end of the memo Woods asked Mulcahy how he was going to help the men who had fought for Collins and who were now prisoners, the people who had aided the struggle but lost their livelihood and the refugees forced to leave the Six Counties. Mulcahy wrote a dismissive reply which disavowed any promises of aid for the Northern IRA that might have previously been made and told Woods that nothing would be forthcoming from Dublin in the future.

With this it was realised that further fighting in the Six Counties was futile. Volunteers who were unable to return to their homes were transferred to the Curragh camp and arms were dumped as IRA Brigades were wound up and became non-existent.

Before he was killed, Collins had attempted to make provision for the preservation of the Northern IRA in the Free State, until the Treaty War was over. He intended there to be another day. Northern volunteers were therefore sent for training at the Curragh Camp and were paid salaries by the Southern Government. Over 500 volunteers came down. Florrie O'Donoghue noted in his account of the life of Liam Lynch, *No Other Law*:

"An agreement was entered into between the Beggars Bush GHQ and the officers in the Second and Third Northern Divisions that the men in these areas should go to the Curragh for a period of intensive training, after which they would return and continue operating in the six counties. Michael Collins, Richard Mulcahy and Gearoid O'Sullivan gave these men through their officers, a very definite undertaking that they would not be asked to take part in the fighting in the South. To their credit be it said that this undertaking was honoured, although many of the officers and men who had come from the North joined the Free State Army. They did so of their own free will.

"But none of the 500 men brought to the Curragh for training was ever sent back to continue the struggle against the Northern government. Given the prospect of any support from outside the area they were ready and willing to return but the outbreak of Civil War in the South ended the possibility of that united support which would have been essential and engaged the parties to such an extent and so far to the limits of their resources that any plans for the North fell to the ground. This phase of IRA activity in the six counties was for all practical purposes ended by the outbreak of civil war" (p.253).

It was only with the death of Collins that the Northern men gave up hope of any renewed Northern campaign and Seamus Woods reported great dejection in IRA ranks in the North with the realisation that Collins's policy had died with him. While some of them went back to fight with 'irregular' units in the North, the bulk of them formed the core of the new Free State army and remained in the South.

After Collins's death the Free Staters called a halt to military activity in the Six Counties and gave the IRA in the North the choice of absorption into the Free State Army or disbandment. By the end of 1923 the Northern IRA had ceased to exist. At the start of 1922 the Northern Ministry of Home Affairs had calculated IRA strength in the Six Counties to be at about 8,000 men. Three years later it was estimated to have declined to less than a couple of hundred. (Lynch, *The Northern IRA and the Early Years of Partition, 1920-22*, p.207.)

The ambivalent policy of Collins, the failure of two Pacts with Craig to protect Catholics from Unionist violence, and then the final withdrawal by the Free State, were very harmful to Northern Republican morale.

The Northern IRA was effectively destroyed by these events and it did not recover until after the events of August 1969.


## Endgame in Donegal

A final tragic episode of the shambles caused by Collins' aborted offensive was what happened to Charlie Daly and his comrades in Donegal. Daly, from Co. Kerry, had been appointed as the full-time IRA organiser responsible for Tyrone and the rural parts of Co. Derry. He was given command of the 2nd Northern Division in the area until early March 1922, when he was removed by Collins because of his opposition to the 'Treaty'. Just before his dismissal he had led a very successful attack that captured the barracks in Pomeroy, Co. Tyrone.

In early 1922, in preparation for the Spring offensive, he was made Vice-Commandant of forces in Donegal. But in Donegal Collins' Northern War met the Commander-in-Chief's Treaty War.

The Free State commander in Donegal, Commandant General Joe Sweeney, on Collins' orders equipped the Northern IRA with hundreds of

British rifles from which his men had chiselled the serial numbers. He gave them to Charlie Haughey's father, Sean, for action in the North. (Interestingly Sean Haughey, from South Derry, was a strong believer in Collins and subsequently fought in the Treaty War on the Government side. This led Frank Aiken, who became an Anti-Treatyite and a founder of Fianna Fail, to detest his son, Charlie, as an "opportunist Free Stater" within Fianna Fail. Aiken believed Charlie to have some of the Collins' deviousness in him, making him "the wrong sort of person" for Dev's principled party. (See Stephen Kelly, *Fianna Fail, Partition and Northern Ireland, 1926-1971*, p. 171.)

General Sweeney then refused to co-operate with Sean Lehane's forces, presumably on Collins' orders, and proceeded to harass the Anti-Treaty fighters who had begun retreating across the Border and been reinforced from Munster.

A meeting was arranged in Drumboe Castle between Sweeney and Tom Glennon (his Belfast Adjutant on the Free State side), and Charlie Daly and Sean Lehane representing the Anti-Treaty Republicans. At the meeting Daly and Lehane asked for an arrangement so that conflict would be avoided between the two forces. But Sweeney told the Anti-Treatyites that they were an unofficial army he could not recognise and they were not welcome in the County. Glennon, the Belfast man, told them: "You are our enemies..." (*Irish Independent* 10.5.22).

Glennon's viewpoint is explainable when one looks at the general Northern outlook about the 'Treaty' split that saw the 'irregulars' as a menace to the national unity they depended upon. From a Northern perspective the Treaty War was meaningless. Frank Aiken, the most effective Northern IRA leader, came south and ended up as one of De Valera's men. But he was neutral in the Treaty War—until he unavoidably got embroiled in it in Dundalk. He had earlier informed Richard Mulcahy, second in command to Collins, that he would not fight for either side, "because that fight would only ruin the country without gaining any ground for the Republic" (Dorothy Macardle, *The Irish Republic*, p.792).

The contentious meeting at Drumboe Castle led to increasing tensions which culminating in a gun-battle in Newtowncunningham on May 4th in which four Free State soldiers were killed. This shoot-out was provoked by Glennon's aggressive actions toward the Southern Anti-Treatyites

The day after Collins began shelling the Four Courts in Dublin, Sweeney's men launched a surprise offensive against the Anti-Treaty men in Donegal, over-running and capturing the static Republican posts and taking several hundred prisoners. Daly tried to halt the spread of the conflict, but when Free State attacks on Republican positions intensified, he was forced to fight.

Sweeney ordered Daly and his Cork and Kerrymen out of Donegal but Daly replied that Liam Lynch had ordered him up to Donegal to wage war in the Six Counties and he would not be leaving until Lynch ordered him to do so.

The Anti-Treatyites, now realising they had been lured up North for a pointless offensive that had been subverted by its own commander in chief, made attempts to negotiate an end to the fighting. However, the conditions proposed by the Free Staters scuppered the negotiations and the Anti-Treaty Republicans remained bottled up in the North-West.

The Free Staters broke up the Republican forces and Republican GHQ bowed to the inevitable and ordered the remnants of their men under Lehane and Daly to evacuate Donegal in late October.

Charlie Daly and his flying column attempted to break out but were intercepted by Free State forces and Daly and three other men were executed by their comrades in the Northern offensive.

The Six County volunteers melted away once the 'Civil War' began in Donegal. They had no interest in it or stomach for it.

Active opposition among Six County Catholics to the Northern Government faded away during the Treaty War. Cosgrave made a number of statements which he meant to be conciliatory to Unionists but which actually had the effect of relieving the pressure on Craig and making the Northern Catholics feel abandoned and helpless in the face of all that had happened.


## Awaiting deliverance

The outcome in the North would have been very different if the independence forces had remained united. The pressure would have been much greater on Craig and on Whitehall. If confronted by greater power from the Southern State, the Boundary Commission could possibly have whittled away parts of the Border Counties and made Stormont less politically viable. Such pressure would have made a greater area look less stable and the smaller area more functional from a British point of view.

Things may have also been different if Collins had not got himself killed in his irresponsible adventure in Cork. The conspiratorial policy he had operated against the North was his policy alone, a policy only he could have pursued, and it died with him. John Regan has described Collins' position from mid-1922 as tantamount to that of a dictator running a military dictatorship through his War Council of Three. Certainly, he was the irreplaceable strongman whom the other Treatyites knew they could not replace and none of them even tried. The new 'strongman' Kevin O'Higgins, who was certainly not a dictator, directed his efforts against Republicans.

Collins' successors were happy to accept the status quo of 'Northern Ireland' and get on with things within the British Commonwealth.

Cosgrave, who replaced Collins, was more a solid administrator than an effective politician, and he believed that the Boundary Commission would act above politics and would adjudicate on a purely academic basis. He did not understand that pressure needed to be applied in order to make any headway in the negotiations and to get transfers of territory.

In the Treaty debates there had been one warning voice that upset the consensus of wishful thinking on the Boundary question. Dr. Francis Ferran, one of the Deputies for Sligo (who later died in a Free State Internment camp at the Curragh) warned:

> "You believe that under the Articles of Agreement you are to get a fair delimitation of boundary. I hold that England is going to trick you in that Article, that Sir James Craig will be left with an equivalent of six counties, and there is not a single guarantee that would not be so" (Treaty Debate, 6.1.22, p. 287).

Up until 1925, some hope remained for Northern Catholics with the impending report of the Border Commission. In believing the Northern entity to be a temporary aberration, Dublin had encouraged Northern Nationalists to have nothing to do with the 1920-1 structures — a policy also pursued by the South itself. And, until 1923, the Free State financed the Northern Catholic community as an extra-territorial part of the Southern State, and a distinct society outside the Stormont system, by, for example, encouraging Councils with Nationalist majorities to not recognise the Unionist Government, paying the salaries of Nationalist teachers in the Six Counties, and producing a flood of propaganda about the temporary nature of Partition and the plight of Catholics arising from it.

But, by the end of 1922, the Southern Government had stopped recognising the Nationalist Councils that flew the Tricolour, ended the paying of the salaries of Catholic school teachers who refused to recognise the Northern Government, and repressed publications, like that of Fr. Hassan, about the grievances of Catholics in the North.

Only after the Treaty War finished, did Cosgrave request that the Boundary Commission meet, and then more out of a sense of duty than with any great purpose. Kevin O'Shiel, the Tyrone Nationalist and Sinn Feiner who was an assistant legal adviser to the Provisional Government and to the Free State Government, urged Cosgrave to take the Border issue to the League of Nations, but the latter allowed himself to be persuaded by the British to let the Imperial Conference deal with the matter. By then the Northern Government had dug in and stabilised its territory.

Because of the Free State's faith in the Boundary Commission, Devlin was forced into a policy of non-recognition of the Northern Government until the Commission reported. And so, between 1923 and 1925, the Northern community continued its boycott of the Six Counties' institutions, even after the withdrawal of Southern support, in anticipation of at least Tyrone and Fermanagh seceding from the Six Counties through the working of the Commission.

The proprietor of the *Derry Journal*, Frank McCarroll, a former Sinn Féiner, later revealed how the Free State encouraged Northern Nationalists with false hope of deliverance, damaging their subsequent interests:

> "The shameful pact of 1925... handed over nationalists to their political foes bound hand and foot... At that point northern nationalists might have struck a bargain for themselves. If they dared to, they could have secured the continuance of Proportional Representation and control of several public bodies in the north now gerrymandered away from them. But they trusted in the people across the border to get the last ounce out of the Treaty and they left them a free hand" *(Derry Journal*, December 1933).

In some ways this was saying the unsayable: that the encouragement given by the Free State to the Nationalist Councils to hold out against the Northern regime had resulted in the Unionist counter-actions, including an end to PR and the use of the process of gerrymandering to counter Nationalist cessation. If the Northerners had not received such false hopes they might have secured a better deal for themselves in a more accommodationist approach to the Unionists.

## Devlinite resurgence

The disastrous failure of Collins in the North, and the subsequent withdrawal of the Free State from Northern affairs, resulted in a Devlinite resurgence. Encouraged by John Dillon, Devlin began moves to lead the remnants of the Parliamentary Party into the new Northern Parliament.

In early 1923 Devlin and Nugent began to remobilize the Hibernians and re-insert them into the vacuum left by Sinn Fein and the Republicans who had gone South. Nugent called the Sinn Fein achievement of the Border Commission "merely eyewash for a deluded people" (IN 11.5.23). In the same month 30 Devlinites travelled to Dublin where they told representatives of the Free State Government that they were to blame for the Unionist reprisals and general treatment of Catholics in the North and their disenfranchised position. They asked why the Free State was delaying with the Commission. The Southerners begged the Devlinites to stay out of the Northern Parliament until the Commission had met, promising that it was imminent.

Devlin's intention seems to have been to make a deal with the Unionist Government which would involve concessions to Catholics in return for the shelving of the Boundary Commission. On 5th May 1923 in a dramatic editorial the *Irish News* called for the abandonment of the Commission in favour of a broader settlement. Two months earlier the editor, Tim McCarthy, defended this position before a representative of the Free State Government on the basis that the stringing out of the Commission had enabled the gerrymandering of Local Government in the North.

But Devlin was blocked by the opposition of the Border Nationalists, who continued to pin their hopes on being freed by the Boundary Commission and who did not wish to legitimise the Northern entity in the meantime. Devlin had to repudiate the *Irish News* editorial, even though he had authorized it as Chairman of the Board of the newspaper.

In May 1924 Devlin became so frustrated with the situation that he signalled to T.P. O'Connor in Liverpool that, if the British Labour Party offered him a seat in Britain, he would take it.

Basically, the division in Nationalist ranks was between the Devlinite East, which feared any minor adjustment the Commission would make in reducing Catholic numbers within the Six Counties and which preferred recognition and entry to the Parliament in the hope of alleviating the Catholic position, and the Sinn Fein West which still had faith in the 'Treaty' and its Commission to deliver the Border Counties to the Free State.

## The Boundary Commission last hope

The 'Treaty' had stated that:

"a Commission shall be appointed by the British Government to determine in accordance with the wishes of the inhabitants, so far as may be compatible with economic and geographic conditions the boundaries between Northern Ireland and the rest of Ireland and for the purposes of the Government of Ireland Act, 1920, and of this instrument, the boundary of Northern Ireland shall be such as may be determined by such Commission".

Those who signed the 'Treaty' agreed that the Commission be composed of three Commissioners, one from the South, one from the North, and a Chairman nominated by the British. Thus great faith was placed in the casting vote of the British-appointed Chairman to support large scale territorial transfers from UK territory. Padraig Colum, an aide to the Irish delegation, later remembered that he had made Griffith aware of the dangerous ambiguity in this part of Article XII:

"I pointed out to him that I considered that the clause was too vague and that it left too much power to the Boundary Commission. I suggested that some unit (such as a Barony or Electoral Division) should be specified, that a vote should be taken in such a unit and that the unit should automatically come to us or stay in the North according to the majority of the votes. He immediately saw the point, but said he did not know whether it would be possible at that stage to have the clause altered. In fact it was not altered (*Arthur Griffith*, pp. 295-6).

Collins and Griffith formed an impression based on wishful thinking that the Boundary Commission was going to deliver vast territorial tracts to the Southern State and that the North would be compelled by economic forces to come into it. This view was based on an obvious misconception about the North—that it was a separate 'state' from Britain—when in fact it was part of the United Kingdom, whose Exchequer could easily guarantee its viability, given the political will. The impression was given to Collins by Lloyd George that there was no will in Britain to guarantee the North, and that it would have to make its own way in the world. But that was said to help Collins sign up to the 'Treaty'.

The Free State Government anticipated large transfers of territory because of its understanding that the boundaries of the Counties were merely administrative divisions going back to the 16th century, and as such would not have been satisfactory as the basis for the creation of an international division.

Twelve MPs in the Northern Parliament had refused to recognise the jurisdiction of the Commission. This number represented half of the eight members from Fermanagh and Tyrone, a quarter of those from County Down, and two of the five from Derry—the areas along the Border. So there was a strong case for major readjustment if the principle of 'self-determination' was applied.

The Free State adopted a very constitutional approach to the Commission. This was in marked contrast to the Unionist return to extra-constitutionalism, in which the threat to revive the UVF was made to dissuade any attempt to deprive 'Ulster' of territory.

The Boundary Commission met for the first time on 6th November 1924. Its chairman was the Round Table/Chatham House member, Mr. Justice Richard Feetham, of the South African Supreme Court. He was assisted by two Commissioners, Eoin MacNeill, the Irish Free State representative, and Joseph Fisher, the representative of 'Northern Ireland', who was appointed by the British Government. The Commission set about taking evidence with a view to making recommendations on how the Border between 'Northern Ireland' and the Irish Free State should be altered.

As the Commission met and performed its investigations, senior English Conservatives declared that the 'Treaty' the Unionist Party had signed with Collins had envisaged no more than a consolidation of the boundaries of 'Northern Ireland', adjusting it by only a few parishes in various localities.

## The Boundary Commission debacle

The final report of the Commission, completed in November 1925, was never published, after disagreements about its recommendations led to the resignation of the Irish Commissioner. (After this the Commission's Report was officially suppressed until 1968 when it was released by the Public Record Office in London.) As a result, no alterations were made to the Border.

The British were intent on making only minor adjustments that would either be rejected by the Free State or give a slightly more secure majority to the Unionists. The Commissioners defined a zone on either side of the Six Counties boundary in which they conducted their 'investigations' and took evidence from witnesses. Presumably they did not expect to make changes outside this 'frontier zone', which they defined as being located only up to 16 miles from the existing boundary. The Boundary Commissioners were not given powers to conduct a plebiscite to ascertain the wishes of the population, as had happened in other areas of Europe after the Great War. There were also different criteria laid down for the transfer of territory. Typically, in areas proposed for transfer to 'Northern Ireland' on the grounds of a non-Catholic majority, the percentage requirement was set at around 60% of non-Catholics in the area's total population. In areas proposed for transfer to the Irish Free State the proportion of Catholics in the total population was set much higher at up to 90% Catholics to be considered for transfer.

In effect, the 'geographic' conditions were allowed to override the 'wishes of the inhabitants'—for instance, the Catholic Mourne mountain area 40 miles to the South of Belfast was taken to be part of the city because it supplied some of Belfast's water.

The belief that the Boundary Commission would act in the way that the Treatyites expected was shattered by the publication of its 'findings' (including a map) in *The Morning Post* on 7th November 1924. The leak of the 'findings' came from Joseph Fisher, the Commissioner appointed to represent 'Northern Ireland', who kept up a running correspondence with Carson, resulting in the mostly accurate information finding itself into the *Morning Post*.

In the Free State there was great shock at the meagre territorial gains forecast by the *Morning Post* and even greater shock at the prospects of having to cede territory, particularly the hinterland of Derry city in east Donegal. The Free State Government feared defeat in the Dáil and an Anti-Treaty revival if the recommendations were accepted. So MacNeill resigned from the Commission on 20th November.

The Tripartite Agreement, signed up to by the Free State, agreed to revoke the Commission and established the boundary as defined in the Government of Ireland Act of 1920. As a sweetener to the bitter pill, the liabilities connected to the Public Debt of the United Kingdom that the Treatyites had accepted on Ireland's behalf under Article V of the 'Treaty' were waived.

But the Free State undertook to assume liabilities and pay compensation arising from the War of Independence and the 'civil war'. The Council of Ireland was abolished and its powers relating to 'Northern Ireland' were transferred to Belfast. Partition was formally accepted.

The Boundary Commission was the final proof of Britain's purpose in establishing 'Northern Ireland'.

The 1920-1 device could have been taken as having served the immediate purpose of luring the gullible self-confident element of Sinn Fein that formed itself around Collins into the 'Treaty'. Its purpose had been served by 1925. Collins himself was broken when Whitehall ordered him to launch a 'civil war' to split the national movement. After his death, the 'Republican' Treatyite element in the Free State Army had been repressed by the Treaty Loyalists in 1924 after the Army Mutiny, leaving just a compliant hulk which was happy to be allowed to throw in the towel and accept the Boundary Commission's consolidation of 'Northern Ireland'.

So, at that point, with all immediate danger past, and with the Six Counties at its financial mercy, Britain was free to do with 'Northern Ireland' what it wished.

There was little point in maintaining the mischievous 'Northern Ireland' facade after 1925, if good government was the objective. But there can be no reasonable doubt that good government was not the objective and the Six County construct had another deeper purpose with the decision to maintain it.

Therefore, the long-term purpose in maintaining 'Northern Ireland' after 1925 must have been connected to the British desire to maintain leverage on politics in the South. Upon the collapse of the Boundary Commission the *Irish News* stated: "we shed no tears over the Commission" because the position had "passed out of a period of uncertainty, deceit... Humbug. They must look ahead... And realise, once and for all, that their fate in Ulster rests with themselves" (IN 4.12.25).

## A Northern view of history

In October 1958 a review of a book on Michael Collins appeared in the *Irish News*. The book was by Rex Taylor. It was serialized in the *Sunday Independent* in Dublin every weekend over a couple of months at the same time. The *Irish News* headline was *'Our Book Review, Why Collins Failed'*. But the reviewer who initialled the review, C.H., who was, presumably, Cahir Healy—that most representative of Northern Nationalists—was more interested in telling the Northern Catholic story than reviewing the book.

And a very enlightening story it was in relation to how Northern Nationalism saw the events that culminated in its predicament—and how different was this view than the traditional Southern Republican one.

It is therefore worth quoting Cahir Healy's history of the North at length:

"It was a double tragedy that Michael Collins should have entered politics. He lost his life at 31 in consequence, killed by jealous or disappointed comrades. He held the fate of nearly half a million Northern Nationalists in his hands, but with little knowledge of their relation to the Irish nation. He was a soldier, with much knowledge of guerrilla warfare, but not a politician, as he admitted...

"The glamour of a Republic—its very name had something magical in it—blinded the extremists to the realities of the situation—Partition.

*"The Shadow and Substance.*

"The Oath became as a red rag to a bull in the ring. In the dreary discussion which went on in the Dail for days, nearly every speaker had something to say as to the horror of the Oath, or a specious and apologetic plea to advance in defence of it.

"The Oath and the harbours mentioned in the Articles for a 'Treaty' are taken as if they were the only things that mattered nationally. The harbours were given back to the people by Chamberlain later without any threat of war. Only one or two speakers timidly ventured to introduce the vital topic of the six divided counties and the people there left without guarantees as to their future or that of their children. Northerners were left to the mercy of their opponents in the two Agreements of 1920 and 1925. The lack of foresight of Dail Eireann was further exhibited when teachers with a National outlook were first advised to refuse to take their salaries from Belfast or give recognition to it; but, after a few weeks, were given contrary instructions. The teachers had, in consequence, to go back upon their knees and accept the salaries they had just refused. That was the sort of light and leading Dublin gave to the North in the critical hour.

*"The Oath a Bogey.*

"Before we blame Collins for that, let us think of the critical position he occupied. Griffith, who knew more of the world and its republics, wanted a settlement.

"He had made a blunder when he gave the Secretary of Lloyd George a private undertaking that 'he would not break on the North'. To Collins the Oath was the unsavoury ingredient of the 'Treaty', because he saw the use his opponents would make of it...

"It is quite clear that he and the other delegates had specific instructions not to decide anything without the approval of the Cabinet in Dublin. They ignored this direction on the plea that the Dail, as the voice of the people, had the last word...

"Of course, the British delegates sized up their men at an early stage. They had had private memos sent from Dublin as to the character of each... It was partly because of this information that they picked upon Griffith and Collins for some private talks. The plea was made later that the Irishmen were confronted with a terrible alternative—'Sign, or we resume the war!'

"Collins never agreed that they were confronted with this threat. 'I did not sign the Treaty under duress... except that the superior forces of England had always been one of duress'.

### *"The Republic not Possible.*

"There was not one of the delegates who did not know before he left Dublin that he could not bring back an Irish Republic... The Irish public would have welcomed any sort of settlement at the time, for they were tired of war. Collins knew how weak his forces in the field were at the truce, and how difficult they found it to make headway against the British assault in its varied forms. He had, however, always been in the extremist camp and wanted to bring them with him now. His desire for peace was such that he had entered into election pacts which he was soon obliged to cancel, as they were unworkable. He was a poor politician.

"If, instead of taking up time in discussing a Republic or the Oath, they had concentrated upon a united Ireland, it is certain that Lloyd George and his associates would never have broken with them...

"The Councils Bill, which had been earlier rejected by the Nationalist leaders as an alternative for Home Rule, was much preferable to a divided Ireland, which is what the Treaty secured.

### *"Councils Bill Preferable.*

"From the Councils Bill we could have gone on step by step to such wider powers as would have left us as much freedom as we needed, if we had only kept the 32 Counties as an indivisible unit. Our demand for a Republic and nothing but a Republic forced the British to put up an easy alternative in a divided Ireland. It is an old game of theirs. So far as Craig and his followers went, they would have made a show of force, in any event, but they would have got little support from the British politicians. The extremists — mayhap unconsciously — offered the British a way out.

### *"Treaty a Stepping Stone.*

"Collins regarded the Treaty as a stepping stone to freedom. He had a foolish idea, too, that the Boundary Commission would have given him about one-third of the Six Counties. It would, if the wording of Clause 12 had been specific enough as to the area within which the wishes of the people was to be ascertained. But the Oath, and the noise that the extremists made over it, turned the thoughts of everyone concerned from the essentials to the non-essentials. It is not the first time that that type of mentality has served the Irish nation badly. Many upheavals left us worse than we were...

"Collins became the glamour-boy of the Revolution. The newspapers, recording his numerous escapes from the Black and Tans, and his disguises, gave him a popularity that was world-wide. I met a Tory M.P. in 1924 who had been sent to Dublin Castle as a sort of secretary in the latter period of the trouble. He boasted of having invented some of the Collins exploits, and related them jocularly to foreign Pressmen in a club or pub. 'I hatched an egg into an eagle', he confessed.

"The truth, perhaps, is that Collins had too much personality for team work. He had been too much spoiled by the amount of space the Press gave him to play the necessary part in a tedious, serious and lengthy political negotiation.

"Looking back upon the events that led to the Treaty, it cannot be claimed that they left the country much better than they found it. Seventy-seven lives had to be sacrificed by the native Government {executions of Republicans, PW} before the Treaty could be implemented. Since then we have had a divided nation, a condition that has not brought either peace or prosperity to North or South.

"Men of goodwill now must look for a solution in a peaceful approach to the problem Collins and his associates left us. If this plan had been followed in 1914 we would have been saved much suffering and bitterness, not to mention the considerable loss of life. We have been left with a truncated country... The people ought to realise that there is no magic in a name. A Republic by any other name might spell freedom. Only a combination of goodwill and hard work can bring peace and prosperity, a fact which some of Collins' comrades have realised—too late" (IN 4.10.58).

This Northern view of the Republican struggle shows why De Valera was so intent in preventing the North from interfering in the struggle for independence after the Treaty. And it also shows why the British believed that the North could be used as a lever over the Republicans in the South.

Cahir Healy saw the people who opposed the Treaty, who stood by the Republic and who went on to form Fianna Fail as "extremists". Ironically, he saw the Council Bill that Joe Devlin's Hibernians had subverted as the lost opportunity of progressing toward a united Ireland. Of course, Healy could say and understand this because he was, after all, an opponent of Devlin's Hibernians at the time and a founding Sinn Feiner, in its pre-IRB days.

Northern Nationalists could not help but see things differently from those in the Independence movement south of the Border. They were unlikely to subscribe to the type of Republicanism that developed in the South. Of course, there were some that did and the Catholic community could swing behind Republican candidates in elections, when they decided that this would be the best way of maximising their punching power against the Unionists. And the ultimate futility of 'constitutional politics' always made Republicanism relevant to the Six County situation.

Healy later summed up the disillusioning experience of it all:

"... we took on to us idols in those years... We were enjoined by the new prophets to 'collar the gods and the Ulster difficulty were gone'. We promptly secured the three deities (de Valera, Griffith and Collins) for three northern seats which, having done, we wandered into our meadows to brood" (Phoenix, *Northern Nationalism*, p.393).

CHAPTER SEVEN

# Cast Adrift

After the failure of Michael Collins, and their abandonment by Dublin, the Northern Catholics found themselves cast adrift in the Six Counties.

Northern Nationalism began to pick itself up after the traumatic events of 1920-5. But what was it to do in the situation it found itself? Was it to act out the part of a subdued and permanent minority that was designed for it within the new construct of 'Northern Ireland'? Or was it to withdraw into itself and have nothing to do with the permanently subordinate and humiliating position that it was placed in?

That was the dilemma that faced Northern Catholics cast adrift of both the Irish and British States within the Six Counties during the next half century.

The Northern Catholics were then confronted by the very peculiar entity that they were trapped within—a *"pseudo-state"* with *"a simulacrum"* parliament in which nothing meaningful could be done.

And, to make matters worse, their attempts to escape their confinement to this state of affairs were frustrated by an understanding South of the Border of the devilish objective of it all, which made the Northern Nationalists untouchable by the object of their desires.

## Formation of Northern Nationalism

It was not until the Boundary Commission had ended that Northern Nationalism had any hope of pulling itself together. The question was: what would become of the political fragments left in the North after the disaster between 1922 and 1925?

The end of the Border Commission produced two responses in the North—a great feeling of desertion and betrayal by Dublin from the Border Nationalists and a sense of relief in Antrim, Down and Belfast that Catholics in the east would not lose their co-religionists in the west of the province.

The *Irish News* in Belfast, representative of the eastern view, appealed to Nationalists to shake themselves out of a feeling of helplessness and despair and make the best of things in the Six Counties. It immediately called for the unity and development of an effective Nationalist organisation.

Its editorial of 17th December 1925 consisted of a review of recent events that was headlined *'The Folly of Despair'*, and was presumably aimed at the Border Nationalists:

"The Treaty made on December 6th, 1921, was a complicated document; Articles V and XII provided ample materials for controversies, disputes, intrigues and negotiations. At the end of four uncertain years the situation is clarified at last... no change will be made in the Boundary set up by the Partition Act of 1920.

"Border hopes... aroused by the existence of Article XII with its provision for the appointment of a Boundary Commission to produce a geographic and economic transformation under conditions capable of many divergent interpretations, have vanished now. The Six Counties are the Six Counties still. All the Nationalists placed under the Northern Government at the end of 1920 are in the same position at the end of 1925. No doubt Irish conditions will be altered to some extent in due course; but the changes will come naturally, gradually and in accordance with developments that cannot be foreseen. And, in the meantime, as MacMahon said when he had stormed the Malakoff fort—'Here we are: here we shall remain' ...

"We are here; there are 450,000 of us. We can recover all that has been lost within the past half-decade, win the respect of opponents while contending manfully for our rights, and help and hasten the realization of national hopes by proving our lot in the land where our lot is cast. But we shall sink lower and suffer more sorely if we keep on railing at others and groaning on our own account instead of coming together and putting our hands to the work that must be done."

The *Irish News* had been worried about the Boundary Commission because it feared the isolation of the Catholics of eastern Ulster, including Belfast, if the Border Nationalists joined the Free State. It wanted the greatest number of Catholics in the Six Counties, in order to maximize nationalist influence in the area they were marooned in and to maintain the possibility of outnumbering the Unionists some time in the future. It opposed the Boundary Commission on the basis that the Catholic minority needed to be as large as possible so that eventually Irish unity could come about.

Perhaps its relief at retaining the maximum numbers of Catholics within the Six Counties produced its greatly optimistic reading of what might be accomplished given unity and organisation.

The reference to the Malakoff Fort concerned General MacMahon's taking and holding of the Malakoff redoubt during the siege of Sevastopol in the Crimean War. This was a defining moment in the fall of the city to the French after the British had failed to take it. MacMahon had been ordered by his commander-in-chief to evacuate the redoubt he had captured but replied with the legendary response: "*J'y suis, J'y reste*".

Marshall MacMahon was a descendant of the Wild Geese who commanded the defeated army at Metz in the Franco-Prussian war, helped put down the Paris commune and rose to become Chief of State in France and the First President of the Third Republic.

I don't know if the *Irish News* meant what it seemed to mean through this analogy—that the Northern Catholic presence, if kept solid and redoubtable, would ultimately result in the fall of the Unionist citadel. That at least was a realistic and practical policy for the Northern Catholics to follow after they had been led to disaster by Collins.

A few lines need to written here about the outstanding writer of these *Irish News* editorials, Timothy McCarthy (1865-1928). McCarthy was a survivor of being 'dragooned' when his silk hat was sliced in two by one of the last English cavalry charges in Ireland and had also been imprisoned for criticizing a *Coercion Act* in 1902. After working for the *Freeman's Journal*, Devlin had recruited McCarthy to run his *Northern Star* in 1897 and in 1906 he made him Editor of the *Irish News*, replacing T.J. Campbell. McCarthy, from Cloghroe in County Cork, had been William O'Brien's Editor at the *Irish People* but lost his position after O'Brien went into one of his periodic retreats from politics in 1903. This must have had a great effect on McCarthy who never forgave O'Brien and became a staunch Redmondite. He held the position of Editor on the *Irish News* for 22 years, until his death in 1928. In this time he became the voice of Devlinite Belfast and the spokesman for the Northern Catholics, a role he performed with considerable flair in his greatly knowledgeable editorials. He is appropriately buried not far from Devlin in Belfast's Milltown Cemetery.

## Cahir Healy

It was in the great let-down after the Border Commission that what became Northern Nationalism and the Nationalist *continuum* in the Six Counties began to be formed. The instrumental force in this was Cahir Healy of Sinn Fein.

The career of Cahir Healy illustrates the 'constitutional'/non-constitutional *continuum* in Northern Catholic politics most clearly. Joe Devlin might have been the most significant politician produced by Northern Nationalism but Cahir Healy was the most representative of his community.

Healy was actually born in Donegal but came to Fermanagh and conducted most of his political life there. He was one Southerner (along with Tim McCarthy) who stood with the Northern Catholics in the bleak generations. He had been an early member of the Gaelic League and the GAA in Fermanagh, a writer in the *Shan Van Vocht*, and was amongst the twelve founder members of Sinn Fein. He was an opponent of the Irish Party and the influence of Devlin's AOH within it.

After Sinn Fein's defeat in the 1907 North Leitrim by-election, Healy gravitated toward the IRB and Michael Collins. During the War of Independence he helped establish Republican Courts in Southern Ulster and played an Intelligence role within the IRA, according to Eamon Phoenix.

After the establishment of 'Northern Ireland', Healy was part of the Fermanagh Council that, expecting to become part of the Irish State, held out against the jurisdiction of the Belfast Parliament, being dissolved by the Unionist Government as a result. The Fermanagh Nationalists assumed that they would be transferred to the jurisdiction of the Southern State. Healy and the Border Nationalists believed they would be part of the South, no matter what, after Collins' promise of the Commission. Healy, who had a personal admiration for Collins, endorsed his view of the Agreement as *"the freedom to achieve freedom"* and, at a specially convened meeting of the Sinn Fein Executive in Enniskillen, held just after the Treaty was signed, he moved the resolution calling on the Dail representatives for Fermanagh-Tyrone to support the ratification of it, even though the Treatyites were about to cut them off from the body politic.

Collins placed him on the Provisional Government's North-Eastern Advisory Committee, established to work out a Northern policy after the military offensive in May 1922 had ended in shambles and catastrophe. Shortly afterwards however Healy was arrested by the Unionist Government and interned on the prison ship, the Argenta, for two years.

While interned Healy was returned for Sinn Fein in Fermanagh-Tyrone, along with T.J. Harbinson, a Redmondite, in the 1922 proportional representation election to the Belfast parliament. He was then elected as an MP in the 1923 British General Election.

Although Healy was returned to Westminster as a Sinn Feiner, the electoral convention which nominated him desired that he should represent the constituency in Westminster. By that time things were swinging away from Sinn Fein in the North. So Healy, despite being elected for Sinn Fein, which he himself had founded with Griffith on an abstentionist basis, took his seat in March 1924, joining the remnants of the Parliamentary Party, Harbinson and T.P. O'Connor, at Westminster. Furthermore, the Government in Dublin gave its approval to Healy in taking his seat.

This act, which has not been generally commented on by historians, was very significant. Healy was accused of betrayal by at least one of his former comrades from the South, but in doing what he did he was instrumental in the making of the character of Northern Nationalism.

In his maiden speech on 19th March 1924, during a vote on providing the Craig Government with a million pound in finance, Healy was repeatedly ruled out of order for discussing matters considered by the Westminster Parliament to be the internal affairs of the 'Northern Ireland' Government.

The *Irish News* saw Healy's taking of the Oath and seat at Westminster for Tyrone-Fermanagh as a vindication of the Parliamentary Party. In its editorial headed, *'The Failure of 'Abstention'*, it held to its view that most of the disasters that had befell Ireland had occurred under Sinn Fein's watch and because of its abstentionist policy from Westminster:

> "Tens of thousands must, like Mr. Cahir Healy, have realised by this time the futility and disastrous folly of the policy labelled 'Abstention' some years ago... 'Abstention's' ghastly failure need not be confessed at this stage; it is painfully evident now; but the proceedings at Westminster constituted an admission that the country may mark, note, and digest with some advantage to its health—even at this late hour" (20.3.24).

Part of the reason why the Free State Government authorized Healy's attendance at Westminster was its belief that this might be useful in relation to the Border Commission. Healy prepared submissions for the Commission, on behalf of the Free State's Boundary Bureau, aimed at gaining Fermanagh's secession to the Free State. But he became greatly disillusioned by its failure and by the willingness of Cumann na nGaedheal to sell out the North for financial concessions from the British. He afterwards accused the Treatyites, in a letter to the *Irish Independent*, of trading in "the liberties and rights guaranteed to the Nationalists by Article 12", which resulted in "the people sold into political servitude for all time" (30.11.24).

The debacle of the Commission totally undermined Healy's confidence in Collins' old Party and marked the beginning of a relationship with De Valera and his anti-Treatyites, whom Healy had previously blamed for the splitting of the national movement, the entrenchment of Partition, and the delay in setting up the Boundary Commission itself.

## Healy and Devlin

In many ways Healy was the personification of Northern Nationalism, spanning the *continuum* from Sinn Fein to 'constitutional' Nationalism. But a personification is merely an individual. Healy was also responsible for bringing about the distinct political movement that is Northern Nationalism by combining the elements of Catholic politics in Ulster to form the *continuum* that was to last for nearly half a century and which was to re-emerge after the interval of the Twenty Eight Year War.

Healy first met Devlin at the Belfast Nationalist Convention called in March 1925. Here it became apparent that Sinn Fein had declined markedly in the North-East since the Collins *debacle* of 1922 and they now represented less than a third of the delegates to the Convention. The balance of power between Sinn Fein and Nationalists had clearly shifted back to Devlin. The electoral pact of 1921 was renewed, but now the Devlinites supplied the majority of candidates and the abstention policy was ended. Individual candidates and local conventions could now decide on this, but all candidates were designated *'Nationalists'* rather than Parliamentary Party or Sinn Fein. Northern Nationalism was born.

After the Tripartite Agreement of December 1925, which formally ended the Border Commission's remit, Joe Devlin's position was that all reason for remaining outside the Northern Parliament had disappeared. But the sense of betrayal by Dublin was much greater in Tyrone and Fermanagh and Cahir Healy said that there would be a temporary retreat from any political action in these areas in disillusionment. Healy then attempted to reassemble the disparate elements of Northern Nationalism which had been broken into political fragments by events in the South during the previous decade.

Eamon Phoenix describes the role of Healy in forming a Northern Nationalist movement from 1925:

"The shattering of their hopes with the collapse of the Commission confronted Healy and the border Nationalists with the reality of lasting partition for the first time. Since 1918, the Northern Nationalists had been badly split between the adherents of Sinn Fein — strongest west of the Bann — and those who remained loyal to the constitutional Nationalism of Joseph Devlin. Devlin, always sceptical of the Collins view of the Boundary Commission, had reversed his earlier policy of non-recognition of the Northern parliament and taken his seat in April 1925. The Unionists had given notice of their intention to abolish Proportional Representation for Northern Ireland parliamentary elections, and by 1927, Healy had come round to the view that only a rapprochement between the Devlinites (centred on Belfast and East Ulster) and his own border supporters would serve the clamant demand of the Catholic community for the constitutional redress of their grievances.

"Throughout 1927, he sought to assuage the bitterness and petty jealousies dividing the incoherent remnants of Hibernians and Sinn Feinism in the North as the prelude to a new united Nationalist Party. Unless the Nationalists 'did something for themselves', Healy told a Fermanagh gathering in May 1928, there was a real danger 'that partition would become an established thing.' His aim was to establish 'a virile and truly national organisation' which would co-operate with any party in the South which was committed to Irish unity...

"The new united Nationalist movement finally emerged as the National League of the North in May 1928 with the rehabilitated Devlin as president and Healy and Patrick O'Neill, the Nationalist MP for Down, as joint secretaries" (From *'Cahir Healy, Northern Nationalist Leader'* in Alan Parkinson and Eamon Phoenix, *Conflicts in the North of Ireland, 1900-2000*, pp.146-7).

In 1925 Healy had been returned to the 'Northern Ireland' Parliament for

South Fermanagh and held the seat until his retirement in 1965. He also represented Fermanagh-Tyrone in 1931-1935, and again in 1950-1955 in the Westminster Parliament.

Cahir Healy was a politician who was able to shift between Republicanism and 'constitutional' Nationalism fairly easily and was continuously elected by his constituents who remained impervious to his changes of party.

In 1941 he was arrested under the *Defence of the Realm Act* and interned in Brixton Prison. It seems a letter of his had been opened by the authorities, resulting in his internment. In it he apparently let slip that he was not totally ill-disposed to a German victory in the war and this was the reason for his confinement. After the war Healy, who was now touching 70, authored the pamphlet *'The Mutilation of a Nation'* which became the propagandist mainstay of the Anti-Partition League. And, as we have seen, he left upon the record the distinctive view of events held by Northern Nationalism in his review of Rex Taylor's *Michael Collins* in the *Irish News* in 1958.

## The 'constitutional'/non-constitutional *continuum*

Once the Northern Government settled down to business, and it was apparent that the Northern statelet was going to survive, the Nationalist Party gradually recovered the seats won by Sinn Fein. Sinn Fein represented the Irish nation in triumph—but in Ulster, the Republicans were less appropriate to the situation and became the minor element in Nationalist politics. This, however, did not stop Catholics moving freely between Nationalists and Republicans as the electoral situation and events dictated.

Catholics returned Republicans periodically in elections as an indication of the knowledge that there would be little likely to be achieved in 'Northern Ireland' without at least the threat of force in the background, no matter how minuscule. It was also recognition that 'constitutional' politics were taken to be ultimately futile.

One of the reasons why the Northern Catholics moved without problem between the two wings of Nationalism was that, after the creation of 'Northern Ireland', there ceased to be any great issue between the two of them. Before 1920 there was a substantial political division between the Home Rulers and the Republicans over the Empire and Ireland's relationship to it. This division had been accentuated during the Home Rule struggle by the development of an Imperialist impulse within the Home Rule movement.

However, once the Empire had decided Irish Nationalism's future relationship with it, and 'Northern Ireland' had been established in semi-detachment from the UK, along with an Irish State taking shape in the South, both 'constitutional' and non-constitutional Nationalists found themselves with a common enemy and a common objective—namely how to escape from the creation of 1920-1.

It was not even that there was a clear division over tactics between the two wings of Northern Nationalism. The Republicans stood for no truck with Stormont or Westminster and a belief in the necessity of force to move the situation along. But, after the debacle of 1922, between 1925 and 1956 there was very little chance that force was going to achieve anything—so the pike was placed in the thatch.

In the 1920s and 1930s 'constitutional' (i.e. non-violent) Nationalism was organised within the *National League of the North*. This was in itself a conglomeration of outlooks. Of the 11 candidates that stood under its auspices at the 1929 elections, 6 came from an Irish Party background and 5 had represented Sinn Fein—and one of the ex-Sinn Feiners had been a Home Ruler before a Republican. That was how fluid and easily transferable Northern Nationalism was.

Between 1926 and 1927 the Nationalists began to take their seats in the Belfast Parliament—eastern Ulster first, followed by the Border Nationalists. The Unionist attitude to the Nationalist entry into the Northern Parliament was to make no concession to it. The Unionists even rubbed the Nationalists' noses in the dirt by deciding to abolish Proportional Representation for provincial elections, which had acted somewhat as a safeguard for Northern Catholics. Devlin was told by the Unionists that Nationalists had insulted the parliament by not entering it in 1921 and would, in effect, be punished for their behaviour. He was assured he could have no complaints about anything that was then done by it after having the temerity to have hoped for its demise.

In response Devlin asked:

> "In what way do we justify our parliamentary existence but by securing concessions and rights for the people we represent? ... anything we have, we have by law, not by your law, but by laws that were passed before this parliament came into operation... what encouragement is it to those who remain outside if those of us who have come in are treated in this way? ...we might as well not be here as far as the total sum of our achievement is concerned" (IN 28.3.26).

At this point half the Nationalist representation was still abstaining from Stormont, despite pleas from the Free State Government for them to attend. The Fermanagh and Tyrone MPs, angry at the Free State over the Boundary Commission, and convinced of the futility of attendance, stayed out. The Unionists were not about to help Devlin get them in. The attitude seems to have been to humiliate the Nationalists inside Parliament and to let those outside stew, not caring one way or another whether they came in.

Despite the futility of attendance in the Northern Parliament, the Devlinites continued to attend—having nowhere else to go. The Border representatives continued their abstention for a while. However, they too entered the Northern Parliament on 2nd November 1927, having put their disillusionment aside and having been influenced by Fianna Fail's entry into the Dail.

Although the Nationalists trooped into the Northern Parliament, the Catholic community responded to the perverse and provocative arrangement they were subject to by thoroughly and systematically detaching themselves from participation in the new jurisdiction and in many areas of life in the province. They naturally became resentful and sullen in their predicament and they could hardly be blamed for being so.

Eamon Phoenix comments on the situation and the political effects it had:

"The abolition of P.R. in 1929 served to increase the bitterness and suspicions of the nationalists, and acted to freeze Northern Ireland politics. It contributed to an electoral situation, consisting of two main parties, whose electoral strength was to remain fairly constant. At times, there was some erosion of Nationalist strength in the Commons by the return of Republican-cum-abstentionist elements and also, from 1945 onwards, of Independents of nationalist outlook; but, considered as an anti-Unionist bloc, the Nationalists and their allies could generally count on having 11 seats in the Commons out of 52. After 1929, the preordained nature of electoral contests in most constituencies, and the reluctance of the anti-Partitionists to appear to sanction the existence of the state, militated against the creation of any durable Nationalist party organisation or machinery on a par with that of the Unionists. The parliamentary group tended to exist from election to election very much on an ad hoc basis, and was particularly susceptible to the problems of disunity, lack of any effective or dynamic leadership, and the chimera of abstentionism, which was to prove a perennial and divisive force" *(Introduction to the Cahir Healy papers* held in the Public Records Office of Northern Ireland, p.10).

## The National League of the North

The National League of the North was launched in St Mary's Hall on the 28th of May 1928. The primary aim of this body was to work *"constitutionally"* (i.e. 'non-violently') for the ending of Partition. With Devlin as President, Archdeacon Tierney as Vice-President and Cahir Healy as one of its Honorary Secretaries, it was largely composed of Devlinites and Hibernians, with a minority of old Pro-Treaty Sinn Fein. In the general election of 1929, the League contented itself with only contesting 11 'safe' Nationalist seats, and large areas of the Six Counties continued to remain without any organisation. Devlin took little part in the affairs of the League, and the bulk of the organizational work was done by Healy.

Devlin, despite his earlier hostility to the Northern parliament and ridicule of it, began to attempt to treat it as a normal parliament, perhaps through a force of habit he had developed at Westminster. He introduced amendment after amendment to try to improve legislation that was being replicated from his old base at Westminster. The Unionists, intent on minimizing any difference between it and Westminster, shot every suggestion down. They saw Devlin as playing a dangerous game in treating 'Northern Ireland' as if it were a state and having little understanding of what he had now decided to participate in.

Devlin, however, did understand that the opposition in the Northern parliament could never be a real Opposition because it could not hope to substitute for the Unionist Government and he declined the job of Leader of the Opposition on the basis that by doing so he would give legitimacy to a permanent Protestant/Catholic division in which he would constitute the permanent opposition. He also believed that in creating a tight opposition he would preserve the Unionist monolith and make the Nationalist/Unionist division permanent.

The Nationalists became increasingly frustrated by merely making up the numbers in the Northern Parliament and being prevented by the Speaker from raising 'reserved' matters (i.e. things reserved to Westminster). After being interrupted by the Speaker at the opening of parliament in May 1932 Devlin, in frustration at not being able to carry on his old work at Westminster, said:

"I only want to say in conclusion that I believe this is the last time we will meet in this House. Well, thank God for that. My colleagues and I who represent democracy have no reason to rejoice at the years we have been here...

"I would like to see this Province prosper. The resentment is founded largely upon the mishandling of the situation. You have a small population of one and a quarter million people covering a very limited space. You have considerable intelligence. You had opponents willing to co-operate. We did not seek office. We sought service. We were willing to help. But you rejected all friendly offers. You refused to accept co-operation...

"This Parliament of fifty-two Members should have been like a corporate body, composed of men of goodwill, sitting round a table discussing these problems in a businesslike spirit, and eschewing political and religious differences unless they were vitally forced with realism on those people. That would be a gathering of wisdom from whatever reservoir it could be drawn as a patriotic contribution to the effective progress of the community. But you went on on the old political lines, fostering hatreds, keeping one-third of the population as if they were pariahs in the community, refusing to accept support from any class but your own, and relying on those religious differences and difficulties so that you could remain in office for ever" (Northern Ireland Parliament *Debates*, vol. 14, cols 44-5).

Three days later, after Cahir Healy was also interrupted by the Speaker, Devlin led his supporters out of parliament. A few of his last words in the Northern Parliament were rather fitting: "I, for one, will take no part in this sham..".

A meeting of the Nationalist parliamentary party then decided that they should resume their seats in the autumn session, but not to render a day-to-day attendance. Devlin, who was very ill at that time, decided that he was not going back to the Northern Parliament again.

And so the Northern Catholics found themselves in and out of the sham of a parliament of a pseudo-state with little to do and nowhere else to go.


## The pseudo-state

What confronted Northern Nationalists between 1921 and 1972 was what Devlin had called "a simulacrum" of a Parliament within what Henry Harrison called a *"pseudo-state"*.

Captain Henry Harrison (1867-1954), OBE and holder of the Military Cross, from Co. Down, went to Balliol, Oxford. He was offered a Liberal candidacy but instead, as an admirer of Parnell, left Balliol to become the Nationalist MP for Mid-Tipperary from 1890-92. Harrison joined the British Army in 1915 and fought in France. After the War he became Secretary of the *Irish Dominion League* and supported the Treaty. He became the Irish correspondent of the *Economist* and wrote a number of books on Parnell and some very interesting works on Ireland's relationship with Britain in the 1930s, including: *The Partition of Ireland, Ireland and the British Empire, 1937, Ulster and the British Empire, 1939* and *The Neutrality of Ireland*.

Harrison set out his argument in *Ulster and the British Empire* that Partition and the treatment of Catholics in 'Northern Ireland' was a poison infecting the relationship between Britain and a potentially valuable ally in the Second World War on Germany.

Captain Harrison recognised something about the Six County entity which has escaped the notice of the top 'political scientists': "Northern Ireland is not really a state... In constitutional theory it is indeed unique" (*Ulster and the British Empire*, p.139)

In his case against Partition, Harrison noted that 'Northern Ireland' was neither "an integral part of the United Kingdom" or "a state". It was, in fact, a "quasi unit"—a semi-detached administrative part of the United Kingdom State, constructed for Imperial purposes rather than good government.

He stated something that dozens of historians and 'political scientists' seemingly missed before and since:

> "First, of course, Northern Ireland is not really a State. It has some of the trappings of a State — a Governor, a Privy Council, a Parliament, an Executive of its own. Yet another Privy Council, another Parliament and another executive are operative in its midst. It cannot either fix or collect the bulk of its own taxes, nor does it even control its own postal service. In constitutional theory it is indeed unique. Again, it is an integral part of the United Kingdom of Great Britain and Northern Ireland, yet it has been permitted to abolish within its own boundaries the whole of the rights associated with the liberty of the subject, which are the historic pride of the British Constitution, the Constitution of that United Kingdom. It may be that it could not govern without doing so. Then if that be conceded, it has proved itself a failure in its exercise of the powers conferred upon it by Britain to make provision for 'peace, order and good government', for whether or not it has secured the first two of these, there can be no dispute but that a permanent suspension of constitutional guarantees is the reverse of 'good government.'
>
> "How… can the conclusion be avoided that, as a polity, Northern Ireland is unique to the point of being little more than a colourable device and that it has failed in the primary purpose of its creation in failing to provide good government" (*Ulster and the British Empire*, pp.139-40).

## What is it?

Brendan Clifford in *Northern Ireland: what is it?* shows how academics in Ireland have taken to writing about the 'Northern Ireland state' as if it exists. In *Northern Ireland: What Is It?* Brendan Clifford says: "The 'Northern Ireland state' is a propaganda construct, designed to shift political responsibility for the creation of the North away from Britain and foist it on somebody else" (p.21).

Nicholas Mansergh, the main writer on British/Irish constitutional affairs, initially rejected the idea that 'Northern Ireland' was a state back in the 1930s but curiously began treating it as such later. He took its abnormalities as something of its own making rather than being inherent in what Britain decided to construct in 1920. His first book, *The Government of Northern Ireland: A Study in Devolution* (George Allen & Unwin, 1936) described what Northern Ireland was in a comparatively honest way.

It didn't say what it actually was, but definitely said what it wasn't: It didn't have independent government. It had no shred of sovereignty attached to it and it was an entirely subordinate structure established by the sovereign Government at Westminster. It was accorded certain powers but had no sovereign right to those delegated powers. The Westminster Parliament remained absolutely the sovereign power. Westminster had the right to overrule legislation of the devolved parliament in Belfast, or to legislate itself on matters which it had devolved to the Belfast parliament.

Harrison noted that the British State decided in 1920 to allow part of itself to govern by means and through institutions that were different in kind from those that had been effective in the rest of the State and which had made up the much-vaunted British Constitution. But it had become clear twenty years after the event that this constitutional experiment had failed in its objective of providing for the 'better government' of Ireland—if that had ever been the objective.

Harrison went on to explain that, despite some appearances, 'Northern Ireland' was a region of the British State, completely under the sovereignty of the Westminster Parliament, with limited authority itself. It was entirely an Imperial construct that administered the workings of the British State in the province and its existence was totally dependent upon the wishes of Westminster. And what went on there, despite suggestions to the contrary, was always a Westminster responsibility:

"Sovereign authority and power in Northern Ireland lie with the Legislature of the United Kingdom of Great Britain and Northern Ireland. Does it not follow that where sovereign authority and power in Northern Ireland affairs lie, there too, lies the ultimate responsibility, moral as well as legal responsibility, for that which is done in Northern Ireland?

"It was this Legislature that, in 1920... accorded to Northern Ireland certain limited powers of self-government... In doing so, however, it reserved to itself full over-riding control in all matters, and a machinery of justice and of financial and other administration which ensured that that control should be a real and effective control. Thus the Government of Northern Ireland is a purely statutory body of limited authority, exercising powers determinable by law, and is unquestionably subject to the British or United Kingdom Government as is the County Council of London...

"These elementary truths are sometimes denied... There have been, in fact, important factions who wished to create a general impression that Northern Ireland, insomuch as it had certain of the organs of self-government, had attained to a position of a British self-governing colony in its pre-dominion status stage of development: and that consequently it was in a position of 'greater freedom and less responsibility' in virtue of some sort of inherent constitutional right. The case of Northern Ireland, however, is clearly distinguishable on all grounds...

"Northern Ireland is... a new and artificial quasi-unit with neither history, tradition, nor organic structure as a distinct community—and this quasi-unit consented to be carved out of, but yet remain part of, the United Kingdom, and willingly accepted certain limited powers and authority from the Parliament of the United Kingdom, in which it continued to be represented and by which it continued to be taxed. It is not an indigenous growth. It has therefore no antecedent pretensions—no claims based on history or tradition or the inherent right of an ancient community—to colour or to qualify its local and subordinate institutions. Its powers and its limitations begin and end in the statute law of the United Kingdom of which it still forms portion" (pp. 61-3).


'Northern Ireland' was still legislated for by Westminster, despite its own Parliament, the bulk of its revenue came from the Imperial Treasury in Whitehall which handled its taxes, and British officials administered all the reserved services for 'Northern Ireland'.

Captain Harrison saw that Britain was letting the pretence emerge that 'Northern Ireland' was a 'state' in order that the formation and conduct of its Government could not be blamed on Westminster and so the Unionists in Ulster would be allowed to have a free hand in governing and policing their minority problem without interference from outside. This led to the convention at Westminster that 'Northern Ireland' business was not to be discussed—giving Stormont even more of a free hand in doing what they liked to Catholics whilst absolving Westminster of the responsibility for this. And in that it undoubtedly succeeded for 50 years.

The establishment of this unique constitutional arrangement of a 'state' within a state, outside its party politics, went against all historical precedent and could only have been a deliberate policy on the part of the great statesmen who organised it. Even if it was accepted that Partition was "*a necessary evil*", the form of government imposed on 'Northern Ireland' could not have been worse.

The politicians who set up the Six County entity: Lloyd George, Winston Churchill, Austin Chamberlain, Arthur Balfour, Lord Birkenhead, were experienced Statesmen of the first order. They were the ruling class of what was widely heralded to be the longest-lasting and most successful democracy in the world, from the "*Mother of Parliaments*".

They could hardly not have realised that 'Northern Ireland' would not function as a normal democracy. The setting up of an alternate state apparatus formally inside of the UK, but outside the party politics of the State ensured that democracy could never really exist in 'Northern Ireland'.

Democracy is not the mere right to cast a ballot every so often. It is a mode by which the state is governed and since 'Northern Ireland' was not a state, it was not a democracy. It was "*a simulacrum*", a mere appendage of a democracy or a democratic façade. And it acted as a kind of false front of the British State in the part of Ireland it continued to occupy.

# Why did they do it?

Sinn Fein wanted to establish a national democracy in Ireland over the whole island. That was a democratic ambition. But Britain frustrated this ambition and corralled the inhabitants of the Six Counties into an entity divorced from both the emerging Irish democracy and the existing democracy of the British State.

States rarely do things for purposes of benevolence and the British State did not get where it was in the world—at the top of it—by being benevolent. States do things for interest, fair or foul. 'Northern Ireland' was a creation of the Imperial interest in 1920.

The establishment of a statelet within a state, based on an artificially engineered permanent majority, was meant to ensure that a part of Ireland would remain under British control, whilst at the same time Anti-Partitionism would continue to flourish. This might seem nonsensical but it was in Britain's interest because it ensured continuing leverage over the bulk of the island, by offering 'Irish unity', conditional on a return to an alignment and allegiance to Britain, when Ireland was threatening to move away from the Imperial sphere of influence.

What it created for the two communities in the Six Counties, was eternal communal conflict within a one-party statelet in which the Protestant majority policed the Catholic minority in whatever manner it saw as necessary and for as long as it was able, while Britain picked up the bill.

The Protestants of North-East Ulster were certainly a complicating factor in bringing about a political settlement in Ireland. But the important point with regard to this is that the British, in the interests of Imperial expediency, were against the bringing about of a lasting settlement and prevented the only other force capable of doing this, the Irish democracy, of bringing it about.

Harrison's account is unusual in that his Anti-Partitionism does not cloud his understanding of 'Northern Ireland' as being a dysfunctional political unit in its own right, quite apart from Partition, and he makes a very sensible suggestion for progressive change that was never acted upon:

> "First, it should be made clear that a change is going to be made—in one direction or another. If it will not be Ireland, then it must be truly United Kingdom" (p.155).

By this statement it is clear that Harrison understood that the most important thing for a functional democracy was that a people should be organically connected to the political life of a state—whatever that state should be—UK or Ireland. That places him head and shoulders above any of our latter-day historians and 'political scientists' whose professional business should be to understand such things but who, in tending to their careers and their financial allegiances, have become disguisers and mystifyers of them.

'Northern Ireland' was undemocratically governed because the Government of the State was completely disconnected from the electoral activity in the Six Counties. What the electorate in the Six Counties did in British elections had no bearing on the government of the State. Democracy is a system in which the electorate in the state decides which party is to govern the state. Elections were held in 'Northern Ireland' but those elections had nothing whatever to do with appointing a party to govern the state, even though there were twice as many elections there as there were in the rest of the British State. The Imperial/Westminster elections were not contested by the political parties that appealed to the British electorate to give them their votes to authorise them to govern the state, nor were the subordinate Northern elections.

Both lots of elections were only contested by Six County parties, a Catholic party and a Protestant party. These provincial parties were essentially the communities organised in political groups rather than the things that real parties in a normal state stand for.

And this peculiar system, that confronted Northern Catholics, was entirely a consequence of what Britain did between 1920 and 1921.

## Churchill reveals all

Winston Churchill actually described the significance of what was done in 1920 with remarkable candour in his *The World Crisis: The Aftermath*:

"The Bill of 1920 was a decisive turning point in the history of the two islands. In important effects it was tantamount to the repeal of the Act of Union after 120 years of friction... Ulster, or rather its predominant Protestant counties, became a separate entity clothed with constitutional forms possessing all the organs of government and administration, including the police and the capacity of self defence for the purpose of internal order. From that moment the position of Ulster became unassailable... Never again, could any British party contemplate putting pressure upon them to part with the constitution they had so reluctantly accepted" (p.286).

Churchill blurted out that the Union was put out of effect by what was done in 1920-1. But the view that: *"Never again, could any British party contemplate putting pressure upon them to part with the constitution they had so reluctantly accepted"* was merely a smokescreen for irresponsibility — as became crystal clear in 1972 when Whitehall abolished what it had put in place in 1920-1 with the stroke of a pen.

Captain Harrison draws attention to something I have not found mentioned in other history or politics books: Churchill's speeches in Parliament which gave something of an indication of what the construction of 'Northern Ireland' was really all about and what Ulster Unionism's role was within it.

In February 1925, three and a half years after 'Northern Ireland' had come into existence, Churchill, as Chancellor of the Exchequer, was proposing the making of a grant-in-aid of 1 million and a quarter pounds to the revenues of 'Northern Ireland'. This was opposed by Philip Snowden, the former Chancellor of the Exchequer, on the basis that such a grant was *"illegal"* and inconsistent with the provisions in the terms of the *Government of Ireland Act* of 1920 (and Treaty of 1921). Churchill justified the 'illegal' subventions to Ulster on the following basis:

> "For many years Ulster's repugnance to Home Rule denied Home Rule to the rest of the island which desired it so keenly, but in 1921 the attitude of Ulster changed. Ulster, not out of any wish on her own part, contrary to her inclinations and contrary to her interest, consented, in the Imperial interest, in the general interest, to accept a form of government which separated the administration of Ulster from the administration of Great Britain, and which established them as a small community in the North of Ireland, with many difficulties, many embarrassments, and many perils which they had to face. I say that that was a great sacrifice on the part of Ulster, and no one who cares about the principle of pacification embodied in the Irish settlement ought ever to ignore or be forgetful of that great sacrifice. It has imposed hardships upon Ulster. They did not want any change, and were contented with the situation that existed" (Hansard, 23.2.25).

A year later, when 'Northern Ireland' required another Imperial subvention from the public purse, Churchill reiterated his point:

> "I think it right to ask the committee to bear in mind the fact that all the inconveniences and difficulties from which Ulster has suffered arose not from any wish of her people. On the contrary, Ulster did not ask for any constitutional change. She was perfectly content to remain in the United Kingdom, and it was only because of the strong movement of Imperial policy and many tragic events, on which I do not intend to dwell, that in 1920 Ulster consented to defer to the wish of the Imperial parliament and to set up a house of her own. From the moment that this took place, from the moment that it was quite clear that Ulster was not in any way standing in the way of the aspirations of the rest of Ireland, but was deferring to the general requirements of Imperial policy, it has always seemed to me that a very strong obligation rested upon Parliament to secure her reasonable help in the difficult and critical years attending the creation of this new government" (Hansard, 22.2.26).

Here, from the horse's mouth, from one of the actual 'architects' of 'Northern Ireland', it is made clear that 'Ulster' had been reluctant to accept Home Rule institutions and had only done so in deferring to the *"general requirements of Imperial policy"*.

Snowden acknowledged Churchill's argument, that 'Northern Ireland' should receive 'illegal' subventions because of the sacrifices she had made to the requirements of Imperial policy, as the only justification for receiving the Treasury's treasure when treasure was in short supply, after the extravagant spending of it in destroying Germany.

The financial arrangements between Westminster and 'Northern Ireland' are one of the lesser-known aspects of the Treaty. Collins was led to believe, as an inducement to signing the Treaty, that it would be impossible for 'Northern Ireland' to opt out from the new Irish Free State due to the lack of financial assistance it would receive from the British Government under the terms of the Treaty. Of course, behind the scenes, assurances were made by the Chancellor of the Exchequer, Stanley Baldwin, to James Craig that extra finance would be forthcoming in the event of it deciding to exclude itself from the Treaty State established in Dublin. This was the beginning of a system, which was developed by purely administrative methods, in which 'Northern Ireland' ceased to make an effective contribution to the British Exchequer but received regular and substantial subsidies or grants-in-aid from the Treasury in Whitehall, for reasons of Imperial interest.

Collins and Griffith were led to believe that this was an impossibility because 'Northern Ireland', as a 'state' had to stand on its own two feet. But 'Northern Ireland' was, of course, not a 'state' and was never intended to be one.

What Churchill was saying was that the Ulster Unionists had agreed to carry the can for the British Imperial interest in Ireland and to do its dirty work in relation to the Catholic minority—a thing Britain did not want the embarrassment of doing itself, lest it antagonise America. And it therefore deserved to have all the money it wanted to maintain the large paramilitary forces it required to do the job of policing the Catholic minority, which Britain did not wish to use its Imperial forces to do or dirty its hands with.

Churchill knew the facts of the matter better than anyone, having been a member of the Coalition Government which passed the 1920 Act and enforced the Treaty, and who then arranged the financial sustenance to the Ulster Unionists as Chancellor of the Exchequer in the Baldwin Conservative Government. Winston Churchill, unlike his father, had been a vigorous Home Ruler who had gone down the Falls to speak up for it and had threatened civil war against the Unionists after the Curragh Mutiny (before drawing back from his bluster when the possibility of a greater war appeared on the horizon).

So it was perhaps only Churchill who could speak up for what had happened, after all the twists and turns of Imperial policy toward Ireland between 1912 and 1922, since he had the greatest understanding and experience of the whole mess, and the devilish thing that had been put together to get out of it. And if anyone was an architect of it all, who had seen the various plans for Ireland consigned to the dustbin of history after events had overtaken the plans, it was he.

## The Horror Story

So 'Northern Ireland' had been created to serve the Imperial purpose with regard to Ireland in the light of the tumultuous events of the decade, 1912-22. The Ulster Unionists had 'taken a hit' and made 'a great sacrifice' in accepting a semi-detached provincial form of Home Rule so that Britain's influence on Ireland as a whole could be maintained in future. A political entity had been created that nobody in Ireland, Unionist or Nationalist, wanted but which would maintain a normal and useful antagonism by the provision of a sizable minority and a Parliament that facilitated the juices to stew. 'Northern Ireland' would also act as a prize that the part of Ireland that was lost would always aspire to, but never obtain without doing Britain's bidding—thereby giving Britain continued leverage and the potential of ideological subversion on the part of the island that it had been forced to let go of.

And Pharaoh said: "*I will let you go, but you will not go far*".

So leverage, in perpetuity, was aimed to be created on that which was lost to Britain by that which was held by Britain—but held out temptingly to that which had been lost in the hope that it would never be completely lost and might be regained, someday, in one way or another.

Harrison sums up the consequences of the horror story very well in this passage:

"Ulster was established with separate institutions in an area partitioned off from the parent Ireland, for Imperial and not for local reasons, and it was subsequently subsidised at the cost of the British taxpayer for the purpose of inducing and enabling it to continue thus to serve British Imperial policy... The Irish nation... was carved up to retard its growth and to impede its progress. And this mutilation was so devised, with its creation of a new minority grievance, as to ensure the perpetuation of the sectional and sectarian rancours which it should be the first duty of all honest Statesmanship to assuage. The conditions necessarily created local irritation. And the fears haunting the privileged majority lest the victimised minority might seek effective redress, forthwith produced the repressive system of such draconian severity as to swell that irritation into a chronic and expiable resentment. If the policy of Partition in Ireland had been honestly intended, as a measure of minority protection, the Partition area would have been much smaller, and the privileged majority ensconced in its new domain would have had fewer causes for fear and much less embarrassment in the administration of its self government" (pp. 40-1.).

The thing that makes Henry Harrison so interesting is that, while he abhorred Partition, he was prepared to give Britain the benefit of the doubt for Partitioning Ireland if it had done it as an honest attempt to deal with the Ulster complication. But he was completely correct in arguing that Britain did not Partition Ireland and establish 'Northern Ireland' as a reluctant necessity but as an active Imperial policy in its own interests, which brought nothing resembling 'good government' to the Six Counties and had disastrous effects for both Ulster Protestant and Irish Catholic.

The establishment by Westminster of the perverse system of devolution at Stormont established the oppression of one community by another as the necessary condition of the continuation of 'Northern Ireland'. It set the peculiar context in which Catholic political activity would take place within an eternal communal conflict with those assigned to be their masters, who held the whip-hand over them.


## Escaping into Fianna Fail?

Having experienced the pointlessness of politics within the simulacrum Parliament in the pseudo-state the Northern Nationalists tried something else to escape their predicament. They made attempts to dissolve themselves into Fianna Fail between 1928 and 1933.

In 1928 Devlin went to Dublin and proposed a merger to De Valera, Leader of Fianna Fail. But Dev would have none of it and even refused to give Devlin any advice on whether to return to Stormont after he had rebuffed his attempt to take part in National politics.

But despite this cold-shouldering large numbers of Border Nationalists crossed into the South in 1933 to campaign for Fianna Fail and they raised fighting funds for De Valera's bid to secure an overall majority in the Dáil. De Valera's bid to secure a majority in the Dáil seems to have been a significant political event in the lives of Belfast Catholics (but which ultimately came to nothing and was largely forgotten). The *Irish News* produced a special Sunday edition to mark Fianna Fail's election triumph in January 1933. The *Irish News* offices were surrounded by a crowd of thousands to view the display of election results on a screen and the publication of the special edition marking De Valera's victory. It was the first time a northern daily newspaper produced a Sunday edition since 1882, after the shooting of Lord Cavendish in the Phoenix Park, Dublin.

In the 1930s, Eamonn Donnelly from Newry, who found himself both a Northern Nationalist MP and Fianna Fail TD, argued for Dev's party to contest elections throughout Ireland. He advocated a policy of boycotting the Belfast Parliament and taking up seats in the Dáil instead. But he was opposed by De Valera who argued disingenuously that organising formally in the North would further split Northern Nationalism. (He was disingenuous because it was clear that practically all sections of Northern Nationalism from Devlinites to Republicans would have welcomed something meaningful to do in National politics.)

The Northern Nationalists put up De Valera as a candidate for South Down in the 1933 Election in the North, even though Dev had decided on a withdrawal strategy from the North by this time and was extremely reluctant to refight his old seat from the Sinn Fein days.

Northern Republicans in Co. Down had no problem with Dev's candidature but it prompted a vigorous response from Southern Sinn Fein, which could not understand why the Northerners were so lacking in a distinct political position on the Treaty divide. Under the heading 'Who let the North down?' *An Phoblacht*, the Dublin Sinn Fein newspaper, launched a vicious attack on Northern Nationalists, who were condemned for their 'anti-national' behaviour and failure to fully embrace Republican separatism:

> "Up to the early part of 1920 the number of active volunteers there was infinitesimal. It was only the sectarian riots in Belfast and Derry which drove large numbers into the ranks of the republican army. It was a gesture of self-defence and nothing more... when the treaty came, nowhere was it supported more scurrilously and venomously than in the Six Counties. The number who joined the Free State Army from the north east was far in excess in proportion to the relative geographical dimension of those who joined in the rest of Ireland" (27.10.33).

*An Phoblacht* suggested that the North had "let itself down" in its "self-pity" and its opposition to Parnell, Devlin's 1916 acquiescence in Partition, and in voting for the Irish Party when the rest of the country had gone over to Sinn Fein in 1918. It had foolishly put faith in the Boundary Commission and had now transferred its "same slavish dependence" over from the Free State to the Republican sell-out, De Valera.

The article showed a complete lack of understanding for the Northern Catholic predicament but it demonstrated the big difference between the political cleavage over the Treaty within Southern politics and the lack of it within Northern Nationalism.

The 'constitutional' Nationalists in the North often agreed with the Northern Republicans that attendance at both Stormont and Westminster was futile and they frequently abstained from attending these chambers. And they also had little problem with the use of force except being of the view that it would be ineffective and counter-productive in the situation in which they found themselves.

Indeed, it would be safe to say that a substantial majority of Northern Nationalists would have backed the use of force if there were any chance it would have got them out of 'Northern Ireland.' In the 1950s for instance, Cahir Healy, who had moved freely between 'constitutional' and non-constitutional Nationalism, told a large convention in Omagh that although he was opposed to the selection of Sinn Fein candidates for the forthcoming Westminster election he was "not opposed to physical force" but "the time selected should offer some chance of success" (IN, 21.5.55).

Anti-Treaty Republicanism and Northern Nationalism were like oil and water. After the events of August 1969 there was a brief confluence between them but then they started to go their separate ways again.

## Southern withdrawal

Academics have largely ignored the position that Southern Republicans, from pre-1927 Sinn Fein to Fianna Fail, took to Northern Catholics. If they have said anything about it, it hasn't been of any significance. A book by Stephen Kelly about Fianna Fail and Partition has just been published. But the only person who has gone into this important matter and said anything worthwhile about it up until now, to my knowledge, is Joe Keenan in the *'Irish Political Review'*.

That is despite the fact that the position that developed within Southern Republicanism with regard to the North, from Collins to De Valera and beyond, had very important implications for the Northern Catholic predicament within the Six Counties.

A day after the Treaty was signed a delegation representing both Sinn Féin and Devlin's surviving remnant of the Irish Parliamentary Party arrived in Dublin with a request for advice. They met Eoin MacNeill, one of Sinn Féin's Northerners who now lived in the South but who had a second Dáil seat North of the Border, and De Valera. But advice was unforthcoming from Dublin on how the Northerners should deal with their predicament, and a general pretence was kept up that everything would be alright in the end, Partition would not last etc.

This seems to have been part of a general movement that was developing in Southern Republicanism to keep the Northerners at arm's length in order not to interfere with the main issue in their eyes—the relationship of the new Irish State with the British Empire. And it was also a product of not really having a clue about what to do in relation to the Northern complication posed by Ulster Protestant opposition.

Of course, Collins had a more direct use for the Northerners, but his erratic behaviour in relation to the Northern IRA between the Treaty split and his death, in which he first used Six County Republicans as an instrument of warfare (or utilised them in preparation for later warfare) and then abandoned them to their fate, when his conspiratorial activity went bankrupt, had lasting repercussions in the North.

The cutting adrift of the North was formalised when the Second Dail, which still had representatives from the Northern Catholic community within it, was subsumed by the 'Parliament of Southern Ireland', as part of the British Treaty requirements, which excluded them.

This was anticipated in the Collins/De Valera Pact which attempted to hold the Republican forces together in relation to the Treaty and the imposed elections of June 1922. The Provisional Government's Law Officer warned Collins that the inclusion of Northern MPs in any future Free State assembly was forbidden by the British in the Treaty. Collins took the advice seriously and excluded them.

Although both Sean MacEntee and Harry Boland raised the issue of excluding the Northern representatives from having a voice on the Treaty and how it would entrench Partition by shattering the integrity of national politics, they were not answered on this point by either Collins or Griffith in the Dail debates over the Treaty. Presumably they gave no answer because they had no answer.

## De Valera and the North

It was in relation to De Valera, who was to fulfil Collins' 'stepping stones' policy when in power during the 1930s, that the longest and most lasting effects were produced by Southern disengagement.

Writing in the 'Irish Political Review' of September 2007, Joe Keenan argued:

"Devlin's Hibernianism survived to thrive in the Six Counties because the pre-Treaty leadership of Sinn Féin was determined that it should do so. That leadership deliberately held back the growth of its own party organisation there in order not to find itself bound by a strong Northern section of Sinn Féin to oppose partition. On the heights of the party organisation, to his fellow mountaineers, de Valera made it clear that he (correctly) favoured an independent over a united Ireland. He was determined to carry Sinn Féin with a partitionist settlement that guaranteed independence for the greater part of the national territory, and entirely willing to sacrifice the nationalists of the Fourth Green Field to that end... The ruthless hypocrisy of de Valera's machinations is disgusting. But at the core of it all his thinking was correct. Ireland could be free of England or it could be united. It couldn't be both… At all events, such remained de Valera's policy throughout his career."

De Valera seems to have formed a position on Partition quickly after the 1920 Act—seeing it as a British device to impede national independence by holding out the prospect of unity on good behaviour. In January 1921 Collins wished to fight the Devlinites in the North but De Valera instead made a pact with them, which effectively ensured their continued existence outside Belfast (a fact that Devlin admitted in a letter to Dillon in April, 1921).

Joe Keenan says that De Valera's policy originated with this 1921 Sinn Fein deal that carved up the Northern constituencies in conjunction with their political opponents, the Parliamentary Party, so that the Six Counties could be kept at this safe distance:

"In 1921 de Valera negotiated Joe Devlin's survival with him. He could easily have left Devlin with West Belfast and taken the rest of the North. He could easily have split the constituencies with him on the understanding that successful UIL candidates would take their seats in the Dáil. But he did neither. He split the constituencies with Devlin on a nod and a wink and the satisfaction of keeping the North at arm's length" ('*Irish Political Review*', January 2006).

## Keeping the North out

De Valera seemed to be aware, from an early stage, of what 'Northern Ireland' actually was and what it functioned as within the Imperial scheme for the whole island. It was there to gain leverage over the part of the island that could achieve independence and Dev was determined it would not by distancing the Twenty-Six Counties from it.

At the first Fianna Fail Ard Fheis in November 1926 De Valera opposed the extension of the party into the Six Counties, despite maintaining that Fianna Fail was intended to be an all Ireland organisation like Sinn Fein. De Valera argued that conditions in the Twenty-Six and Six Counties were very different and they required different treatment. Sean Lemass and Gerald Boland were eager that Fianna Fail should extend its operations into the Six Counties but they bowed to Dev's insistence that a representative conference of Republicans in that area be convened prior to establishing the party in the North. This was, in essence, a holding operation by De Valera.

In early 1928 a committee of Fianna Fail members, including Lemass, Boland and Sean T Kelly, travelled to the Six Counties to investigate the possibility of the party contesting the forthcoming elections. The Bishop of Clogher, Dr. McKenna, reported that the time was opportune for Fianna Fail to set up in the North and there seems to have been great enthusiasm amongst the prominent Nationalists they met that they did so. However, the committee recommended that organisation should be postponed for the immediate future, until Fianna Fail achieved power in the South.

But, when Fianna Fail took power in 1932, the party no longer debated the issue of Northern organisation. The main reason given thereafter for non-participation in the Six Counties was that Fianna Fail's aim was to "consolidate" and "not divide Northern Nationalism" (see John Bowman, *De Valera and the Ulster Question, 1917-73*, p. 133).

In his exclusive interview with the *Irish News* in its special Sunday edition after his election victory of January 1933, De Valera stated that the North could "look forward with hope" because "forces greater than the will of any individual are making for the restoration of National Unity" which "will prevail". He had been asked by the *Irish News* "if he had any plans in regard to Partition and if he would initiate any negotiations with the Northern Government with a view to ending Partition?" De Valera replied:

> "The time has not yet come. The majority in the Six Counties have not yet shown the disposition to consider this matter in a reasonable spirit. We can afford to wait" (IN 29.1.33).

That reply must have been dispiriting for the Northern Catholics who had so enthusiastically greeted De Valera's majority. The *Irish News* hoped that "National Unity" would be the uppermost issue in "the next stage of Ireland's national development". But it seemed that it was a case of the North must wait!

When Cahir Healy requested Fianna Fail intervention in 1934 in by-elections in Belfast, Tyrone and Fermanagh he was fobbed off.

Stephen Kelly in *Fianna Fail, Partition and Northern Ireland, 1926-1971* notes how De Valera continued to resist his party's involvement in the Six Counties. Throughout the 1930s Eamonn Donnelly persistently called on Fianna Fail to organise on an all Ireland basis and he was incensed at De Valera's refusal to extend the party's organisation across the border. Donnelly had been Sinn Fein's chief organiser during the early 1920s and was a founder member of Fianna Fail. He heckled De Valera at the Fianna Fail Ard Fheis in 1933 and shouted: 'What about the North?'

In 1938 Northern Nationalists hoped that De Valera's negotiations with Chamberlain would take in the issue of Partition as well as the Treaty Ports, annuities and trade. Cahir Healy and others went to London to press the importance of this on Dev. But De Valera's main objective was to consolidate and enhance Twenty-Six County independence and he was careful not to let the Partition issue interfere with the negotiations. He got Healy to organise a series of rallies in the Autumn of 1938 to support the launch of his Anti-

Partition campaign in Britain.

With the British declaration of war on Germany, some meetings were held between De Valera and a delegation of Northern Nationalists led by Cahir Healy, under the auspices of Cardinal MacRory of Armagh. Dev made it clear to the Northerners that independence and sovereignty could not be risked in the pursuit of unity. (Kelly, *Fianna Fail, Partition and Northern Ireland 1926-1971*, pp. 95-6).

De Valera also maintained his opposition to the extension of Fianna Fail to the Six Counties. In July 1939, at a meeting at the Fianna Fail parliamentary party, he stated his view that members should not agree to select Fianna Fail candidates to run in the elections in the North. During the Second World War further calls for Fianna Fail to be reconstituted on an all Ireland basis were rejected by the party hierarchy. And at the 1939, 1944 and 1945 Ard Fheiseanna, Fianna Fail supporters expressed anger that the organisation was not making any attempt to set up branches in the Six Counties.

After 1945 Fianna Fail's leadership continued its boycott. In 1948, in the party's National Executive Publicity Subcommittee, Eoin Ryan and Basil Clancy recommended that the organisation be extended into the Six County area but they were ignored by De Valera. Further motions put forward during the Fianna Fail *Ard Fheiseanna* in 1949 and 1953 for the extension of the Fianna Fail organisation into the North were similarly opposed by the party leadership.

Stephen Kelly notes:

> "Speaking in 1953, de Valera admitted that Fianna Fail had considered the establishment of the organisation in Northern Ireland, but decided that it would be 'far better to stand aside, and to allow the people of the Six Counties to form a political organisation which would suit their own needs.' If Fianna Fail crossed the border, he explained, it was likely to 'create more difficulties than the solution of difficulties, and would be very unwise.' 'The people in the Six Counties', he said, 'have different problems from a political point of view.' He was adamant that such a venture was politically futile considering that from a practical point of view little success could be made given the Ulster Unionist dominance of Northern Ireland politics....'" (p.36).

Kelly reveals that Tommy Mullins, Fianna Fail's General Secretary from 1945 to 1973, concluded shortly before his death in 1976 that Fianna Fail's decision not to extend its organisation into the Six Counties "was a major 'mistake.' 'Representatives from the North', he explained, 'advised us that it would only worsen matters if we organised Fianna Fail in the North. We accepted this advice... but looking back I feel we did the wrong thing. We should have organised there long ago.'" (p.36).

Neil Blaney suggested that the Southern-based Northerners active in the party, like Sean MacEntee and Frank Aiken, had a significant say in preventing the organisation from extending into Northern Ireland. Kelly concludes:

> "For many supporters the Fianna Fail leadership's reluctance to establish the party in Northern Ireland represented a paradox; Fianna Fail was preaching anti-partitionism and unity, the orthodox policy for such a party would be to organise throughout the thirty-two counties and adopt an abstentionist policy in Northern Ireland elections..." (p.37).

## De Valera's admission

De Valera avoided stating his policy explicitly but it was disclosed years later, on the 7th February 1939. The admission occurred in a Seanad debate initiated by two Independent Senators, Frank MacDermot and Ernest Alton, who were looking for compromises to be made by the South to assuage the Ulster Unionists in a hope of reconciling them to a united Ireland. However, an Amendment was introduced to their motion by a Fianna Fail Senator, Sean O'Donovan, who was unhappy at De Valera's lack of vigour on Anti-Partitionism, and who called for Britain to immediately evacuate the Six Counties and for the Free State to assume control of them.

In the course of a long speech in which De Valera outlined his views on the evils of Partition and the Anti-Partitionist efforts his Government had made in relation to influencing the British Government and internationally the Taoiseach stated that he was no pacifist with regard to the Border and would use force, if he had enough of it at his disposal, to incorporate the Border regions where Catholics were a majority and desired to be part of the Free State. His argument was that these regions, as opposed to the predominantly Unionist parts of Ulster, were held by force, and therefore it was legitimate for force to be used to free them.

However, De Valera said he would never sacrifice an *'Irish-Ireland'* i.e. the restoration of the Irish language, in an attempt to end Partition as that would lead to *"absorption"*:

> "And there is another price I would not pay. Suppose we were to get unity in the country provided we were to give up the principles that are here in this first Article of the Constitution—the 'sovereign right of the nation to choose its own form of Government, to determine its relations with other nations, and to develop its life, political, economic, and cultural, in accordance with its own genius and traditions'—I would not sacrifice that right, because without that right you have not freedom at all. Although freedom for a part of this island is not the freedom we want— the freedom we would like to have, this freedom for a portion of it, freedom to develop and to keep the kernel of the Irish nation is something, and something that I would not

sacrifice, if by sacrificing it we were to get a united Ireland and that united Ireland was not free to determine its own form of Government, to determine its relations with other countries, and, amongst other things, to determine, for example, whether it would or would not be involved in war. Our people have the same right as any other people to determine these vital matters for themselves and they ought not to surrender them in advance to anybody or for any consideration. Certainly, as far as this Government is concerned, we are not going to surrender that right—for any consideration, even the consideration of a united Ireland" (*Seanad Debates*, 7.2.39, col. 989-90).

This was De Valera giving the most explicit indication of his policy that Anti-Partitionism should never impinge on the Nation's march to sovereign independence and if there were ever a conflict between the two objectives of Irish unity and independence there was no contest. And, in effect, because of the Imperial design and purpose of 'Northern Ireland', that meant that Irish independence would, through necessity, have to be Partitionist.

Eamon Phoenix's work in the archives backs this up. He found that the minutes of an "interview between An Taoiseach and a northern Nationalist Deputation" record De Valera stating to the Northerners that "the retention of the 26 county status was considered to be of such value that the loss of it could not be risked in any effort to reintegrate the country..." (*Northern Nationalism*, p. 389).

After De Valera's comments and at the request of Eamonn Donnelly a special meeting of Fianna Fail's National Executive was convened to discuss the party's attitude to Partition. A similar motion to Donnelly's amendment in the Seanad was presented to it but De Valera managed to persuade the Executive not to endorse it.

As a result of this Donnelly left Fianna Fail, went North, and stood for Sinn Fein in the Falls district, being elected on an abstentionist basis as a Stormont MP in 1942.

De Valera's pursuit of independence through Irish neutrality in Britain's Second World War on Germany emphasised Dev's position to Northerners of not allowing affairs in the Six Counties to affect the march of the Irish State toward sovereignty. This led Healy to complain in The Irish Press that Fianna Fail had "washed its hands" of Northern Catholics as the Treatyites had in 1925 (29.9.44).

## Sacrificing the North for independence

Joe Keenan makes the following comments on De Valera's strategic approach to the North:

"De Valera was entirely correct that freedom from English politics and

English wars was incompatible with the compromises the strong Unionist minority, which unity would have saddled him with, were sure to demand and win... Partition was the essential precondition of a Republic in the greater part of Ireland. De Valera knew that. And de Valera said that, in only slightly coded form, in the smoke-filled rooms of high political life. He never said it publicly. Publicly he always denied it. And publicly he always appeared to be working to undo partition while privately he did his best to shore it up. Tomorrow was no doubt to be another day when all manner of wrongs would be put right. But tomorrow never came" (*Irish Political Review*, September 2007).

The *Catholic Bulletin* (whose driving force, Fr. Timothy Corcoran, had taught De Valera and was a close friend) writing in 1938, in '*The History of the Struggle Recalled*' (by *Fear Faire*) was of the opinion, with De Valera, that the North was the last piece in the National jigsaw. But the jigsaw needed completing before the last piece was added, lest putting the last piece in prematurely might spoil the rest of the jigsaw.

Perhaps Dev's policy could be compared to Lenin's and Stalin's in consolidating power within the territory it was possible to hold before moving forward in pursuit of the fuller objective at some future date.

What De Valera achieved was an effective buffer to Northern interference (and in consequence, British interference) in Twenty-Six County affairs and his independence project. It prevented Northern Republicans muddying the waters with talk of Partition and diverting energies away from the national struggle which De Valera believed must be achieved in the rest of the island before Partition could be tackled.

But it also sealed Northern Catholic politics off into a kind of Devlinite Ice Age, interrupted by short periods where frustration boiled over into electing Republicans.

Fianna Fail claimed a right of sovereignty over the Six Counties in its 1937 Constitution but it never possessed an army to put it into effect. However, it also chose not to stand candidates in the North in any formal way and to show everyone how things should be done.

It chose then, to all intents and purposes, to be 'a hurler on the ditch' in relation to the North.

That coupled with Britain's enforced exclusion of the Northern Catholics from the party politics of the UK ensured that they were cut adrift from State politics in both jurisdictions. They were effectively sealed into a box marked: "Closed in 1921. Not to be opened under any circumstance"

They would have to fight their way out of that box themselves.

# 1935 — The Catholic predicament illustrated

The Catholic political predicament in 'Northern Ireland' was illustrated by what happened in 1935. In the previous couple of years there had been a sharpening of the communal antagonism brought about by factors like economic depression, rising unemployment, and perhaps Nationalist enthusiasm over De Valera's political successes. In 1932 there had been attacks on Catholics journeying south to the Eucharistic Congress. It seems that a small rise in Catholic confidence after a decade of disaster could not be borne easily by Unionism within the sectarian framework of the Six County construct.

This was followed by a number of provocative speeches made by the Stormont Minister of Agriculture and future Prime Minister of 'Northern Ireland', Sir Basil Brooke. Brooke told Unionists not to employ Catholics who he described as "99 per cent disloyal" and "out to cut their throats if opportunity arose" (Hepburn, *Conflict and Nationality in Northern Ireland*, p.164) When Cahir Healy at Stormont described this statement as "a disgrace to the government", the Prime Minister, Lord Craigavon, shocked the Nationalists by fully endorsing Brooke's sentiments on behalf of the government, stating "there is not one of my colleagues who does not entirely agree with him" (Stormont *Debates* March 1932, v., xv., cols 612-8).

Nationalists saw this as an economic pogrom but were quickly confronted by a physical one in July 1935. Its organisers included a new militant Unionist organisation called the Ulster Protestant League, which was inspired by the activities of the SA (Sturmabteiling) in Germany. Over four hundred Catholic homes were burned, a dozen lives lost and hundreds put out of their jobs.

T.J. Campbell asked Craigavon for an Inquiry into the disturbances, during which British troops were deployed, but was refused. Craigavon blamed "a certain section in our national life who are disloyal to the Throne and Constitution in these Realms" for the trouble (*Fifty Years of Ulster*, p.31). The Nationalists then attempted to bring their case to Westminster, and there was an all-party meeting held in Committee Room 14 in the House of Commons, attended by over 100 MPs.

The employment of British troops on the streets of the Six Counties, for the first time since the Unionists were handed responsibility for these aspects of law and order, drew attention to 'Northern Ireland' in Westminster. The all-party meeting passed a resolution calling for an extensive Inquiry into the disturbances. However, Stanley Baldwin, the Prime Minister, rebuffed the demand by referring to the matter being,

"... entirely within the discretion and responsibility of the Government of Northern Ireland and for fundamental Constitutional reasons the possibility of holding an inquiry by the Imperial Government is completely ruled out"

(Fifty Years of Ulster, p.33).

Having been frustrated in drawing attention to their plight by the State that held overall responsibility for what went on the Six Counties, the Northern Nationalists went south to try to obtain a hearing. However, De Valera was just as unresponsive to the Catholic predicament in the North. He declined to meet a delegation of Northern MPs at the height of the crisis and to become involved in Northern affairs which were, for the Leader of Fianna Fail, matters for decision "in the areas immediately concerned". And De Valera maintained continuity with the Free Staters in refusing to raise the grievances of the Northern Catholics at the League of Nations in Geneva (Staunton, Northern Nationalism, p.380)

The events that occurred between De Valera's taking of power in the South in 1933 and the Pogrom of 1935 made it clear to the Six County Catholics what a tight spot they had been placed in by the establishment of 'Northern Ireland'. They had been quarantined, not only by the Imperial Government, but by the part of the Irish Nation they had been cut off from. They were the fall guys for the mess that had resulted from the events of 1912-25. And it was determined by all and sundry that their plight should not be allowed to contaminate the destinies of those who had believed they had escaped that mess.

# CHAPTER EIGHT

# Marooned

There is one consistent and reliable source, which gives a good account of the social and political life of Northern Nationalists over the last hundred years. That is the community's only and, consequently, representative daily newspaper, the *Irish News*.

For a brief period of fifteen months there were two Northern Catholic newspapers after the *Irish News* was launched on 15th August 1891, in opposition to the *Morning News*. This occurred during the Parnell split in the Home Rule Party. Those who controlled the *Morning News* supported Parnell, but the popular Nationalist base, particularly in Belfast, was strongly clericalist and anti-Parnell. The new *Irish News*, which took up the motto *'Pro Fide et Patria'*—For Faith and Fatherland—and emphasized the connections between Catholicism and Nationalism, quickly put its rival out of business.

It remained the primary voice of the Northern Catholics ever since.

## Fifty Years of Ulster

During 1941 the *Irish News* published T.J. Campbell's autobiography, *Fifty Years of Ulster, 1890-1940*. T.J. Campbell was the most influential Nationalist politician in the thirties and early forties, following the death of Joe Devlin, and his views were entirely consistent with the general outlook of Northern Nationalists during the period. His autobiography is the most useful account of Nationalist politics during the early Stormont period.

After talking about his early life, his work for the *Irish News* and the trauma of Partition, Campbell gave the following summary of Nationalist politics in the Six Counties:

> *"Nationalists and the Six County Parliament*
>
> "At the first General Election in Northern Ireland on 21 May, 1921, the Unionists captured 40 seats, the Nationalists 6, and the Sinn Feiners 6... All 12 declined to take their seats... The second Parliament was opened on 14th March 1925. A fortnight later Joseph Devlin and Thomas M'Allister (afterwards Senator) attended the temporary Parliament House in the Assembly's College, College Green, Belfast, in response to a call from a representative conference in Belfast of Nationalists from Belfast and County Antrim, at which I took the chair. Three other Nationalists joined them in March 1926. In October and November, 1927, four others took their seats...

"In these two Parliaments the Nationalists declined to constitute an official opposition. This tradition has been consistently observed. They never elected a Sessional Chairman, an office which Parnell held in the Irish Parliamentary Party. Devlin would not accept the office. In actual practice, however, he was called upon to preside at their meetings...

"During the debate on the Budget on the 11th May, 1932 Devlin and his colleagues walked out of the House in protest against the Speaker's ruling that the Reserved Services could not be discussed. Devlin did not return. He never sat in Stormont.

"The Parliamentary and Administrative Buildings at Stormont were officially declared open by the Duke of Windsor—then Prince of Wales—on 17th November 1932. The Nationalists did not present an appearance at Stormont until 3rd. October, 1933, and only did so after mature deliberation.

"In the parliament which met after the General Election in January, 1934, the attendance of Nationalists, with three or four exceptions, slackened. In the Parliament which met after the General Election in January 1938, abstention was the rule, except in the case of Alderman Byrne and myself, who gave intermittent attendance conditioned by questions affecting school and working class and other interests coming up. I went there of duty, not of desire.

"In the 1938 election conventions in South Down, South Armagh and Mourne—three Nationalist constituencies—resolved to nominate no Nationalist candidate and appealed to Nationalist voters to keep away from the polls. The three seats were lost to the Unionists...

"If a minority anywhere are to regard themselves as condemned to be in a permanent minority in Parliament, with no inducement to tempt ambition or ability into their ranks, they will inevitably become discouraged and indifferent. A parliamentary constitution depends on the continuation of parties, and if this factor is eliminated the constitution will of itself cease to exist. Parliamentary government will fall into contempt. The system will collapse..." (pp. 105-7).

What Campbell wrote in his last paragraph was very true and it was indeed prophetic in the last sentence. The Stormont system could only end up breeding disillusionment and discontent within nationalist political life.


## Single issue politics

The Nationalist Party's policy was directed toward one end—achieving reunion with the rest of the country. All other matters were secondary and futile.

Joe Devlin had imagined that he could utilise social reform against the Unionist Government but in the early years of the 'Northern Ireland' Government Craig gave priority to establishing parity in social welfare with

Britain. R.J. Lawrence's book, *The Government of Northern Ireland*, tells how the Unionist Government took over an area in which social services were well below British standards and set about improving them to the level of Britain. Westminster would have readily allowed the North to drift along with a much more rudimentary degree of welfare but the Unionists insisted on Britain taking its responsibility in maintaining the social services of the 'Northern Ireland' region of the state. In 1932 during the Great Depression there was considerable trouble in both Protestant and Catholic areas of Belfast during the Outdoor Relief Strike but, once the Unionist Government forced the Belfast Guardians to raise their rates, politics returned to the normal communal conflict.

The only issue in 'Northern Ireland' elections was whether the Six Counties should remain a part of the UK or unite with the rest of the island. There was never a question of how the state should be governed—as is the case in normal democracies. The Northern Catholics really only turned up to vote to register their existence, to indicate that their existence had increased (through breeding at a higher level than Protestants) or to score a small victory over the Unionists by maximising the effect of their votes through more effective electoral practice.

They felt and instinctively understood who it might be best to vote for in particular circumstances and times and as a result transferred their votes from 'constitutional' Nationalists to non-constitutional Republicans and back again without paying too much heed to their political programmes—which were unrealisable in 'Northern Ireland' in any case.

Elections were always shadow-boxing and largely point-scoring events with no chance of a knock-out blow being landed by either side.

The British had established the Anti-Home Rule Unionists in dominance within the territory it was possible for them to dominate. But the minority which they had to dominate to remain in existence was so large that the Ulster Unionists had to remain a solid bloc at all events.

This, in turn, ensured that the minority was predisposed to remain as solid as possible a bloc to counter their domination. And so politics could go nowhere else but this communal routine that resembled the war of attrition on the Western Front.

The battle-lines were drawn in perpetuity, every periodic battle was for minor tactical advantage and the battlefield was always Partition.

As Campbell's book reveals, Northern Catholics were an intensely political community. The fact that the Nationalists did not wish to involve themselves in the affairs of the Belfast Parliament did not make them any less so.

The Catholic community, eager for politics, wished to immerse themselves in the politics of the Free State, and tried to accomplish this through

Fianna Fail. But, while the Catholic community wished to live apart from the Stormont system, and were given every encouragement to do so by Unionists, they remained avid and enthusiastic for politics, as T.J. Campbell's autobiography shows.

## The futility of 'constitutionalism'

The ultimate futility of the 'constitutional' approach was reflected in the lack of party organisation in the Nationalist Party, which had little organic life outside Stormont. One observer of this later noted:

> "The Nationalist Party at Stormont… was purely a parliamentary group. It had no constituency units. When an election was called, a constituency convention was summoned, generally under the auspices of a Catholic priest, and the delegates representing the various Catholic parishes decided whether to contest the election and whether the selected candidate should take the seat if elected. If elected and in attendance, the M.P. was then accepted as a Nationalist M.P. That was the system, and of course it broke down easily. Procedural disagreements at conventions were frequent with several candidates emerging, thus creating an electoral split which enabled Unionists to win Nationalist seats. Nor could the system withstand any organised takeover bid, and whenever Sinn Fein decided to contest Westminster seats there was no machinery to oppose them" (Michael McKeown, *The Greening of a Nationalist*, p. 18).

The contrast with the rigorously organised Northern Home Rule Party of Joe Devlin and his Hibernian shock-troops, who conquered as far south as Cork, could not have been stronger. Decades of fruitless political activity after Northern Nationalists had been cut out of the political life of the State led to 'much ado about nothing' — great flurries of political activity at election time which were ultimately rendered useless by the inability to bring about any substantial change.

And, of course, even if the Nationalist Party had been the slickest electoral machine in history it would have mattered little. Their political activity would have still been rendered entirely futile by the political system within which they were trapped, which cut them off from the meaningful political activity that was taking place in the real states to the south and to the east.

In April 1936 the *Irish News* conducted a survey of Northern Nationalism. At this point, just after the death of Joe Devlin, the futility of the 'constitutional' approach was becoming apparent to Northern Catholics and they had swung over to the Republicans at the 1935 Westminster Election.

This is the time when Cahir Healy had contacted De Valera with a mind to get the Taoiseach to try and organise Northern Nationalists under one movement—assuring him that most Border Catholics were Fianna Failers. Healy's action demonstrated how Northern Nationalists tended to follow developments in the South—Healy having previously been a supporter of Griffith, Collins and the Treaty.

The special correspondent of the *Irish News* found Northern Nationalism broken into factions. He divided them into "the peace with Stormont group" and the "no truck with Stormont" group. The nearer to the Border he got the more the latter increased and the more "plantation-conscious" people were. At the frontier in Fermanagh, Tyrone and Armagh the Plantation dominated everyday existence for the Border Catholics, whereas in Belfast it had become merely a "historical fact". This was reflected in the attitude toward Stormont.

In Belfast there was a belief that Stormont was "here to stay in our generation" and a much stronger willingness to engage with the Northern Parliament on social and economic issues. One Nationalist representative contrasted the poor attendance of the Party at Stormont, where only two or three now bothered to attend, to the time, before the establishment of the Northern Parliament, when the Irish Parliamentary Party had engaged with the "great social and economic issues" in the State (IN, 14.4.36).

When Britain declared war on Germany in September 1939 there was absolutely no enthusiasm for fighting for the Empire—as there was in 1914/ 5. A large and successful campaign against the threat of conscription was mounted which united all Northern Nationalists, 'constitutional' and non-constitutional, until Churchill concluded that it would be more trouble than it would be worth to attempt the same thing as in 1918.


## Orange Terror

The most significant expression of the plight of Northern Catholics in the Six Counties came in the form of a pamphlet entitled *'Orange Terror'* by 'Ultach' (Joseph Campbell), which first appeared in the *Capuchin Annual*, 1940 and 1943.

*'Orange Terror'* described how ordinary Catholics in 'Northern Ireland', however willing they might have been to live the quiet life of a peaceable private citizen, came to suffer periodic terror and intimidation through the normal functioning of state authority over them that drove them from their natural conservative nature into a rebellious mentality.

*'Orange Terror'* is significant because it described how the everyday conditions of life for Catholics in 'Northern Ireland' made a peaceful existence impossible. It was written by a middle class Catholic who was predisposed to be an ordinary decent and law-abiding citizen but who was put into an antagonism with the British State in Ulster by its constitutional character.

'Ultach' wrote of his continued regard for the other community:

> "... they have assaulted me, they have tried to shoot me, they have evicted me from my home, they have ruined the prosperity of my family, they have killed my relations, they have reduced me and mine to miserable poverty, and I still find them agreeable and obliging—yes, the very same individuals... So my estimate of the situation must accept all this...
>
> "I do not belong to any political party or organisation. Indeed rightly or wrongly, I am one of those who think all politics in the North to be rotten. In fact, I am very ordinary, and that is why I might be a victim of any of the acts of persecution and oppression" (pp.1-2).

The pamphlet was not an ideological Republican criticism of the Six Counties but a description of why Catholics were alienated from 'Northern Ireland' by the way its political and judicial functioning impacted upon their ordinary lives.

The criticism 'Ultach' made of the Northern Partitionist entity was quite distinct from the usual Anti-Partitionist one. He made the point that the mode of government that operated in 'Northern Ireland' was reprehensible and dysfunctional in its own right, quite apart from the injustice Northern Catholics felt from Partition itself:

> "I should like it to be understood clearly at the outset that I do not regard the present intolerable position of Catholics in the partitionist area as being a necessary consequence of partition as such, but rather the result of a particular form of administration" (p. 7).

'Ultach' described Northern Ireland as a 'totalitarian state' like the Soviet Union or the Third Reich in Germany but with a novel feature absent from these aforementioned regimes:

> "In the Six Counties the Orange-Unionist Party commands the State: the state is its instrument. It has been in control of the state since England established it. But Craigavon did not make the mistake (from the point of view of outside propaganda) of abolishing all other parties in the area. Other parties may exist. New parties may be formed. They may 'contest' elections. There are 'elections' at the usual intervals. The people vote with as much enthusiasm as is shown anywhere these days. The whole business has all the outward marks of a 'democratic' regime: and the whole business is a farce. There is not the slightest chance of any other party gaining control" (p.8).

The Unionist one-party regime which contained so many of the trappings of fascism was the logical working out of the Stormont system imposed on the province by Westminster. 'Ultach' understood that what was peculiar about it was that the undemocratic and totalitarian system of the Six Counties existed within a democratic state that continuously exhibited to the world great propaganda in favour of democracy.

Britain was at war with Fascism—so it said—but within its own territory it established a carefully protected enclave that had many of the hallmarks of Fascism.

It was a practical assumption of the Unionist Government that rebellious tendencies would be generated in the large, frustrated Catholic minority whose energy had no outlet into the democratic life of the State. The routine of 'politics' consisted of the Unionist community voting itself into office at every election in order to remain semi-attached to Britain. The Catholic community played no part in the process because there was no part for it to play. Its role was to be kept down. But it was far too large a minority to be kept down without a continuing sense of unease and generating an atmosphere of threat to the existence of the Northern entity.

The Northern Catholics were therefore subjected to close, intimate supervision by the 'Peelers', made to feel the weight of the 'Specials', and reminded that the UVF, which had brought about their predicament, had never gone away, you know.

The attitude among the Unionist establishment was that it was unfortunate that there should have been such a large body of Catholics within the Ulster idyll, but Fenians will be Fenians, and had to know their place. Of course Croppies should lie down, but it was no matter for great surprise or resentment when they didn't: Hence the very substantial security apparatus that was maintained at the disposal of the Stormont regime.

'Ultach's' pamphlet seems to have been a major event in the life of the Catholics of the Six Counties. This can be seen in the type of people who contributed to the discussion comments printed after his article. These included Bishop Mageean of Down and Connor, Count Plunkett, Maud Gonne MacBride, John Nugent, Ernest Blythe, Maurice Walsh of 'The Quiet Man', T.J. Campbell, Denis Ireland and Eamon Donnelly among others.

Britain did not lack the executive or legislative power or the appropriate means of securing a just and peaceable existence for the Catholics in 'Northern Ireland'. It could have vetoed or suspended any Bill presented by the subordinate Parliament. The 1920 Act also gave the Privy Council the power to test any powers of the Stormont administration it wished and Section 75 provided the means of producing over-riding legislation from Westminster. And there was always the power of the purse held by H.M. Treasury in Whitehall. But Westminster lacked the will to do any of this and continued to allow the sub-Government at Belfast to police the Catholics as they saw fit.

# Jack Beattie, West Belfast and Labour

There was another possible escape route from 'Northern Ireland' and 'Orange Terror'.

Jack Beattie was elected in West Belfast to Westminster in a by-election in 1943 as a Northern Ireland Labour candidate. He was a Protestant elected with Catholic votes. He defeated the Republican candidate by a massive majority and reduced the Unionist vote by a third.

In 1945, after falling out with the NILP, he was re-elected as an 'Independent Labour' candidate. Beattie took part in the great social reform that was occurring, claiming to be a member of the (British) Labour Party. But that Labour Party, in 1948, refused to grant him the Whip, maintaining that, because his home was in Belfast, he did not qualify for membership. However, he still voted with Labour against the Tories on all its reform measures, while the Ulster Unionists voted against. Frustrated with British Labour's attitude, he joined the Irish Labour Party. He lost West Belfast on that ticket in 1950, regained it in 1951, and lost it again in 1955.

Beattie was also a Stormont MP, representing Pottinger in East Belfast. He looked forward to fighting the Unionists there on the same measures that he fought them at Westminster, where they trooped behind Churchill into the lobby against Labour's great reform measures in the interest of the working class. But what happened was that the Unionists re-enacted and rubber-stamped at Stormont as a matter of course all the social reforms which they opposed at Westminster.

Beattie was perplexed at this and he taunted the Unionists at Stormont for acting as Socialists and introducing the self-same legislation that they voted against at Westminster:

> "Mr. Beattie: I am asking the question now, what is a Unionist, and what is a Conservative? If you decide to follow the path of... Churchill and company you have every right to do that. But you have got to play straight... This straightforward path in Unionist politics does not exist in Northern Ireland. You are playing fast and loose with the policy of your party. You know perfectly well that... the major part of the legislation you brought in here was part and parcel of the Socialist policy for the last forty years... Conservatives would not have looked at it...
>
> "The Prime Minister: The hon. Member asked what was a Unionist... He failed to ask what was a Socialist. I think the answer... depends on what you mean by Unionist or Socialist. It is a thing you could argue about for a very long time. We are planning social services which have been agreed upon by all parties on the other side... I think the hon. Member for Pottinger (Mr. Beattie) said that was entirely a Socialist Measure..." (Stormont *Debates*, 10.2.48).

And that is how it was in 'Northern Ireland'. It was an integral part of the

British State for social reform, and many other purposes. And then it had its own peculiar politics, which could never be anything but a communal squabble within which no development was possible.

The Unionists, led by Craigavon and then Brookeborough, minimised the activities of the devolved Parliament, so that the Catholic community could possibly exist without bothering with politics. They did this by taking long holidays and acting as a mere rubber-stamp for Westminster legislation, particularly in maintaining parity with Great Britain in social welfare provision. Lord Craigavon, who set up the devolved Government and ran it for a generation, knew very well that 'Northern Ireland' was a thoroughly abnormal concoction which could not bear very much political activity without there being trouble ahead. The understanding was that 'Northern Ireland' was not a democracy and notions of this sort should be discouraged by inactivity whenever possible.

Lord Craigavon has been famously denounced for saying that Stormont was *"a Protestant Parliament for a Protestant people"*. But that is all it could have been. He simply made the mistake of saying it outright and gifting Nationalists a slogan they could throw in the Unionist face. After Craigavon had set it functioning, what happened in 'Northern Ireland' as a matter of routine was that the Protestant community returned a Unionist majority to Stormont, and the Stormont legislature then re-enacted Westminster legislation, regardless of which party was in power in London.

Whilst the minimalistic approach of Craig and Brookeborough to politics failed to prevent Catholic alienation from the statelet it, at least, had the advantage that it prevented an explosion for nearly half a century.

'Northern Ireland' was excluded from the political life of the British State, though it remained part of it. Pointless political debate was engaged in at Stormont. But social and political reform did not depend on the political debate within the North. It came to 'Northern Ireland' as the outcome of the political debate in the rest of the state.

Political debate in 'Northern Ireland' was therefore doomed to futility. Nothing of any consequence depended on it. The measures of social reform came to the Six Counties as a product of the state from whose politics it was excluded. It was excluded from the politics that produced the measures, and that would undoubtedly have given rise to a substantial body of cross-community political unity, based around people like Jack Beattie, if it had been included.

British Labour closed off another possible escape route for Catholics from their political predicament in 'Northern Ireland'. Catholic West Belfast was willing to vote for Labour in conjunction with Shankill Protestant working class voters disillusioned with Orangeism and the Unionist Party. It produced and elected politicians like Frank Hanna, Harry Diamond, Paddy

Devlin and Gerry Fitt who all would have neatly fitted into the Labour Party at Westminster. They could still have maintained their desire for Irish unity and worked to persuade Protestants in Labour ranks of its desirability.

The Church Hierarchy, the *Irish News* and Catholic bourgeoisie were all opposed to the policies of the British Labour Government, including the construction of the welfare state, the National Health Service and the extension of secondary education. There was talk of Communism and *"sinister influences at work"* and people prevented from helping themselves. But the Catholic working-class ignored the scare-mongering and voted for Beattie, socialism and its own material interests.

Beattie's victories in West Belfast were reminiscent of the Joe Devlin era in the commitment they involved from local people and the celebrations they produced upon victory. Bonfires were lit, there were large firework displays and processions of 15,000 marched along the Falls Road (K. McPhillips, *The Falls, A History* p.32).

By refusing Beattie and West Belfast being part of the great Labour movement that was enacting comprehensive reform in the working-class interest, British Labour maintained the Catholic-Nationalist monolith in the North and prevented the development of class politics across the two communities.

Not only that, by supporting the Unionist Government's step-by-step approach to implementing Labour's welfare state in the North with the required financial assistance, it actually ensured the Unionist Party's hegemony over Protestant workers, who associated material improvement with the Orange State. It, therefore, helped preserve the Protestant monolith under the party which opposed socialism at Westminster but which implemented it at Stormont to facilitated its all-class alliance.

And so, despite the efforts of Beattie, British Labour determined that Catholics remain a communal bloc, dominated in perpetuity by a more numerous and more powerful communal bloc in the provincial backwater it would allow no discussion about.

## Northern Irish Action

After the World War, when De Valera re-launched his Anti-Partitionist campaign, Eamonn Donnelly, now representing the Falls for Sinn Fein, demanded that Fianna Fail establish a committee on Partition that included Northerners. But De Valera refused to let Northerners sit on any Anti-Partition committee his Government was establishing.

This prompted the Northerners to establish their own home-grown *Anti-Partition League* which was convened at a convention of 500 delegates at Dungannon in November 1945.

The main effect of the *Anti-Partition League* in the North was to reconcile the different factions of Northern Nationalism. Devlinites such as T.J. Campbell and T.S. McAllister, Fianna Fail supporters such as Cahir Healy and Eddie McAteer, and some former Republicans—all reunited for the new political project which generated a feeling of purpose amongst ordinary nationalists.

To coincide with this one of the leaders of the Northern Nationalists, Eddie McAteer, launched a plan for civil disobedience, *'Irish Action—New Thoughts on an old Subject'*, published by the *Donegal Democrat* (see *'Irish Action'* republished by Athol Books).

Eddie McAteer's brother, Hugh, had been Chief of Staff of the IRA during the 1940s and contested Westminster elections as a Republican in 1950 and 1964. This was further evidence of the fact that there was a *continuum* between 'constitutional' Nationalism and Republicanism. When the IRA launched a sensationally successful arms raid on Gough Barracks in Armagh during 1954, Eddie, the 'constitutionalist', remarked to Conor Cruise O'Brien of the Department of Foreign Affairs, that this was greatly welcome for "keeping up morale amongst a population which had been cowed and defeated" (cited in Henry Patterson, *Ireland since 1939*, p. 133) This perfectly illustrated the *continuum*.

And it could hardly be said that there was competition between the two wings of Nationalism when elections were shared out between them even within families.

In his *'Foreword'* to the plan for 'Irish Action' Eddie McAteer wrote:

> "I am a member of the Irish Anti-Partition League and I am extremely proud of that organisation. It is, as everyone knows, an entirely constitutional movement and despite provocation it has remained constitutional. In about two years it has accomplished, by a happy combination of good luck, good guidance and good hard work, a grand job in publicising the existence of a border in this small island. It has forced the Partitionists to scurry here and there in frantic efforts to counteract a movement which they professed at the outset to disdain. I hope and pray that the League will continue with its mission despite its many difficulties and the lack of helpfulness which is sometimes imposed from quite surprising places.
>
> "There is, however, an undoubted undercurrent of feeling amongst a growing section of the Irish people that extra-constitutional efforts should be made in order to supplement the League's work." (See Appendiz.)

I don't think that the last sentence could be represented as a threat in any way. It was simply an observation of reality on McAteer's part. The fact that it proved prophetic is neither here nor there. Its real significance lay in emphasizing that there was little real political division within Northern Nationalism despite the factionalism that existed.

Although the *Anti-Partition League* was a development independent of De Valera and Fianna Fail it suited the Taoiseach's insistence that Northerners should be kept at arm's length. The Northern Anti-Partition League complemented Dev's own efforts, could be used as an instrument of his own campaign and had absolutely no influence within Fianna Fail or the Southern State due to its independent character. And that is why Dev liked it so much.

An unwelcome development for De Valera's control of Anti-Partitionism occurred with the establishment of the *Clann na Poblachta* party, led by Sean MacBride, former IRA Chief of Staff and son of one of the executed leaders of 1916. It sought to outflank Fianna Fail on the national question and by being more socially radical and it pledged that if elected it would allow Northern Nationalist MPs entry into the Seanad with audience rights in the Dáil. Sean MacBride wrote to Cahir Healy describing this as "the most constructive" proposal ever put forward from the South and saw it as the way of uniting Northern Nationalism with a renewed purpose (Enda Staunton, *The Nationalists of Northern Ireland*, p.62).

This was something De Valera was intent on preventing after refusing requests by Healy and Devlin for Northern participation in Dáil Eireann in the 1930s and demands within Fianna Fail itself for the right of Northerners to actually take seats in the Dáil.

Fianna Fail described the Clann proposal as a "mock remedy" and "absurd" and its National Executive insisted that all *Cumann* supported party policy on the North and trusted Dev in "getting back the Six Counties as he had the ports". But Fianna Fail were voted out of office in the election of February 1948.

## The Anti-Partition League

The return of a Fine Gael/Clann na Poblachta/Labour Coalition, which included Sean MacBride as Minister for External Affairs, ushered in a new phase in Anti-Partitionism which placed the Border centre-stage.

The decision by the Taoiseach, John A. Costello, to repeal the External Relations Act and declare Ireland officially a Republic provoked the last Westminster interference in the affairs of 'Northern Ireland' for two decades. The 1949 Government of Ireland Act retaliated for Ireland's leaving of the British Commonwealth by recognising the right of the Stormont Parliament to decide on behalf of the people of the Six Counties whether to stay in or leave the UK and Commonwealth.

The Coalition Government then set up an *All-Party Anti-Partition Committee*. MacBride aimed to take Anti-Partitionism out of the party conflict in the Republic by establishing a broad based campaign and consensus on it.

Stormont responded to these moves by calling an election for February 1949.

The Anti-Partitionists held a spectacular conference in the Mansion House, Dublin, on January 27th. It was decided to launch a massive propaganda campaign against Partition led by Frank Gallagher. A book by Gallagher, *The Indivisible Island*, was later issued along with a string of pamphlets with titles such as *'Ireland's Right to Unity'*, *'The Orange Card'*, and *'Discrimination: A Study of Injustice to a Minority'*.

An election fund for Northern Catholics was set up, and it was decided to take collections for it at Catholic Churches throughout the Country the following Sunday. The money collected for the election was given to the Church to keep up an accurate electoral register of Catholics qualified to vote. To select candidates in local constituencies, the clergy called a convention with every Catholic organisation having two delegates.

The result of the election was, however, another predictable victory for the Unionists, and even bigger than usual. The *Northern Ireland Labour Party* was all but wiped out in the polarised atmosphere of the Anti-Partitionist campaign and the Orange vote was encouraged to come out in large numbers to demonstrate their opposition to Dublin rule.

The ratcheting up of Anti-Partitionism and the obvious reverse suffered afterwards, in the Northern election result and the passing of the *Government of Ireland Act* confirming the Unionist veto, encouraged De Valera to wind up his own Anti-Partition campaign in 1950.

By 1951 the *Anti-Partition League* began to fragment in the great anti-climax of achieving nothing and De Valera, who came back to power, began to abandon it and establish contacts with Stormont for mutual benefit instead. Eddie McAteer was outraged and, according to Conor Cruise O'Brien, denounced the new policy as "fraternization" (*Ireland Since 1939*, p.32)

At this point Michael O'Neill, one of the two Nationalist MPs at Westminster, made representations to Dublin to admit Northern Nationalists to the Dail, so that the energies that had been released by the Anti-Partition campaign could be channelled into politics rather than elsewhere. But he was swiftly rebuffed by De Valera like all attempts before had been.

The Nationalists had not been prepared to carry McAteer's policy of passive resistance through to its logical conclusion, and the refusal of the Dublin Government to let them into the Dail destroyed their only other option for purposeful activity. But still Northern Nationalism was not prompted into drawing the only possible conclusion from all this—that they should cease to rely on the South for deliverance and look to themselves for it. It was not until the events of 1969-70 that this conclusion was drawn and really taken in earnest.

The Nationalist Party was challenged by a new republican grouping which, unlike Sinn Fein, recognised the Twenty-Six County State. Liam Kelly of Pomeroy succeeded in capturing Mid-Tyrone, whilst T.B. Agnew, polled well in Mid-Derry. Kelly had been supported by MacBride's Clann Na Poblachta and was subsequently imprisoned for making a seditious speech in Carrickmore.

Kelly's imprisonment led to the launch of a new republican party, *Fianna Uladh*, with a policy of abstentionism from Stormont and recognition of the Dail and support for physical force. In July 1954, the decision of the Dail to return Kelly to the Seanad prompted Cahir Healy to make representations to the Taoiseach, John A. Costello on the setting of a dangerous example in which the physical force policy was being given approval in the South. But Kelly was still able to speak as a Senator, in support of a motion that all elected parliamentary representatives of the people of "the six occupied counties of Ireland" should be given a right of audience in the Dáil or in the Seanad.

## A Fianna Fail Border Campaign?

The Anti-Partitionist campaign of the previous decade had worked up passions in Nationalist Ireland that were not easy to turn off when it ended in failure.

Even within Dev's party there were plenty of people who, having seen the futility of 'constitutional' efforts to end Partition, decided that only other methods were now functional.

The Memorandum of the *Tomas O Cleirigh Cumann* of 1955, sent by Charles Haughey to the Fianna Fail National Executive as a proposal for a more vigorous Fianna Fail policy on the North, is a prime example. This *Cumann* included George Colley, Oscar Traynor, and Harry Boland as well as Haughey, the Hon. Secretary. George Colley's wife, Mary, later told Stephen Kelly that the policy was put together by her husband and Haughey jointly.

The policy, noting De Valera's acknowledgement that Partition could not be ended by "diplomatic measures", argued that the only "policy open to us which gives reasonable hope of success" was the use of force (p.1). It contended that, if the Fianna Fail Government did not take steps to act on this understanding, then it would be responsible for others, i.e. the IRA, acting on it. It went on:

"There is a noticeable and growing discontent with National Inaction in relation to Partition... At present, young people who feel strongly on this question of Partition have no outlet for their feelings of national outrage except the IRA... we believe it is the duty of the Fianna Fail Organisation to provide the leadership and the organisation of such national feeling, and that if it should fail to do so, it will be responsible for the consequences..." (p.1).

It recommended a Government-sponsored military guerrilla campaign, concentrating on Border areas with Catholic majorities, and a campaign of Civil Disobedience involving Northern Catholics. Such a campaign—

"should be controlled and directed by the Irish Government, either openly or secretly. The object of such a campaign would be to create an international incident which could not be ignored by the British Government. The campaign would be based on that adopted by Sinn Fein, i.e. non recognition of British or Stormont sovereignty in the area or areas selected; non-recognition of the Courts, and the setting up of 'Sinn Fein' courts; the withholding of rates and taxes..." (pp.3-4)

The Memorandum then advised that the Irish Government and its small Army should prepare for a campaign of guerrilla warfare as the next stage in the campaign:

" An important preparation would, of course, be in the military sphere. While there is a reasonable hope that negotiations could be forced before the necessity for military action arose, nevertheless it would be criminally negligent to embark on a campaign without having made preparations in our power to deal with every contingency likely to arise. In this connection, we advocate the laying-in of the greatest possible stocks of arms and ammunition suitable for guerrilla warfare, the closest possible study of British military installations likely to be of particular importance in relation to the areas in which the campaign will be carried out..." (p.6).

This would also involve the arming of Northern Nationalists by the Irish Government so that "local forces" could:

"Work in conjunction with the Army in making simulated and diversionary attacks on British military installations if required, plans for the destruction of official British and Stormont records in regard to rates and taxes in the selected areas etc. it would of course be essential to organise nationalist opinion in the Six-counties in general and in the selected areas or areas in particular. We believe that given a positive policy with full support from the South, both materially and spiritually, the necessary co-operation will be obtained from the Northern Nationalists..." (p.6).

Finally, it advocated the setting up of "a committee of experts" to organise the assimilation of the liberated Border areas in preparation for complete unification;

"In this connection, your attention is drawn to the action of the Egyptian government which unofficially organised a liberation Army, consisting of irregular volunteers, but which is believed by many to have consisted mainly of regular army units" (p.6, The Memorandum is quoted in Kelly, *Fianna Fail, Partition and Northern Ireland, 1926-1971*, pp.170-7.).

Many years ago, when I submitted my thesis on Irish Republicanism for the award of a PhD to Queen's University, I was told by Paul Bew that the External Examiner, Professor John A. Murphy, objected to my understanding and depiction of Scelig, Brian O'Higgins, and the IRA as more vigorous spirits within Irish society. Professor Murphy had a view of them as unrepresentative extremists, completely detached from the mainstream Nationalism of Fianna Fail.

I think the Memorandum produced by the *Tomas O Cleirigh Cumann* shows where the truth lies. The IRA's *Operation Harvest*, launched in 1956, was the smaller private enterprise version of what many in Fianna Fail would have liked to see the Government doing, if it had the will.

Unfortunately, no record exists of De Valera's response to the Memorandum, but Haughey was subsequently appointed to Sean Lemass' *Standing Committee on Partition Matters*. It produced a very different Memorandum, which recommended closer co-operation with Stormont particularly on economic practicalities, including the lifting of tariffs and the opening up all-Ireland free trade area. Dev also rejected this new approach.

And so things began to let rip.

## The IRA Border Campaign

The British General Election of 1955 produced a swing in Nationalist politics, from the 'constitutionalists' to the Republicans. The endorsement of Sinn Fein candidates by Nationalist Conventions represented a vote of no confidence in the 'constitutional' approach that had demonstrably failed over the previous decade, and it enabled Sinn Fein to claim a mandate for the launch of a Border campaign in 1956.

Then, between 1956 and 1962, the IRA tried to achieve by military force what the *Anti-Partition League* could not by its 'constitutional' and 'extra-constitutional' methods with a cross-Border campaign. The IRA received a new lease of life from the failed efforts of the *Anti-Partition League*.

The character of the Border campaign was that of a small invasion from the South. What is significant about it was the absence of any activity of significance from Northern Republicans or any action from the Northern Catholics in support of it. (The smaller Republican grouping, *Saor Uladh*, led by Senator Liam Kelly from Pomeroy, was a more Six County affair. But it was opposed by the Southern Anti-Treaty IRA because it recognised the Twenty-Six County State.)

If the IRA had hoped to spark off a rising in the North it was sorely disappointed. There was nothing of the risen people of 1969 about the Campaign. It was a Southern event, waged across the Border by the Southern IRA, with massive funerals in the South for the volunteers who were killed and all-party support in Books of Condolences.

After the Brookeborough Raid, and the massive show of support by Nationalist Ireland at the funerals of Sean South and Fergal O'Hanlon, many Fianna Fail *Cumann* and Councils expressed votes of sympathy and solidarity with the IRA men. This led De Valera to attempt to restore discipline in the ranks by calling a meeting of the Parliamentary Party. The Parliamentary Party, including over eighty deputies and all Senators, convened over an eight-hour period, with Dev chairing proceedings. According to Stephen Kelly the meeting was the most hostile in the party's history, with TDs openly quarrelling with one another over whether the use of physical force was a Fianna Fail policy and many expressing sympathy for the IRA campaign. (See Kelly, *Fianna Fail, Partition and Northern Ireland, 1926-1971*, p.200).

It was Sean Lemass, rather than Dev, who brought the meeting back to order. But his intervention only had a limited effect, according to Kelly:

"Lemass's intervention at the parliamentary meeting did not prove altogether successful... After considerable debate, those present decided that 'there could be no armed force... except under the control and direction of the Government' and that 'the employment of force at any time in the foreseeable future would be undesirable and likely to be futile'. Paddy Hillary remembered that while it was a 'decision not easily arrived at', party members had 'definitely' agreed that 'whatever happens in the North we're not going in there.' His recollection is, however, at variance with the official minutes of the parliamentary party meeting. The minutes record that 'concerning the feasibility of the use of force by any future Government as a means of solving partition... no definite decision was taken'. It is apparent, therefore, that at the conclusion of the meeting de Valera had failed to secure agreement from those present that the Fianna Fail Party was against the use of physical force to secure Irish unity, if, in the future, the suitable circumstance arose.

"This was significant, not least because... lengthy meetings were a classical example of de Valera's leadership techniques, in which he always... sought... unanimity by the simple process of keeping the debate going, until those who were in the minority, out of sheer exhaustion, conceded the case made by the majority. On this occasion, however, this technique was unworkable, for the fact that too many Deputies could not agree that the use of force by a future Fianna Fail Government was not a legitimate policy" (Kelly, *Fianna Fail, Partition and Northern Ireland, 1926-1971*, pp.201-2).

However, a year later in February 1957 Fianna Fail returned to government, after the 1956 Campaign had run itself into the ground, and enacted the *Offences against the State Act* which led to the interning of the IRA Army Council, GHQ Staff and Sinn Fein Ard Chomhairle. The IRA campaign was later effectively brought to a halt by Charlie Haughey, who had become Justice Minister in the Lemass Government after Dev's retirement in 1959. Haughey reactivated the Special Criminal Courts and instituted a propaganda drive against Republicans that drained away support for them.

In 1955, twelve Sinn Fein candidates in the Westminster General Election received 150,000 votes and two were elected. But, by 1959, with the Border Campaign fading, Sinn Fein lost their seats and half their vote in the British General Election. Northern Catholics deserted the Republicans when their chances of success diminished and returned again to the Nationalists of the 'constitutional' variety.

In West Belfast support for Republicanism was very limited, even in the 1955 Election, when it was at its height in the rest of the North. The Republican candidate, Eamonn Boyce, made a poor showing, only disrupting Beattie's vote enough to let in the Unionist. The Belfast West seat remained in Unionist hands until Gerry Fitt won it back in 1966.

The IRA Border Campaign was the last hurrah of Anti-Treaty Republicanism in the South. It was a Southern event that marked the exhaustion of the Anti-Partitionist impulse within that society. This had something of a reawakening in response to events over the Border a decade later. But that was very much a Northern Catholic event. The Northern Catholics looked on with curiosity in 1956-62 at the efforts of the Southern Volunteers but played little part in The Patriot Game.

## 1958: What is to be done?

In August 1958 there was a rather innocuous Summer School Conference of what there was of a Catholic intelligentsia in Ireland, held at Garron Tower on the North coast of Antrim. (Garron Tower was a mock Rhineland Castle, built by the Londonderrys 50 years previously, which became a Catholic boarding School, St. MacNissi's College.) It was entitled *'The Citizen and the Community'*.

The August 1958 Social Study Conference occurred when the Anti-Partition campaign, in its political and military forms, had all the appearances of having exhausted itself. All means available, 'constitutional' and unconstitutional, had been applied over the previous two decades to end the predicament of Northern Catholics. The whole gamut of Anti-Partitionist activity had proved inadequate to destroying the Northern entity and the question needed asking was: *'What is to be done?'*

This Conference has been ignored or passed over by historians as being of little consequence. G.B. Newe, who was one of the most prominent Catholics who participated in 'Northern Ireland' as Secretary of the Northern Ireland Council of Social Services, and Mary McNeill delivered speeches and Cahir Healy and Joe Stewart made contributions for the Nationalist Party.

But a closer study of the debate that it provoked in the political sphere reveals that there was some understanding of what might happen if Catholic politics in the North were to embark on the new departure which the intelligentsia was now urging upon it.

The debate caused a bit of a stir largely because the Dublin *Sunday Independent* lent its pages over a period of three months to interested parties, debating the issue of what should be done about 'Northern Ireland' now that all else had failed in trying to destroy it, and more specifically considering what should the Northern Catholics do in the light of the reality of this fact.

The original airing of the new departure proposal was an article in the Dublin *Sunday Independent* by Basil Clancy, entitled *'New thoughts on Partition?'*

Basil Clancy was Editor of *Hibernia* magazine in Dublin, a religious publication. He had been born in Coalisland in Co. Tyrone in 1907 and had authored a book on foreign affairs entitled *Ireland among the Nations* published by the *Kerryman* in 1948. He was a member of Fianna Fail. In Mainchín Seoighe's *'Odds and Ends'* column in the *Limerick Leader* (18.11.50), Clancy is mentioned for his national work. (Mainchín Seoighe or Mannix Joyce was the biographer of Sean South, killed on the Brookeborough raid in 1957: *Maraóidh Seán Sabhat Aréir*.)

Basil Clancy was a solid patriotic Nationalist of Fianna Fail and Irish-Ireland. In 1958 he became the main proposer of the new departure in Catholic politics, very different to what Sean South would have desired. Clancy argued in the *Sunday Independent*:

"The way to end Partition is to accept it. This is the paradox that sums up 'the breakthrough' in Nationalist thinking which has just found expression in the remarkably frank and significant discussions at Garron Point, Co. Antrim... For the first time since the division of Ireland into two states an audience of Nationalists comprised of Northern and Southern Catholics representative of every shade of political opinion from moderates to extremists heard Catholic and Protestant speakers—Nationalist and Unionist—putting the case for the acceptance of the constitutional position of Northern Ireland and, afterwards, engaged in a reasoned and sincere discussion of the proposition...

"From now on there will be a growing number of Nationalists with a new conception of their responsibility to the whole community of which they form a part and who visualise a new plan of action, a plan which will enable them to play a full and acceptable part in the life of Northern Ireland, and at the same time work towards the ideal of full co-operation between all the people of Ireland for the welfare of the whole country...

"The policy of abstention, of segregation, of non-participation and of unwillingness to cooperate with the regime was a policy which was incapable of being expressed constructively.

"Now it is seen that the policy was based on three false hopes: —

    (1)  that the State would not last;
    (2)  that pressure from outside would abolish the Border, and;
    (3)  that physical force would do the trick.

"Hopes one and two slowly faded away and now the unexpected reaction to the actual attempt on the part of extremists to try physical force is that it is seen to be the most hopeless and unacceptable prospect of all.

"The happy result, therefore, of these unhappy Border incidents is that there is a growing realisation of the urgency of discarding policies and attitudes which are defective... and to replace them by a policy which will express a positive, constructive and Christian Nationalism—a Nationalism which will seek not to live apart from the rest of the Northern community and plot to overthrow the constitution by force...

"Another quite unexpected result is a corresponding reaction among Unionists of goodwill...

"It is in Belfast itself... that the situation has changed most... there is far more readiness now to recognise the value of the contribution which the Catholic community could make to the welfare of the Northern State... far more willingness on the part of Catholics to consider acceptance of the idea of working within the existing constitutional framework and of playing their full part as citizens in the community.

"It is a time of great opportunity, therefore, for the leaders of the Northern Government, the religious leaders of all denominations, business directors and political thinkers and policy makers, for now they can work hopefully towards the elimination of the antagonisms between the two main components of the Northern community and lead the way to the elimination of any idea of conflict between North and South as a preliminary to a true union of mind and heart in some future working arrangements that will respect the rights of all parties" (SI 17.8.58).

Clancy's article prompted a reaction in the *Irish News* editorial of the next day. It called Clancy's view "a false picture" of Northern Nationalists but carefully avoided the substance of what Clancy was proposing. Clancy replied in a letter to the Editor but from then onwards the *Irish News* ignored the debate that raged—it acted as if it was not happening. All the action concerning the future of Northern Nationalism took place in the Dublin *Sunday Independent*.

What was interesting was how the *Irish News* of Belfast and the *Sunday Independent* of Dublin treated this event and another, the publication of

Rex Taylor's *Michael Collins*, which occurred at the same time. The response of the *Irish News* to the Michael Collins book has been examined in Chapter 6. It was dismissed in a short review by Cahir Healy that consisted of the story of how Collins and the Southern Republicans/Free Staters had let the North down over the years in pursuance of a Republic to the neglect of the Northern Catholics. The *Sunday Independent* produced a three month serialisation of the book which celebrated Collins and his derring-do in the most extravagant fashion, while airing proposals for Partition to be recognised.

With regard to the proposal for Catholic recognition of the North made at Garron Tower, the *Sunday Independent* pursued the issue for all it was worth whilst the *Irish News* ignored it to the extent of not even reporting Eddie McAteer's or Brian Faulkner's comments on the subject.

I think this was very illustrative of the gap in perception that was opening up between Southern and Northern Nationalism by 1958 as the traditional Anti-Partitionist approach was being seen as bankrupt in the South.

## Faulkner and Blythe show their hands

The Unionist Chief Whip, Brian Faulkner, expressed scepticism about the substance of the Catholic reform and recognition proposal saying that it was worthless unless it had the official backing of the Catholic Church. He said in a speech at Raffrey, Co. Down:

> "The editor of an Irish Roman Catholic journal contributed an article to a Dublin paper last weekend in which he said: 'The best way to end Partition is to accept it'. He referred to Nationalists who visualise a new plan of action, a plan which will enable them to play a full part in the life of Northern Ireland and at the same time work towards the ideal of full co-operation between all the people of Ireland.
>
> "There is the approach to politics which is advocated by those who argue that co-operation in the running of the country is the proper course for Roman Catholics.
>
> "They do not want to strengthen the constitution. They want to overthrow it. Force has failed, they say, and how right they are. So the theory runs: Let us co-operate in every way until we so penetrate the machinery of government that we are in a position to achieve our ultimate aim—national unity.
>
> "Mr. Faulkner went on: 'there is no fundamental change in the Nationalist outlook. Evidently there are some people in our midst who would like to run with the hare and hunt with the hound. They must do some straight thinking.
>
> "Do they want a united Ireland or do they want Ulster in the United Kingdom? That is the primary decision to be made. It was made in 1920 by the Ulster people. Some of those who have lived here for 37 years and

accepted the benefits of that Government are evidently prepared to bury their heads in the sand, but fortunately the great bulk of the Ulster people view the constitutional position with the same clarity of vision as was shown in 1920" (SI 24.8.58).

For Unionism there was black and white and any shades of grey were unwelcome.

On 31st August Ernest Blythe made a contribution to the debate. (He was described by the *Sunday Independent* as "an Ulsterman born in Magheragall, County Antrim, in 1889, …Vice President of the Executive Council… Minister of Finance and Posts and Telegraphs in the Free State Government, 1927-32… TD for North Monaghan 1921-33… a Senator from 1934 to 1936").

Blythe, an Ulster Protestant, had been a strong critic of the Anti-Partitionist League believing it to be futile. He believed that Britain would never coerce the North into joining the Republic and that if Britain left the Protestants would fight. Having experienced the events of 1922 Blythe believed that IRA guerrilla activity would simply lead to a massive expulsion of the Catholic population. He saw Anti-Partitionist propaganda as only solidifying the Unionist regime and making the hard-core of Unionism harder; and the only remaining policy was peaceful persuasion over generations.

Blythe's contribution appeared in the Sunday Independent under the headline: '*SCATTER would be my watchword for regrouping Nationalist forces in the Six Counties*'. He argued:

"Heretofore Nationalist organisations in the Six Counties, by seeking to have Northern Protestants brought not with their consent but against their will, under the authority of all-Ireland parliaments and governments, have ensured that every Northern election in a reasonably mixed constituency should be almost a formal mobilisation of all Catholics against all Protestants.

"Many Southern Nationalists and indeed many Northern Catholics continue to accept the old propagandist contention that only the Unionist political leaders are completely committed to Partition, and that large numbers of Northern Protestants, if left to themselves, would agree to what is called a settlement.

"The idea has no foundation whatever.

"At the present time, Six County Protestants stand more solidly for the maintenance of the Border than ever.

"This is not astonishing when we remember how maladroit our general attitude towards them has been, with our futile, rather smeary, propaganda campaign against the government freely elected by them, with the gunning and bombing activities of our extremists, with our implied and often express calls to Britain to impose financial penalties upon the Six Counties and with our demands that England should withdraw from the North, without the agreement of the local majority, the garrisons which, rightly or wrongly, they deem necessary for their protection.

"There is no prospect of the reunion of Ireland being brought about or hastened by armed action, though the illusion that violence can still achieve results persists and feeds on the most extravagant fantasies...

"If we are not to rely on force, we must rely on persuasion. There can be no intermediate course which is not futile and self-defeating...

"That means that Northern Catholics, who are the key to the whole situation, and who more than any others, desire a change, and have good reason to desire a change, should no longer crowd into one Anti-Partitionist party or group of parties which, broadly speaking, no Protestants will touch, and which so long as it is confined to members of the minority must always remain incapable of achieving results. Instead, they should deliberately scatter into various parties which will, for the time being, have no kind of Anti-Partition policy and which can, therefore, remain or become religiously mixed parties and bring politico-religious segregation to an end.

"... refusal by Catholics to cling to the old ideal of monolithic unity in elections would in time, bring about completely new political groupings in the North and lead to the emergence of a new majority in Stormont.

"What is needed now is to understand that we shall accomplish nothing if we fail to realise that the roots of Partition go back well over 100 years, that 800,000 people want it, and that getting rid of it will be a very slow and infinitely troublesome task, which few of those already grown-up will live to see fully accomplished.

"It may be said, however, that if practically all Nationalists North and South could abandon the still widely cherished hope of reunion by coercion, which, by the way, is the principal cause of continued discrimination against Catholics, a change of atmosphere would begin to manifest itself and reunion would, as it were, be able to grow out of friendship and co-operation so that when the time for the final political act arrived, there would be no heart-burning and little excitement" (SI 31.8.58).

Blythe had a realistic view of Northern Protestants but his main proposal for a multitude of Catholic parties to replace the monolithic Nationalist Party as a device for out-maneouvering the Unionists proved to be misconceived. This situation actually came about in the mid-1960s and, whilst some Protestants were attracted to the ranks of some of these groups, they dissolved themselves into a new 'constitutional' monolith, the Social Democratic and Labour Party, as soon as the situation necessitated.

## Big Eddie declines 'the soup'

The criticism of Northern Nationalism and the placing of the blame on the Catholics of the Six Counties for their own predicament were all too much for Eddie McAteer, who was at that time Nationalist Party Deputy

Leader and the MP for Derry City. He wrote an extraordinarily frank rebuke to the proposers of the new departure in Catholic politics in the *Sunday Independent* of 7th September. It is worth reproducing almost in its entirety for the plain speaking it exhibited:

"Of your charity spare a little pity for us uncouth Northern Nationalists.

"We are so unrefined and so far removed from the genteel tinkling of intellectual coffee cups and the purifying air of Garron Towers that we go on protesting at the organised day-to-day Unionist theft of our rights. And, crowning Sin of all, we don't even co-operate in the system of planned discrimination that passes for Government in the Six Counties. In other words we won't co-operate in the Unionist schemes for our own degradation.

"There is nothing new in this recent outbreak of supercilious chatter about co-operation. Since the first invader polluted our shores each and every generation has had the choice of co-operation. Dermot MacMurrough was a notable co-operator. Those who 'took the soup' as an alternative to starvation for the Faith would also be high on the list of co-operators....

"I know it is tiresome to complain constantly of the evil system under which we are made to live, but anything is better than spiritless acceptance of our second-class citizen status. Monotonous our complaints may be, but unceasing is the discrimination daily and hourly practised on us.

"I am no expert on moral law, but it seems to me that you'd come dangerously close to condoning evil if you agreed to accept and live with it. It seems as simple as that.

"The 1958 epidemic of superior thinkers seems to be classifying Northern Nationalists—and, of course, the leaders whom they persistently elect—as dour lovers of feudin' and fightin'. We are preoccupied with old grievances— we don't give the Orangemen the love which will make them love us in return—we don't say that previous generations were stupid to resist—we sulk outside the Irish Garden of Eden where shamrocks and orange lilies grow lovingly side-by-side—We're... Oh so impossible!

"What a slander on a steadfast people who pay dearly for their adherence to principle. The Northern Irish love peace as much as anyone. They like to work and to rear their families to become useful citizens. They dig deeply into their pockets to preserve for themselves the right to have their children schooled in the Faith of their fathers. They are practising Christians who abhor strife just as much as those who seek to lecture them.

"But, and it's an impossible but, they have long experience of their Orange overlords and of their methods. Through the forest of olive branches they still see the hard facts of life in the North...

"Let Derry be the proving ground of the Unionist desire for a new deal.

"The violence campaign is the well prophesied product of the cheating and frustration which have emptied Six County democracy of all hope of redress for the marooned minority. Violence begets violence, and British-backed Unionist scheming over many years in the North is the root cause of the unrest in the North.

"Now for a plain, last word on this discussion: No matter about the surface differences or the views of newspaper letter writers, there is a very deep and satisfying unity of purpose among Northern Nationalists. And however exasperating it may be to the watchers on the sidelines we will continue to expose and resist the Unionist schemes for rubbing our noses in the mud" (SI 7.9.58).

After Eddie McAteer told them, the Unionists told them. W.A. Douglas, Secretary of the Ulster Unionist Council, made a reply in the *Sunday Independent*. He was as uncompromising as Eddie McAteer from the opposite position in the 'Northern Ireland' spectrum.

## Faulkner warns of the greatest danger

Most interestingly, and prophetically as it turned out, Brian Faulkner, the Unionist Party Chief Whip was greatly concerned at the possibility that the Northern Catholics might actually adopt the policy of 'co-operation' with Unionists and accept the 'state'. He saw it as a much greater danger to the existence of 'Northern Ireland' than the routine of the Nationalist Party or the IRA.

The *Sunday Independent* reported Faulkner's address to delegates of the Young Unionist School at Portrush in a way intended to open up a cleavage in Unionism over the proposed new departure in Catholic politics. The article was headed with the wishful-thinking banner, *'Unionist confusion in Six Counties, Article in Sunday Independent is perturbing to Minister'* (perhaps confirming the Unionists in their suspicions that it was all just Anti-Partitionism in a new guise). It reported:

"Unionist Party men all over the Six Counties report confusion in the ranks following attempts by the Party Headquarters to switch policy because of the fear that the traditional Anti-Partition policy might be succeeded by a de facto recognition of the Border.

"Most outspoken statement so far came from Mr. A.B. Faulkner, Unionist Chief Whip... He referred to the recent article by Basil Clancy in the Sunday Independent. His statements may create a wide cleavage between moderate Unionists and extremists at Party Headquarters.

"For years the Unionist official position has been to deplore the failure of the Northern Nationalist and the Dublin Government to recognise officially Stormont's existence as a separate government. Recent moves at Garron Tower and elsewhere have been hailed by Unionists and Unionist newspapers, but Party Headquarters fear that this move might upset the traditional balance between the majority and minority.

"Mr. Faulkner referring to the 'neo-nationalist policy' whose advocates, he said openly proclaimed that the best way to end Partition was to accept it and work for a majority decision; said that this is 'the greatest danger which Northern Ireland has yet faced'.

"'The proposition' he said 'was put in crystal clear terms in a Dublin newspaper article in the *Sunday Independent* the other day by the man who presided at the Roman Catholic Social Study conference in the North this summer'... commenting on the article Mr. Faulkner said: 'This is the greatest danger which Northern Ireland has yet faced. This is the policy of the fifth column which penetrated so successfully into the countries of Europe before the last war'.

"'Because the policy of co-operation has an attractive refrain', Mr. Faulkner said, 'it had an appeal for those who did not face up to the fact of political life in Ulster'.

"'But' he said 'it is a policy designed to lull us into a false sense of security. This is the song that the Sirens sang. This is the lure that might at last succeed in destroying the Ulster ship of state'..." (SI 2.10.58).

An interesting aspect of this is that, when the possibility of a Catholic reform movement which accommodated itself to the Stormont system was advocated, it produced horror in the minds of Unionists. The inference was that Unionism was well able to cope with open military and political assaults on its positions and all the Anti-Partitionist propaganda the Southern State could throw at it, but a Catholic acceptance of the system in order to change it would be incapable of being dealt with by the system without it imploding.

This must surely have been noticed by Nationalists and got them thinking.

A few months on the Prime Minister, Lord Brookeborough, told a meeting of the Grand Orange Lodge that there was " a certain confusion caused by those who put forward the idea of accepting the present position in order to change it and those of the minority who have advocated co-operation with the Government... Loyalists should distinguish clearly between the two and keep the implications of both clearly in mind" (BT 11.12.58).

But Unionism found itself incapable of doing this when it was actually confronted with the ambiguity of the civil rights movement a decade later. They took it to be *"the policy of the fifth-column"* and a new Anti-Partitionist manoeuvre. And by doing so they turned it, in effect, into one.

## Clancy Repeats

Clancy penned another article in October for the *Sunday Independent* towards the end of what the paper called *"the great debate on Partition"*. It was entitled *'I REPEAT; the way to end Partition is to accept it...'* by *'the man who set them all talking'*:

"In the existing circumstances of the Partition of Ireland the most satisfactory way of effecting the unity of the country is for the majority of the people of Ireland to accept the fact of the legal existence of the two states and to work within the framework of their two Constitutions for an all Ireland Government and Constitution...

"Therefore, the ending of Partition can best be achieved by its acceptance for the time being—the recognition of the Northern Constitution and insistence on the same full rights of citizenship for the Nationalists in the North as are enjoyed by all the citizens in the 26 Counties of the Republic.

"Since... the majority of the people of Ireland exclude the use of force, the only alternatives are permanent partition or a United Ireland accepted by a Northern majority. The consequence of this truth is recognition of Northern Ireland.

"The basic position of those who think as I do and they are increasingly rapidly is that the Northern Unionists of the various Protestant denominations are Irishmen... We have sufficient confidence in the democratic idea... to believe that in a democratic State, where unconstitutional and external threats to its stability are absent, unjust and undemocratic discrimination against the minority must cease...

"To Mr. McAteer I can only reply that I cannot and will not accept the distinction implied in his opposition of the two terms 'Northern Irish' and 'Orange overlords'. My belief in a future United Ireland is founded upon my conviction that the men he calls 'Orange overlords' are in fact Irish." (SI 12.10.58)

Clancy made two fatal presumptions that had significant repercussions when his proposal was taken on by a Catholic reform movement which came into existence a few years later. Firstly, there was the view that the Ulster Protestants were an integral part of a one and indivisible Irish Nation. As the Unionists told him in the columns of the *Sunday Independent*, they weren't and did not feel themselves part of such a thing. That would have fundamental implications for any strategy based on such a presumption.

Secondly, there was the view that 'Northern Ireland' comprised a normal state which would revert to standard operation if the overt Anti-Partitionist threat, external and internal, was removed from it.

Although the Civil Rights Movement and those within the Republican Movement who were to advance it did not subscribe to Clancy's and Blythe's analysis that Anti-Partitionism was at the base of Unionist discriminatory practice and gerrymandering, they made a similar calculation about the effect of the removal of such practices. This, they believed, would result in the emergence of a normal 'state' in which real politics could be engaged in with progressive results for all concerned.

This was an idealist fantasy that informed those who pushed on the catastrophe that was to come once Basil Clancy was taken in earnest and his proposal put to the test.

# CHAPTER NINE

# A New Course

In the mid-1960s a new departure was embarked on by Northern Catholics. The Nationalist Party agreed in 1966 to accept the status of loyal opposition in the Stormont Parliament that Joe Devlin and the previous leaders of Northern Nationalism had always been careful to avoid and which Eddie McAteer had, only a few years earlier, likened to *"taking the soup"*. But all the indications are that the Nationalist Party formally recognised 'Northern Ireland' unwillingly and with good reason, as it turned out.

Sean Lemass, the new Taoiseach, had not taken the trouble to think about the nature of 'Northern Ireland' before exhorting the Nationalist Party to engage in the charade of loyal opposition to it.

The Northern Nationalists, having never developed a substantial independent will of their own, despite their desertion by the Southern State in 1925 and De Valera's distancing of Fianna Fail from them, did not have the character to refuse. That was even though they knew from long experience that 'Northern Ireland' was not a normal state, and that Stormont was only *"a simulacrum"* Parliament, and that opposition was futile within the structures of the self-government which had been farmed out to an all-class alliance of the Protestant community.

The fact that the Nationalist Party did Dublin's bidding with little more than a murmur showed how much Northern Catholics had been reduced to a dependency of the Southern State. But all the participation at Stormont did was to bring out the futility of it all when the Nationalist Party went on a new road . . . to nowhere.

## Nationalist politics

The Nationalist Party by 1964 was a cautious body which had little expectation of there being any great changes in 'Northern Ireland.' Its new Leader, Eddie McAteer, said at the start of that year: "if government policy here changes even slightly we will be satisfied we have done a good day's work" (IN 4.1.64).

Northern Nationalism was in a rut by this time. The full gamut of Nationalist politics had been exercised in the Anti-Partition cause during the 1940s and 1950s and nothing had come of it.

The narrow confines of the Nationalist Party struggled to accommodate the frustrated politics of a community, particularly its growing younger generation, and divisions began to emerge about where Catholic politics should go that were more potent than those that existed before.

The result was a proliferation of Catholic parties centred on strong personalities eager for politics — as Ernest Blythe had advised. Apart from the *Nationalist Party* there was the *National Democratic Party* formed from the *National Political Front* in 1965, the *Republican Labour Party* of Gerry Fitt and Harry Diamond formed in 1960, a number of *Independent Nationalists*, as well as a growing participation of Catholics m the *Northern Ireland Labour Party* and the *Ulster Liberals*.

But there was little movement or sign of change despite the new political manifestations and activity — things had been the same for so long it seemed that they would never be any different.

Michael McKeown, a middle-class Catholic who believed that a new approach should be tried, established *National Unity* — a pressure group aiming to re-establish unity around greater engagement within 'Northern Ireland'. In 1962 National Unity organised a debate around the motion: '*That the government of Northern Ireland should be recognised*'. It was supported by Ernest Blythe and opposed by the Leader of the Nationalist Party, Eddie McAteer, in a repeat of the 1958 debate. McKeown remembered:

> "Speaking from the floor I was very supercilious about big Eddie's contribution. Essentially he counselled a quietist attitude of dumb insolence on the grounds that no pleas would be listened to, and it would then be dangerous to raise the expectations of the nationalist community. This was a very easy attitude to attack fairly scathingly. Less than six years on, I recognised the wisdom of what he had to say" (*The Greening of a Nationalist*, p.21).

Stephen Kelly has revealed that Lemass supported this new movement from its inception, viewing it as a welcome departure from the routine of the Nationalist Party. The Taoiseach received a copy of McKeown's pamphlet, '*Unity, New Approaches to Old Problems*', which argued for acceptance of the need to win Protestant consent before unity could be achieved. Some in the Republic's Department of Foreign Affairs believed that Lemass was "flirting with heresy" by supporting this view. The Taoiseach helped organise private funding for the movement's periodical, *New Nation*, to avoid having a Dáil vote on public finance that would expose his support for it (Kelly, *Fianna Fail, Partition and Northern Ireland, 1926-1971*, p.230).

*National Unity* was based around the idea of winning Protestant 'consent' for a united Ireland — a novel idea in Northern Nationalism in the early 1960s. But it was an idea that had a strong effect on John Hume and others who were looking for a new departure from the Nationalist Party. *National Unity* subsequently manifested itself as the *National Democratic Party* (the NDP) which in many respects was a forerunner of the SDLP and inspired many of the latter's original policy positions.

But the SDLP could not have come into existence in 1964. It needed something drastic to occur to shake everything up.

The start of this shake up came with a major innovation in Irish politics, an innovation which was to have a great de-stabilizing effect on North and South for three decades. In a real sense, for both Catholic and Protestant Ireland, it was the beginning of a new course.

## Lemass makes believe

Stephen Kelly says this about Lemass' attitude to Northern Nationalism:

"On becoming Taoiseach Lemass's relationship with Northern Nationalists was... frosty... he had little time for those he regarded as being as conservative and sectarian as Ulster Unionists. In particular, Lemass disliked Northern Nationalists' unwillingness to participate as the official opposition to Ulster Unionists at Stormont. He maintained that if his federal approach to a United Ireland was to prove successful, Northern Nationalists would be required to play an active role in the electoral politics of Northern Ireland. By the early 1960s Lemass had become increasingly exasperated by Northern Nationalists' attempts to influence the Fianna Fail government's Northern Ireland policy. This was a matter that Lemass believed was for the government alone. Just as de Valera had explained in the 1950s, Northern Nationalists should know their place and would not be permitted to have any direct input into policy-making.

"His criticisms were justified.... there was no Nationalist Party organisation in the strict sense of the word; no constituency organisations such as the Ulster Unionist Party or the Northern Ireland Labour Party; no party officers, no headquarters, no secretary, no membership cards and no members. Instead there were only individual MPs at the Northern Ireland parliament who came together in a loose form of parliamentary party organisation " (*Fianna Fail, Partition and Northern Ireland, 1926-1971*, pp. 227-8).

Whether this represents Lemass' view of Northern Nationalism or Kelly's, or both, it is very unfair.

For one thing, Nationalists in the North had no problem with playing *"an active role in the electoral politics of Northern Ireland"*. They contested elections in the North for 40 years, however much this proved to be a futile exercise in just making up the numbers. They did so primarily to register the existence of a large and discontent minority, that could not be totally ignored if its presence was revealed every couple of years, in the large number of elections the Six Counties had.

As to being *"conservative and sectarian"*, what else did the system require both Unionist and Nationalist to be but communal blocs eternally contesting the issue of the Border? They had been cut off from both body politics in 1921. The British political parties had excluded them both from normal party politics of left and right and Fianna Fail had blocked all attempts made by Nationalists to integrate themselves into the party system of the Southern State and its political institutions. The term *"conservative"* is really meaningless in the 'Northern Ireland' context, particularly in relation to the fact that in any other context the Nationalists would have been seen as revolutionary, desiring the destruction of the 'state' within which they contested elections.

Lemass had two real and actual points of contention with the Nationalist Party, beyond the rhetoric. Firstly, he believed that it had no right to feel that Northern Catholics could influence or play a part in the Southern body politic, even in respect of the policy of the Southern State in relation to the North. Lemass wanted to continue, as De Valera had done, keeping them at a distance, merely to periodically use them as an instrument of State policy in the South whenever the Anti-Partition issue needed a rattle.

The second point of contention between Lemass and the Nationalists was that they refused to act as a proper party of state, which the Taoiseach seemed to imagine would be useful for his new Northern policy, or fantasy. They persisted in seeing the Six Counties and its Parliament as nothing more than it actually was—a pseudo-state that did not deserve a proper political party to legitimise it.

So what the Northerners were actually being criticised for was not being able to keep up with the vacillating requirements of Southern policy from 1921 to 1965.

But, in response to Lemass' bidding, the Nationalist Party began to pretend it was a real political party. In November 1964 it announced that it would establish formal constituency structures and even hold an annual party conference (up until then Nationalist conventions had been called, when necessary, to agree on candidates, often under the auspices of the Catholic Church).

McAteer even produced a kind of election manifesto, *'The Thirty-Nine Points'*, the first policy statement issued by the party. It included policies on employment, housing, agriculture, local government and fisheries as well as equal rights for Catholics in the North prior to an ending of Partition (IN 21.11.64).

The Party had never bothered with this sort of thing prior to Lemass telling them to do so. It seemed pointless for a party that would never form a government to have a manifesto of promises it could never institute.

It was released, rather appropriately, when a popular song *'It's All Only Make-Believe'* was in the British music charts.

## Lemass and the new road

On 14th January 1965 Lemass, met the Northern Premier, Terence O'Neill, in Belfast. It had been kept a closely guarded secret (even from the Stormont Cabinet), and the *Irish News* described the meeting as "one of the most sensational events in Irish politics since the establishment of the border".

After the historic meeting a statement was released by the two Prime Ministers, saying:

> "We have today discussed matters in which there may prove to be a degree of common interest, and have agreed to explore further what specific measures may be possible or desirable by way of practical consultation and co-operation. Our talks which did not touch upon constitutional or political questions, have been conducted in a most amicable way, and we look forward to a further discussion in Dublin."

The Taoiseach said: "How far the road may go is not yet known. It has been truly said, however, it is better to travel hopefully than to arrive" (IN 15.1.65).

Lemass said that Britain's declaration that it had no interest in Partition meant "many old arguments and attitudes will now be seen to have become irrelevant" (IN 27.1.65).

He did not recognise Stormont as legitimate. If he had done so, he would have endangered his own support within Fianna Fail and the South in general. (Both Fine Gael and Labour were strongly nationalist at this time and ever eager to play the green card if it could be used to remove Fianna Fail from Office.)

It has been presumed that Lemass had it in mind that his meetings with O'Neill, and subsequent meetings by other members of his Government with their opposite numbers at Stormont, would be the beginning of a pragmatic development in the course of which the old antagonisms would wither away. The idea being that extensive cross-border networks would ultimately make the Border an irrelevancy as North/South relations improved and overt nationalist posturing declined.

There is interesting information in Michael Cunningham's *Monaghan, County of Intrigue* in relation to Lemass' views. He quotes from a letter by Peggy Lemass O'Brien, Lemass' daughter, to the *Irish Times* and *Irish Press*. The letter came in response to a review of Kevin Boland's book, *Up Dev!* by Paddy Harte TD, and a review by the *Irish Times* itself, in 1978. Lemass's daughter said that the reviews had claimed "that my father, Sean Lemass, changed the direction of Fianna Fail and implied that he abandoned the idea of Irish unity when he paid his visit to Terence O'Neill" (IT 5.1.78).

Peggy Lemass O'Brien refuted this view and said that her father had very different intentions in 1965:

> "Both reviewers are wrong; their opinions are very much at variance with the facts. So for the benefit of both correspondents, and perhaps for Kevin

Boland himself, I would like to define my late father's policy regarding the Six Counties.

"Firstly, he believed that it was unreasonable to expect the people of the Six Counties to have any enthusiasm for Irish unity while this part of the country was much poorer and much less developed than theirs. I think your reviewer will accept that he expended himself to alter the situation with some success.

"Secondly, he had a theory that in an intractable situation one had to do 'something' and so alter the situation, so that new solutions might be tried. When the opportunity to visit Terence O'Neill arose he took it in the hope of altering a situation which had become static and so renewing public interest and allowing new solutions to be sought for a new situation.

"Some months after that much-publicised and apparently much-misunderstood visit, he made a speech at Queen's University. This particular speech gave some offence to the nationalist organisations but illustrated his thinking at the time. He berated the Nationalists for their constant bickering and fragmentation, and he told them that it was largely their own fault that they were second class citizens in their own land. He told them that his government could not give support to the aims of one faction against another, but if they could come together in harmony in pursuit of a few generally accepted political policies, then they would have his full support.

"But, perhaps more important still, my father saw the EEC as the strongest single instrument which could help to persuade the British to withdraw from Ireland. In an effort to copper-fasten that idea he paid a visit to each of the six counties and told them that when he came to conduct our negotiations we would insist that, if at some later date British application was accepted, the Six {EEC Member States at that time, PW} would have to ensure the departure of British troops from Irish soil before we could accept partnership with her in the EEC.

"Both Adenaeur and De Gaulle promised enthusiastic support for this stance, as did the other leaders of the Six. Unfortunately, my father died before our negotiations took place and one of the principal ambitions of his whole career was allowed to be forgotten by default.

"I think these points demonstrate adequately that Sean Lemass, far from accepting the partition of our country, was actively engaged in trying to end it, by making overtures to the Unionists, urging the Nationalists to unite and finding powerful allies to pressure the British to leave our country.

"In conclusion, on the day that my father's successor was chosen in 1966, he made the uncanny prediction to members of his family. He forecast that the Nationalists in the Six Counties were at the limit of their endurance of tyranny and discrimination. He said, 'They will rise up in 1969; there will be no end to the bloodshed and it will continue in various forms until the British withdraw.' How prophetic that command was we are all too well aware... He said the British would have Croke Park-type Bloody Sundays and Black and Tan type atrocities, and thousands would be murdered and maimed. He prayed that the Irish people would not forsake the Republican tradition and allow this to happen.

"Constant misrepresentation of my father's ideals, particularly that which charges him with abandoning the idea of a united Ireland, have forced me to set the record right for once and for all..." (cited in *Monaghan, County of Intrigue*, pp.81-3).

Michael Cunningham reckons that Jack Lynch, who succeeded Lemass, made a lot of republican-sounding noises just after the publication of the Lemass letter. He says that Lemass' successor used a whole *This Week* programme on RTE to set out his 'Republican' policies in order to attract criticism from the North and Britain that would bury the revelation that Lemass differed so much from Lynch. Cunningham also suggests that responses to the letter were suppressed by the *Irish Times* and *Irish Press* to prevent discussion on the matter.

A reading of the *Irish Times* in January 1978 shows what Cunningham has to say to be accurate: it published the transcript of the entire Radio interview with Lynch in which he called for an amnesty for Provisional IRA prisoners. This, and the other Republican posturing he indulged himself in, attracted a series of published letters that quickly drowned out comment about the Lemass letter. In the same broadcast he denied knowledge of Lemass's EEC policy in relation to Britain and nobody bothered to delve into the truth or otherwise of this very significant claim.

## Lemass and the explosion

In recent years the story has been developed in the South that Lynch continued Lemass's work in 'recognising Partition' before being interrupted in his efforts by the Fianna Fail 'backwoodsmen' of Haughey, Blaney and Boland. That is wishful thinking from those who want to create a picture of Saints (Lemass and Lynch) and Sinners (Haughey, Blaney, Boland etc.—or perhaps just Haughey!) in relation to subsequent Irish political developments. It is also wholly misplaced as it seems that Lemass, far from heralding a new *rapprochement* with Ulster Unionism, helped to reactivate the Anti-Partitionist struggle on a much higher plane than traditional Fianna Fail under Dev could ever have done.

And, according to his daughter, he not only intended to unsettle Unionism but predicted privately the catastrophic outcome of his policy!

Lemass may have sought more co-operation and dialogue with the North but he still held the position that the Six Counties was both an artificial and illegitimate entity, despite his encouragement of Northern Nationalists to give de facto recognition of it.

So why is Lemass worshipped so much by the revisionists and Haughey so detested? After all Haughey only picked up the pieces of Lemass' Republican initiative that had had the effect of destabilising North (and South) and spent his political career minimizing the consequences of it.

Peggy O'Brien's letter puts a very different complexion on Lemass' overtures to O'Neill. Cunningham suggests Lemass was suspicious of Lynch and thought he would let the North down and desert the Catholics there if the bit came to the bit—or when the bit came to the bit?

Lemass seems to have wished to put some fluidity into the situation on the island in 1965 in the general Republican interest. He wished to replace the negative and sterile Anti-Partitionism that had gone nowhere with a more positive innovation. Perhaps he had read Basil Clancy and thought it was worth a try.

But Lemass undoubtedly acted at the level of Republican idealism and showed how little he knew of 'Northern Ireland' and what it was. He did not intend what happened in August 1969 to come about as a result of his unfreezing of the situation. But that was the consequence of the train of events he set in place.

Apparently, Lemass was very dismissive of the civil rights movement saying that "two or three wet days will finish things" (John Horgan, *Sean Lemass; the Enigmatic Patriot*, p.342). He had no understanding of its potential to produce the political momentum that the Six County system could not handle without disintegration.

It is no accident that Lemass' departure from the policy of De Valera had the revolutionary effect on the North that it did. Lemass stopped Anti-Partitionist propaganda altogether in the pursuit of 'co-operation' with the Unionist regime. Dublin no longer collected statistics on discrimination against Catholics in the North and shelved McAteer's pamphlets on the plight of his community, as it all felt so inappropriate to the new policy of *detente*.

The result of this was that Northern Catholics, despite no discernible improvement in their lot, felt abandoned by Dublin. There is a strong element of this in the correspondence of Eddie McAteer, who later wrote:

> "In my role as leader of the Nationalist people, I made many trips to Dublin for talks and consultations with Dublin Ministers. I got hospitality but little real support. There was less than enthusiasm to get involved…When I returned home after my post-O'Neill talk with the Taoiseach I was more worried than ever. I got neither the encouragement nor understanding of our position…Lemass said that it appeared to him that Catholics in the North were just as intractable as Protestants. It was hardly the reaction I expected from a Taoiseach with his Republican background to the representative of the oppressed Irish minority in the six Counties…I came away with the conviction that as far as Sean Lemass was concerned, the Northern Irish were very much on their own" (Frank Curran, *Countdown to Disaster*, pp.37-38).

Northern Catholics felt that there was no longer an appreciation of their position in the one place that there always had been in the past, with the resultant loss of important moral support.

And yet their position was the same as it always was. Were they just going to lie down under O'Neill's "carpet slippers" as they did under Basil Brooke's *"hob-nail boots"* (to use Gerry Fitt's evocative phrases) in the interests of Sean Lemass?

The effect of this was two-fold: they were forced to do something actively themselves about their position internally and they were also encouraged to direct their political energies in the direction of Westminster. And this created the explosive mix that would come to blow everything apart in August 1969.

Lemass' policy of opening up the North through a strategic departure that would shatter the routine of politics therefore succeeded. It succeeded by introducing an activism into the political system in the North that the system could not cope with and which proved catastrophic to it. It might be said, to paraphrase Goethe: that the tragedy was that Lemass achieved his heart's desire, in what he set in motion back in 1964-5.

## Big Eddie 'takes the soup'

Lemass persuaded Eddie McAteer to lead the Nationalist Party back into Stormont and accept the role of Official Opposition, which they announced they would on 23rd January 1964.

The Nationalists did so reluctantly. A couple of months before McAteer had been questioned on that very subject and said: "We are going to examine all our sacred cows. This ticklish question will be examined properly at the convention, but if we do contemplate that step we will never go into parliament as the representatives of a subject or second-class people" (IN 21.11.64).

And yet within two months the Nationalists were Her Majesty's Official Opposition at Stormont on Mr. Lemass's bidding, without any discernible change in status for the North's Catholics.

Northern Nationalists were unsure of what to make of the Lemass visit to Belfast but it was certainly the case that it represented something of an unwelcome disruption in the routine. McAteer made the best of having to accept the role of Her Majesty's Official Opposition with a ludicrous pretence:

> "Stormont must be seen as a federal or regional Irish Parliament to continue in existence until the fears of an All Ireland parliament are finally resolved. There must be co-operation to ensure that...the existing Parliamentary machinery operates for the common good. For all practical purposes this will mean little change in existing practice and will enable us to advance the policy programme we have already issued. Our fidelity to a United Ireland ...remains unaltered by this decision. Pursuit of this aim is an entirely lawful

political objective in no way inconsistent with full community status. Cooperation will not and cannot be carried beyond the brink of national principle" (IN, 3. 2.65).

This thought had obviously been implanted in McAteer's mind by Lemass and it begged the question why Nationalists had stayed away from the Northern Parliament for most of the previous 40 years.

But McAteer was justifiably concerned at where Lemass' road might go. In the political manoeuvring that took place after the Lemass/O'Neill talks, it was the Nationalists who were the most keen to point out that 'constitutional' questions had not been discussed.

Seven years previously, in March 1958, at a Nationalist Party meeting there had been a proposal from the Belfast Nationalist MPs, Frank Hanna and Harry Diamond, for the Party to take up the role of Official Opposition at Stormont. Some others including Cahir Healy and Joe Stewart backed the motion and there was a majority in favour of it. McAteer threatened to leave the Party if the motion was carried. A great deal of pressure was put on Stewart to withdraw his support for the motion: he was told he would end up like T.J. 'Judas' Campbell, being despised for having accepted a judgeship, and his children would bear the stigma of 'collaborators' to their graves. Stewart cracked under the moral pressure, changed sides and was elected Leader of the Party (see Enda Staunton, *The Nationalists of Northern Ireland*, p.212 for an account of this).

In response to Basil Clancy's proposal of co-operation, McAteer had compared the proposers to Dermot MacMurrough and those who took the soup. Seven years later McAteer took up the role of Leader of the Opposition upon Lemass' orders.

The *Irish News* took three years to reveal the concern it had had over the meetings between Lemass and O'Neill. It maintained a diplomatic silence during the time of the talks, to give the Northern Nationalists the least discomfort and did not reveal its true feelings until mid-1968. Its editorial on 29th June 1968 said:

"For almost 50 years we of what is known as the minority have lost no sleep over the question of our unpopularity and have borne and countered the hardship and unprofitability as best we could. What has helped us to laugh at the one and sustain the other has been the knowledge that we are in the right and that time will, as it always does, see the right triumph, that the tag of minority is really a misnomer because we accept oneness with the rest of the Irish people and constitute in fact the majority, and, finally, that we have behind us the full moral support of our fellow Irishmen and women in that part of the nation where the writ of native government runs.

"This feeling that we have behind us in our stand the loyal and determined backing of the vast majority of Irish people is of vital importance, but there have been occasions in recent years when one has got the impression that the interest of their leaders in the position which obtains in the little North-Eastern corner of our island is somewhat lukewarm. This is an observation we felt constrained to make at the beginning of last month when commenting upon a visit paid by Mr. McAteer in order to discuss with Mr. Lynch matters of common interest. An Taoiseach had, in fact, precisely nothing to say of interest to us in the North."

## Northern 'backwardness'

The Northern part of the Irish nation was its most backward at that point. This was nothing to do with the internal character of the Northern Catholic community. It was the result of a unique combination of historical circumstances which sealed it off from the developments that would have affected its evolution. Even before Partition, the Catholic community in the North differed substantially in its social position from the rest of the nation, arising from the effects of much of it being a migrant community within a rapidly developing industrial society with which it could not merge. But after Partition the gulf between South and North widened.

In many ways Northern Nationalists had led the Nation in the Home Rule campaign and were the most enthusiastic proponents of it. West Belfast was the power behind Joe Devlin and Devlin was the main substance in the Home Rule Party. If Home Rule had come about, there was every chance that the North would have been in the vanguard of the Nation and done much to determine what Home Rule Ireland would have been. But then Partition cut them off from the Nation they were about to take the lead of.

In 1920 the Catholics of the North had no wish to be separated from the rest of the Nation and wanted to participate fully in the developments which were occurring within it. But the Northern Catholic community could or would not take part in the four great political events which did so much to develop the national character: the destruction of the Home Rule Party by Sinn Fein in 1918, the Treaty War of 1922-23, the triumph of Fianna Fail in 1932, and the neutrality policy during the Second World War that established effective independence.

As a result, the Northern Catholic community remained part of the Irish Nation although it could not take part in its making. Nationalism in its political development was frozen at the pre-1914 level.

The only way Northern Nationalism could remain part of the nation was by emphasizing its distinct character—which largely meant its Catholic character: the distinction which it held from the rest of the North, and by stressing the similarity it had with the Free State. As a result the great National events it participated in — The Centenary of Catholic Emancipation in 1929, the International Eucharistic Congress in 1932 and the Catholic Truth Congress held in 1934 — were of a religious and communal nature. As a consequence, the best the Northern Catholic community could do was to tail-end what was happening in the rest of the nation, reproduce its Catholic character, often to a greater degree, and wait for deliverance in the long run from across the Border.

The only alternative open to it was for it to swallow its pride and take part in the affairs of the Northern statelet as a permanent minority, with the community which had deprived it of its historical destiny always forming the Government. So, with a choice of being a dominated minority in a Protestant province and being a backward part of the Catholic nation, awaiting deliverance from the South, it naturally opted for the latter.

If a third alternative had been available to Northern Catholics, things might have been very different. If, instead, it had become one of the many minorities, along with the Protestant community, within the United Kingdom and had been able to take part in the system of representative government through the party politics of the State, another development might have been possible. The Northern Catholics could have linked up with the Catholic community in Britain, which had begun to exert a discernible influence on British politics, and also within the British Labour movement, into which Irish emigrants had begun to flock. A substantial secular, liberal democratic, and socialist influence would have emerged in Northern Catholicism (without the fear that this was a victory for Unionism), which would have had a positive effect on reconciliation in the North and given a great boost to the national unity of Ireland in the long term. And the Northern Catholics might have been to the forefront of developments instead of having to follow the Free State.

Because it did not happen that way, Lemass and the Fianna Fail leadership was the advance element of the Nation and the Northern Nationalists were its rearguard. And they would have preferred the certainties of the old, rather than the challenges of the new, when they entered Stormont on 2nd February 1965, on the bidding of Mr. Lemass.

## The great illusion

The Nationalists quickly found out that Stormont was no ordinary Parliament with the conventional relationship between Government and Opposition. For one thing, they found there was little the Official Opposition could actually do when legislation was faithfully reproduced by the Unionists as it had been made in Westminster. Any political conflict could only take place on matters of secondary importance — matters which did not disrupt the social welfare integration achieved by Craigavon.

Opposition was therefore something of an empty exercise. Some believed there might be some basis of party conflict but the role of Opposition was stifled. J. O'Hare, the Nationalist Senator, complained in a Senate debate that the Joint Exchequer Board was nothing more than "a rubber stamp". J.G. Lennox said that "year after year he was disappointed to find that the Government did not use its discretion to retain a portion of the money collected in income tax for the benefit of industry here" (IN, 30.6.65).

Lemass in effect succeeded in encouraging the Nationalists to treat 'Northern Ireland' as if it were a real state — and a functional democracy at that. He therefore began a development of Catholic activism which, when combined with O'Neill's similar pretensions of governing the province as if it were a state, put everyone on the road to disaster. By encouraging ambitions in Northern Nationalists that could never be fulfilled within the political framework it operated, the fuse was lit which was to explode just a few years later.

In October 1965 O'Neill called an election. McAteer having the old instincts of contempt for this playacting at parliaments called it "a needless waste of money".

During the months before the election O'Neill led a very vigorous campaign against the Northern Ireland Labour Party, simultaneously stealing its social policies and banging the Orange Drum against it. It could only be the case that O'Neill believed the NILP to be a potential alternative Government of the province and wanted to crush it.

Kenneth Bloomfield, who served as O'Neill's private secretary, later explained the Prime Minister's actions to Peter Rose:

> "It was because of the moves he had made towards the Catholics. He had to take out an insurance policy with the Unionists by obtaining a big win in the General Election (1965). But where would he get new seats other than from the Labour Party?" (Peter Rose, *How the Troubles came to Northern Ireland*, p. 43).

This was a very good illustration of the perversity of the Stormont set-up. O'Neill believed he had to break up the small non-communal middle ground of politics in order to make any reform possible. Without bolstering Unionist confidence by destroying the NILP, the Nationalists could not be accommodated.

O'Neill obviously thought a Unionist/Nationalist division in the politics of the province would be a preferable one, in which a permanent majority could be guaranteed. And so he set out to cultivate the Nationalists as an Opposition, knowing they could never possibly form a Government at Stormont. Such was the perverse political thinking of O'Neill, which took sectarian headcounts as a basis for representative government, in what he began to believe was a functional 'state' in which activist politics could be conducted as if it were Westminster or the Dail.

Some Nationalists seemed to have been taken in by these delusions of Lemass/O'Neill and see possibilities in the election for the formation of an alternative Government. Addressing the Queen's University Labour Club, two Nationalist MPs called for a Coalition of Opposition Parties to oust the Unionists. Paddy Gormley said the Unionists needed only to lose 8 seats for there to be a change in government (IN 15.10.65).

## The great disillusionment

The election held on 25th November 1965 showed vividly the charades that were Stormont elections. In the 52 seats there were only 28 contests between 2 candidates, and one between 3. Twenty-three Stormont MPs were elected without even a poll being necessary. Sixteen Unionists were returned unopposed. When the poll was taken, the Unionists won 36 seats to the combined Opposition's 16 (Nationalists 9; NILP 2; Liberals 1; Republican Labour 2; National Democratic Party 1; Independents 1).

The *Irish News* editorial on 27th November, '*After the Poll*', summed up the great disillusionment felt in Nationalist circles:

"Although Northern Ireland is often described as a place where the unexpected always happens, 'Ulster', through its government defies all description. In the results of its elections the expected always happens. The same party is always returned to power.

"There is joy in Government ranks now that it has won two seats from N.I. Labour. Mr. Wilson's victory at Westminster had no prestige value for a party that has worked hard but finds the big battalions in local politics too much for it.

"Captain O'Neill is satisfied with his victory and has reason to be. He can have new towns according to the tastes of himself and his fellow Ministers. Others may protest. Protests go for nothing. Stormont gets its mechanical majority once more except it is bigger now."

For the Catholic community, Stormont elections were invariably great anti-climaxes. The weeks preceding polling day showed what a political community the Northern Catholics were with vigorous conflicts between strong personalities and the usual calls for unity against the Unionists. Every time there were political disputes and schisms, often only resolved at the last minute. The *Irish News* reported the wheelings and dealings among prospective candidates weeks before the elections and there was a real sense of elation as the community readied itself to send out its best men for the contests. And then the election took place, the Unionists won as always, and a great sense of disillusionment set in—a disillusionment that was greater this time because of the expectations that had been raised by Lemass/O'Neill.

Partition remained the only real issue in Northern elections because it was deliberately arranged that it should be so. So-called elections were never anything but referendums on whether the region should be part of the British state or the Irish state. They were unconnected with the governing of the state, which is what democracy is usually all about. In the British State that was done through the operation of the party system, with usually one party as the Government and the main other as a Government-in-waiting. The other parties are marginalized unless there is an electoral stalemate.

The party-system of the State formally excluded 'Northern Ireland' from its operations in 1920. Voting in the Six Counties was therefore disconnected from the actual democracy of the State. But electoral activity in the North had nothing to do with governing the State. Elections were only convoluted referendums on the question of whether the region should belong to the British state or to an Irish one. They were referendums conducted under the disguise of elections to give the appearance of democracy when all the time they were just sectarian headcounts. And, in order to remain within the British state Unionists had to secure 'party' majorities within the devolved system. Devolved Governments were elected, but government policy played little or no part in the voting. And the conducting of referendums in the form of the election of devolved Governments ensured that both Protestants and Catholics remained cohesive communal blocs ready to engage in conflict eternally.

The NILP during the 1960s made the best attempt possible under the circumstances to establish political conflict in the province on the lines of the British party-system. But their task was an impossible one, since real social conflict at the level of the state was conducted at Westminster and working class advances were automatically registered by the Unionists at Stormont. When O'Neill buried the NILP in 1965, he also buried the illusion that provincial Labour could achieve anything positive (though the shadow of it still persisted for some time afterwards). But, by doing so, and by promoting the communal division, he hastened the downfall of his own Parliament and Government.

It made little practical difference whether Nationalist representatives sat in Stormont or abstained. The Stormont Parliament was not the source of government of a state. The major institutions of the State remained under Whitehall control, and some of the more substantial powers which Westminster sought to devolve to Stormont were actually reintegrated by Stormont back into the Whitehall system. This was the one significant achievement of the Ulster Unionist Party in the 1920s and 1930s. But it meant that the matters on which any form of class-based politics might have developed were not dealt with by Stormont because the Stormont Parliament simply copied Westminster legislation, whether Tory or Socialist.

The real decision-making assembly for most matters affecting the state in 'Northern Ireland' was Westminster. But Northern Ireland representation at Westminster was not allowed within the parties which wielded power at Westminster, and was therefore futile.

## The Opposition charade

The 1965 election also dispelled another illusion. In most Parliaments of the world the Opposition Parties content themselves with their role, because they can presume that they can return to government in time. The fact that this is the case exercises a moderating influence also on government, since the party in power is constantly restrained from exercising its powers in a despotic manner which would always bring a similar abuse from the other parties on their return to power.

In the Stormont system there could only ever be one government—the Unionist Party—and one Opposition—the Nationalists—given the communal basis of politics laid down by Westminster in 1920/1. A change of Government would have meant a change of state.

And on the limited issues on which there were political conflicts (sectarian ones such as the locating of new universities and the naming of new towns) there was no deterrent in exercising power, which the possibility of being ejected from office would bring. In many respects, the devolved Parliament at Stormont and the boycott of the political Parties of State gave the Province the worst of all politics. There could be no party conflict on substantial social issues because Stormont was merely a rubber stamp and all argument centred around the sectarian disputes which naturally surfaced. (This, of course, is not an argument that more powers than the minimal ones should have been transferred to Stormont. Only an Independent Ulster would have given Stormont the role of a Parliament of a state.)

The facts of life in the Stormont Parliament were made clear very quickly to the Nationalists. The Unionists had not made provision for a salary to be paid to the NILP when it was the Opposition in Parliament, on the basis that the 'real Opposition' was boycotting Stormont. But, when the Nationalists took up the position of Official Opposition, and Eddie McAteer applied for his salary as leader of Her Majesty's Opposition, O'Neill refused it.

It must have not been a pleasant experience to have turned up for the soup only to be denied it.

The Nationalist MP, Paddy Gormley, said at Stormont: "he had heard that the Unionist attitude was that there could never be a change of Government and that was what motivated their attitude towards the opposition" (IN 10.6.65). There was little one could say against this view.

After a year of Official Opposition, the Nationalist Party was in a peculiar position. They were committed to remaining in Stormont, but realised they could never become even part of a coalition government; they had little influence on the legislation passed there, and were part of little more than a rubber stamp. So it was natural that the Party turned to its internal organisation in 1966 as an outlet for some kind of activity which would divert attention from the real causes of the Party's impotence at Stormont.

On 6th February, 1966 the Nationalists held a private delegate meeting in Belfast, at which their *Thirty Nine Point* plan was adopted. Its basic principle was the re-unification of the country. Eddie McAteer said that, under the new re-organisation plan, constituency organisations would submit resolutions and nominations to the Party Conference before April 1st. The Party would continue to put forward alternative policies to the Government, "for example, in the field of education and economics, with the prospect remote as it may now seem of one day forming an alternative government".

McAteer said, however:

> "If we don't get some token from the Unionists that they are going to normalise conditions we might have to take our troubles to Westminster again. Despite efforts of the government to maintain abnormality we are canalising politics along conventional political lines and taking a fuller part in public life. We are coming out from our tents...
>
> "In our efforts to find and co-operate on matters of general good we find much misunderstanding. The Government seem reluctant to accept any ideas arising outside the narrow limits of their own Front Bench and I am wondering lately whether they really want parliamentary opposition. At times they seem to be yearning for the good old days of growl and glare... Perhaps we will some time have to review this brave experiment in normalisation" (IN 7.2.66).

But if the Nationalists thought O'Neill was going to normalise politics in the province they were to be sorely disappointed. Craigavon and Brookeborough had accepted the abnormality of 'Northern Ireland' as an accomplished fact, whose effects they set out to minimise by operating the Stormont Government to the minimum. O'Neill's peculiar innovation, however, was to accept in principle the abnormalisation of the province and, under pressure from Whitehall, use the Unionist Party to embrace the abnormal as the norm and enhance it.

This was because O'Neill had begun to believe that Ulster Unionism was a distinct political philosophy, which was preferable to the normal politics of the British party system.

The *Irish News* commenting on the re-organisation of the Nationalists in its Editorial on 8th February said:

> "It would be easy to say that the party should have set up the full machinery of party long ago, since we have had Nationalist MPs at Stormont for over 40 years. But this would fail to take account of the political climate here. Over the years there seemed little need for a party, as such, when political

endorsements were quite predictable. They still are to a major extent. But we have been moving on."

What had been "*moving on*" was the Nationalist Party's willingness, under orders from Lemass, to indulge in the O'Neillite fantasy of normal government based on abnormality. It was a position which the Nationalists could only really sustain for a short period. And in the meantime they had to take their "*troubles to Westminster again*".

In September 1967 McAteer visited the British Home Secretary, Roy Jenkins, in London. The *Irish News* reported the Nationalist Leader as complaining that after a full year "there is little outward evidence of the reforms for which we were hoping" (13.09.67). McAteer, according to the *Irish News* (14.09.67), received assurances that the Home Secretary would speak to O'Neill, but Jenkins had no intention of putting any pressure on O'Neill.

Opposition having brought nothing for the Nationalists, they became reduced to wishful thinking with regard to British Labour.

## New Catholic politics

Prior to the 1960s, aside from a few 'Castle Catholics' practically the whole Catholic community was Anti-Partitionist. But by 1964 there were a number of things making for a sea-change. There was the feeling that, after the failure of the Anti-Partitionist campaign of 1948-62, the Border was going to be there for a long while and life in 'Northern Ireland' should therefore be made the best of. There were the beneficial aspects of the British Welfare State which were being widely availed of by the Catholic community, and which stood in contrast to lesser welfare provision in the Republic at that time. There was the extension in working-class education begun by the 1945 British Labour Government that was producing more Catholic students at University. And there were the effects of Vatican II, which had begun to undermine the old dogmatic Catholicism which had looked on liberalism and socialism as a form of heresy, and which opened the way for more radical expressions of politics.

In 1964 RTE commissioned a film to be made by Michael Viney about the changes which were taking place in the Northern Catholic community. On his travels Viney met a young Catholic teacher called John Hume. Viney was impressed with Hume and his views and persuaded him to write some articles for the *Irish Times* about Northern Catholics. These were printed in May 1964 under the title '*The Northern Catholic*'. Here are some extracts:

"The crux of the matter for the younger generation... is the continued existence of great social problems of housing, unemployment and emigration. It is the struggle for priority in their minds between such problems and the ideal of a united Ireland with which they have been bred that has produced the frustration and the large number of political wanderers that Michael Viney met on his tour. It may be that the present generation of younger Catholics in the North are more materialistic than their fathers, but there is little doubt that their thinking is principally geared toward the solution of social and economic problems. This has led to a deep questioning of traditional nationalist attitudes.

"Weak opposition leads to corrupt government. Nationalists in opposition have been in no way constructive. They have—quite rightly—been loud in their demands for rights, but they have remained silent and inactive about their duties. In forty years of opposition they have not provided one constructive contribution on either the social or economic plane to the development of Northern Ireland...

"There has been no attempt to be positive, to encourage the Catholic community to develop the resources which they have in plenty, to make a positive contribution in terms of community service... Unemployment and emigration, chiefly of Catholics, remain heavy, much of it no doubt due to the skilful placing of industry by the Northern government. But the only constructive suggestion from the Nationalist side would appear to be that a removal of discrimination will be the panacea for all of our ills. This this lack of positive contribution and the apparent lack of interest in the general welfare of Northern Ireland that has led many people to believe that the Northern Catholic is politically irresponsible and therefore unfit to rule.

"One of the great contributions, therefore, that the Catholics in Northern Ireland can make to a liberalising of the political atmosphere would be the removal of the equation between nationalist and Catholic. Apart from being factual, it ought also to be made fashionable that the Catholic Church does not impose upon its members any one form of political belief. There is nothing inconsistent with such acceptance and a belief that a 32 county Republic is best for Ireland. In fact, if we are to pursue a policy of non-recognition, the only logical policy is that of Sinn Fein. If one wishes to create a United Ireland by constitutional means one must accept the constitutional position...

"People who discriminate through prejudice believe that they are justified. Catholics can contribute to a lessening of prejudice by playing a fuller part in public life, as some of our religious leaders have been urging. Undoubtedly in the beginning they will be neither wanted nor welcomed in many spheres of public life in Northern Ireland. But public life means more than service on statutory or local government committees. It means the encouragement and participation in community enterprises designed to develop the resources of the community and done in conjunction with all those in the community who are willing to co-operate.

"If one wishes to create a United Ireland by constitutional means, then one must accept the constitutional position.... Such an attitude, too, admits the realistic fact that a United Ireland, if it is to come, and if violence, rightly, is be discounted, must come about by evolution, i.e. by the will of the Northern majority. "

Much of this was an echo of Basil Clancy's argument. But John Hume was not a man of mere words. Originally he had gone to train to be a Priest at Maynooth and when he decided this wasn't for him left and became a teacher—the traditional routes of upwardly-mobile Northern Catholics. But then he went out and helped found a Credit Union in Derry and a Housing Association, as well as setting up a small business in salmon smoking. And being one of the most vigorous and talented young men in his community, he naturally gravitated toward politics.

The kind of things Hume said in his articles for the *Irish Times* would not have been said by a Northern Catholic before the 1960s. It was not simply the case that the 'Protestant State' alienated Catholics who always wished to play a full part in it. In response to their predicament of being excluded from the Southern and UK states, the Northern Catholics had secluded themselves as far as possible from the statelet in which they were marooned and contacts with the non-Catholic elements in society were minimal.

Largely under the auspices of the Catholic Church, and originally inspired and financed by the Free State, the community had aspired to make itself independent by providing a comprehensive social framework (segregated schools, Catholic health provision and poor relief) in which Catholics might live in readiness for their transference into a future all-Ireland state.

John Hume sensed a feeling in his community that this situation had finally run its course by 1964. He felt that the Catholic community should now attempt to take its place within the society it had boycotted for so long, and that this would be the most effective demonstration to the Protestants that they had no longer anything to fear from Catholics and no excuse to discriminate against them on the basis of disloyalty. And he pointed out that it would be to the benefit of the entire community if the Catholic middle class rectified the lack of industrial and business development in Catholic areas by putting their efforts into economic activity outside the traditional confines.

Hume was only one individual in the movement from out of the ghetto that was taking place. By the mid-1960s, 'Northern Ireland' Catholics were explicitly demanding British standards of justice and democracy in the province. (For instance, in 1963 a Dungannon doctor's wife, Mrs. Pat McCluskey founded the *Campaign for Social Justice*. This body compiled documents on discrimination against Catholics in housing and employment in rural Ulster.)

It is possible that Hume and others would not have emerged if it weren't for Lemass's initiative and the Nationalist Party recognising Stormont. But, with McAteer having become "a co-operator" at the bidding of the Taoiseach, he hadn't a leg to stand on against John Hume. The Nationalist Party attempted to lure Hume into its ranks. But Hume thought better of it. He saw the Party as "coterie politics" and determined to organise a new form of politics that the Nationalist Party was incapable of.

Up until the end of 1968 Hume maintained a distance from the developing Civil Rights Association. He refused to endorse the October march in Derry, took no part in the organisation, and attended only as an individual. But Hume was frustrated in his efforts at developing a different form of Catholic politics when the Unionists refused to meet him half-way. The Unionist decision to block a new university in the second city and opt for Coleraine, coupled with the refusal to sanction the building of a new housing estate for homeless Catholics in Derry made Hume give up on O'Neill and finally throw in his lot with NICRA.


## Northern Nationalists and British Labour

In January 1964, the Nationalist Party made the first attempt in its history to meet representatives of the main British Parties in London. Both the Conservatives and Labour refused to formally meet the Nationalists when they arrived and they had to content themselves with an unofficial meeting with a number of sympathetic Labour and Liberal MPs on the 31st of the month.

Despite the fact that the new Northern Premier, Terence O'Neill, had made reforming noises when he took over the Unionist leadership from Brookeborough, there had not been much forthcoming in his first year of Office (apart from his recognition of the Northern Committee of the Irish Congress of Trade Unions). In March, an attempt by the Nationalists to reform the system of housing allocation was defeated by 25 votes to 12 on a party division. In April, a Republican Labour motion calling for one man, one vote in Local Council elections at age 18 was voted down by 20 votes to 14. It would have been very useful to Unionism if it had put these two issues to bed at that point while Anti-Partitionism was in the doldrums.

The *Irish News* did not see any benefit for the Nationalists in the possibility of a Labour victory in the impending British General Election. After Anthony Greenwood, the Chairman of the Labour Party, said that if the Party won the next election, "it will make certain that Northern Ireland receives top priority over any part of the British Isles when it comes to putting men into work", the Editorial of the *Irish News* commented: "No Labour government is likely to channel aid to an area where its representation is small, at the expense of its followers in Wales, the North-East and. Scotland" (4.5.64).

There should have been some hope of a Labour intervention. The incoming British Prime Minister, Harold Wilson, was known to have Irish nationalist sympathies. In July 1964 he had written to Patricia McCloskey of the *Campaign for Social Justice in Northern Ireland* promising to introduce impartial procedures for the allocation of public housing and assured her "that a Labour government would do everything in its power to see that infringements of justice are efficiently dealt with" (IN 3.10.64).

The view of the *Irish News* was close to the mark, but it might have been more accurate to say that the British Labour Party was not likely to do much for the Six County area when there were *no votes* to be won or lost in it.

From 1964 a number of Labour backbenchers, including Hugh Delargy, Paul Rose and Kevin McNamara, attempted to raise various issues concerning 'Northern Ireland', including allegations of Stormont discrimination against Catholics in elections, jobs and housing.

Early in 1965 the *Campaign for Democracy in Ulster* was formed. The aim of the CDU was to break the Westminster convention, dating from a 1923 ruling by the House of Commons Speaker, that questions specifically involving 'Northern Ireland' transferred matters could only be asked in Belfast and not be discussed in the British Parliament.

The backbenchers attempted to bring up 'Northern Ireland' issues into debates about overall UK matters and by introducing amendments to Bills. In one such attempt on 26th October 1965, the Under-Secretary at the Home Office, George Thomas, emphasised that the Wilson Government had no intention of departing from the convention against discussing Ulster's 'internal affairs' in the following way:

> "It is of the utmost importance that we should establish right relationships between the subordinate Parliament and... the Imperial Parliament. When we have governments of different political colours in the subordinate Parliament and the Imperial Parliament it is all the more necessary for all to tread carefully to ensure that conventions established over long years are not trampled upon" (IN 27.10.65).

This idea that there were *"governments of different political colours in the subordinate Parliament and the Imperial Parliament"* was, of course, a great pretence. The subordinate Parliament always dutifully passed the legislation of the Imperial Parliament whether the colour of the Government at Westminster was blue or red.

The convention excluding discussion of Ulster had actually no basis in law. Section 75 of the 1920 Act made it clear that the Imperial Parliament could legislate for whatever it chose in 'Northern Ireland'. It had done so in the *Prices and Incomes Act* of 1966 against the wishes of the Stormont Parliament. So there were no constitutional barriers to interfering with 'Northern Ireland'. It was simply a continuation of the policy laid down in 1921.

The reason for the continued existence of the convention was simply that the British Executive continued to indulge it. And Wilson indulged it during 1965 and 1966 in the same way as the previous Tory Government had in 1964, only this time thwarting his own backbenchers.

'Northern Ireland' figured significantly in Whitehall's preoccupations only once during the mid-1960s—when O'Neill and RUC Special Branch, attempting to deflect attention away from the efforts of the Labour backbenchers to expose injustices in Ulster, encouraged Wilson to believe there was an impending security threat from the IRA connected to the 50th Anniversary of the Easter Rising. No attacks either in Britain or the Six Counties, of course, materialised.

This seems to suggest a general acceptance by both Ulster Unionists and Britain that the primary lever in 'Northern Ireland' politics has been, and remained, force or the threat of it.

The persistence of the parliamentary convention was another consequence of the insulation of Britain from 'Northern Ireland.'

## Gerry Fitt's maiden speech

A very important event in the Northern Catholic experience was the election of Gerry Fitt to Westminster on a *Republican Labour* ticket to the West Belfast seat on 1st April 1966.

Fitt got up during the debate on the Queen's Speech on 25th April and skilfully used the tradition that a maiden speech is not interrupted to lambast the Unionist system. That was not something that was conceded to Cahir Healy when he gave his maiden speech forty years previously but it was allowed to Fitt.

The Speaker also unusually declined to stop him despite having ruthlessly suppressed Labour MPs in raising Ulster issues. It was two and a half years until any other speech of this character was permitted in the House of Commons.

In 1983 Gerry Fitt told the *Daily Express*: "I believe the maiden speech I made in the House of Commons was a landmark in Irish politics" (18.7.83). This is what he said in that speech:

> "Since the election I have read in sections of the British Press that I have been classified as an Irish Republican... To classify me as an Irish Republican is not strictly correct. The Irish Republican Party in Ireland does not recognise the authority of this House in any part of Ireland and its members would, indeed, refuse to take their seats in this House.
>
> "I have not given up hope, and have not yet determined to follow the line of the Irish Republican Party, because I believe that during my term as the representative of West Belfast in this House I will be able to appeal to every reasonable member of this chamber, and, through them, to every reasonable member of the British public. I feel certain that at the end of this parliament

dramatic changes will have taken place in the North of Ireland.

"Having arrived at this House... and having listened to the speeches made... from both sides, I marvel at the normality which exists in British politics. Serious questions are discussed... This atmosphere does not exist in the constituency which I represent. In Northern Ireland, at every succeeding election there are no economic issues involved. In this island of Britain, the recent election was fought on the different policies and philosophies of the Conservative party, the Liberal party, and the Labour party... In Northern Ireland, no such issues entered the contest...

"At every election at which I have been declared victor, the bigoted mobs have attempted physically to assault me... This is something which people in Britain cannot understand and it is something in which I intend to educate the British people. It is something in which I hope to elicit support... from both sides of this House, because I am convinced that there are on all sides in this chamber honourable men who have acted in their political life with the upmost rectitude, political honesty and sense of fairness. I make an appeal to each and every one of those members in this House to ensure that we in Northern Ireland are afforded the same opportunity to fight elections on the economic issues involved and that we will be free from all threats of physical violence."

Fitt then asked whether the Labour Party had ever considered amending the 1920 *Government of Ireland Act*:

"The changing social conditions over the past 50 years make the Government of Ireland Act completely unworkable. When we realise how every concept of British democracy is being flouted in Northern Ireland we conclude that now, immediately, is the time to amend that act"

The only amendment which he proposed was the extension of the 1949 *Representation Of The People Act* to the province in order to abolish the property franchise in provincial elections:

"... We have an anti-democratic electoral system. This system would not be tolerated in any other freedom loving country. In Northern Ireland the same people are elected to administer the different Acts—the one applicable to Northern Ireland and the one applicable for imperial elections. Can we expect the same people to administer their own electoral laws, on the one hand, and then to wear a different hat and administer the 1949 Representation of the People Act? The first aim of the Northern Ireland Unionist Party is to perpetuate its own existence there.

"It is generally accepted that when an area of Britain is threatened with economic depression... it will return Labour, or even Communist, representatives... Northern Ireland has consistently returned Tory representatives. I suggest that those members are returned not on the issues involved, but by a completely unacceptable system, and that the only issues discussed during the contest concern the question whether one is a Catholic or a Protestant.

"In West Belfast I fought the recent election on the platform of Republican Labour. I am a socialist... I intend to vote as a Socialist... But having done so... I shall ask for support of hon. members on this side of the House to help me initiate the same system in Northern Ireland. If I believe in socialism for England, Scotland and Wales I must be afforded the right to believe in socialism for my own country."

Fitt said that people in 'Northern Ireland' had to own a home to have a Local Government vote:

"The people there are British subjects and are entitled to the same privileges as are possessed by any other persons living in these islands.

"To perpetuate its own majority the Unionist Party in Northern Ireland has devised an electoral system which for local government purposes can give six: votes to one person and yet deny a single vote to another... Not only does it deny a vote to a person who does not own a home; from this root stems all other social evils. If a person does not own a home he does not have — a local government vote, and if the party in power considers him to be an enemy or an anti-Unionist it will ensure that he will not get a home... I have no hesitation in predicting that... within the next two or· three years further council estates will be built in my constituency and the houses will be given to government supporters with the intention of unseating me. This is the atmosphere which I am trying to break through" (Hansard, 25.4. 66. In fact, it was rate-payers, rather than property owners who had the vote, which is not quite the same thing.)

A year later in the House of Commons Fitt told the Home Secretary that his only objective was "... to ensure that we are all treated as British citizens. That is all we ask" (IN 26.10.67).

Two years later, in October 1968, Fitt made a speech, this time to the *'Campaign for Democracy in Ulster'* at Blackpool in which he said:

"I do not consider I am making any outlandish requests. All I am asking for is that the same rights and privileges which are enjoyed by the people of Doncaster should be afforded to the people of Dungannon and Derry and that the same electoral system which is enjoyed by the people of Birmingham should also be made available to the people of Belfast."

The reasonable implication of Fitt's argument was for 'equal citizenship' to be extended to the people of 'Northern Ireland'. He wanted the 1920 Act amended so as to deprive the devolved Government of authority over electoral processes within the devolved structure. He wanted Westminster to resume direct control over an area in which power had been devolved, so that United Kingdom subjects in 'Northern Ireland' might enjoy the full rights of the state in which they lived. And, furthermore, he wanted elections in 'Northern Ireland' to be fought over the economic and social issues which were preoccupying people in the rest of the United Kingdom.

It was reported that Fitt might take the Labour Party whip. But the Secretary of the Labour Party said that this was reserved for members of the Party only and the British Labour Party did not take members in 'Northern Ireland' (IN 5.4.66).

## How Parliament kept the Six Counties out

Fitt spent 1966-67 cultivating the British Labour Party. On 22nd May 1966 he proposed twenty amendments to the British Finance Bill to draw attention to things in 'Northern Ireland'. He began pressing at Westminster for Imperial intervention but, on 9th August, the British Government issued a statement to say that in no event could there be any question of the UK government interfering with matters delegated to the Stormont Parliament. The British Government view was that such a course would "do harm to relations between the two governments" (IN 10.9.66).

A month earlier a debate involving Fitt showed how Westminster kept the Six Counties out.

The debate arose during the Consolidated Fund Bill (which allows MPs to raise virtually any issue they wish except involving specific calls for legislation). Fitt opened the debate by quoting Section 75 of the *Government of Ireland Act*, 1920.

Fitt told the Deputy Speaker, Sir Eric Fletcher, that Section 75 gave,

"... ultimately an overriding responsibility to the Parliament of the United Kingdom, and as the representative of Belfast, West... I stand here to demand of the British government that they accept the responsibility which they themselves have written in to this Act of 1920."

However, the Deputy Speaker, would have none of it and stopped Fitt in his tracks, telling him:

"Section 75... does not confer a responsibility on Her Majesty's ministers in the United Kingdom over matters within the competence of the Northern Ireland government. My predecessors in this chair have ruled repeatedly that matters within the competence of the Northern Ireland government, and therefore matters for which Her Majesty's ministers in this House are not responsible, are not subject to the debate in this House."

The convention that matters relating to 'Northern Ireland' could not be discussed dated from a ruling given by the Speaker of the House of Commons, J.H. Whitley, in May 1923. Here is what the Speaker said then:

"With regard to those subjects which have been delegated to the Government of Northern Ireland, questions must be asked of Ministers in Northern Ireland, and not in this House. In the case of those subjects which were reserved to this Parliament, questions can be addressed here to the appropriate Ministers—for instance, the President of the Board of Trade, the Postmaster-General, etc. The policy of voting money here in aid of Irish services may be discussed here, but, subject to the responsibility that attaches to the Chairman of Committees in that matter, I would say that this right does not cover matters of administration for which a Minister in Northern Ireland is responsible" (3.5.1923 vol. 163, cc1623-5).

The question to which the ruling related came from a Liberal MP, Mr. Frank Gray, who was concerned at the spending of the Belfast Government, which Westminster did not seem to be able to enquire about. He had previously asked questions relating to control of the RUC and its religious composition and had been rebuffed.

Gray asked simple pertinent questions in his short parliamentary career that lasted from 1922-4. He was something of a free spirit. After being educated at Rugby and becoming a solicitor, he entered the British Army during the Great War. He refused a commission, and served as a private soldier until the Armistice. After the war, he worked as a farm labourer, living with Warwickshire miners. After leaving Parliament he toured the local Workhouses of Oxfordshire as a tramp and wrote the book *The Tramp: his Meaning and Being* (1931).

Gray was elected as the MP for Oxford in the 1922 General Election and was made a Liberal Whip. He was accused of corrupt practices in the 1923 General Election and, following a petition, he was unseated in May 1924, a few weeks after he had elicited the Speaker's ruling on the convention (although he was acquitted of the charge).

After Gray left Parliament there was no appetite for asking these questions again until the 1960s.

As regards the *Consolidated Fund Bill* in 1966, after the Speaker made his ruling, Michael McGuire, a Labour MP, then stood up and argued that if the Home Secretary was satisfied that it was right to intervene directly in the affairs of 'Northern Ireland' he would be the supreme authority delegated with the powers given to him under Section 75 to do so. Maguire told the Speaker:

"Your ruling seemed to me to suggest that he does not have that power but I suggest that Section 75, in anybody's clear interpretation, gives the ministers in this house overriding authority over the parliament at Stormont."

The Deputy Speaker told him that his confusion arose because he had failed to distinguish the position between the United Kingdom Parliament and the United Kingdom Executive:

"The 1920 Act in Section 75... gives this parliament supreme authority over matters in Northern Ireland and enables the United Kingdom parliament to legislate on matters affecting Northern Ireland. On the other hand, the responsibility of the United Kingdom government as regards matters in Northern Ireland is limited and her Majesty's ministers in this country have no responsibility for matters which are within the exclusive jurisdiction of the ministers of the government of Northern Ireland."

The Speaker argued that MPs could not raise matters for which Ministers at Westminster were not responsible.

Fitt then called on the Junior Minister from the Home Office present to note the remarks that have been made during the debate and he asked the Deputy Speaker if he could:

"In any way help us to rid ourselves of the conventions which exist in this House and which prevent me discussing the welfare of my constituents? I find it rather frustrating when I look to this house for justice for my constituents because I know that any plea I make in the Stormont will certainly fall on deaf ears."

The Deputy Speaker replied to Fitt:

"It is perfectly competent for this parliament to intervene, in any legislative sense, in Northern Ireland. The competence of the sovereignty of the United Kingdom parliament has been preserved by Section 75 which would therefore, for example, enable this legislature to revoke or amend that Act; but that would involve legislation. It is not permissible, in debating the Consolidated fund Bill, to introduce matters which involve legislation."

So, even when it was possible to talk about 'Northern Ireland', it was not possible to talk about legislative change!

The Junior Minister at the Home Office present in the chamber, Alice Bacon, who was responsible for 'Northern Ireland', declared:

"In no event can there be any question of the United Kingdom government interfering in transferred matters without legislation... to put it as simply as I can... the government have powers in those matters reserved to us. We have not powers in those matters that have been transferred to the Northern Ireland government."

So the British Government could not interfere in the affairs of the 'Northern Ireland' Government without legislative authority — and legislation was not allowed to be discussed in the debate! And, of course, the convention was that in normal debates 'Northern Ireland' was not allowed to be discussed.

So Westminster had built itself into one of those concentric mediaeval castles where if one wall was successfully penetrated there would be another, then another, then another...

Bacon then put on record in the clearest possible statement that, despite Labour's pledges in opposition to bring about reform in the Six Counties, the Government had no intention of taking any action:

"I should like to remind the House that there has never been an occasion in which legislation on transferred matters has been applied to Northern Ireland against the wishes of the Northern Ireland government. Section 75 of the 1920 Act provides authority for it to be done. It could be done by this parliament according to Section 75. But it would do great harm to relations between the two governments... successive governments have taken the view, however, that so long as Northern Ireland retains its present constitution, it would be wrong for the United Kingdom government and parliament to interfere in matters for which responsibility has been delegated to the Northern Ireland government and parliament... The Prime Minister... prefers the method of informal talks with the Prime Minister of Northern Ireland" (House of Commons *Debates*, vol. 733, 8.8.66).

## 'John Bull's political slum'

To coincide with the Queen's visit to Ulster in July 1966, the *Sunday Times* (3.7.66) had published an investigation into the state of the province under the headline *'John Bull's Political Slum'*. The article was one of the few in the British press which made a genuine attempt to warn Britain of the consequences of the failure to tackle Catholic grievance. Because of the party boycott of the province, and the consensus that largely existed at Westminster to leave Northern Ireland alone, the British media showed very little interest in the predicament of Catholics and the character of the Stormont regime.

The *Times* article talked about "the underlying sickness that will remain" after the Queen's visit was over. It said:

"When the flags are hauled down after the Royal visit, Mr. Wilson's government will be confronted with a sharp alternative: whether to use reserve powers to bring elementary social justice to Ulster, or simply allow Britain's most isolated province to work out its old bizarre destiny. During the last 45 years since Partition the latter course has been negligently adopted with what often look like disastrous results."

The article went on to give detailed evidence of gerrymandering, discrimination in employment and housing against Catholics and bias by the Stormont Government in making decisions in favour of the Protestant community. It noted that "the most curious aspect of religious discrimination in Ulster is that the Westminster parliament is prevented by convention from discussing it".

It advised Wilson: "the Loyalist cheers for the Queen tomorrow should not be allowed to soften a very hard line on John Bull's political slum".

Another press intervention occurred in March 1967 from the *Catholic Herald*. This was significant because the article in question was written by the political correspondent of the *Sunday Telegraph*, Ian Waller, who was known to be on close terms with the British Prime Minister. It was reproduced by the *Belfast Telegraph* under the ominous heading, *'Irish Unity is Wilson's dream'*.

It referred to the irritation the 11 Ulster Unionists at Westminster caused Wilson and referred to them as "the faithful slaves of the Conservative Party". Waller revealed that: "... one of the most powerful ambitions in the minds of many Labour MPs and ministers is either to eliminate or at least greatly reduce the power of this group..."

However, there was apparently a greater ambition at Whitehall:

> "... another far more important consideration that I know the Prime Minister feels very deeply: the need for a far-reaching constitutional change that would finally end the century old Anglo-Irish quarrel. It would indeed be a feather in Mr. Wilson's cap if he could go down in history as the man who re-united Ireland...
>
> "Mr. Wilson's hope is obviously pegged on solving the Irish issue as a whole, but pending that a great deal of thought is being given to possible constitutional changes that would limit the right of Ulster MPs to speak and vote on issues that are delegated to the Ulster Parliament, and also to define more strictly those functions of the UK government which are also applicable to Northern Ireland, and to restrict the Ulster voting to those issues" (*Catholic Herald* 17.3.67).

Wilson, in his first term of Office, with his slim majority of 4 in the House of Commons, had found his room for manoeuvre curtailed by the 11 Ulster Unionists. However, once he had obtained a much more substantial majority in the election of 1966, his willingness to deal with this problem slackened off. It is likely, therefore, that these suggestions were just warning shots across the bow of the Westminster Unionists. In any event Wilson did nothing to curtail the powers of the Ulster Unionists at Westminster or embark on greater constitutional change with regard to 'Northern Ireland'.

The *Times*, under its new Editor, William Rees Mogg, a Catholic, had begun to take an interest in events in the province. However, having revealed it as Britain's *'Political Slum'*, a *Times* Leader during May 1967 entitled *'The Trials of Ulster'* warned the Wilson Government on no account to "wade in". The *Times* Leader was written by Owen Hickey, a Catholic from County Kildare, who had been writing Leaders for the *Times* since the 1950s.

Hickey seems to have reasserted the traditional British policy with regard to 'Northern Ireland', over his Editor, to head off where all this talk of discrimination was leading. *'The Trials of Ulster'* warned everyone to leave well alone with regard to 'Northern Ireland', because the system was there for a purpose, and things should therefore be left to O'Neill:

> "The credit of the Unionist administration... is bound up with the person of the present Prime Minister. He is known to be working towards a reduction

of suspicion between the two religious/political communities in the province and towards a relationship of functional co-operation and common courtesy with the Republic...

"Meanwhile, at Westminster there is the urge to interfere, intensified by the arrival on the scene of Mr. Gerald Fitt, the Republican Labour member for Belfast West. It has not so far penetrated the procedural defences of the House. Nor has the government caught it. Mr. Wilson is having a series of informal meetings with Capt. O'Neill and has expressed himself satisfied at the way they are going. The deprecators of bigotry and discrimination have an ally in Capt. O'Neill and Mr. Wilson's way of exploiting the alliance is a good deal more sensible than Mr. Fitt's.

"Overt interference at the present time would do no good, though it may be helpful to remind people, if any have forgotten it, that religious discrimination and gerrymandering are well documented in the Six Counties. If things were getting worse they are, or even if they were not getting better, there might be a strong case for setting aside the constitutional provisions which make the matters complained of matters for the provincial parliament. As it is, Westminster should think of this before wading in: since 1922 MPs here have had no experience of ordering a society in which much political opposition takes the form of opposition to the basis of the constitution; and before that date they had little success and no joy in trying to do so " (*The Times* 2.5.67).

The warning the *Times* Leader was sending out to the British Establishment was: interfere with the 1920 constitution at your peril. The system established in 1920 was done so with a purpose and that purpose, although it might have become obscure to most and a distant memory to others, remained primary in the interests of the British State. Other matters which had recently come to the attention of Westminster and the British public, due to the efforts of Gerry Fitt, were of transient and secondary consideration.

The British State works in obscure and mysterious ways. It maintains great continuity in its behaviour and activities without seemingly having to work much at it. There must be people within it that look after such things so that the temporary occupiers of political office within the democratic system don't do things that should not be done. That is the only conclusion one can reach in relation to Wilson and the *Times* with regard to their drawing back on 'Northern Ireland' during the mid-1960s.

## British Labour and Northern Ireland

Gerry Fitt, undeterred by the rebuffs he had received at Westminster, visited the Labour Party Conference in 1967. The *Irish News* reported him as telling a meeting that if reforms were not forthcoming "some people might resort to extra-parliamentary methods" (5.10.67).

The 1967 Labour Conference was notable for the fact that the Nationalists clearly recognised that the power of state lay with the Parties of State and it was only by influencing them that 'Northern Ireland' could be reformed. It was evident that they still had hopes of doing so, in the light of Gerry Fitt's efforts over the previous year.

But the Nationalists were to find out that lobbying the Labour Party was not going to influence it all that much.

At the end of the Conference the *Irish News* reported:

"This year's Labour Party conference ended today leaving behind it a very definite feeling that Northern Ireland had been given, to say the most of it, a lukewarm shoulder to cry on. Yesterday could have been Northern Ireland's day with a major debate on discrimination. Time, however, destroyed any hopes that week of really bringing the region under the spotlight -and closer to democracy. This sense of remoteness is the general impression which local observers will bring home with them. But it is also an impression which is to a large extent understandable in the face of significant issues like the common market, Vietnam and the car industry.

"These problems, and the obviously high-tension competition between personalities involved in them, have demonstrated forcibly what a small fish in the big political sea Northern Ireland really is.

"At the same time, there is undoubtedly a real reluctance, and a timidity— possibly the result of misunderstanding and lack of knowledge -about getting to grips with the problems of Northern Ireland. 'The point that any previous Prime Minister—for instance, Gladstone—who had moved on the Irish problem had found himself in trouble, was put to Mr. Wilson's Private Parliamentary Secretary, after one conference session.

"He replied: 'That is true, but their trouble was that they were not sincere'. Gladstone, he said only began thinking about Ireland when he found he needed Irish votes to retain his position" (7.10.67).

The Labour Party had no votes to be won or lost in 'Northern Ireland' so the province was not a priority for its consideration. That was the bottom line. Gerry Fitt was the most influential 'Northern Ireland' politician who ever had dealings with the Labour Party and yet he still could not gain its interest in reforming the province, even with the threat of *"extra-parliamentary methods"* waiting in the wings.

## Separating Catholic from Nationalist

*"One of the great contributions... that the Catholics in Northern Ireland can make to the liberalising political atmosphere would be the reversal of the equation between Nationalist and Catholic"*, John Hume had said in his *Irish Time*s articles.

But, going into the New Year in 1968, it was not easy to see how this could be achieved.

In 1968 there were only two agencies which could have achieved the separation of Nationalist and Catholic politics within the Six Counties. It was conceivable that a Catholic reform movement might have developed, demanding democratic reform at the same time as making it clear that the state was being recognised, and that the community wanted to play as full a role as possible in its functioning.

This was what was being suggested by Hume and tentatively by others. But, although the Catholic demand for democratic politics was growing, by necessity it was contained within the institutions of the communal division. (It obviously could not be articulated by Catholics joining the Unionist Party as the Louis Boyle case demonstrated.)

Therefore, it tended both to give the Nationalists a stick to beat the Unionists with and consequently to be seen by the Unionists as another tricky Nationalist plot. And even those who made great attempts to move away from the shibboleths found it hard not to be a tool of Anti-Partitionism and to be regarded as such by the Unionists as a result. That was the routine of the communal conflict that 'Northern Ireland' had created, after all.

It seems to have been the view that British liberalism and social democracy were vulnerable to protest by the Catholic minority. But, in fact, they were intensely indifferent to it. Protest at Stormont was certain to be voted down, and protest at Westminster was not allowed, because the "*convention*" was that Stormont was the appropriate place for it.

What was wrong with Stormont was its essential structure. And nobody should have needed to draw Westminster's attention to that because it was Westminster who had devised it. 'Northern Ireland' was a region of a State, an area for which a peculiar form of government had been devised which could only function through the conflict of two communities, with the larger Protestant community exerting dominance over the smaller, but growing, Catholic community. It is inconceivable that the British statesmen who set it up did not know what they were setting up.

British opinion, which is largely moulded by the party conflict in the State, was almost completely indifferent to protest about 'Northern Ireland' in the mid-1960s. It was only when protest led to trouble on the streets in 1968-9 that it began to take heed and even then it did nothing until conflict on the streets led to gunfire and burning in Belfast in August 1969.


## British Labour's missed opportunity

According to Enda Staunton:

"Ernest Blythe had for long being canvassing the idea that northern nationalists should dissolve their identity within the British Labour movement and the sphere of Irish cultural activities, in order to defuse unionist fears that they constituted a 'fifth column' for a foreign state. In the process of doing this, he contended, their grievances—which he felt were overstated anyway—would be eliminated. Late in 1956 he circulated the nationalist MPs with an extensive memorandum setting out his ideas" (*The Nationalists of Northern Ireland, p.216*).

Blythe had apparently received a sympathetic reply from Cahir Healy, who had been previously rebuffed by Fianna Fail, and said he agreed with much of Blythe's argument.

But how could Northern Catholics accomplish this without being admitted to the Labour Party?

It was probably only the British Labour Government which could have provided the means by which Catholic politics could evolve out of the sectarian cocoon and by which a peaceful reform of the statelet could take place. In those days the Labour Party was a very powerful force in the State, harnessed to the powerful Trade Union movement, and Irish Catholic involvement within it was very significant.

But the Labour Party was determined to stay aloof from the problems of 'Northern Ireland', and see the liberal and socialist strains in each community bottled up within the communal blocs and used merely as weapons in the service of Unionism and Nationalism, rather than as substantial growths within the organic life of the Six Counties, developments which might have begun to overcome the communal division without prejudice to the national demand.

Catholics would have taken part in the democracy of the State if it had been open to them to do so. But, in the convoluted referendums in which a vote to remain attached to Britain could only take the form of a vote for the Ulster Unionist Party (the communal party of the Protestants with the Orange Order at its core), only a minuscule number of Catholics could be expected to vote for the British connection.

And so the Catholic third of the population remained a coherent Nationalist community, sustaining an Anti-Partitionism as its politics, because there was nothing else for it to become within the actual political context to which the Six Counties was consigned. The Protestant two-thirds remained a coherent Unionist community because it was required to return a Unionist majority at every election to 'defend the Union'.

It was a feature of the 'Northern Ireland' system that Partition could never be taken entirely for granted and political life conducted with regard to the governing of the existing state. If the territory excluded from the Irish State had been limited to two or three Counties, containing a much smaller Catholic minority and remaining an integral part of the UK, this might have been possible. But, within the Six County 'Northern Ireland' as it was constructed, the large Catholic minority could only vote against Partition, because they would otherwise be voting for their own humiliation.

If, in 1968, the Labour Party had involved itself in the Six Counties by taking members there, putting up electoral candidates, and reforming the Province to bring it into line with the rest of the UK, it might have separated the democratic demands of the Catholic community from Anti-Partitionism, and provided for the attraction of increasing numbers of Catholics into the Labour movement where they would be joined by their Protestant fellow workers. It is possible that the next three decades of conflict could have been averted. But the Labour Party retained its detachment, as did the British State, and the rest, as they say, is history.

It was just possible for a settlement to have been made in the late 1960s in 'Northern Ireland' within the State. The UK was a successful multi-national state and was perhaps better suited at that time than the Irish Republic to produce some kind of accommodation between the communities. It was the institutions of the British State that made life tolerable for the Catholic minority, along with its cultural links with the South. However, the element that made the UK a successful multi-national state was the very thing that the British political establishment withheld from the Six Counties.

Catholics did not refuse to take part in UK politics—they were excluded by Britain from any participation within it.

In the late 1960s the greatest opportunity to accomplish this arose. It was clear that Catholic politics in the North were in flux. The Nationalist Party was no longer adequate to the ambitions of the Catholics of 'Northern Ireland' and there was nothing much else available to them. If a purposeful attempt had been made at this point to facilitate Catholic participation within the party politics of the State, what subsequently happened might possibly have been headed off. But after Britain was found wanting in this respect only damage limitation was possible.

The Northern Catholics were disrupted in the mid-1960s by an external intrusion—the Lemass initiative. But Catholics, told to be an Opposition, found they had been led up the garden path. The whole point of Opposition is that some day it might form a Government. This is what makes Opposition bearable and functional in any normal state. But 'Northern Ireland' was not a normal state or indeed a state at all. And without the possibility of Government Opposition was intolerable.

In such circumstances Catholic politics had to go in a different direction and, having the British direction closed off to them also, this direction turned out to be Republican.

# CHAPTER TEN

# Civil Rights

When my *From Civil Rights to National War* was published in 1989, it was criticised by Bob Purdie, who was at that time writing a book on the Civil Rights Movement to be called *Politics in the Streets: The origins of the civil rights movement in Northern Ireland*. That criticism was contained in a review in *Fortnight* magazine. It centred on Purdie's desire to show that the Civil Rights Movement was not a "Communist, Republican conspiracy", which he claimed had been argued.

It was certainly the case that Unionists believed *NICRA* — the Northern Ireland Civil Rights Association — to be a Republican conspiracy, and perception is very important in these matters. But it is also the case that Unionists helped confirm NICRA as a Republican manoeuvre by the attitude they took to it.

Communists and Republicans were indeed behind the Civil Rights Movement and the chief theorist of it was Charles Desmond Greaves of the Communist Party of Great Britain. But it was meant to produce a situation entirely different to what it did produce, and they lost control of the momentum it developed long before August 1969 when it became an insurgency.

What was possible in 'Northern Ireland' except conspiracy? There were two autonomous communities with no medium of interaction between them, pursuing completely separate objectives within a façade of democracy. In a constitutional structure which ruled out the pursuit of reform through electoral swings and changes of Government, reform could only be pursued outside the established routines, by means which the other side would see as conspiracies.

Even in asking the question: was the Civil Rights Movement a Communist, Republican conspiracy? Purdie is being naïve. He presumes 'Northern Ireland' to be a normal 'state' where conspiracy is some kind of aberration. In 'Northern Ireland' conspiracy was the medium of politics in the absence of functional alternatives.

The nature of the state in Northern Ireland made the Civil Rights movement subversive in fact, regardless of intention. And, just as Brian Faulkner had predicted back in 1958, before Greaves had even dreamed it up, active Catholic participation aimed at reforming the Six County 'state' was the thing most dangerous to it, far more dangerous than Anti-Partitionism.

That is what made a very moderate reform demand into a powerful subversion whose consequences continue to work themselves out.

# Gerry Fitt's other speech

On 25th February 1967 Fitt gave a speech to an *Irish Democrat* Conference in London. It, rather than his maiden effort in the Commons, is a landmark in the career of Gerry Fitt. It retained some of the democratic features of his Commons speech, but it set them in a framework of Nationalist resentment, a framework which gave a totally different meaning to his demands.

Since this speech was more representative of Fitt's subsequent career, and gives an insight into his political thinking it is worth quoting at length.

The Conference itself was organised by Desmond Greaves and the *Connolly Association*, a front organisation for the Communist Party of Great Britain. It was sponsored by 29 MPs, and was attended by delegates from 15 Constituency Labour Parties, 9 Trades Councils and the District Committees or Branches of 13 Trade Unions, as well as delegates from various other CPGB fronts.

Fitt said:

"If Northern Ireland is, at the moment, constitutionally an integral part of the UK, then I must demand for my constituents in Belfast the same rights and privileges as are enjoyed by those in Coventry, Wales, Glasgow or any other part of the UK. But I realise, and the Unionist Party realise, that in making such a reasonable request, I am, in fact, asking for the downfall of the Unionist administration in N. Ireland, because if you have British standards made applicable in the six counties of N. Ireland, the same Electoral law, the 1949 Representation of the People Act, because once you do have this brought into Northern Ireland, it cuts away the whole basis of Unionism.

"So let us be quite clear what I am asking for is, that British standards as they apply in the island of Great Britain, should be made applicable to N. Ireland. And what Conservative, Liberal or Labour representative at Westminster dares deny these rights for my constituents?

"I was born and bred in N.Ireland, I know that some day the 'crunch' has to come. It may not be this year, or next year, or the year after it, but come it will in relation to the existing state of affairs in N. Ireland and particularly in relation to the overall responsibility of the British Government. We cannot get away from the fact, because until the Irish question is resolved, it will always be with the British people...

"Many people in Northern Ireland have a Sinn Fein outlook, and indeed in years gone by I have disagreed with them on the question of violence. As an Irish Socialist, I do not want to see one Irishman shooting another Irishman. I do not believe that that will solve the Irish question. But these people certainly have a principle—they say that the Partition of Ireland has existed now for forty-seven years, that it is useless to try to talk to a British Government, that they will not listen, that they themselves created the problem and they are unwilling to take any steps to solve it, and I have been told time and time again that the only answer to the Partition of Ireland, lies in the hands of Irishmen themselves and it can only be reunited by force.

"I would sincerely hope that the day will never come when we, once again, have to take to the gun in Ireland. But I do say this, that at the end of the lifetime of the present Parliament, if I have to go back to N. Ireland and say that I have spent four, four-and-a-half, or five years talking to the British Government... if l feel, in all honesty, that I have achieved nothing, I will be the first man to say that I have achieved nothing and I am not willing to go back to Westminster again. I am neither intimidated by, nor enamoured of Westminster—I am there to do a job, to try to highlight the injustices which exist in N. Ireland...

"Ireland, for over 700 years, has had... a troubled relationship with the island of Gt. Britain. It is born in every Irishman... to seek the right to govern his own country... Britain drove the Irish natives from their own lands, particularly in the North-East corner of Ulster. They then began a Plantation. English aristocracy was planted in the parts of North Eastern Ireland. They have been there quite a long time now. They have not been assimilated into the Irish race, though they do not call themselves English either. They call themselves Ulster-Scots.

"But I view the Partition of Ireland from the Socialist angle. Since the day and hour I was able to understand politics, I have been a disciple of James Connolly..."

"I am willing to stake my political reputation that if the British Government were to initiate.... an enquiry they would find that democracy as it is known in the island of Gt. Britain does not exist in N. Ireland. In the House of Commons I have listened to many speeches on the situation in Rhodesia, and how the British Government are prepared to take a stand against the Smith regime. I thought then and I say now that the British Government should take a stand against the Fascists who control Northern Ireland (applause).

"I have here, Mr. Chairman, the six principles which we have heard so much about in relation to the Rhodesian problem. One {is} the principle of unimpeded progress to majority rule... There can be no question that the majority of people in Ireland want the island united. Every one of these six principles are applicable to N.Ireland... the British people are aware of the problem, but do not want to trouble themselves to take any steps to remedy it.

"...in Northern Ireland, we have a system of electoral franchise which is the envy of Ian Smith in Rhodesia—he could not improve upon it. We have a position where one man can have six votes because he is a property owner... On the other hand, another person...is denied the right of a local government vote on the grounds that he does not pay rates to the local authority... The Unionist Government realise that if they build homes for the homeless, they are also going to give them votes. They know well that those votes will be against the Unionist administration. So they take the easy way out, and in my estimation the most savage and inhuman way out. They don't build houses at all. So if you are suspected of being an anti-Unionist in Northern Ireland you are denied the right to have a home for your wife and children."

Fitt then explained the Local Government gerrymander in Derry city. He said that Harold Wilson had expressed concern about it to Terence O'Neill, and that O'Neill said: "he would just love to bring about reforms", but he would have to proceed slowly because of Paisley. But the Unionists were intent on stalling until "a Conservative Government is returned and then there will be no need to initiate any reforms at all..."

"Most of you know about this man Ian Paisley. Paisley has been charged with being an extreme Unionist. He is an embarrassment to the established Unionist Party in Northern Ireland. But I know, because I was born and reared in Northern Ireland, that Paisley is not an extreme Unionist. Paisley is the fundamental expression of Unionism. What Paisley says in public other Unionists say and think in private (Applause)...

"The Unionist in Northern Ireland has a siege mentality. He realises that he is there by no right. He is not there by right of being an Irishman, because he disclaims Irish nationality. He is not there because he is an Englishman, because he doesn't act like an Englishman and refuses to accept British standards. He is there because he wants to maintain this little oasis of Fascism in Northern Ireland. Last year he became aware that his privileged position was endangered. This was the reason for the hysteria which crept into the Northern Ireland political atmosphere...

"The Englishman has his freedom and he is determined to protect it. But Northern Ireland freedom is only given to one section of the community, those who support Unionism. In 1922 there was put on the Statute book the Special Powers Act. This act was supposedly designed to protect the security of the State. But the Northern Ireland Unionists equate the security of the State with the security of the Unionist Party. So they use everything they are empowered to do under this act to protect, advance and perpetuate the cause of Unionism in Northern Ireland. In Great Britain this would not be tolerated. But I have here with me a cutting from the South African Parliament 'Hansard' of April 24th, 1963. The late Prime Minister of South Africa Dr. Verwoerd was busy pushing through the Apartheid laws, which are anathema to everyone who believes in the concept of democracy. He was meeting some opposition in the South African Parliament and he got up and said:- 'If honourable members were to say to me now that this legislation...is far reaching then I will agree with them at once it is drastic, but.. .I am prepared to give up every single clause of this legislation for one clause of the Northern Ireland Special Powers Act of 1922'. This is certainly some commendation coming from that source and I don't know if the Northern Ireland Government are proud to ally themselves with such friends.

"...But it is no good pointing at the problem which exists if you haven't anything constructive to put forward to end it; and I think I have something constructive to put forward....It costs the British taxpayer 117 million pounds per year to subsidise Northern Ireland. Northern Ireland could not exist for five minutes were it not for such massive subventions from the British exchequer.

"In 1964-66 the British Labour Government had a majority as low as three, two or even sometimes one. During this period...you had twelve Northern Ireland Tories coming over to Westminster and voting on every single issue from the Rhondda Valley to the Highlands of Scotland. In division after division they were out in the lobbies with their Tory counterparts trying to bring about the downfall of the British Government which was giving them a hundred and seventeen million a year for doing it.

"I can't understand the reason in this at all. I come over here as the representative of West Belfast and can put down a question about what is happening in Hammersmith or Camden. I have to be answered because I am a representative in the British Parliament. But the only constituency that I cannot put down a question about is my own, or for that matter any other Northern Ireland constituency... I was told '...you can't ask about unemployment in Northern Ireland—but you can ask about unemployment in Wales, Scotland, or London or anywhere else'. This is called a convention. Now what is a convention? A convention is something that has been built up over a period of years. It has no legal standing whatever. A convention cannot override a statute, and the statute which relates to Northern Ireland affairs is the 1920 Government of Ireland Act, Section 75 of which is quite clear. Now some people think that a convention which has been built up over 46 years in Westminster should not be tampered with. It certainly works to the advantage of the Tories in Northern Ireland. It keeps the spotlight of public opinion away from Northern Ireland...

"They don't want anybody to know what is going on in Northern Ireland. All they want is that the British Government should give them one hundred and seventeen million in every year to keep them and their supporters happy in Northern Ireland. So the answer to the problem is that the British Government controlling the purse strings should make it quite clear that reforms must take place, otherwise the subsidies to Northern Ireland will be stopped. This seems to me the easiest and most logical solution to the problem.

"There is no time far delay... Those people in Northern Ireland who are at the moment British subjects and citizens of the U.K. are not being treated as such, and are looking to the British ·Parliament for reforms. If reforms are not forthcoming who could blame them for taking whatever action they see fit in the circumstances? I for one, Mr. Chairman would certainly not blame them."

In his Closing Statement, Fitt said:

"I am a member of the Republican Labour Party. I am not a member of the British Labour Party... Therefore I have no say in its Party Conference. Now I realise that although I have made many, many friends in the House of Commons, in the final analysis I could be left standing completely alone, as an Irishman fighting for a solution to the Irish question...

"Now to the many Trade Unionists and members of the Labour Party this

289

evening, I make a special plea, to move resolutions, either at trade union level, or at Labour Party Conference level..., and then we will get the Executive of the Labour Party to come out into the open and we will know where we stand. (Applause)

"One of the speakers said...that there is too much of a religious internecine war going on in Northern Ireland. This is a question of status.... The Protestants have the jobs, where the Catholics do not have the jobs. This is the root of the problem, not the question of worship, but the question of first and second-class citizenships, where there is a large Catholic opposition to the Unionist Party, and the Unionist Party have certainly made it a practice since 1920 to deny those areas industries.

"Put yourself in the position of the Protestant worker in Northern Ireland. It's no good trying to get away from this. Put yourself in the position of Protestant worker...After all he is only a human being. He wants the best standard of life which is possible under the prevailing circumstances, and if he joins the Orange Order, he knows it will open up the door to a job. Once you become a member of this organisation, you are a member of the same organisation as the Prime Minister. You are one of the boys, so, therefore, you can ask and receive a little bit more favour. Why should such a worker vote Labour? This is why there have been twelve Tories from Northern Ireland, four from the industrial city of Belfast

"I want to finish, Mr. Chairman; by stating very clearly where I stand. I am only a Nationalist because I am a socialist. I am a disciple of Connolly..."

## Political chameleon?

It has been said that Gerry Fitt was something of a 'political chameleon', playing the democrat at Westminster and the Republican to other audiences.

But it cannot be discounted that Fitt was attracted to an ordinary reform of 'Northern Ireland' and an infusion of British Labour politics to shake up the system for the betterment of both Catholics and Protestants. And, if Westminster and the British Labour Party had not put up so much determined resistance to this, then Fitt might have found himself pursuing this course with some degree of success, whether he wanted it or not.

If we were to give Fitt the benefit of the doubt on this, we should say that the fortress put up against Fitt by the British political elite impelled him toward the obscurantist *mélange* of British Labourism and Anti-Partitionism that became his characteristic politics and which proved so effective against Ulster Unionism in the latter part of the 1960s.

It seems that Fitt had two objectives that could have been complementary in the best of all worlds—bashing the Ulster Unionists and getting democratic rights and equal citizenship for Catholics within the State. But, due to the stonewalling of the British State, and the Labour Party in particular, those twin objectives could only be in conflict and lead in a very different direction in advancing the Anti-Partitionist struggle to a higher plane.

So Fitt, finding the democratic door shut firmly in his face and needing something to do politically, pushed at the more open door of bashing the Ulster Unionists in the Anti-Partitionist interest.

Gerry Fitt encapsulated the predicament of the Catholic community in the North. It was deprived of a democratic political outlet for its energy in the politics of the State, and the Stormont system was nothing more than a system of communal Protestant over-lording of Catholics. And so Northern Catholics were compelled by the circumstances imposed on them by the Partitionists to continue to be only Anti-Partitionist. And so Gerry Fitt was 'Republican Labour' and not 'Labour'.

If Jack Beattie had been let into the British Labour Party politics during the 1940s, the North would have been connected with power in the State. And the gravitational pull of power in the State would have brought significant alterations in political life in the Six Counties. But the Labour Whip was refused to Beattie. 'Northern Ireland' remained locked up in itself and detached. And that was the situation Fitt worked within.

These were the political circumstances which made Gerry Fitt both an Irish Republican and a British Socialist. If Beattie's demand had been conceded, Fitt might have ended up a Junior Minister in Harold Wilson's Government and might have taken up the work which Joe Devlin had been cut off from in his prime. He was in many respects an archetypal British working-class Labour politician. But he lived as a Catholic in 'Northern Ireland', and that made him a 'Republican' as well.

That is how it appeared to Unionists who disregarded the distinctions Fitt, and Joe Devlin before him, had made, and that is substantially how it therefore was.

## Gerry Fitt's confusion

Many of the criticisms made in the speech by Fitt to the *Irish Democrat* Conference were valid. They were the genuine concerns of Catholics trapped in the political slum of 'Northern Ireland'. However, this speech placed these genuine concerns within a broader Anti-Partitionist context that would ensure what Fitt was saying would be viewed as a new, more sophisticated, Anti-Partitionist manoeuvre by Unionists. If they saw what Clancy and Blythe had being saying in 1958 as Anti-Partitionism by any other name, it was not surprising that they would see the 'Connolly Socialist' similarly.

In the House of Commons, Fitt declared the issue to be the extension of the 1949 *Representation of the People Act* to 'Northern Ireland'. Outside the

Commons, the Unionists saw him declaring the issue to be the unification of Ireland. It is not possible that Fitt could have confused the two. The first was quite a minor reform. The second was something which could only possibly be achieved by warfare, and the destruction of 'Northern Ireland'.

The ending of the property vote had no connection with the ending of Partition. More Unionists than Nationalists were disenfranchised under the old Local Government system (see Hewitt, in *British Journal of Sociology*, Vol. 32, No 3, 1981, p.363-7). The actual establishment of *"one man one vote"* would not have advanced the Anti-Partition cause an inch—it most probably would have resulted in the reverse by removing the grievance.

The confusion of basic democratic demands which could have been met and aims which could only be realised through war was a dangerous misrepresentation. And all it did was convince Unionists all the more that Civil Rights was not sincerely wanted and it was all just another Republican tactic.

If Fitt's objective was to achieve full democratic rights for Catholics, what he was doing became counter-productive. In the deteriorating situation of 1968-69 Nationalist politicians accused the Unionists of slandering the Civil Rights Movement by calling it a Republican front and yet any Protestant reading the speeches of Gerry Fitt would find it difficult to escape that conclusion.

Fitt was accused of being a chameleon by both Terence O'Neill and the Fianna Fail TD for Donegal, Neil Blaney in 1968, after making a rare foray into Southern politics. He intervened in the Southern Referendum over Proportional Representation, criticising Fianna Fail for seeking its replacement with another electoral system. This broke the golden rule that Northerners keep their noses out of Southern affairs. Blaney said of Fitt at the time:

> "He is something of a chameleon who rings his colours up and down as it suits his purpose. He criticises the Taoiseach for referring to partition and says this has strengthened the Unionist case and could be very injurious to the Civil Rights movement. I question Mr. Fitt's motives in regard to the Nationalist population of Derry city for he no sooner got himself batoned in Derry than he was off over the border to use this incident in a most despicable and dishonest way in relation to the referendum" (IN 9.11.68).

Blaney was an honest Fianna Fail Republican and he saw the deceit Fitt was indulging in as unprincipled. And, as if to prove Blaney correct in his view of him, Fitt replied:

> "Over a great number of years I have been appalled at the deafening silence that has emanated from Fianna Fail sources in relation to the situation in Northern Ireland. I do know from quite authentic sources in the Republic that Fianna Fail supporters had been advised not to associate themselves

with the Civil Rights movement in Northern Ireland. And now at this rather late stage, after the overwhelming defeat in the referendum, Fianna Fail now proclaim themselves as the great Republican Party of Ireland. I think their past inactivity in this matter is sufficient to condemn them out of hand" (IN 11.11.68).

So, Gerry Fitt admonished the Taoiseach when he mentioned the Civil Rights Movement in the same breath as Anti-Partitionism, and then criticised Fianna Fail for not being Republican enough, and for not involving themselves in the Civil Rights struggle.

If Fitt's maiden speech had been made in earnest and been taken up as such by British Labour, and if he had campaigned within West Belfast in support of the aims he expressed in it as vigorously as he had campaigned to discredit Stormont before British public opinion, he may have made a difference in a different way than he subsequently did.

But perhaps that was too much to expect. Fitt, once he encountered resistance from the British political establishment, did not campaign in West Belfast in support of advance through the development of normal British politics in the province.

He had complained in his maiden speech that the Unionists did not allow normal British politics to develop in West Belfast, but he never put it to West Belfast that it should advance against the Unionist Party in the ranks of the Labour Party. If he had, in the circumstances of 1970 when much of the Catholic community was in a state of political indecision before the IRA got organised, it is possible that he would have carried some of that community with him and attracted substantial support from Protestants who were fed up with the Unionist Party. But by that stage he was part of something bigger and he chose to ride the tiger.

If Fitt had demanded that the Labour Party should organise in the province so that normal British politics could develop there, the Labour Party would have found it much more difficult to have kept up its boycott of the province. He was immensely influential in that period—much more influential than any other Irish politician since. But he did not do so. So, while he complained of the absence of normal British politics, he did nothing to demand the means by which normal British politics might actually develop.

Presumably, Gerry Fitt wanted British rights but not British politics. However, effective rights and political structures are not separable in the real world. British rights without British politics would have meant either continued domination by the Unionist Party or the Direct Rule situation which later came about. That would have been an improvement on the Stormont system but the abnormal politics of 'Northern Ireland' would have continued. In 1969 'Northern Ireland' got British rights and by 1970 it was on the verge of civil war.

It seems, therefore, that Fitt settled for British rights merely to disrupt the Unionist regime in a way that would be advantageous to the ending of Partition. The rights themselves, of course, had no Anti-Partitionist significance. So Fitt can only have believed that the Nationalist resentments worked up in connection with them, and the disturbances which would occur with their establishment, could be exploited for Anti-Partitionist purposes, with Fitt being the left-wing of the movement.

That was very much the stuff of the Desmond Greaves/Connolly Association strategy and it could have been that Fitt saw his activities as part of that scheme. Greaves had made contact with Fitt when he was first elected MP and impressed upon him the importance of raising issues about the North at Westminster.

In an interview with Michael A. Murphy, the chief political biographer of Fitt, a colleague of Greaves, Anthony Coughlan, confirmed:

> "There was a close political connection between the Connolly Association, Desmond Greaves and Fitt from 1961/2 onward, and possibly earlier... The Connolly Association had been seeking to expose Unionism in Britain since 1958, and indeed earlier, and yet there was very little support for or response to that from the Six Counties itself until Fitt's advent in Britain following his election as an MP. His arrival in Britain from the 'belly of the beast' in the Six Counties was of great practical and symbolic importance at the time. The Connolly Association campaigning since the mid-1950s had led to the emergence of a significant anti-Unionist element among British Labour MPs at Westminster by the mid-1960s, but the Six Counties themselves seemed to be virtually somnolent so far as civil rights issues were concerned. So when Fitt was elected to Westminster he found himself in the congenial company of quite a number of Labour MPs who knew what he was talking about and were sympathetic to his anti-Unionist message. But it had taken a decade of hard work in Britain, overwhelmingly by the Connolly Association and the bodies it was affiliated to and influenced- the NCCL (National Council for Civil Liberties) and MCF (Movement for Colonial Freedom) — to bring that situation about. It contrasted fundamentally of course with Labour's wholesale endorsement of the Unionist position by means of the Ireland Act 1949, when the Labour Party had been overwhelmingly pro Unionist" (*Gerry Fitt—A Political Chameleon*, p.103).

In *Gerry Fitt—A Political Chameleon*, Murphy comes to the conclusion that Fitt was fundamentally a British Labourite trapped in the Irish Nationalist *milieu* by the disengagement of Britain from the North. For an Irish Nationalist, Dublin had no appeal to him and he had little interest in Southern politics. His orientation was always toward Westminster and his antagonism was directed against Ulster Unionism, but never Britain.

And that goes a long way to explaining how the 'Connolly Socialist' ended his days in the British House of Lords.

## Greaves and Republicans

Greaves not only influenced the 'constitutional' Nationalism of Gerry Fitt, he also exerted a guiding influence on Republicanism.

With the failure of the Border campaign of 1956-62, the IRA Chief of Staff had resigned. The new Republican leadership of Cathal Goulding and Tomas MacGiolla who filled the vacuum left vacant by imprisonments and disagreements, were open to new ideas to keep the movement in existence when military activities were impossible.

Goulding was contacted by a socialist intellectual, Roy Johnston, who had been active in the Connolly Association in London during the 1950s. Johnston was a colleague of Greaves, a theorist of the Communist Party of Great Britain. During the Second World War the Connolly Association had been taken in hand by Desmond Greaves on behalf of the CPGB and he ran it for the CPGB for the next 40 years.

Some connections were established between the Connolly Association and Republicans after the failure of the Border campaign, and Johnston and Anthony Coughlan, another member of the Connolly Association, helped establish the *Wolfe Tone Societies* in Ireland, where they engaged with Republicans to commemorate the bicentennial of the birth of Wolfe Tone in 1963.

At this time the Republican movement was engaging in a campaign in defence of economic independence and against Irish entry into the European Common Market. It was also hostile to the meeting of Lemass and O'Neill which took place in January 1965. Greaves and Johnston began to convince the Republican leadership that the Lemass/O'Neill talks, the movement toward EEC membership, and the signing of the Anglo Irish Free Trade Agreement of 1965 were part of the one process. They represented a developing alliance between compromising Irish Nationalism and Imperialism that would culminate in the reintegration of Ireland economically and politically into the British sphere in a new federal relationship (an aim of Lemass was a federal Ireland).

This big idea gave the Republicans a new political focus in opposition to the 'new Imperialism', in defence of Irish Protectionism and National Sovereignty against the compromising mainstream of Irish Nationalism, particularly in Fianna Fail and was to have significant effects later on, in relation to the North.

Roy Johnston joined the Republican movement and became its Director of Education. The intention of Greaves and Johnston was not to convert the Irish Republican movement, which they saw as the inheritor of the "anti-imperialist" tradition in Ireland, into a Communist movement, but rather to utilise it as an ally in a broad-based National Liberation Movement.

Greaves' Communism was a highly nationalist variation of Marxism but he was keenly aware that any talk of Communism in Ireland would alienate large sections of the population and make the building of the kind of movement he desired impossible. So he and Johnston, while educating the Republicans in politics, took great care in deterring them from declaring for a Workers' Republic, or anything sounding too Communist, as politically damaging.

The Republican campaigns in defence of economic independence proved to be a failure. However, the re-education of the Republican Movement by the Marxists proved all too successful.

## The Greaves Plan for the North

Desmond Greaves also had an 'anti-imperialist' plan for the North. In 1963 Greaves wrote a pamphlet called, 'The Irish Question and the British People'. It addressed the problem of Partition and how to end it.

Greaves noted how the IRA campaign to defeat Unionism by pure force had been unsuccessful. As an alternative, he outlined a plan whereby what could not be achieved by force might be achieved by other means.

Greaves argued that the way forward for Anti-Partitionists was through a Civil Rights campaign in 'Northern Ireland'. Greaves saw two advantages to such a plan. He thought that, if the British were made aware of the situation in 'Northern Ireland' by a Civil Rights campaign, they would be encouraged to re-evaluate the *Government of Ireland Act* of 1920, which he saw as maintaining the Union. Secondly, he believed that, if the campaign was successful, sectarianism would disappear and the combined masses, Catholic and Protestant, would overthrow the Border.

Greaves believed the masses to be inherently "anti-imperialist". The Protestants, he took to be under the false consciousness of a Tory-Unionist clique, who diverted them from their natural 'Irishness' and the spirit of their forefathers in the United Irishmen. A similar outlook predominated in the *Northern Ireland Communist Party*. Its 1965 Programme, *Unite*, conceived of a "progressive Stormont which could act as an anti-imperialist force independent of Westminster" (p.14). It also suggested: "Paisley, so long as he disrupts the Unionist ranks can be regarded as ally... his supporters... can be won for a genuine radical and national stand in the long run" (p.15).

The strategy of Johnston and Greaves was founded on the belief that Protestant workers would be receptive to the Republican message but, because *Sinn Fein/Republican Clubs* was banned in the North, it was necessary to remove the repressive legislation through a civil rights agitation. And the Republican Movement needed to be detached from overt Catholicism to make it more amenable to Protestants, so Rosary-saying was suppressed from Republican commemorations, much to the annoyance of traditionalists.

The theory was that, when the Civil Rights Movement had broken down certain features of the Unionist 'state', Republicanism would be made more attractive to Protestants. So Sinn Fein was to get involved in everyday issues and the Republican movement was to be the vehicle for the converts in the Protestant community to become effective anti-imperialists. Or, at least, that was the plan.

Just prior to the launching of the Civil Rights movement, Johnston produced an internal document for Sinn Fein in 1967, outlining the direction in which such a movement should develop for Republican purposes. Under the heading, 'The Struggle for Democratic Rights', it said:

> "The Unionist leaders will try to concede the minimum. They are in an extremely awkward situation. Let us make it as much more awkward for them as we can. On the one side they are caught by the changing demands of Britain's policy towards Ireland as a whole, and by the bad publicity they are getting in Britain —where people are demanding to know why British taxpayers' money should be used to subsidise a Tory gang in the North while Britain's own economy is in crisis. On the other hand the Unionists should be squeezed by popular demands from the disenfranchised, the gerrymandered, the discriminated against, the oppressed Catholic and Nationalist minority within the North itself, demands for reforms, for Civil Rights, for genuine democracy and opportunities of free political expression.

> "There can be no doubt that the policy of Republicans must be to ensure everything is done to make this demand strong, vigorously organised, widespread, well-expressed and heard not only in the North itself, but in Britain and throughout the world. Force O'Neill to CONCEDE MORE THAN HE WANTS TO DO OR THAN HE THINKS HE CAN DARE GIVE without risking overthrow by the more reactionary elements among the Unionists. Demand more than may be demanded by the compromising elements that exist among the Catholic leadership" (*Republican Educational Manual*, Vol. III, p.39).

This had originally appeared in an article by Anthony Coughlan, called 'Our Ideas' in the Wolfe Tone Society newsletter, *Tuairisc*, of 31st August 1966. A copy had been obtained by the Inspector General of the RUC and was shown to Terence O'Neill, with the Prime Minister's attention being drawn to the pages containing the above passage. It was intended to send it to the British Home Office but it was deemed "too risky" to do so (PRONI 25.10.66, Cab/9B7201/14).

The Greaves strategy went something like this: An Anti-Partitionist manoeuvre was to be conducted under the cloak of a campaign for democratic reform. Republicans were to ensure that, whatever was conceded by the

Unionists, it should not be accepted until Unionism was divided, and then a campaign could be conducted on a higher plane to end Partition. And at all costs democratic reform was not to be allowed to take place before an Anti-Partition campaign had gained momentum.

The *Northern Ireland Civil Rights Association* (NICRA) was set up by a number of conferences organised by the Republicans (through front groups, the *Wolfe Tone Societies*) and came into existence on 29th January 1967. It was, of course, composed of much more than Republicans. If it were made up of Republicans, it would have been completely ineffective in what it set out to do. Its first Executive included 3 members of the CPNI and a number of middle-class Catholic reformers.

Only one Republican joined it, because it was important that the IRA was distanced from NICRA. (Billy McMillen, Officer Commanding of the Belfast Brigade, sensibly declined a position on it.) At the same time, however, it would be possible for them to determine its direction since only they and the Communists had a purposeful political orientation on it, the strategy thought out by Greaves.

But NICRA was initially very cautious. For its first 18 months hardly anyone knew of its existence. The Communists, who still had a base in the Protestant working class, were concerned at not alienating support and confined themselves to sending letters to Stormont and Westminster demanding reform. To the irritation of the Republicans, NICRA's approach posed minimal problems for Unionism.

The Greaves analysis was an idealistic fantasy in its belief that 'Northern Ireland' could be democratised so that Protestant workers would unite with Catholics for Republican objectives. Greaves saw progressive possibilities in Stormont as an 'Irish' institution detached from the UK State, which he believed could be normalised through putting pressure on the State to normalise it. The plan was successful, however, in producing a more devious and flexible approach against the Stormont system which shattered the all-class alliance that sustained it by exploiting the differences between the Stormont system and the democratic projections of the British State.

So Greaves was right in thinking the Civil Rights approach could cause divisions in the Unionist Party, but was very mistaken in his idea of what this would lead to.

## Austin Currie begins the war

In a speech during October 1967, Austin Currie, the Nationalist MP for East Tyrone, told an audience at a meeting of the *Economic and Political Studies Society* in Magee University College, Derry, of the feelings in the

Catholic community towards O'Neill:

> "No politician in the history of this state has aroused hopes and
> expectations to the same extent as has Captain O'Neill. For the first time we
> seemed to have a Prime Minister who could shake off the shackles of the
> past and look to the future" (*Belfast News Letter*, 24.10.67).

Currie warned that O'Neill had a 12 month deadline in which to "weed
out injustice and intolerance" and that, if he failed, a "grave militancy" would
develop in the Catholic community. As events proved, 12 months was
accurate nearly to the day. Currie warned:

> "There will be more squatting, more acts of civil disobedience, more
> emphasis on 'other means' and less on traditional Parliamentary methods.
> And Terence O'Neill and his Government must carry their responsibility.
> The Prime Minister could leave a record of real achievement or, if he refused
> to act, he will be recognised as the political confidence trickster... and
> stuntman of this generation".

Then the issue of direct action was raised. At a *National Council for
Civil Liberties* meeting held in Scarborough in October 1967 Paul Rose of
the *Campaign for Democracy in Ulster* acknowledged that parliamentary
methods had been shown to have failed: "Unless action is taken in the lifetime
of the present Labour Government to right injustice against the minority in
'Northern Ireland' many people in the province will be tempted to turn to
extra-parliamentary methods" (BT 4.10.67).

On 19th June 1968, with the help of local Republicans, Austin Currie
occupied a house in Caledon to protest at its allocation to a single Protestant
woman by the local Council. Currie argued that his action was to highlight
discriminatory allocation practices by the Unionists.

This is how Currie saw the significance of what he had started, writing
in the first page of his autobiography, *All Hell Will Break Loose*:

> "On Wednesday 19 June 1968, near the end of an acrimonious debate in
> the Stormont Parliament, I was ordered by the Speaker to leave the House.
> As I left, I angrily threw my speaking notes at the jeering Unionist benches
> and shouted, 'All hell will break loose, and by God I will lead it' ... I didn't
> wish to hang around anyway. I knew what I had to do.
>
> "Had I known the consequences of what I intended to do later that day, at
> Caledon, would I have proceeded with it? I have asked myself that question
> many, many times over the years. Would I have gone ahead had I known, or
> even suspected, that the action I was about to take would initiate a process
> that would lead to the loss of nearly four thousand lives? Would I have gone
> ahead had I known that my intended action and other actions stemming
> from it would transform the political scene in Northern Ireland and destroy

a political regime which, at that time, appeared permanent and unchallengeable?... These are some of the questions I have wrestled with for more than thirty years..." (p. 9-10).

This is all very honest — although Currie answers his own question that he would not have occupied the house at Caledon and brought direct action into play against the Stormont system if he knew all the trouble he was going to cause in doing so.

But this also suggests that, without the trouble, there would still be the same *"political regime"* that appeared *"permanent and unchallengeable"*.

So it seems that the Republican War was a necessary event in the Great Transformation of the Catholic community even from the perspective of 'constitutional nationalism'.


## The Nationalist Party ponders

A week later, at the *Nationalist Party* Conference in Belfast, Currie proposed that the Party should support a campaign of non-violent civil disobedience. This is the report from the *Irish News* of 24th June 1968:

> "Proposing the motion Mr. Currie said they had been complaining about discrimination in housing, jobs and other things for 50 years. When Mr. O'Neill came to power many of them had high hopes, but for 5 years now all they had got was pious platitudes and damn all else.
>
> "Mr. Barney McShane (Newry) said they should take stock of where the motion would lead them. Did Mr. Currie mean that they should not draw unemployment benefit and not pay the stamp?
>
> "Alderman Jack Harvey (Derry) said he was not frightened by violence, but a constitutional party was not the place for it. The only body with the right to use force was the Irish government, he said. Unfortunately that government seems to have more loyalty to party than country, he said. How was a civil disobedience campaign to be kept non-violent? He asked. You can take it from me boy, it can't be done.
>
> "Some doubted popular support for such a campaign. One delegate feared 'a return to 1956'. 'It was not much fun for our people' he added. Conference decided to instruct their Executive Committee to study the implications of a non-violent civil disobedience campaign."

The *Irish News* editorial commented:

> "While the Nationalist Party have been soldiering on, their opposition has been a hopelessly inadequate outlet for the securing of any redress of minority grievances — Mr. Currie's squat being an example. Mr. McAteer seems to be wondering if opposition at Stormont is worth anything. The non-violent civil disobedience campaign which he advocates is rightly a

matter for deep consideration, and the convention was wise to ask the Executive to undertake a study of the implications of the policy."

Where was opposition to go once it had tried and failed at Stormont— only to civil rights agitation on the streets?

## Legitimising the system

The taking up of Opposition by the Nationalists helped to both legitimise the Stormont system and give the British an excuse for non-intervention in 'Ulster'. During June 1968 Lord Stonham, Minister for State at the British Home Office, paid a three-day visit to the province to see if the natives were indeed restless.

According to the *Belfast Telegraph* report (7.6.68), headed *'No pressure on Stormont over bias',* Labour had discounted interfering in Stormont affairs partly because of the assumption of the role of Official Opposition by the Nationalist Party. Stonham said in the interview:

"Capt. O'Neill was not being pressurised by Westminster on the question of discrimination... that would be wholly wrong... but we can certainly give advice... such interference would be equally resented by the Opposition leader Mr. McAteer as by Captain O'Neill... The curse of Cromwell is a thing of the past... things are very much better than I anticipated. You don't advertise yourself very well here."

The *Belfast Telegraph* further reported:

"Referring to his meeting earlier with Mr. McAteer, Lord Stonham said he believed Stormont now had an effective opposition which was so essential to any democracy."

So, the assumption of Opposition by the Nationalist Party on the instructions of Lemass, had helped to bolster the façade of 'democracy' in the Six Counties. Taking the soup had, after all, involved supping with the devil.

How much the Nationalists had helped legitimise the system for Whitehall can be seen in the fact that an article appeared in the *Times* as late as in August 1968 by the constitutional historian and Labour MP, John Mackintosh, which used the example of Stormont as a great success story which he argued proved that devolution for Scotland and Wales should hold no fear for Westminster:

"The Stormont system started as something no one wanted, and has become positively popular. It is significant that the demand for Dominion status heard in the 1930s has gone, but so has the desire to be completely incorporated into Britain" (*The Times* 6.8.68).

R.J. Lawrence's *The Government of Northern Ireland* appeared out of Queen's University in 1965, just after the Nationalists had taken up the role of Opposition. It noted:

> "Single-party government and all it implies is distasteful to liberal-minded men... It has, indeed, been argued that the transfer to London of Ulster's affairs would weaken Unionist domination... and heal social divisions more rapidly because Westminster would be more willing than Stormont to redress Nationalist grievances. That, however, seems too simple a prescription for a deep-seated malady... one party has been in power since 1921 simply because Nationalists repudiated a constitution that perpetuates partition. By changing this attitude they could gradually make party politics less rigid and partially less defensible. The decision by the Nationalist Party in 1965 to accept the role of Official Opposition at Stormont could have a profound effect on Ulster politics" (p.168).

The decision did indeed have *"a profound effect"*. Just as Stormont seemed to reach the pinnacle of its democratic pretensions with the legitimacy conferred upon it by the Nationalists, it began to unravel.

## The New Departure

In mid-1968, the campaign for Civil Rights was about to enter a new phase. With the failure of the Nationalist Opposition at Stormont to gain anything, and Gerry Fitt's rebuffal at Westminster, this was inevitable. And it was also clear that the Nationalist Party were far too set in its ways to lead the campaign which Austin Currie was wanting. Politics went onto the streets.

At the end of April 1968 Currie, on a NICRA platform in Armagh, at a meeting held to protest at the banning of Easter Commemorations by the Unionist Government, outlined a suggested 'New Departure' in Catholic politics:

> "Such a movement would not confine itself to constitutional methods if by these words is meant the type of political activity we have been involved in over the years but would use all the weapons in the arsenal of non-violent civil disobedience... We will have justice or we will make a governmental system based on injustice unworkable" (IN 29.4.68).

In his autobiography Currie saw the New Departure as "invoking the development, under Charles Stewart Parnell, of a national movement involving the Land League, the Irish Parliamentary Party and elements of the Fenian movement" (*All Hell Will Break Loose*, p. 100). On the platform with Currie were Eddie McAteer, Gerry Fitt and members of the Republican Clubs.

The obvious question was: could the new 'Fenians' be controlled as well as Parnell managed it?

NICRA organised a march from Coalisland to Dungannon on 24th August to demand '*one man, one vote*'. It was attended by about 4,000 people and went off peacefully. Republicans provided 70 of the stewards for the march. Another march was set for Derry on 5th October. This, however, was banned by William Craig, the Minister for Home Affairs at Stormont.

The cautious NICRA Executive was in favour of calling off the march, and would have done so, if the Republicans, and a number of activists centred around Eamon McCann in Derry, had not declared their intention of going ahead regardless. In the interests of the campaign, it was decided that the inevitable confrontation should not be avoided. As McCann later said, the march was aimed "to provoke the police into over-reaction and thus spark off mass reaction against the authorities" (*War And An Irish Town*, p35). NICRA, of course, were not entirely in agreement with this, but it decided to sponsor the march nonetheless.

October 5th is the date on which the Northern Ireland Civil Rights Movement became known world-wide. And it was undoubtedly the case that October 5th was a great propaganda victory for NICRA. In the conflict between marchers and the police, nearly one hundred were injured and, more important, the whole scene was captured by British television crews, and shown on screens throughout the United Kingdom and abroad. What the British public saw was peaceful protesters, led by three MPs, demanding '*one man, one vote*', being attacked by a 'British' police force in the UK. It was not surprising that NICRA rose from obscurity to worldwide recognition in one day.

Those more traditional Republicans who could see little or nothing of value in the Civil Rights Movement suddenly saw its potential. Seamus Rodgers of Donegal Sinn Fein told a meeting in Strabane in December 1968 that "the civil rights movement has done more in a few weeks to damage the Unionist state than decades of IRA activities" (Bishop and Mallie, *The Provisional IRA*, p.56).

## The Civil Rights demands

The fundamental element in the Greaves strategy was the undermining of the Unionist Government in the eyes of the British. There was little doubt that discrimination was practised in 'Northern Ireland' and it was this which NICRA set out to exploit. The Civil Rights Movement conducted its propaganda at the level of pure formal democratic principles, presenting Catholic grievances as evidence of a reactionary Unionist regime. But the facts were not as simple as that.

The Civil Rights demands by themselves did not constitute the reasons for what happened subsequently. It was the political momentum they produced, particularly when Unionism chose not to address them, that blew the system apart.

The great Civil Rights slogan of *'One Man, One Vote!'* played well on the international media, but it was actually much ado about nothing. What it mainly referred to was not voting in either the State or the Stormont elections, but an element of plural votes in Local Government elections which had been ended in Britain some years earlier. The conceding of that demand would have changed next to nothing. The astonishing thing is that the UUP did not concede such an insignificant demand the instant it was made.

The Unionists probably thought that it was of so little consequence that it was not worth conceding, since it would not satisfy Nationalists and granting it would only annoy the Unionist base. But that was a big mistake because its value was in the propaganda it allowed, rather than the political effect of abolition. When it was conceded by O'Neill, in 1969, it was treated, by those who had raised it, as being of no consequence at all.

The slogan, as played in the British, Irish, and international media, suggested that the Northern Catholics were deprived of voting rights *en masse*, as were blacks in South Africa and the Southern USA. The Civil Rights leaders must have known very well that this was not the case, and that the element of disfranchisement was fairly trivial, and was not even one-sided. But the obtuseness of the UUP made the issue an effective wedge for splitting the whole Northern situation open.

The gerrymandering of Derry Corporation and some other council areas provided the strongest case for accusations of discrimination. But this was largely confined to local government rather than parliamentary elections. Parliamentary constituencies mitigated more against smaller parties and if anything aided the representation of the communal parties.

The grievances about economic discrimination were also not fundamental to the problem. The hostility of the nationalist community to the devolved system had economic consequences, as John Hume noted. The Catholic community boycotted many of the institutions of the statelet after Partition. There was a reluctance to join the security forces, the judiciary, the Northern Ireland civil service, and other Stormont agencies, because Nationalists saw these institutions as illegitimate, temporary and the instruments of oppression. Catholics were much more likely to work in the UK reserved services, such as the Post Office. The devolved institutions became bastions of Loyal Protestantism and then reproduced themselves with a strong communal character, as most areas of life in the Province did. When the entire apparatus of state became British and less Ulster Unionist in 1972, Catholics became much more likely to move into these areas of public employment and soon began to flourish in them.

As Hume also noted, Catholic industrial development tended to be weaker than Protestant development for a number of reasons, quite disconnected with notions of 'discrimination'. There were historical factors that led to Catholic economic development in towns being confined to certain trades. There were geographical factors that aided industrial growth around the port of Belfast and therefore largely in Protestant areas. And it would be naïve to think that religions as different as Calvinism and Catholicism would produce through their schools economic results that were identical, when they encouraged ways of looking at life that were so different.

The type of discrimination which took place in the province was, in fact, widespread across the UK, particularly in relation to immigrants and women—but generally not religion. Religion had become a matter of little consequence in England since its anti-Catholicism was de-institutionalised in the 17th to the 19th Century. It caused minimal trouble there and was easily legislated away without causing a revolt from the indigenous population. Since 'Northern Ireland' was such a divided society, in which the two communities largely lived separate existences, it was quite natural that they would both look after and employ their own kind and be reluctant about doing otherwise.

Communal politics led to sectarian allocation of resources such as housing and public service employment where these functions were provided by Local Councils dominated by one side or another though predominantly by Unionists, and there were no votes to be gained, and some to be lost, in the rewarding of those who would potentially vote for you. The inevitable consequence was discrimination and a strong sense of inequality among Catholics.

NICRA concentrated on persuading the British that what they were protesting about was the Unionist prevention of Catholics taking their full part in the processes and institutions of the state and its economic life, as Blacks were prevented from doing in many US states. The Civil Rights case was based on an abstraction—but what was important was to make sure it was this which the British accepted as the true situation, not the more complex historical context. It was, of course, no concern of NICRA to help the Unionists with a broader, more complex picture that might complicate its message.

The beauty of the NICRA approach was that it persuaded the British that here were people being batoned by a British police force for doing nothing more than demanding the same rights and privileges as the rest of the United Kingdom. It was no wonder that, against the perceived liberal standards of the British State, the Unionists looked to be a gang of backward reactionaries.

The Civil Rights demands were conceded before 1970. And there still was a War—which tends to suggest that the War was not about Civil Rights at all, or was only connected to them in a superficial way.

In fact, the trivial Civil Rights demands were totally inadequate to the situation in which the North found itself by 1968-9. They were met and the whole place still went into flux. And then a War was launched without any reference to them.

The British were always open to addressing these Catholic grievances because they could place the blame for them on local Protestants. They were useful diversions from the real issue from the point of view of the British State, particularly since the architect of the cause of Catholic second-class citizenship was actually Westminster and the abnormal political conditions it imposed in a region of the UK rather than the local Unionists, who simply operated the system on Britain's behalf and upon whom London wished to place responsibility.

But what Westminster found difficult was cajoling the Unionist Government into taking steps that the Protestant masses found difficult to stomach.

Whilst the civil rights demands were comparatively trivial, the Civil Rights Movement was not. Northern Nationalism had finally extricated itself from its position of being a mere adjunct of the Southern State. It had at last produced something of its own that was outside the control and direction of Dublin. It was the independent political expression of Northern Catholics. And things would never be the same again, as a result.

The reason why the Civil Rights Movement in the North was beyond the influence of Dublin was that the South had ceased to have a policy with regard to the North. Dublin had, of course, a strategic Anti-Partitionism but it also had a tactical desire to maintain Partition, lest the 'extremists' in the North destabilise things. The policy Dublin sank into with regard to the North was one of 'moderation', and 'moderation' is not really a policy at all. So for the first time the Northern Catholics struck out on their own and Dublin had nothing to offer them as an alternative - either to deter them or to take them in hand.

## Nationalist Party walks out

After the events in Derry, there were increasing signs within the Nationalist Party of disenchantment with having taken up the mantle of Official Opposition at Stormont. The success of the street politics at Derry showed up the impotence of the Opposition at Stormont. After Derry, Eddie McAteer, said: "it is clear that the Nationalists' Party must reconsider what its role should be, whether in fact there is any use in parliament in providing a cloak for what is a one-party system here" (IN 7.10.68).

On 10th October, Derry Nationalists, by an overwhelming majority, recommended that the Party should withdraw from the role of Official Opposition at Stormont. On the same night, Austin Currie, Nationalist member for East Tyrone, speaking at a Constituency Meeting in Cookstown said that:

"... the party would cease to be the official opposition. The decision to become the official opposition... had been taken in the aftermath of the O'Neill-Lemass talks as an earnest gesture of the party's dedication to the ideal of good community relations and in the belief that the new atmosphere would lead to government intervention to ensure social justice.

"For the nationalists, official opposition had been a degrading one-way process of all give and no take. As far as he was concerned the experiment had already ended. Derry was just the last nail in the coffin... In a normal democratic community, Mr. Currie said change would take place through the normal channel of parliamentary debate. But this was not a normal community and those who desired change had not been able to achieve it through Parliament. The same changes had been demanded over 40-odd years and had been constantly refused. It was for this reason and this reason only that civil disobedience had been used in an effort to bring social justice. If the Unionist Party continued with its 'not an inch' policy, civil disobedience would inevitably spread. The theme for an increased number of people in the future would be: If we cannot have justice, then we must make a system based on injustice unworkable" (IN 11.10.68).

On 11th October, the Nationalist Party Executive recommended to the Parliamentary Party that they should withdraw from the status of Official Opposition at Stormont. Total abstention was not recommended, although there was a distinct possibility the Party would decide on a policy of partial abstention.

The *Irish News* commented:

"Mr. Austin Currie has described the Nationalist Party's role as official opposition at Stormont as a 'degrading, one way process of all take and no give' While we do not think that the party degraded itself by making the gesture it did in the pursuit of good community relations we certainly agree that the process has been very much one sided, and that to continue to act as official opposition would not merely be farcical—it would, in addition and more seriously, be morally wrong, because in effect what it would be doing-and all, in fact, that it was ever expected to do—would be to give an appearance of democracy to utterly undemocratic proceedings... The question is where do we go from here?" (12.10.68).

Where indeed?

On 15th October, after a Debate in Stormont over the events in Derry, the Nationalists declared that they would cease "to function as the official opposition until such times as the Government gives further concrete evidence of its sincere desire to remedy the present situation".

On his meeting with Mr. O'Neill, Eddie McAteer said "I asked for bread and I got a very small crumb" (IN 16.10.68).

The Nationalists had realised that the charade of 'opposition' was over and that sitting on the Benches at Stormont had been nothing but an indulgence in the Lemass/O'Neill fantasy of 'state' politics. They had given credibility and "pathetic gratitude" (in Michael Farrell's phrase) to O'Neill, when none was deserved, and had received nothing of substance in return. In a Debate on Brookeborough's retirement during February, McAteer ruefully stated:

> "In some way or another I am reminded of a very recent experience which I had discussing—with a veteran Nationalist some of the difficulties surrounding the new soft-line approach. I talked for some time and I recall he looked at me sorrowfully and said, 'Ah, sure, Eddie, there is hardly any such thing as politics now at all'..." (NI House of Commons *Debates*, Vol. LXVIII, col. 1140).

When the Nationalists had given up their traditional role and entered Stormont they had given up politics to take part in a fantasy. But they were to find that it was easier to trade in the politics for the fantasy, than it was to trade in the fantasy for politics—because, while the hands of time had stood still in the fantasy world, politics had been moving on outside.

The Nationalist Party announcement, on 17th November, that it was leaving its role as Official Opposition and was going over to a policy of non-violent civil disobedience, seems to have prompted O'Neill to act.

On the 22nd he announced a Five Point plan of reform, including the appointment of an ombudsman to investigate citizens' grievances, the re-organisation of Local Government within 3 years, the abolition of the company vote in local elections, the advising of local authorities to adopt a points system for housing allocation, and the replacement of Derry Corporation by an appointed Development Commission.

The *Irish News* editorial on 23rd November, 1968, the day after O'Neill's Five Point Programme, said:

> "... now, after the years of frustration, after the fair words which were never backed by appropriate action, after the contemptuous treatment which drove the Nationalist Party out of the role of official opposition into a policy of civil disobedience, after Dungannon and after Derry, this hazy, hedging statement of a reform programme is just not enough.
>
> "We want more, and we want it now. We want full democracy for everyone—and not in the seventies or eighties."

On November 25th NICRA rejected O'Neill's scheme too.

The reform movement had built up such momentum that it could no longer be satisfied with the concession of the formal demands with which it had begun.

O'Neill followed up his concessions with an emotional speech on television which was known as the *'Ulster at the Crossroads'* broadcast where he appealed for the moderate centre to come forward and save the situation. But 'Northern Ireland' was not conducive to the assertion of a 'moderate centre'.

Two days later, O'Neill sacked William Craig, the Minister responsible for the banning of the Derry March. In response, NICRA announced a Christmas truce, and Nationalist caution became evident.

The Civil Rights campaign had undoubtedly reached a watershed. The substance of its demands had been met, or was in the process of being met, and it was now impossible to proceed without bringing more overt Anti-Partitionist demands to the fore. Opinion was divided. The more reformist elements wanted to give O'Neill time to manoeuvre so that reforms would be forthcoming. Others, whose interest in the reform campaign was more concerned with how it advanced Anti-Partitionist objectives, wanted to push on.

The confusion on the ground is entirely understandable because of what confronted the civil rights agitators. The obscure construct of 'Northern Ireland' confronting them produced a welter of contradictory notions and intentions that made for general confusion. In the circumstances the only movement that seemed appropriate was a forward one of pushing at the Unionist regime, after some momentary hesitations. And if the Civil Rights Movement did not do the pushing, others stepped forward to do it instead.


## Enter People's Democracy (stage left)

It was at this stage that the student group, People's Democracy, entered the scene. PD was a coalition of various elements. There were Socialists who were Civil Righters and Socialists who were first and foremost Nationalists. Then there was the bulk of the rank and file, who were students caught up with the radicalism of the 1960s. They became a great variety of political things subsequently from Provos to University Professors and from Revolutionary Socialists to the Alliance Party.

Ed Maloney stated in a collection of memoirs about the Civil Rights Movement published in 1988 that People's Democracy "had little to do with nationalism or republicanism, if anything, we were trying to make Northern

Ireland more British, not less" (Michael Farrell, *Twenty Years On*, p.138).

That might have been the formal position—although it was rarely articulated in such terms—but, in December 1968, the political line which predominated within PD was the militant Nationalism of Michael Farrell and Cyril Toman. PD was also supported by the Republicans who suggested in the *United Irishman* of January 1969 that things should be pushed on: "Nationalists and Capt. O'Neill would have the Civil Rights marches stop: republicans would have them continue until something tangible is gained."

After much political manoeuvering, the PD leadership decided to march from Belfast to Derry to ratchet up the pressure on O'Neill.

Opinion in NICRA was almost unanimously against this highly provocative course of action. Alderman Frank McCarroll of the Nationalist Party said:

> "I feel that someone should say publicly what many Civil Rights supporters are saying in private, namely that the proposed march is ill-advised and further, that the truce involving the cessation of street demonstrations should be extended, at least until it is seen clearly that there remains a need for such demonstrations... If those who, for one reason or another seek trouble, should be successful in their attempts to make use of legitimate demonstrations in order to distort clear-cut issues by the intrusion of sectarian strife there would be much to lose and nothing to be gained" (IN 28.12.68).

Eddie McAteer commented:

> "I would rather they didn't {march} but it is up to them now. I think it isn't good marching weather in more senses than one and I feel the public has become browned off with marches and that they have lost their novelty" (IN, 30.12.68)

But the radical PD leaders had a Trotskyite abandon and were out to destroy Unionism first and foremost. Michael Farrell was afraid that NICRA was about to accept O'Neill's reforms, and there would be an end to agitation and so to revolution. The march was designed to prevent the reforms, and plunge Ulster into a "revolutionary situation", in the general spirit of new left student radicalism of the time, that had been seen on the streets of Paris.

Everyone, PD included, knew the likely consequences of a march from Belfast to Derry, by people seen as Republican, through Protestant townlands. Most in PD naively thought this to be simply an attempt to break down political divisions, and build a new cross-community movement. Others, who knew what was what, understood it would provoke rank-and-file Protestant opposition which could be of use to the general Anti-Partitionist/ revolutionary objective. This element unfurled a tricolour as they marched through the Protestant areas.

The march was harassed as it entered Protestant villages and at Burntollet Bridge, six miles outside Derry, it was seriously attacked. The RUC did not intervene (except to participate in the attack) and made no arrests among the attackers. Rioting broke out in the Bogside in response to the TV pictures, and barricades went up in Derry for a week.

A week after Burntollet, Newry PD organised a march "to capitalize on the emotions engendered by Burntollet", as T. Keene, their local Chairman revealed. There was, again, violence at the march as marchers clashed with the RUC. John Hume said after Newry that "at the moment it would appear that mass demonstrations were distracting attention from the central issues of the Civil Rights movement" (IN 15.1.69). A week later he said: "the Civil Rights movement was at a crossroads and this was now the time for all those who supported it to restate clearly what it stood for. All that they sought, he continued, was the creation in Northern Ireland of a just society in which Catholics, Protestants, and Dissenters could freely discuss their differences without a return to the prejudices of the past" (IN 22.1.69.)

But the conflict was now assuming a momentum that rendered the NICRA demands irrelevant.

## Ulster at the Crossroads

On 6th February, 1969, O'Neill called a General Election. This decision by the 'Northern Ireland' Prime Minister raised great concern in Whitehall, where total reliance had been placed on O'Neill. Richard Crossman, one of Wilson's Cabinet, summed up the reason for the fear at Whitehall in his diary: "... because O'Neill is the man we are relying on in Northern Ireland to do our job for us—to drag Northern Ireland... out of its 18th century Catholic Protestant dispute" (Peter Rose, *How the Troubles came to Northern Ireland*, p. 136)

Kenneth Bloomfield, O'Neill's private secretary, called O'Neill's decision "the phenomenal risk of appealing to the electorate" (*Stormont in Crisis*, p. 103-4)

On the BBC's *Panorama* programme, Robin Day, explained the peculiarity of the Ulster election to the British democracy:

"Normally an election in Ulster does not arouse immense interest anywhere, even in Ulster. But this time it is different. The Prime Minister, Captain O'Neill, is fighting for survival against a challenge from within the ruling Unionist party... so, unlike a normal democratic election, the object of this one is to decide not which party will govern, but how the governing party will be led..." (Rose, *How the Troubles came to Northern Ireland*, p. 137).,

The election that O'Neill called in an attempt to strengthen his position, but which weakened it, illustrates the peculiarity of the Stormont system. In a normal Parliament an election is a contest between parties, usually two, for political power. But this election was called, not to automatically return the Unionist Party to power, but for O'Neill to engineer a mandate for his policies within the Unionist Party itself. The Prime Minister used a coupon system in which he either supported, or did not endorse, individual Unionists in his Party. And he took the same selective approach to Unionists who put themselves up against his party, endorsing some as his supporters against members of his own Party who he decided not to support.

So, having encouraged the Nationalist Party to become the Official Opposition, O'Neill, in his conduct of the February 1969 election, showed what a sham the whole exercise was by treating elements in his own party as the main opposition to himself. The election revealed that the whole system was designed to be a Unionist democracy: Protestant voters deciding on which shade of Unionism benefited them most and whether or not to give some small concessions to the Catholics, who did not count at all.

It showed that Nationalists were completely reliant on the Unionist leader and the decision taken by the Protestant electorate for their general conditions of life. Who they elected themselves was largely inconsequential.

And, of course it ended in a complete muddle for O'Neill, that did not do him any good at all.

A month or two before the election O'Neill wrote to his aide Kenneth Bloomfield:

"As I look in the glass darkly I see demonstrations, counter-demonstrations, meetings, rows, and general misery. In such an atmosphere of hatred would one in fact wish to continue this job—I doubt it. The only solution—direct rule from London—will of course never materialise and so we shall drift from crisis to crisis" (Ken Bloomfield, *Stormont in Crisis*, p.108)

In early 1969 O'Neill found himself trapped by the system he had elevated to a fatal purposefulness. And he found the only escape route barred by his masters in London. He, as an individual, had a means of escaping it. But the two communities did not.

O'Neill's depression in the face of those who barred the escape route was well-founded.

## End of the Nationalist Party

The election that had nothing to do with Nationalism put an effective end to the Nationalist Party.

John Hume stood as a candidate in Foyle against Eddie McAteer (and Eamonn McCann of PD) on the platform of:

"1. The formation of a new political movement based on social-democratic principles, with open membership and elected executives to allow complete involvement of the people in the process of decision making.

"2. A movement that must provide what has been severely lacking at Stormont- a strong energetic opposition to conservatism—proposing radical social and economic policies.

"3. A movement that must be completely non-sectarian and committed to rooting out the fundamental evil in our society—sectarian division.

"4. A movement that would be committed to the idea that the future of Northern Ireland should be decided by the people and that there should be no change in its constitutional position without the consent of its people" (IN 7.2.69)

Catholics voted for Hume and rejected McAteer and McCann. The *Nationalist Party* lost its leader and three of its nine seats, suffering a mortal blow. There was a new crop of Catholic MPs including Hume, Fitt, Paddy Kennedy, Paddy Devlin (NILP), Currie and Paddy O'Hanlon (and Ivan Cooper, who was a Protestant Civil Rights activist).

The playwright Brian Friel wrote a letter of commiseration to McAteer after his defeat by Hume. The Nationalist Leader replied:

"I do not mourn the loss of a seat at Stormont but I have a throaty feeling that so many of our people seem to have turned their backs on that lovely indefinite thing which I mean by nationalism. But I think that they will return when they have filled themselves with the mess of British rights and Welfare Benefits. There have been other times in Irish history... when all seemed lost but our faith blossomed again. " (Staunton, *The Nationalists of Northern Ireland*, p. 259)

McAteer further elaborated on this view in a letter to Corinne Philpot in March 1969:

"I do not believe myself that Irish nationalism will die, although its complexion may change. The Civil Rights campaign, of which we hear so much at present, is simply an efficient takeover of the work which has been carried on for many years by us. The takeover was aided by the folly of ex-Minister William Craig, the all-convincing power of television and our own lack of guile in thinking that the Civil Rights Movement was really non-political" (ibid, p.260)

The *Irish News* gave this epitaph to the Nationalist Party:

"Since the emergence of the Civil Rights campaign and the street marches, the Nationalist Party has been subject to close scrutiny, and its weaknesses and human failings continually cited in support of its ultimate disappearance by those who could not remember, nor wanted to be told, of the party's tireless efforts to keep alive National ideals and to resist, however impotently, the heavy hand of Orange-Unionist domination.

"With the emergence of new movements and more radical thinking, every effort has been made to capitalise on the Nationalist Party's imperfections. Much of the party's thunder has been stolen by the Civil Righters who will now have their spokesmen—Hume, Cooper and O'Hanlon—at Stormont" (IN 27.2.69)

There was something of sadness in the *Irish News* editorial which bemoaned the demise of the Party. The Nationalists had done their best within the Stormont set-up and now it was the chance of Hume, Cooper and O'Hanlon to show if they could do better. The *Irish News* seemed to think not.

The *Irish News* was the voice of traditional Catholic-nationalism in the North and it appeared to be a little uncomfortable with the new men. They were articulating a demand which Nationalists had never even considered— full and equal rights within the UK State. These were not normal things for Nationalists to do, and the paper which stood for '*Faith and Fatherland*' did not quite know how to take the new movement, not knowing where it would lead.

## O'Neillism and Catholics

Terence O'Neill believed that Unionism was an all-embracing political philosophy, which was superior to the class politics prevalent in British society. He thought that Catholics could be cultivated into good Unionists— or at least passive citizens—by treating them like Protestants. But the Catholic politicians who were replacing the traditional Nationalists were not articulating a Catholic Unionism; they were voicing a demand for the type of politics which prevailed in Britain.

John Hume's object at this time was to create a kind of movement in 'Northern Ireland' which already existed in Britain, in the form of the Labour Party. He was not aiming to convert the Catholic community into a lot of flag-waving admirers of the British royal family. It was not that aspect of British society which attracted Catholics. (That aspect repelled them.) It was, as the *Irish News* noted, the fact that the British State was a normal one, with substantial welfare provisions and the Politics of State, which was encouraging them to favour it as the Nationalist Party disintegrated.

The Civil Rights Movement had developed because a new generation of Catholics had become quietly reconciled to many aspects of the UK, despite the barrier of 'Northern Ireland' that the British had put up between them.

The Ulsterish character of 'Northern Ireland' repelled them. They had relegated national aspirations to a secondary level and decided to press for full rights within the State in preference to the perverse political structures which they were subject to in 'Northern Ireland'.

But the British political establishment refused to facilitate the move Catholics were eager to make from local communal into UK party politics, and so they effectively strengthened the hand of those involved in NICRA who wanted to confuse the issue and use the demand for democracy as a lever for a push for an Anti-Partitionist manoeuvre.

Around this time Sir John Chilcott was commissioned by Wilson and Callaghan to make contingencies for British military intervention in the Six Counties, including all the legal aspects. He had earlier been asked to draw up plans for Direct Rule from Westminster, just in case O'Neill had fallen and could not be replaced with a compliant Unionist leader. He later said in an interview: " I remember there was relief over O'Neill's liberal policies and North-South rapprochement. The civil rights protests came as a surprise, an unwelcome surprise to the Unionist government" (Rose, *How the Troubles came to Northern Ireland*, p.153)

The unwelcome surprise was the activism of the Northern Catholic community. This was the one thing the 'Northern Ireland' setup could not cope with.

O'Neill raised the expectations of the Catholic community and hoped to fulfil those expectations within the political philosophy of Unionism, and within the confines of the Six County statelet. But the Catholic community, which was ripe for a new departure, had aspirations which could not be fulfilled within those confines. Catholics would have fitted into an all-Ireland state, or also, increasingly easily, into British party politics. If they were left in the backwater of Ulster provincial political life, after being stimulated into activity, there was bound to be a build up in pressure. And since the pressure had no outlet there was bound to be an explosion. In February 1969 that explosion was not far away.

O'Neill encouraged an incendiary pretence in the ability of the Stormont system to be an outlet for Catholic political energies, and the 'constitutional' Nationalists humoured him.

And so it came to pass that in the long run the Unionists were not able to govern what they had never desired to govern. The Catholic minority, which was much bigger than the Protestant minority would have been in all-Ireland Home Rule state, was placed in a predicament by British policy and Ulster Unionist compliance with it. It could only remain quiescent by staying at home and confining itself to a private existence—as in fact large numbers of it did, for a couple of generations. But this could not go on indefinitely, particularly when it was subjected to annual reminders of its defeat and subordination. There was bound to be a build up of the confined energy that, when released by the lighting of a fuse, was going to result in an explosion.

Ulster Unionism, which was in 1920-1 constituted into a governing power by the Parliament against which it had rebelled seven years earlier, did not address this possibility. It felt it could settle down in its perfect world and let its substantial police force do its job. The problem of how to make its authority tolerable to the Catholic third of the population, that could play no part in its governing system, was ignored as it operated the simulacrum Parliament which Britain conferred on it without any understanding of the effect this necessarily had on the large Catholic part of the population it was charged with governing.

It responded to any tentative suggestions of reform to alleviate the position of Catholics with an uncomprehending hostility right to the bitter end. It had its Ulster idyll, and it instinctively felt that any change would open the way for the deluge, as it indeed did.

Even a people with a great talent for politics would have found it hard to operate the poisoned chalice that Imperial Britain handed the Ulster Protestants in 1920-1. And it has become very apparent since 1920 that the Ulster Protestant may have many talents but political skill is not prime amongst them.

## Old Wine in New Bottles?

The new crop of Catholic politicians was fatally confident that they could make the Stormont set-up succeed where their predecessors in the Nationalist Party failed.

Addressing a crowd of 3,000 at a victory rally in Coalisland, Austin Currie, the individual with the greatest pretensions toward treating 'Northern Ireland' as a 'state', was reported by the *Irish News* as saying:

> "Many able and vigorous young men would sit on the opposition benches when Stormont reconvened. There now was, he said, the nucleus of a political movement which could transform politics in the 6 Counties, not only at parliamentary level, but in local government and at the grass roots as well. An opportunity had been presented and those who failed or refused to see this would deserve to be reviled by this and future generations.
>
> "In the past, Mr. Currie said, the Government had not been prepared to treat the Opposition as an opposition and it was largely on account of this that there had been no alternative to street politics.
>
> "He hoped the Government had now learned the lessons, but if the message had not yet seeped through he would reinforce it with a warning: 'If the

government is not prepared to treat the Opposition as an opposition and if it contrives to drag its feet on reforms and if it is not prepared to take the necessary steps to ensure social justice for all in this community, then the Opposition will take to the streets' Mr. Currie said" (IN 1.3.69.)

But it was not because O'Neill did not treat the Nationalists as a real Opposition that Catholic political aspirations were frustrated. It was simply because the Opposition at Stormont was not actually an opposition at all, in the accepted sense of the word and 'Northern Ireland' was not a real state. No matter how generous O'Neill was in his treatment of the 'Opposition', the non-Unionists could never form an alternative Government at Stormont, let alone a real government at the level of state.

And it was not the case that street politics had come about because of the absence of political opposition at Stormont. It was precisely because the Nationalists had taken up this role in the first place, and had shown it to be a sham, that street politics had taken its place. There had been no street politics in the 50 years prior to the Nationalists taking up the role of Her Majesty's Opposition. Craig and Brooke had realised that Stormont was a sham and had not encouraged the Nationalists to entertain any such illusions about it. They didn't and things were stable.

But the new breed persisted in the dangerous expectations and illusions that had developed and, if anything, they were true-believers in the Lemass fantasy that had been foisted on the sceptical and reluctant Nationalists.

Currie greatly looked forward to the new Stormont with its many independents, smaller parties and divided parties. He thought that this situation had progressive possibilities with the demise of the monolithic blocs.

Currie called for a new united Opposition as "a real radical alternative to the Unionist Party". John Hume said that such an organisation would have to have "a name that would suggest left of centre" (IN 4.3.69). Earlier Currie had said that if the new Party was not a left-wing one, he would have nothing to do with it.

Nationalists had persisted throughout the 1960s with the delusion that the Unionist Party was a conservative Party (or, indeed, was the Conservative Party in 'Northern Ireland'). This was partly because they saw the Labour Party as their potential allies in Westminster, partly because most of the young Catholic politicians were of a social-democratic disposition, and partly because the Conservative Party was still called the *Conservative and Unionist Party*.

Whatever the case, they believed they could make a class-based division in 'Northern Ireland' out of the sectarian division, with Unionist equalling Conservative and Nationalist equalling Labour.

But there were very good reasons why this could not come about. Despite the historical animosity between Nationalists and the Tories, a good section of the Catholic community were certainly more of a conservative disposition than a Labour one in social and economic matters, and a substantial number of Protestants were Labour-orientated and socialist-inclined, rather than being natural conservative voters.

Indeed, Austin Currie had given a very good explanation of why the Unionist Party was not the Conservative Party in Ulster when a member of the Unionist Party had said on a Twelfth platform that they would defy the British Prime Minister if necessary. The *Irish News* of 15th July, 1968 reported:

> "Mr. Currie said the leader of the Conservative and Unionist Party, Mr. Heath, ought to be challenged for his views on this type of threat from one of his supporters in Westminster. He should be asked promptly how he could accept the support of the leader of a section of his party, prepared to incite violence in order to thwart the wishes of the democratically elected British government. Mr. Heath might also be asked about Mr. Orr's statement that he became a politician to further the Orange institution and 'was an Orangeman first and a politician second'. 'Did Mr. Heath agree that a Conservative and Unionist MP should have entered politics to further the cause of a secret sectarian society? If this was the case, can he explain the position of Catholics in the Conservative Party? It would be interesting to hear Captain Orr himself in view of his admissions how he presumes to represent the large Catholic electorate in South Down' said Mr. Currie."

But, if Austin Currie's scheme for making Nationalist politics Labour, and Unionist politics Conservative, were realised, this situation would have logically persisted. (This was the time of the Louis Boyle case. Louis Boyle, a Catholic, had joined the Unionist Party and tried to become a Unionist candidate, and failed to gain nomination, despite O'Neill's 'ecumenism'. Further information on this incident can be found in the *The O'Neill Years*, by David Gordon.)

The idea that the Unionist Party is a Conservative party, and Protestants are born Tories, while the Nationalist Party is a Labour party, and Catholics are born Socialists, is not one that can be taken with any measure of seriousness. To underline this point one need only refer to the attempts of John Hume and Austin Currie to form a united Catholic left-of-centre party in 1969. After meetings with the Nationalists, James O'Reilly (Nationalist Party) revealed:

> "It would be a gradual process involving long negotiations because of radical differences separating some of the opposition parties and their divergent views on such questions as integrated education and the eventual

re-unification. Nationalists in some areas, he said, had a strong mandate to work for a united opposition, but they had no mandate to turn themselves into Unionists. 'However progressive we may feel we cannot dispense with tradition'..." (IN 4.3.69).

## NICRA at the crossroads

On 23rd April 1969 O'Neill conceded the main Civil Rights demand of 'one man, one vote' after a Stormont vote on the issue. By this time there had been several resignations from NICRA. John McAnerney, Betty Sinclair, Fred Heatley and Raymond Shearer had left the Executive after the PD element put pressure on them to increase marches through Protestant areas. Michael Farrell and Kevin Boyle of PD replaced them on the Executive. John Hume and Ivan Cooper resigned as Chairman and Vice-Chairman, respectively, of the *Derry Citizens' Action Committee.*

The Civil Rights Movement was now becoming more overtly Anti-Partitionist and the Catholic moderates were leaving it. NICRA was now demanding the repeal of the *Special Powers Act*, the withdrawal of the *Public Order Bill*, the disbandment of the B Specials, and the disarming of the RUC. In short, it was calling for the abolition of the defence mechanisms of the Unionist statelet — something that Unionism would never concede.

In the *New Left Review* of May 1969, Farrell and McCann admitted the developing nature of the confrontation to be a sectarian one. McCann wrote:

"... the civil rights campaign must acknowledge that it had failed in its primary task of building bridges to the Protestant working class. We have alienated them {Catholics} from their Protestant neighbours more than ever before... We keep saying parrot-like that we are fighting on working-class issues for working-class unity... It was a lot of pompous nonsense... The consciousness of the people who are fighting in the streets at the moment is sectarian and bigoted... Everyone applauds loudly when one says in a speech that we are not sectarian, we are fighting for rights of all Irish workers, but really that's because they see this as the new way of getting at the Protestants" (pp.33-4).

In the same article Farrell observed, almost incidentally, that NICRA always ensured "that there was a pet Unionist on its executive". Cyril Toman added: "It may seem rather unfortunate if one puts it like that, but if we are going to have a socialist workers' republic then we have got to have Protestants in it" (p.42).

PD's activism had created a 'revolutionary situation'. But it was very much the illusion of revolution, in those few heady months. Things went into great flux and intense revolutionary feelings flourished. There was an idealistic belief that a break with the past had happened and all would be new and utterly different from then on. But the revolution, though televised, changed little of substance and merely helped to bring the pot to the boil with the basic ingredients unchanged.

In a video of *'The Troubles'* made by Thames Television in 1981 Michael Farrell is a prominent commentator. He keeps referring to the 'Northern Ireland State' in the manner of a revolutionary who was challenging for state power, like a Lenin. But 'Northern Ireland' was only the façade of a state and state power is not possible in a façade. As such it was never a possible arena of socialist revolution. The façade might be overthrown—as it was—but the State would continue as it had done for centuries.

The apparatus of the British State had never ceased to operate behind the 'Northern Ireland' façade. When the façade crumbled, the State appeared and it was taken on by a new IRA –the Provos. And Michael Farrell and the revolutionaries disappeared to the margins.


## Republican views

Dublin Sinn Fein, which had similar 'revolutionary' illusions, made this comment in its monthly:

> "Cooper and Hume beware, and learn this lesson—the Civil Rights Movement's place is on the streets... The People's Democracy is now striving hard to be seen as 'a new socialist force' with its drive to cut across religious barriers (something not evident in the make-up of its own leadership). Its insistence is that partition is not today an issue in the direct colony of Britain: the Twenty-Six Counties is its neo-colony. The struggle for all progressive forces in the Thirty-Two Counties is a struggle for self-determination against British Imperialism" (*United Irishman*, March 1969)

It is clear in this passage that the Republican Movement was in utter confusion between Civil Rights, Socialism and Anti-Partitionism. Or else it was keen to let the Anti-Partition cat out of the Civil Rights bag to see off the Student revolutionary upstarts.

The month after, the same publication made this remark:

> "The prospect of continued infighting in the Unionist Party could lead to increased emphasis on Craig-Paisley UDI tendencies and increased activity by the UVF. The Civil Rights Movement is better placed than ever now" (*United Irishman*, April 1969)

The cohesion of the Unionist ruling class had been destroyed by the trivial Civil Rights demands which it had proved incapable of conceding without fragmenting. The Revolution was on! But what then? Certainly not Socialist Revolution or the clearing of the false consciousness from the minds of the Protestant working class that would make them into good Irish Republicans.

More likely was conflict between the two nationalities—National War.

By this stage the Republicans had become badly disorientated by the British Marxism that Desmond Greaves and Roy Johnston had imported into the movement and the obscure alien ideology had disabled their minds. And this made them incapable of responding effectively to the raw events that were to suddenly occur as a result of Desmond Greaves' Leninist fantasy.

## O'Neillism without O'Neill

On 28th April, O'Neill resigned and was replaced by his cousin, James Chichester-Clark.

O'Neill's downfall was triggered by two main events. A series of loyalist bombs exploded at waterworks and electricity installations and were blamed on the IRA, putting further pressure on O'Neill. Then his Minister of Agriculture, Chichester Clark, resigned because of the timing of the abolition of the property vote at Local Government elections.

The diaries of Richard Crossman give a good flavour of the thinking within the British Cabinet at that point in time. It would all be so laughable if it were not leading to great tragedy:

> "Crossman: Would it be a good thing with the possibility of civil war and suppressing the Catholics or not suppressing the Catholics if we know something about Northern Ireland?
>
> "Callaghan: I don't think we really need that. After all I am seeing Chichester Clark every day...
>
> "Crossman: If we have to know about Russia and every other country in the world, we should at least spend some money finding out something about Northern Ireland...
>
> "Healey: frankly, Northern Ireland has completely different conditions from Britain and we shall be as blind men leading the blind if we have to go in knowing nothing about the place."

Crossman also records:

> "As we went out of the room, Healey said to me, 'You have no idea what it was like before you came on to the Committee. The Prime Minister was always demanding active intervention early on, with this crazy desire to go in there and take things over, that we should side with the Roman Catholics and civil rights movement against the government and the RUC, though we know nothing at all about it" (Rose, *How the Troubles came to Northern Ireland*, pp.155-6).

(A word should be said about Peter Rose's book, *How the Troubles came to Northern Ireland* at this point. It is one of the more informative books to appear about the crucial period in which the Labour Government shirked its responsibilities toward 'Northern Ireland' at the vital hour. However, it still lies firmly within the British understanding of things—seeing British intervention to have been potentially effective if it had been done earlier, therefore making more substantial intervention unnecessary. Whilst there is much concentration on the *1920 Act*, the lack of a full understanding of its strategic purpose in relation to the island of Ireland as a whole leads to an acceptance of the principle that responsibility can be a limited liability.)

In the light of this atmosphere there was much wishful thinking with regard to 'Ulster'. Wilson convinced himself that Chichester Clark would succeed where O'Neill had failed. According to Wilson he "quickly became the Prime Minister who would see it through" (Harold Wilson, *The Labour Government*, p.675).

In early May a *Times* headline declared, *'New policies bring calm at last to Ulster'*:

> "After months of bitter weekend clashes, the proposed reforms announced last week by Major Chichester Clark seemed to have taken the steam out of militants on both sides... an air of normality has returned to the Province. Civil rights marchers seem content to sit back and wait for concessions and that the extreme Protestants have accepted the situation for the present was shown on Friday when Paisley's victory meeting attracted only 400 people" (12.05.69).

But during May 1969, despite all the false optimism in Britain, the situation in the Six Counties began to deteriorate rapidly. Confrontations were occurring regularly in Belfast, assuming a greater significance in the situation. At the end of June the marching season started, building up the potential for conflict even more.

Evictions became regular happening from July onwards with families moving to safer areas amongst 'their own'. In early August crowds assembled on the Shankill when they heard reports that a junior Orange Lodge had been attacked at Unity Flats. Serious confrontations broke out that shattered the mixed housing experiment.

At this point old reflexes were produced: there were growing demands for the security forces to go into the Catholic areas of Belfast to sort out the 'troublemakers' and preparations began to be made for such an occurrence on the Shankill.

Gerry Adams, a Republican involved in the Civil Rights agitation, later noted:

> "The older people in nationalist areas had been through all this before, and they knew what we were going to bring down upon ourselves and upon

them. As the situation began to build up once again, it must have felt to many of them that we were going for a rematch in a deadly fight which they had always lost. Even if anyone had articulated any of this, it probably would not have changed my attitude. But no one did, though one old barman said to me, 'Forget about asking them for civil rights. Take their money instead'. And a year or so later, with a fatalism that perplexed me, another man said, 'Forget about trying to change things: it will all be the same in a thousand years'. In many ways our ignorance, our higher expectations and our lack of experience, combined with the sheer exuberance of youth, made everything seem possible... I felt that a tide was flowing which would sweep away the old conditions that had constrained our lives" (*Before the Dawn, An Autobiography*, p.96)

Before the events of the late 1960s the Catholic community in the North had been reduced to fatalism by the system they had been forced to endure.

What happened next, in August 1969, was to prove the great pivot for the rise of the Catholic community, in which it threw off its despondency and transformed itself beyond all recognition.

## On the One Road... to God knows where

After his meeting with the Prime Minister of 'Northern Ireland' the Taoiseach, Sean Lemass, having unfrozen the North, predicted: "How far the road may go is not yet known. It has been truly said, however, it is better to travel hopefully than to arrive" (IN 15.1.65).

Lemass had deviated from De Valera's policy of letting 'Northern Ireland' be. And he met with a kindred spirit in O'Neill. Lords Craigavon and Brookeborough had had a policy: to minimise political activity in what was called "*the Northern Ireland state*" because it was not a state and there was no possibility in it of evolutionary political life.

Lemass and O'Neill departed from these policies, South and North and, by doing so, they caused the explosion from which everything else has followed.

Lemass pressed the Nationalist Party to take on the role of Official Opposition at Stormont, and that was the beginning of the end for the "*the Northern Ireland state*". The Nationalists knew in their bones they were indulging in a farce, but evidently Lemass did not.

Lemass took 'Northern Ireland' to be a viable political entity and obliged the Nationalist Party to participate in his grand illusion. He has been called a pragmatist by his admirers, but "pragmatism" is hardly the right name for what he did. The thing about pragmatism is that it is supposed to work. The thing about 'Northern Ireland' is that when it was operated in earnest it did not work, and in fact it exploded.

There was no material for political development in 'the Northern Ireland state' and its simulacrum Parliament. The matters which were the substance of political development elsewhere were "reserved" matters in 'Northern Ireland', dealt with by British democracy through party conflicts from which the local façade was excluded, and the outcomes were applied administratively in it as a matter of routine.

'Northern Ireland' elections (referendums on the Border, in fact) always decided to retain this mode of attachment to Britain through the entrenched Unionist majority. Then after the election there was really nothing more to be done but wait for the next election/referendum. But Lemass, the "pragmatist", could not see that pragmatic fact and he forced the Nationalist Party to play a make-believe game of Government and Opposition at Stormont in which it always came off second.

The pragmatic effect of the Taoiseach's initiative was to blow away the Constitutional fig-leaf which the preceding generation had kept in place by inaction.

The Catholic genie had been bottled up for half a century by leaving the cork in the bottle. But, once the cork was out, the genie was loose and it wanted to escape the bottle.

The Catholics of the Six Counties had never wanted to be part of what was constructed there in 1920. They had not wanted to be cut off from the Irish Nation and neither had they wanted to be placed under a *"Protestant Parliament for a Protestant people"*. They had sought numerous means of escape, through Michael Collins and the Free State, through De Valera and Fianna Fail, through British Labour. But they had been bottled up.

What happened in the 1960s was that they had been induced to treat 'Northern Ireland' as a state. In the course of this they had produced something out of themselves for the purposes of political activism and the testing of the pretensions of the 'state' they were part of. The pseudo-state could not cope with being treated as a real state and the real state chose not to interfere and appear in its actual substance from behind its false front until it was too late.

The road that Lemass opened led first to August 1969 and then far beyond for the Northern Catholics. There was great uncertainty about where that road would lead but it was certainly felt that it was worth travelling. Any road out of 'Northern Ireland' would do.

And, nearly half a century later, they are still on that same road the Taoiseach opened—although much further along.

# 'Irish Action' (Extracts)

*'Irish Action, New Thoughts on an old Subject'* by Eddie McAteer' (from the *Donegal Democrat*, October 1948);

"Most Irish people who are active in seeking freedom used to believe that it would come to us by force of either constitutional agitation or by violence. Then the mighty spirit of the late Mahatma Gandhi pointed a third road—non co-operation, non violence. Maybe we could follow that road and be proud to draw inspiration from its pioneer.

"What I have to suggest is mainly for the Free Irish in the British—occupied Six Counties... Even in the carefully carved Six Counties, 35% of the people are opposed to the British-controlled puppet Government at Belfast. That is a very considerable percentage-quite big enough, if sufficiently determined, to render government impossible...

"I yield to no man in my admiration for the heroic revolutionaries on the past—the men who went out against hopeless odds in the certainty that their deaths and sufferings would be an inspiration to torpid spirits. But I do not believe that such terrible sacrifices are necessary today... I do not want to see a handful of our best men die so that the majority maybe shocked back onto the road to national freedom.

"No more unsuccessful Insurrections, please. And no unnecessary risks, either...

"It is not necessary that this new campaign be formally organised. Indeed, in my opinion, formal organisation has distinct disadvantages... each individual must constitute a complete action cell. If you resolve within yourself each morning that you will do something during the day to render the British occupation of Ireland more trouble some or more expensive you may rest assured that your enlivened imagination and more active thought will suggest a means. Where there is a will, there is most certainly a way.

"What can you do?

"It is neither possible nor desirable to lay down a definite action program. The situation is ever fluid. Every day is full of little opportunities which must eagerly be seized and turned to advantage. The success of a pin-pricking campaign lies not in the actual size of the pin-pricks, but in their number and frequency.

"The old boycott idea springs to mind at once and it must be practised to the maximum degree by each individual. Those who support the enemies of our freedom are guilty of a small act of treason. Do not delude yourself by saying 'oh, but so-and-so s a very nice man to speak to'. It is not unusual to find a man 'nice' to you when he is making something out of you. Business is rapidly becoming competitive again and the advantage is passing to buyers.

"A merely commercial boycott is not enough. All pro-British functions must be shunned like the plague. However fond you are of music or the arts, you must avoid concerts, etc, where they insist that an artistic feast must be digested with the help of the British National Anthem. Irish people must not be spectators at militant tattoos, parades or any functions under Occupation auspices. Are attitude must be the attitude of the French to the Germans whilst France was under German occupation. If circumstances place you as a spectator you must contrive to show your disdain and disapproval.

"It follows that you must develop a well-defined treatment for individual members of British Forces here... Join nothing that will give Britain any encouragement to think that she is welcome here. Let only those who love English rule so much themselves man the garrison in Ireland...

"Now let us consider the non-military aspect of the Occupation. Nowadays, governmental machinery works largely though the agency of Myriads of forms which are showered on the helpless citizens... All such forms must be lost...

"A note of caution. If completion of these forms brings financial benefit or is otherwise obviously to your advantage, then complete them by all means... Be selective in this form of action. If it pays you to fill a form, fill it. If it doesn't, throw the form in the fire. Increased cost and difficulty in administration here will quickly make itself felt in Whitehall...

"Do you know one answer to the numerous bans inflicted on us? Forbidden to march in procession, it is still possible for a few thousand of us to appear on the streets. Surely we can walk (not march) on our own streets, and if we all walk in one direction and in perfect silence, what law do we break?... Shuttered shops, black flags, are all ways of showing disapproval...

"I have finished... if I succeed in adding one per cent to the cost of British or British quisling administration here I shall have succeeded beyond my best expectations..."

# Select Bibliography

## Newspapers/Periodicals

| | | |
|---|---|---|
| Belfast Newsletter | Irish Democrat | Round Table |
| Capuchin Annual | Irish News | Studies |
| Catholic Bulletin | Irish Independent | The Times |
| Catholic Herald | Irish Political Review | Ulster Herald |
| Church and State | Irish Times | United Irishman |
| Derry Journal | New Left Review | Worker's Republic |
| Freeman's Journal | Northern Star | Worker's Weekly |

## Books/Pamphlets

A.O.H., (1967) *The Ancient Order Of Hibernians*

Dáil Éireann, *Irish Bulletin* Volume 1, Reprint of official newspaper of Dáil Éireann with War Reports. (Aubane Historical Society, 2012)

Dáil Éireann, *Irish Bulletin* Volume 2, Reprint of official newspaper of Dáil Éireann with War Report. (Belfast Historical Society & Educational Sociaty, 2014)

Beaslai, Piaras, *Michael Collins and the Making of a New Ireland*, Vol. I. (1926)

Beckett, J.C., *The Making of Modern Ireland 1603-1923*. (1981)

Lovat Fraser's Tour Of Ireland in 1913. Belfast Historical and Educational Society (1992)

Beaverbrook, Lord, *Politicians And The War*. (1932)

Bergin, J.J., *History of the Ancient Order of the Hibernians*. (1910)

Bew, Paul, Gibbon, Peter, Patterson, Henry, *The State in Northern Ireland*. (1979)

Bishop, Patrick and Mallie, Eamonn, *The Provisional IRA*. (1987)

Bloomfield, K., *A Tragedy of Errors, The Government and Misgovernment of Northern Ireland*. (2007)

Bloomfield, K., *Stormont in Crisis*. (1994)

Blunt, William Scawen. *My Diaries*. (1931)

Campbell, T.J., *Fifty Years of Ulster*. (1941)

Carroll, Dennis, *They Have Fooled You Again— Michael O'Flanagan, Priest, Republican, Social Critic*. (1993)

Casement, Roger, *The Crime Against Europe*. (1915)

Childers, Erskine, *The Framework Of Home Rule*. (1911)

Churchill, Winston Spencer, *The World Crisis 1901-1914*. (1932)

Churchill, Winston Spencer, *The World Crisis: The Aftermath*. (1923)

Clifford, Brendan, *The Cork Free Press In The Context Of The Parnell Split*. (1997)

Clifford, Brendan, *Ireland In The Great War*. (1992)

Clifford, Brendan, *Joe Devlin; What Now?* (2007)

Clifford, Brendan, *Northern Ireland, What is it?* (2011)

Clifford, Brendan, *Whither Northern Ireland?* (2010)

Clifford, Brendan, *William O'Brien and his World*. (2010)

Colum, Padraig, *Arthur Griffith*. (1959)

Colvin, Ian, and Marjoribanks, Edward, *Life Of Lord Carson*, 3 Vols. (1936)

Coogan, Tim Pat, *Michael Collins*. (1990)

Crossman, Richard, *Diaries*. (1970)

Cunningham, Michael, *Monaghan, County of Intrigue*. (1980)

Currie, Austin, *All Hell Will Break Loose*. (2004)

Dwyer, Ryle, *Michael Collins and the Civil War* . (2000)

Ewart, Wilfred, *A Journey in Ireland*. (1922)

Fanning, Ronan, *Fatal Path, British Government and the Irish Revolution, 1919-22*. (2013)

Farrell, Michael, *Twenty Years On*. (1988)

Farrell, Michael, *Northern Ireland: The Orange State*. (1976)

Farrell, Michael, *Arming the Protestants*. (1983)

Foy, Michael, unpublished M.A. thesis, Queen's University Belfast) '*The Ancient Order of Hibernians: an Irish Political-Religious Pressure Group 1884-1975*'. (1976)

Gallagher, Frank, *The Four Glorious Years*. (1953)

Gallagher, Frank, *The Indivisible Island*. (1957)

Glennon, Kieran, *From Pogrom to Civil War, Tom Glennon and the Belfast IRA*. (2013)

Gordon, David, *The O'Neill Years*. (1989)

Greaves, Desmond, *The Irish Question and the British People*. (1963)

Gwynn, Denis, *Life Of John Redmond*. (1932)

Gwynn, Denis, *The History Of Partition*. (1950)

Gwynn, Stephen, *John Redmond's Last Years*. (1919)

Harrison Henry, *Ireland and the British Empire, 1937—Conflict Or Collaboration*. (1937)

Harrison Henry, *The Neutrality Of Ireland*. (1942)

Harrison Henry, *Ulster and the British Empire*. (1939)

Hart, Peter, *Mick—The Real Michael Collins*. (2005)

Henry, R.M., *The Evolution Of Sinn Fein*. (1920)

Horgan, J.J., *From Parnell to Pearse*. (1948)

Horgan, J.J., *The Grammar Of Anarchy*. (1919)

Joy, Henry, and Bruce, William, *Belfast Politics*, Athol Books edition. (2010)

Kelly, James, *Bonfires on the Hillside*. (1995)

Kelly, Stephen, *Fianna Fail, Partition and Northern Ireland, 1926-1971*. (2013)

Kenna, G.B., *Facts and Figures of the Belfast Pogrom 1920-22*. (1922)

Lawrence, R.J. *The Government of Northern Ireland*. (1965)

Lynch, Diarmuid, *The IRB and the Easter Rising*. (1957)

Lynch, Robert, *The Northern IRA and the early years of Partition, 1920-22*. (2006)

Macardle, Dorothy, *The Irish Republic* . (1937)

McAteer, Eddie and Campbell, T.J. *Irish Action* from *Donegal Democrat*, 1948. (1979)

McCann, Eamonn, *War and an Irish Town* (3rd ed.). (1993)

McDermott, Jim, *Northern Divisions; The Old IRA And The Belfast Pogroms, 1920-22.* (2001)

McKeown, Michael, *The Greening of a Nationalist.* (1986)

McMahon, Sean, *Wee Joe, The Life of Joe Devlin.* (2011)

McNeill, Ronald, *Ulster's Stand for Union.* (1922)

McPhillips, K., *The Falls, A History.* (1992)

Mansergh, Nicholas, *The Government of Northern Ireland.* (1967)

Moore, Frank Frankfort, *The Truth about Ulster.* (1913)

Murphy, Michael A., *Gerry Fitt—A Political Chameleon.* (2007)

NI Communist Party, Unite. (1965)

O'Byrne, Cathal, *As I Roved Out.* (1946)

O'Connor, Fionnuala, *In Search of a State—Catholics in Northern Ireland.* (1993)

O'Connor, Seamus, *Tomorrow was Another Day.* (2000)

O'Donnell, Peadar, *The Gates Flew Open.* (1968)

O'Donoghue, Florrie, *No Other Law.* (1954)

O'Loughran, Reverend Robert, *Redmond's Vindication.* (1917),

Patterson, Henry, *Ireland since 1939.* (2010)

Phoenix, Eamonn, *Northern Nationalism.* (1994)

Phoenix, Eamonn, *A Century of Northern Life,* The Irish News *and 100 Years of Ulster History.* (1995)

Phoenix, Eamonn and Parkinson, Alan, *Conflicts in the North of Ireland, 1900-2000.* (2010)

Redmond-Howard, L.G., *Six Days of the Irish Republic.* (2006)

Regan, John, *Myth and the Irish State.* (2014)

Rose, Peter, *How the Troubles came to Northern Ireland.* (2001)

Shea, Patrick, *Voices and the Sounds of Drums.* (1981)

Staunton, Enda, *The Nationalists of Northern Ireland.* (2001)

Ultach, *Orange Terror.* (1940 and 1943)

Walsh, Pat, *Ireland, 1921* by Lionel Curtis. (2002)

Walsh, Pat, *The Catholic Bulletin and the Politics of Pre-War Europe.* (2004)

Walsh, Pat, *From Civil Rights to National War.* (1989)

Walsh, Pat, *Irish Republicanism and Socialism.* (1989)

Walsh, Pat, *The Rise and Fall of Imperial Ireland.* (2003)

Walsh, Pat, *Britain's Great War on Turkey.* (2009)

Walsh, Pat, *Remembering Gallipoli.* (2010)

Whitford, F.J., *Joseph Devlin, Ulsterman and Irishman.* (Unpublished M.A. thesis London University)

Wilson, Trevor, *The Political Diaries of C.P. Scott, 1911-1928.* (1970)

Winterton, Earl, Orders Of The Day. (1953)

# INDEX

# Available from Athol Books:

*Joe Devlin*: **What Now?**, *His Confrontation of the British Parliament, After The 1918 Election.*Edited by *Brendan Clifford*

**Orange Terror**, *The Partition Of Ireland* (1943) by *"Ultach"*.
A Reprint from *The Capuchin Annual*

**The Grammar Of Anarchy**: Force Or Law—Which? by *J.J. Horgan*. **Unionism, 1910-1914**. Introduction by *Brendan Clifford*

**The Christian Brothers' History Of The Great War**, first published in monthly instalments in 1914-18, edited by *Brendan Clifford*

**The Fighting Irish And The Great War**, "Lest We Forget" by *Brendan Clifford*

**Roger Casement**: *The Crime Against Europe.* With *The Crime* Against Ireland

**Traitor-Patriots In The Great War: Casement & Masaryk** by *Brendan Clifford*

**Casement, Alsace-Lorraine And The Great Irredentist War** by *Brendan Clifford*

**Connolly And German Socialism by** *Brendan Clifford*

**Ireland In The Great War**, The Insurrection Of 1916 Set In Its Context Of The World War by *Charles James O'Donnell (1849-1934)* and *Brendan Clifford*

**Northern Ireland What Is It?** Professor Mansergh Changes His Mind
by *Brendan Clifford*

**The O'Neill Years**, Unionist Politics 1963-1969 by *David Gordon*.
A detailed study of events within Ulster Unionism during Captain O'Neill's period as Prime Minister at Stormont

**Belfast Politics (1794)** by *Henry Joy & William Bruce*. First complete reprint. Introduction, *Brendan Clifford*. Includes *Thoughts On The British Constitution*

**Whither Northern Ireland?** by *Brendan Clifford*

**Ulster Presbyterianism**, The Historical Perspective, 1610-1970 by *Peter Brooke*

**The Economics Of Partition**, A Historical Survey Of Ireland In Terms Of Political Economy by *B. Clifford.*

**The Dublin/Monaghan Bombings, 1974**, *a military analysis*,
by *John Morgan, Lt. Col* (Retd.)

**The Arms Conspiracy Trial**. Ireland 1970: the Prosecution of Charles Haughey, Capt. Kelly and Others by *Angela Clifford*

**Elizabeth Bowen: "Notes On Eire"**. Espionage Reports To Winston Churchill, 1940-42; With an extended Review of Irish Neutrality in World War 2
by *Jack Lane* and *Brendan Clifford*.

**Dáil Éireann,** *Irish Bulletin* Volume 1, Reprint of official newspaper of Dáil Éireann with War Reports (Aubane Historical Society, 2012)

**Dáil Éireann,** *Irish Bulletin* Volume 2, Reprint of official newspaper of Dáil Éireann with War Report (Belfast Historical Society & Educational Society, 2014)

**https://www.atholbooks-sales.org**